The Mountain Guide Manual

What I've always loved about the guiding community is the focus on sharing tried and true techniques with the goal of improving safety and efficiency. This book is an aggregate of skills, tips and tricks that are the result of years of training, experience and collaboration between some of the most qualified guides and instructors in the business. It is sure to become a "must-have" manual for those who want to improve their technical rope skills for both climbing and guiding.

—Marc Piché, technical director, Association of Canadian Mountain Guides

The Mountain Guide Manual

The Comprehensive Reference— From Belaying to Rope Systems and Self-Rescue

Marc Chauvin
Rob Coppolillo

GUILFORD, CONNECTICUT

FALCONGUIDES®

An imprint of Globe Pequot
Falcon and FalconGuides are registered trademarks and Make Adventure Your Story is a trademark of
Rowman & Littlefield.

Distributed by NATIONAL BOOK NETWORK

Copyright © 2017 by Marc Chauvin and Rob Coppolillo

Photos by the authors unless credited otherwise

British Library Cataloguing in Publication Information Available

Library of Congress Cataloging-in-Publication Data Available

ISBN 978-1-4930-2514-5 (paperback)
ISBN 978-1-4930-2515-2 (e-book)

♾™ The paper used in this publication meets the minimum requirements of American National Standard for Information Sciences—Permanence of Paper for Printed Library Materials, ANSI/NISO
Z39.48-1992.

Printed in the United States of America

"Perfection is achieved, not when there is nothing more to add, but when there is nothing left to take away."

—Antoine de Saint-Exupéry

"Order and simplification are the first steps towards the mastery of a subject."

—Paul Thomas Mann

Contents

Acknowledgments

I would like to acknowledge the core group of instructors I got to work with at the inception of the AMGA Guide Training Courses: Alan Jolley, Mark Houston, Kathy Cosley, SP Parker, Steve Young, Alain Comeau, KC Baum, Eric Craig, Dave Staeheli, Bela Vadasz, Jean Pavillard, Karl Klassen, and Colin Zacharias. The foundation of this book was laid in those early days.

More recently, Jay Philbrick was crucial, taking many of the photos, and can't be thanked enough. The models who helped set up the shots in North Conway: Nicole Wrobel, Justin Guarino, Andrew J. Blease, Holly M. Blease, and Jane Chauvin. Finally, all the candidates and AMGA Instructor Team members I have worked with over the years in the guide training courses and exams.—MC

Without all my instructors, examiners, and mentors within the climbing community, editing and writing this book wouldn't have been possible. Tim Brown, Joey Thompson, Bill Wilkin, Markus Beck, Lee McNeely, Mike Arnold, Eli Helmuth, Trey Cook, Doug Nidever, Dale Remsberg, Brian Lazar, Paul Rogers, Colin Zacharias, and everyone I've missed—thank you.

Sincere thanks to FalconGuides for undertaking such an endeavor. And here's to the certified guides who commit to the standard and refine the craft daily.

Justin and Berndt, thanks for the endless patience and modeling. You helped a below-average photographer—me—shoot some OK stuff. Emilie, Silas, Angela, PattyP, Howie, Morrone, excellent contributions, appreciate the shared wisdom. And the friendships.

Sean and Azissa, great job on the double duties of writing *and* modeling. Remember me when you blow up!

Jay Philbrick—your images help make the book. Thank you.—RC

Introduction

We love to climb and ski in the mountains. It challenges us and creates fantastic memories, and it also carries a measure of risk. Most things do, but it's simple fact that climbing and skiing usually incur more than the rest of our daily lives.

So first we must realize that if something is truly risky, it means even if we do everything correctly, something bad can happen. Or put another way, not everything that could go wrong is in our control. Some people call this "objective hazard," or even more dramatically, an "act of God."

Some risks, however, we *can* control or at least mitigate through our actions. As climbers and skiers we should learn, nurture, and develop these tools. Technical systems like belaying, anchor building, and short-roping all help to manage risk. Learning these strategies and systems proves the easy part. Far trickier can be having a realistic perspective on our competencies with those systems. Are we as good as we think we are? Do we sometimes look for a technical solution to a problem we could solve more simply?

We encourage you to devote the time and energy to amass wisdom and sound judgment in the mountains—there are no magic shortcuts. What can help, though, is feedback from those with experience, people who've made the mistakes, learned from them, and progressed.

What we present here loosely follows the organization of coursework in the American Mountain Guides Association (AMGA) training program. Just as guide candidates begin their studies with fundamentals like gear, anchors, belaying, and rope systems, in this book we introduce an overall system, beginning with those topics and progressing into more complicated subjects like bigger terrain, glaciated peaks, waterfall ice, and even self-rescue.

We often hear or are asked, "What's the AMGA way?" We definitively state: There is no "AMGA way." Certified guides teach and practice a range of technical systems and decision-making systems. We strive to implement "the right technique at the right time," and within that there is a wide array of skills that are appropriate and vetted.

In short, we present a modern system that will occasionally seem familiar, many times completely new, and hopefully eye-opening in other instances. It may feel like two (or three!) steps back when learning some of the unfamiliar techniques, but in general we trend toward faster and safer through simplicity rather than "rope trickery." As with any new skill, learn in a low-pressure situation and accept that things may feel complicated or clumsy at first. Trust, though, that with time you'll master the new skills and in doing so, your horizons will broaden.

So, onward . . . deeper and higher into the mountains. Thanks for taking the journey with us.

CHAPTER 1

Body, Mind, and the Toolbox

The Three Solutions

As the climbing situations we face become more complex, we must prioritize risks accurately, something that can be greatly influenced by our experiences, (mis)perceptions, and biases. Once the risks are prioritized, we turn our attention to mitigating them or "solving" them. No solution is perfect, though, so we guard against exposing ourselves to a greater hazard when devising a solution.

For example, pitching out a section on a climb might improve security from the risk of falling, but if it guarantees our getting benighted, it might dramatically increase our exposure to another risk like hypothermia or bivying with your unwashed partner—yuck. Here again is a place where a previous experience or personal bias can derail us via our human factors and/or personal habits and heuristics.

We climb and ski in a wide variety of terrain, which makes the *use and application* of our tools the complicated component of our systems. Learning individual tools (rappelling, lowering, placing gear, and hauling, for example) isn't all that challenging, and with diligent practice the tools help us create good solutions. But before we approach those challenges, we need a big-picture perspective on the categories of tools we use in the mountains: the physical, the technical, and the psychological.

The physical primarily focuses on movement skill and fitness level: the athlete's ability to rock climb, ski, or ice climb, and his or her aerobic fitness, balance, and athleticism. For many, this is what climbing (and skiing) are all about. Superior movement and elite fitness usually improve our

risk management. Simply put—no fall, no problem! Falling hazard involves much of the risk in the mountains, but there are many others to consider. Movement skills alone do less to mitigate rock- and icefall, avalanches, and weather hazards.

Technical skill is easiest to understand in rock climbing, but it has importance in all climbing. In rock climbing, fall-protection systems (rope, gear placements, etc.) comprise the bulk of the technical skills. Using the rope and equipment to protect you and your partner requires technical expertise. Technical skill in the mountains can also involve reading weather maps, land navigation, lightweight bivy tricks, avalanche rescue, and even knowing how to repair gear in the backcountry.

Psychological skill requires the ability to perform at your best, often while under intense stress (just ask any guide candidate on his exams!). Generally, fear causes that stress—fear of heights, falling, and failure being the primary examples. Managing these fears (and many others) requires solid psychological skills within our mountain sports.

Play to Your Strengths, Work on Your Weaknesses

Whenever we begin to analyze any subject, we first need to dissect it—but ultimately, it is the whole that we're trying to understand and communicate. The three skills—physical, technical, and psychological—are inextricably connected, and understanding them separately only gives you part of the picture.

For years watching candidates go through the guide program, we've seen how connected these skills are. Succumbing to stress causes technical errors or diminished movement skills. Movement weaknesses create fatigue and mental exhaustion, or invite lapses in technical systems or their application. We often advise a candidate after a course to "play to their strengths and work on their weaknesses." This advice works for the recreational climber, too.

Strength in one skill can help you manage weakness in another, just as easily as a weakness can derail a strength. That said, a serious imbalance in your skill set can be devastating. Movement is often the easiest to develop, not because it is easier, but because it is often the focus of our sports and it's fun. Climbers in a gym or skiers at a ski area don't necessarily need a high level of technical or psychological skill and can work on their movement in a simplified environment.

This is not an indictment of those venues, but a caution. Once someone can move well, they're better able to access bigger, more challenging ski lines and climbing routes. For many, improved physical skill becomes a potential hazard, because more interesting terrain often requires a greater range of competencies. Deficiencies in technical and psychological skills can have serious consequences in unforgiving settings like steep skiing and high-commitment climbing.

Of course, other imbalances can be just as serious. While less common, seeing someone with poor movement or technical skills fearlessly traveling in the mountains can be nerve-wracking. Or take the "engineering type" that has all the right equipment: She tries to solve every problem with the latest device. Yikes!

Human Biases and Experience

Our movement skills, technical systems, and stress-management capacities help manage our risk. Our personal biases and experiences, though, often work against these skills. Just like making mistakes, we all succumb to our personal biases. (There is a tremendous body of research on this topic, but it'd be another book entirely, so dive in on your own and do some reading elsewhere.) We sometimes over-emphasize our experience, too. "Trusting our gut" isn't always the sage advice it seems.

Having a realistic, honest self-perception of our skillset helps to derail these biases, or "human factors" as avalanche educators often call them. Our biases can cloud our judgment and dim our perception of the risks we face. If we can't accurately perceive a risk, then how can we prioritize it against others? We're constantly prioritizing risks on a climbing route or ski tour. Avalanche hazard, nightfall, weather hazards—we need to be constantly assessing these and mitigating them, which requires accurately determining if it's an immediate risk or something we can "back-burner" for the moment.

Experience, Education, and Educated Guesses

We often rely on our experience, or our personal "education," to make decisions. But what is that education? It's really just the limited things we've done and seen in our lives. The broader these experiences have been, so the argument goes, the more "educated" our guesses can be.

Problem is, all experience is anecdotal; in random, chance events can appear as a trend. If you were to toss a coin a hundred times, you would get pretty close to a 50-50 probability, but if you were to look at a small sample, you could easily see what appears to be a trend of heads or tails. In the big picture, most of us are working off a pretty small sample size.

To put the example into the context of alpinism, let's imagine you're deciding between two variations on a climbing route. You observe the route from base camp for a weekend and witness several rockfall events on the "left variation." From your limited experience you might deem this particular variation the more hazardous.

What you might not know is that historically there has been far more rockfall on the "right variation." The rocks you saw on the left were an aberration and, in fact, that particular variation is the safer of the two. Reliance on your experience alone, in this instance, might convince you to climb the more hazardous section because you've taken your two days of experience to mean more than they should. You've overestimated the education in your educated guess.

Our experience and personal education sometimes get in the way of devising solutions and assessing risk. Augmenting our education becomes an important component to sound decision making.

Human Factors, Heuristics, and Mitigating Them

In addition to our natural bias toward our own experiences, we need to consider other powerful ones when making risk-management decisions. Numerous papers and studies on human biases illustrate their powerful and often subtle impacts on our decision making.

A bias is simply a prejudice or tendency toward something—the word *prejudice* carries lots of connotations, but prejudging in this context reveals an unconscious judgment. This unconscious aspect concerns skiers and climbers the most, because if we're not aware of our tendencies, we can't watch out for them.

Imagine trying to stop and make a careful, reasoned decision for every choice in life. You couldn't get out of the house in the morning! Research shows that we humans leave thousands of decisions a day to habitual, automatic responses—what social scientists call *heuristics*. Consider a few decisions from your day that might not even register as conscious choices: what cereal to eat in the morning, pants on backwards or forwards, look both ways when crossing the street, which route to take to work. These heuristics are helpful, enabling shortcuts that let us navigate a complicated, busy life, essentially freeing up our awareness for other tasks.

They can also be shortcuts to disaster if we let them make life-or-death decisions. You take for granted that the brake lights on your car are functioning properly when leaving home, but do you assume your tie-in knot is done correctly every time? We hope not! You and your partner check each other's harnesses and knots, because a shortcut or heuristic in this circumstance could lead to disaster.

So experience isn't as accurate as we'd like. OK, now what? In guiding we put a high priority on planning and preparation, and that includes getting information about the frequency, severity, and location of objective hazards—in effect, augmenting our experience or even overriding it in certain circumstances.

Just as we must augment our own experiences with planning and prep, we need to recognize when to turn off the heuristics and practice a more reasoned, thoughtful approach to making an important decision.

Communication and Teamwork

Avalanche practitioners have developed effective processes for detecting and correcting a team's biases and mistakes. Based on decades of development in the avalanche world (based on research poached from aviation, medicine, and economics), it seems nothing insulates you and your partner from problems better than open communication and teamwork.

Whether a five-member ski posse or just a twosome out for a day of ice climbing, everybody in your team should have a voice in decision making and everyone should have a veto, too. Shared input means more eyeballs on a problem or decision, which tends to catch mistakes more frequently. Giving every person in the team a veto ensures any misgivings about an objective or decision at least gets discussed, if not heeded.

Team members need to be open to changing their minds, as well as being "wrong." This can be really difficult, but we have to remain open to the idea that each of us can miss something, have an "off" day, or simply blow it. Trust in partners isn't just about giving a good belay or anchor-building skills; it's as much about honesty in speaking up and integrity in taking responsibility for a mistake or omission.

THE PRE-MORTEM (AND AN UNPLEASANT MAN-BIVY)

An invaluable tool for sound decision making is the "pre-mortem." Academics designed the exercise to produce "prospective hindsight" by imagining that an event has already occurred, then looking at what might have gone wrong in the planning and execution stages. Simply put, it's the practice of stopping at a decision point and then imagining an outcome in an effort to glean the 20/20 vision of hindsight, without having to risk the consequences of that outcome. Huh?

We all know a *post*-mortem is simply an autopsy—doctors and students study a person's death, in an effort to discover the cause and avoid other deaths in the future. Helpful for med students, but not so great for the cadaver! The pre-mortem, on the other hand, gives us the opportunity to learn something before we have a corpse to deal with. In business settings, it's been shown to help improve identification of "reasons for future outcomes" by 30 percent. That is, it helps a team to identify the reasons something might happen, like an avalanche accident or not summiting a peak, by nearly a third.

It goes like this: You and your team take a two-minute break, either at a predetermined decision point (it's great to build these into tour plans) or any time your team wants to check in with the day's progress. Let's say you're two hours behind schedule, moving slowly, and worried about your chosen objective—the *Resolution Arete* in Red Rock, outside Las Vegas (a long, adventurous route, but one known for overnights and epics).

"Well, we got a late start and I got off-route after the second pitch. We're behind our time estimate," you might say.

Your partner responds, "Wait, didn't the weather forecast say a 30 percent chance of rain this afternoon? We better think about this. Let's imagine we end up on top of Mount Wilson after dark and have to call for a rescue. If it's raining, we're probably out here all night. No bueno."

You: "OK, so we're behind schedule, started late, weather possibly coming, and we're onsighting this thing."

Partner: "I'm not liking the sound of this. Why don't we use our bail option—rappelling the route *Inti Watana*—and come back another day?"

You: "Good thing we did our pre-mortem, dude. We might've just avoided a heinous man-bivy in the rain."

Your 20/20 prospective hindsight saved the day. Good job.

Judgment

We know we have biases and deficiencies in our education and experience—and that's when we're thinking "clearly." Keep in mind, though, the environment can affect one's judgment just as much. We believe that many apparently foolish decisions can be partly attributed to physical stress. Dehydration, hypothermia, hypoglycemia, heat stroke, hypoxia, lack of sleep, and fatigue all have as an early symptom the lowering of higher brain function.

So often we look at accounts of accidents and see actions that are seemingly insane. The first reaction is to vilify the people in the accident, which often gives us the ability to believe that we would never be so foolish—yet seldom do we consider that the victims may have been so completely stressed by one or more of the above factors. There are certainly foolish people out there, and the Dunning-Kruger effect is alive and well in our community, but we also think that physical stress is an important factor.

Irritability, another symptom of physical duress, impacts the effectiveness of a team, too. Not only do you need to recognize your own testiness or impatience, you must also tolerate your partners' overreactions and outbursts. Your team's communication and attitude are too important to take personally the rants of a person under these physical stressors. If your partner barks at you during a tough day or moment, blow it off and revisit it later, when you're both rehydrated, relaxed, and you've survived another adventure.

Mitigating "the Suffering"

Fortunately, these physical stressors can be easy to manage. Keep yourself in good condition and anticipate symptoms if you're growing fatigued, you've run out of water, or you're starting to "suffer."

Hydration presents a tricky problem for any ambitious climber. Carrying enough water for a 12-hour climb is nearly impossible, so then you're confronted with "suffering through," bringing a filtration system or even a stove.

When you sense yourself starting to suffer or entering the "pain cave," this might be the time to use acquired judgment to your advantage. This is where your past experiences can have a positive impact. When confronting a decision, an experienced person can run through similar events from his personal history. If with that experience you also remember your self-evaluation of those times, you might see the right response to the current situation. Since memory isn't as affected by these physical stressors, drawing on past experience can be an effective way to derail the effects of these stressors.

The Toolbox

For any job, we bring our toolbox. This book assumes you already have a good set of tools, ones that work for you and ones you've used in countless solutions in your climbing. Over the ensuing pages we'll introduce you to a few new ones, but before we get going, we want to make sure you've wired a few necessary techniques to make sense of some advanced topics to come.

If you find yourself lacking in one of the baseline tools described below, consult a reputable book, hire a certified guide to help, or solicit advice from a more experienced friend. You *might* check the chaos of the Internet for video help, but beware—there's more kookery out there than good info.

Staying Hydrated

Dehydration sneaks up on all of us, and alongside mental stress, it's probably the most pernicious influence on our performance during a big day.

One strategy to avoid dehydration is to keep your pace at a reasonable level throughout the day, thereby avoiding sweating. Stripping layers can go a long way toward staying cool and comfortable on a long day, too.

We try to avoid drinking plain water on any outing longer than three hours. Using an electrolyte-replacement drink helps keeps salt and potassium levels topped off. The Boulder-based brand Skratch Labs makes an interesting "hyper-hydration" product, too. Saltier than you'd drink in your regular bottle, you consume the solution all at once, slamming a full 16 or 32 ounces just before leaving the trailhead. The fluid then passes directly into your bloodstream, "hyper-hydrating" you. It's awfully salty and only suited for long, hard days. If you have any problems with salt (think high-blood pressure), consult your doc before trying any of these products.

As with most complicated tasks, the individual tools themselves aren't especially tricky to learn—it's knowing which tool to use and when. In short, application.

The Rope

No book on technical systems can get too far without first talking about the rope itself. Modern climbing ropes are not only strong, but also more importantly, very dynamic. We often simplify "dynamic" to mean "stretchy," but stretch is only part of the story.

Dynamic climbing ropes indeed stretch, but what's important about the stretch is it dissipates force. How? Manufacturers make modern ropes of nylon, and more importantly, they weave and construct the nylon in very specific ways to facilitate this ability to dissipate energy. They begin with a braided nylon core and then wrap it in a nylon sheath.

Without veering into mechanical engineering, material dynamics, and—uh oh—physics, let's just say that the way the nylon fibers are initially made and then braided into a modern rope gives the rope amazing capacity to dissipate energy. That energy, of course, comes in the form of falling. We have to be clear here: This is a very basic and elementary explanation, and like all things that are simplified, not nearly the whole story.

TAKEAWAYS FROM ROPE PROPERTIES

This basic understanding, however, helps us explain some consequences of this construction. The first takeaway is that the rope needs to feel the force of the fall to stretch; this seems very basic but it is important to remember. Second, the more rope holding the fall, the more the rope stretches. The more the rope stretches, the less force is delivered to the climber and the system.

Let's take, for instance, a leader falling 20 feet. If the leader were 100 feet up the pitch when he fell, then 100 feet of rope would stretch to reduce the force. If the leader were only 50 feet up the pitch,

half as much rope would be able to stretch. To compare the shock-absorbing capacity of the rope of the two falls, we use a simple formula: length of the fall divided by the amount of rope available to hold the fall. The number derived from this calculation is called the "fall factor."

A higher fall factor results from less rope in the system, which means less stretch and less dissipation of force—and that means more force transmitted to the climber, the belayer, and the protection piece that holds the fall.

So in the first example, $20 \div 100 = .2$; in the second example, $20 \div 50 = .4$. The highest fall factor one can generate in normal fifth-class climbing is 2. That only occurs when a leader falls prior to clipping her rope into any protection. Imagine a leader 10 feet up the pitch with no protection clipped; if she falls she'll drop 20 feet—but only 10 feet of rope is available to hold that fall. After doing the math, you will see that is a fall factor of 2.

We will be referring to fall factor and how it impacts our climbing as we talk about anchors and protection, as well as other parts of our system.

ROPE SYSTEMS

Besides rope construction, we also need to understand the characteristics and applications of the different rope systems. In climbing we use:

1. Single ropes
2. Half ropes
3. Twin ropes

A single rope is just that; it is designed to be used alone. Half and twin ropes are designed to use two ropes together. Teams of two often prefer either of the two-rope systems on routes with long rappels. By climbing with two (usually skinnier) ropes instead of a single, the two-rope systems allow a team to rappel the full length of the rope rather than doubling over a single rope. A single, 60m rope, for example, only allows a team to rap 30 meters, while a twin-rope, 60m system will allow a 60-meter rappel. Useful if the team finds itself retreating!

We use twin ropes together, meaning we clip both ropes into every piece of protection on a pitch. Half ropes, on the other hand, are made to be clipped into alternating pieces of protection. Most climbers, however, don't necessarily alternate clips; they use them in a way that creates two independent, separate lines of protection up the cliff.

Imagine two cracks running parallel up the cliff and a route that wanders back and forth between the two cracks. You start up the cliff with a half-rope system, one rope being red and the other blue. You tie into the red rope on the right of your belay loop and on the left with the blue. You climb the pitch, using both cracks, but for any protection in the right crack, you clip the red rope, while for protection in the left crack, you clip the blue. This might mean two or three pieces in the right crack before moving left and placing several pieces. You wouldn't alternate clipping the ropes; you would protect the right crack with the red rope and the left crack with the blue rope.

This approach reduces the need for long slings on the pieces, but it's technically not the way half ropes were designed to be used. Using half ropes in this way, though, really offers benefits on wandering routes with protection spaced to either side. Applying half-rope technique in this manner requires a competent belayer who can both manage two ropes at once and help the leader keep the ropes straight and separated. As we said, though not the way half ropes were designed, this is a very common "non-approved" use of them.

TWIN AND HALF

Each rope type has a testing regime set forth by an international body, the Union Internationale des Associations d'Alpinisme (UIAA). Rope technology has advanced to the point where manufacturers can make one rope that passes all three testing standards. These ropes can be used in any of the three configurations: single, half, or twin.

It is our understanding that due to the costs of getting ropes tested and approved in each classification, most manufacturers seldom have their ropes tested for all three. Several manufacturers seek both twin and half systems for several of their ropes. This allows a leader to choose whether to separate or not, depending on the terrain and protection. A fairly straight pitch allows the leader to clip both ropes, keeping her system nice and simple. On wandering pitches with protection far to both sides, she can elect to protect herself with two independent lines. Separating her half ropes might also reduce the number of slings she needs, reduce rope drag, or even protect her follower more completely.

ROPE TECHNIQUES FOR PARTIES OF THREE

Moving beyond the three UIAA classifications of ropes, we use three main techniques when climbing in a party of three:

1. Caterpillar
2. Parallel
3. End-roping

Caterpillar is the traditional, and was at one time by far the most common, way a party of three climbs. This system has a rope between each climber. The leader leads on one rope and belays a second who is trailing a rope to the third climber. Once the second arrives at the anchor, the third climber is then belayed. In this system only one person is climbing at a time, and this method therefore adds approximately 50 percent more time than a party of two.

In a parallel system the leader climbs on two ropes and belays both seconds at the same time. In most cases the leader is using two single ropes and clips both ropes into all the pieces of protection. Even though this at first looks like a twin rope system, the leader is almost always belayed only on one rope. A single rope stretches and dissipates the force of a climbing fall, but if the leader clips two single ropes into each piece and takes a belay on both, the ropes don't stretch enough to dissipate forces. This in turns leaves too much force in the system, which increases fall forces on the top piece of protection, the climber, and the belayer. Not good!

So, in the parallel system we clip both ropes into the gear, but only take a belay on one. Because we trail two ropes, we can then belay both seconds simultaneously. This system substantially reduces the time it takes for all three to climb a pitch—not quite as fast as a party of two, but so close that an efficient party of three can outpace a similarly skilled, but inefficient, party of two.

End-roping involves the leader climbing on one rope, with both followers attached at and near the end. One follower ties into the end with the other 10 to 15 feet above, attached to the rope with what is commonly called a "cow's tail." The cow's tail is simply a bight knot, usually an overhand on a bight with a clove hitch or slip hitch, tied in the loop and clipped into a carabiner system on the belay loop.

We tie a clove hitch or slip hitch to reduce the chances of cross-loading the carabiner system. The clove or slip hitch holds the carabiner in its long axis, so it can't rotate into its weaker, cross-loaded configuration.

Some might ask, "Why have the bight knot at all?" The bight creates an independent connection off the main line of the rope, giving a little freedom of movement to the climber clipped into it. It gives the cow's-tail climber about half a step up in movement so the climber isn't stopped instantaneously by the lower climber if he's moving more slowly. Although this doesn't seem like much, it does help the flow of movement and is worth using.

When connecting via a cow's tail, we recommend a minimum of one locking carabiner and one regular carabiner, with their gates opposite and opposed. Some use two lockers opposite and opposed. Others use one triple-action locking carabiner with a captured eye, like the Black Diamond GridLock Magnetron. We don't commonly end-rope in fifth-class rock; it is reserved for fourth-class

or easy slabs of fifth-class and is very useful in snow and low-angled ice.

The Tools

We could spend dozens of pages listing everything you should know to get the most out of our book. Instead, let's imagine our "average" reader is an avid climber, probably already owns a book or two on the topic, can climb multi-pitch trad on her own, has tackled a few longer routes . . . and now wants to go bigger, faster, and better. In short, she's a fairly competent climber looking to jump to the next level on rock, in the mountains, on ice, and/or a skier hoping to augment her systems for ski-mountaineering.

If you're a little ahead or behind this "average" climber, no worries. So long as you're highly competent with the fundamentals of belaying, placing gear, rappelling, and anchors and you're committed to improving, you're in the right place.

Let's start with a few basics you probably already know and then progress to some lesser-known techniques.

FRICTION-HITCH BACKUP

We will use a friction-hitch backup dozens of times in the book. If you don't have a tried-and-true method in your arsenal, it's time to get one. Many climbers use a dedicated sewn loop like Sterling's Hollow Block, but most just have a tied-off loop of 6mm nylon (or 5.5mm tech cord) 12 to 18 inches long. The key here is choosing a material and sticking with it. It helps to know how your chosen loop grabs different ropes. Eventually you'll know how many wraps to use on all your ropes, but if you're constantly changing materials and techniques, it makes the process harder.

For a dry rope, we prefer the autoblock or French Prusik when building a backup. Note we're building a backup, not a friction hitch that will hold a climber's full weight; we just need the hitch to grab the rope with enough force to let our belay device or Munter hitch hold the climber's weight.

On a skinny or wet rope, or in a situation requiring more holding power, we bump to the klemheist or traditional two-to-three-wrap Prusik. Your own judgment will dictate what you need and when. If in doubt, use a hitch with greater holding power like the klemheist and Prusik.

TYING OFF A BELAY DEVICE

Any time we're belaying with a device, we should know how to tie it off quickly and securely. This method works well and stays tight against the belayer's locking carabiner.

1. Blocking a device. Pull the brake strand through the locking carabiner on your belay device to create a bight of rope.

PHILBRICK PHOTOGRAPHY

3. Pull the second bight through the first, cinching it down against the spine of the locking carabiner. Make sure you tie it off against the spine of the carabiner, not the gate.

PHILBRICK PHOTOGRAPHY

2. Pull the brake strand through the bight you just created to form another bight of rope.

PHILBRICK PHOTOGRAPHY

4. Finish it off by tying an overhand around the load strand of the rope.

PHILBRICK PHOTOGRAPHY

MUNTER MULE OVERHAND

The Munter hitch, blocked off with a mule and overhand knot, is an indispensable tool for lowering transitions and self-rescue. It's useful because it's releasable under load, meaning even if we're hanging on it, we can untie it and use it to lower.

You must remember that the Munter flips between "lowering" and "belaying" modes. That is, the hitch rotates through the basket of the carabiner in which it's built depending upon the direction the rope is moving. This becomes important when building it as a releasable hitch.

When building a tied-off Munter mule overhand, you need to tie it in its lowering configuration. If you space this and build the Munter in its belay position, you'll tie the mule overhand, weight the hitch, and then the Munter tries to flip, snarling itself into a mess.

The fix is easy. If you're going to tie off a Munter, most of the time you're using it to lower, so make sure the hitch is in its lowering configuration before tying the mule overhand. If you remember to build the Munter on the load/climber strand, it's already oriented correctly for a lower.

1. Munter mule overhand. Take the brake strand and form a loop by putting a half twist in it against the load strand.

3. Cinch the mule knot as tight to the Munter hitch as possible.

2. Take the brake strand and pass it around the load strand and then put it through the bight formed in the previous photo.

4. Take the bight and tie an overhand around the load strand and cinch that tight.

"FLIPPING A PLAQUETTE"

We trust you're pretty familiar with your guide-style belay/rappel device—what we call a *plaquette* throughout the book. We'll eventually use it in a few ways that might be new to you. For example, we can "flip" our plaquette from belay/rappel mode to "guide mode" to use it as a quick and reliable ascender.

Imagine you're rappelling a formation and you realize you've gone past your next set of anchors. First, tie an overhand on a bight into your brake strands and then clip it to your belay loop with a locking carabiner. This is your backup in case you blow it on the next move.

You'll now flip your device and use it as an ascender. First, clip a locking carabiner through the "ear" of the device—the large hole just beside the two rope channels—then clip that carabiner to your belay loop. Now you carefully unclip the locking carabiner capturing the ropes from your belay loop *without unclipping it from the ropes.*

If you were using a friction-hitch backup while rappelling (we hope you were!), you can remove this and bump it above your plaquette to use as a foot loop. If it's easy, slabby terrain, you can "walk" back up the rock while pulling slack through your plaquette without using the foot loop. Either way, it's a good idea to clip in directly to the ropes every 10 feet or so, just in case something weird happens with the plaquette.

1. Flipping a plaquette. We assume you start this maneuver with a tied-off belay device. Once you're there, attach a locking carabiner (black in this shot) to the ear of the device and then clip it to your belay loop. PHILBRICK PHOTOGRAPHY

2. From your belay loop, unclip the locking carabiner (orange in this shot). **PLEASE NOTE:** *Extreme caution is necessary during this step. You're opening the carabiner attached to the rope. If you inadvertently unclip the orange rope, the leader will fall. Note that in the self-rescue chapter, we describe how to back this process up simply and easily.* PHILBRICK PHOTOGRAPHY

3. The finished process. The plaquette can now be used as an ascender. PHILBRICK PHOTOGRAPHY

1. Flipping an extended rappel. A rappel device extended with a friction-hitch backup.
PHILBRICK PHOTOGRAPHY

2. From an extended device, simply clip the ear back to your belay loop—and note you do not need to open the rope carabiner at any point.
PHILBRICK PHOTOGRAPHY

3. Once you've removed your friction-hitch backup, you're ready to ascend the rope.
PHILBRICK PHOTOGRAPHY

Learning the Ropes

by Azissa Singh

Azissa Singh COURTESY AZISSA SINGH

"So now you untie and feed the rope through the rings!"

"I untie? Like, my knot?"

"What?"

"Like I untie *my* knot?"

"Yeah!"

Sitting at the top of my first outdoor sport climb, I stare at the mess of rope, slings, carabiners, and quickdraws with only the indistinct, shouted directions from the ground to decipher it all. At this point, I'm wondering why I ever came up here in the first place.

Like many of my contemporaries, my climbing career started at an indoor wall. Indoors at the University of South Carolina, I was climbing 5.11 on toprope and leading 5.10. I felt totally ready to climb outside. On this particular, sweltering southeastern day in March, I had traveled almost two hours to some of the closest outdoor rock climbing—Crowders Mountain State Park just outside Charlotte, North Carolina. The route was *Opinionated*, a 5.9 with awkward stances and some spacey bolting. It was a classic first outdoor lead among our group, if only because it was one of the few mostly bolted moderate lines in western North Carolina.

If you're not a climber, this scenario sounds a bit like a horror story: stranded 50-plus feet off the ground having instructions yelled from below about a complex process involving ropes, knots, and carabiners. And yet I'm sure many readers are reminiscing about their own experiences as they read this account of learning to rappel. Most of us have been a part of this story on one end of the rope or the other—shouting or whimpering depending on our role.

Over four years have passed since that first rappelling encounter. I've sat at the top of countless pitches since. Thankfully I have also been through many trainings, a couple AMGA courses and assessments, and benefited from some great mentors.

These days I have far more refined tools for getting down than shouted directions and a whole lot of hope. I've learned to extend and backup my rappels, which is thankfully becoming a more common practice. I generally accomplish this with some combination of a double-length sling extension and a friction hitch.

More recently I've also embraced the practice of lowering through permanent anchors in certain situations. As organizations such as the American Alpine Club compile more data detailing the numbers of rappelling accidents, the argument for lowering becomes increasingly compelling. The process is not only simpler and faster, but allows the climber to stay on belay the entire time. These options give me the freedom to use both hands, unencumbered by other responsibilities, on my descent.

I've found occasion to use these skills plenty as I've ventured into bigger, more committing terrain. Just before Rob and Marc finished this book, I was descending the East Face of Longs Peak in Rocky Mountain National Park, and we didn't hit the ground until nine rappels later. My rappel extension did double duty as the perfect tether for intermediate rap stations on the way down, but the system really shone when I managed to pass a rap station and had to ascend the rope for 10 feet. Aside from being totally exhausted after such a long day and having perhaps not the most reliable brake hand, I now really needed to go hands-free to accomplish the shenanigans I needed to transition from descending to ascending. Much sweat and heavy breathing later, I managed to make it up to the rap station.

As just one example, I have found the versatility achieved by extending and backing up a rappel invaluable in my many days in the mountains and at crags. Skills like these not only make me a safer climber—I get more climbing done in a day and it's more fun, too.

—Azissa Singh began climbing in 2010 on clean North Carolina granite. Her guiding career began in 2014 in NC, and she has since moved to the Front Range to guide for the Colorado Mountain School.

LOWERING WITH A PLAQUETTE (REDIRECTING THE BRAKE STRAND)

We'll also use our plaquette to lower climbers. Most folks have already lowered their partners for one reason or another, usually off their harness and redirected through a carabiner on the anchor.

We typically opt to lower directly off the anchor, with the plaquette hanging on our cordelette or quad. This makes for a smooth lower, but with the plaquette orienting downward, we need to redirect the brake strand. One easy way to do this is to simply loop the brake strand through the carabiner on which the device hangs (pictured) or through a carabiner on the anchor.

We usually back up this type of lower with a friction-hitch backup on the brake strand, as it comes out of the rings or carabiner and down to us.

Redirecting the brake strand through the carabiner on which the plaquette hangs creates a simple, smooth lowering system.

CHAPTER 2

Gear and Strategy

By far the most common form of roped climbing is rock climbing. If you were to include gyms, sport climbing, traditional cragging, and multi-pitch climbing, you would likely include every climber in the United States. Of course, there are climbers who only scramble or ice climb, for example, but that number is small. For many, rock (including gym) climbing is the gateway to all the various forms of climbing and mountaineering.

Many pursue sport climbing and cragging without venturing into other disciplines, and this is awesome. As authors of an advanced book, however, we are less focused on those genres of climbing as stand-alone endeavors and more on committing, complex routes in a variety of terrain.

Using some of the techniques and skills from this book in cragging and sport-climbing situations isn't inappropriate or high-risk, but there will be less benefit than when you take them into the mountains. On the other hand, this book has ways of looking at problems and solutions that may increase risk for little or no real benefit when taken out of the context of time pressure created by the size, remoteness, and environmental conditions on bigger, more committing climbs.

Of course, we aren't suggesting the techniques herein are dangerous, but they do at times straddle a line, requiring a level of training and understanding that is not necessary to go cragging and sport climbing. In short, these techniques are less applicable in venues like the Gunks and Joshua Tree, but really begin to shine in Eldorado Canyon, Red Rock, and Yosemite Valley.

These advanced techniques require practice, and the relatively controlled environment of the crag offers a good place to do just that. As an added benefit, you just might find you get far more climbing in on any given day, too.

For the most part, though, we will focus on advanced systems to better manage risk on longer routes. Rock climbing doesn't get much more advanced than leading long, remote, multi-pitch routes. Even routes with relatively modest grades present serious challenges and much more commitment than far harder routes on roadside crags. We're talking about objectives like the *Casual Route* on the Diamond of Longs Peak, the *East Buttress* of El Cap, *Black Orpheus* or *Epinephrine* in Red Rock, the *Arête des Papillons* in Chamonix, and *Moby Grape* on Cannon Mountain in New Hampshire. Classic, beautiful undertakings, and a bit more serious than the usual crag outing.

Practicing Small for Going Big

People often miss the opportunity to practice on smaller terrain for larger objectives. It's a common mistake. Acquiring essential skills in the more controlled setting of your "backyard crag" makes you a much better climber on the big routes. When cragging we often take extra gear, leaving some at the base depending upon the route we choose. We might do a few routes in a day, customizing our rack each time we leave the ground—a nice luxury and totally reasonable, but doing so underprepares you for longer routes like the ones mentioned above.

Why? Bigger, more complex routes make returning to the base of the cliff or peak unrealistic. What we have when we leave the trailhead is all we have for the day. Climbing in this style requires a level of planning that can seem daunting without practice and experience. How large a rack, what rope system to take, how much food and water, your clothing system, what emergency gear? These questions should be answered before leaving the trailhead, because every pound we carry into the vertical means less stamina and reduces our movement skill.

Packing

For starters, we recommend treating your cragging days as if they're bigger undertakings. Pack as if all the routes you'll do amount to a single, bigger objective. The luxury of leaving a pack with extra gear at the base of the cliff can make us lazy in our planning. Instead of thinking through choices of food, water, rack size and type, and rope system at the car or at home, we bring extra knowing we can just leave it at the base.

If you find this difficult, then on your next few cragging days take note of what you leave at the base and of those things what you actually use and how much. This is especially important with water, food, cams and nuts, and other things on your rack. This starts you down the road of knowing what you really need and use.

Once you have a good idea of what to pack, start making a point of climbing with everything you bring to the crag. This will help you learn how the weight affects your movement, stamina, and pace on the climb. Less weight on a climb is essentially free strength and fitness—but it's a double-edged sword, too. Skimp on the wrong gear, and it can be anything from annoying to dangerous!

Compromise

Once you've made the commitment to train for bigger objectives, you need to consider your equipment choices. Longer, more involved routes demand compromises in your gear—you simply can't take everything you want. A good habit is to compromise on the least important part of the equation when selecting gear.

For example, when choosing your pack, do you bring one big enough for the kitchen sink or one that climbs well? We all enjoy a comfortable pack on the approach and descent, but climbing safely and efficiently trumps comfort on a challenging route. For bigger routes, we suggest compromising on comfort and taking the pack that allows you to climb better—easy choice. Save the cushy, comfy pack for casual days.

MORE ON THE PACK

So, while we're on the topic of our pack, let's finish the discussion. For huge days in the mountains or long linkups closer to home, we tend to go with a smaller pack that expands rather than a bigger one that compresses. That means if you are using a twin- or double-rope system, it needs to fit one of those ropes, half the rack, your harness and helmet, plus the food, water, clothing, and any emergency equipment for the day.

For a hybrid system, you could bring a superlight summit pack inside your larger pack. Overall this adds a few ounces to your system, but if you're going to bivy for a night or two in one spot, it might make sense. Stuff your sleeping bag into the summit pack, and shove those into the bottom of your approach pack. For something like Mount Shuksan's *Fisher Chimneys* or bivying at the base of the Rainbow Wall in Vegas, this might make sense.

Fewer straps, bells, and whistles saves weight and makes a cleaner carrying pack, too. It's nicer for hauling as well.

The Rack

Think of the rack as a tool designed to build anchors and protect pitches, kind of like a socket set with a bunch of individual pieces. Often we carry a standard rack; we have our favorite pieces, and importantly, except for special pieces we use on odd pitches, climbers carry the same rack for every climb. Now we need to be more strategic and build the rack from the ground up, based upon our objective.

Begin with the basics: The rack needs to consist of enough pieces to build two anchors and protect a pitch. Let's say we average three pieces per traditional anchor—that means we will use six pieces for anchoring. If we on average place one piece for every 12 or 15 feet of climbing, we need to know how long a pitch of sustained difficulty is on this route. This is something we can get a pretty good idea of through our research when we are doing our planning and prep. For our purposes let's say we have a sustained pitch of about 150 feet—that means we need ten to thirteen pieces, making a total need of sixteen to nineteen pieces if we add the anchors.

In a perfect world, we'd carry nineteen pieces and that would be enough. We all know, however, we need to carry extra to make sure we have the right sizes. So our next goal is to study how we can manage the use of the rack to minimize how much extra we carry.

Good rack management is probably the least discussed skill a leader needs, and it is a very advanced concept. In most cases when we stop to place a piece of protection, we have a choice of sizes and types of protection that we could place. By using that choice, we can strategically leave pieces behind that allow us to keep a representative size range and type remaining on our rack. Good rack management requires these three skills:

1. Keeping a good inventory

2. Understanding how the various pieces overlap in size and how they can fit similar and different shaped cracks of the same size

3. Knowing which pieces are the most valuable, either because the pitch requires a lot of the same size or because a particular piece doesn't have much overlap on your rack

Keeping a precise inventory of your gear from the start of your lead until the end is the foundation of good rack management. You cannot manage the rack if you don't know what pieces are already in use. We can always tell a leader with advanced skill when we climb because when she takes over the lead, she takes note of what we used in our anchor. These leaders are making a mental note of what pieces they're "missing" on the upcoming pitch.

When a leader looks at a crack, most note the size and shape and imagine what piece would fit, then grab that piece from the rack. Someone with lots of experience and practice gets it right most of the time. Someone less practiced at remembering what's on his rack might see a spot for a .5 cam, for example, and reach for it, only to discover it's at the anchor below. This ends up wasting time and mental energy, not to mention physical energy if placing at an awkward or strenuous stance. Without a good inventory, not only will you waste that time and energy, but it is also nearly impossible to accomplish the next two rack-management skills.

Sizes, Shapes, and Strategies

Understanding how the various pieces in your rack overlap in size and how they can fit similar and differently shaped cracks of the same size affords us choices. When you're using one company's gear, this is pretty easy to do. But let's say you want to carry doubles in a certain size range and for weight and bulk reasons instead of doubling up on spring-loaded camming devices (SLCDs), you decide to bring three or four Tricams or hexes. Knowing how these relate to the SLCDs and wedges you carry allows you to choose between pieces more effectively.

Tricams can be a great way to enhance a rack in the midrange without adding much bulk or weight. Since they can be placed in constrictions like a nut (in two orientations), they can duplicate some of your larger nuts. They also cam, which allows you to use them to duplicate your spring-loaded cams.

Tricams: Lightweight and Versatile

We suggest you consider carrying the .25, .5, 1, and 1.5 (black, pink, red, and brown) CAMP Tricams. As cams, they fit between several sizes of Black Diamond Camalots. The .5 Tricam fits between the Camalot .5 and .75; the 1 Tricam fits between the Camalot .75 and 1; and the 1.5 Tricam fits between the 1 and 2 Camalot. When placed as a nut or wedge, the .5 Tricam fits the same-size crack as the BD Stopper size 11, the 1 Tricam is like the 12 Stopper, and the 1.5 Tricam is like the 13 Stopper. Tons of versatility in the Tricams at a fairly light weight, *and* if you end up leaving gear, they're far cheaper than cams.

If you are looking to add larger pieces to your rack but don't want to add the weight or bulk of large SLCDs, hexes can be a good compromise. The larger hexes are lighter than the corresponding size of SLCD or Tricam. The downside is that a hex, when placed in its wide configuration, requires a constriction in the crack; if the area where you will be climbing has more parallel cracks, hexes might not be effective.

Another piece of gear that is often added to a rack to increase its diversity is Omega Pacific's Link Cam. These SLCDs have a very wide size range, and by adding two of these cams you can duplicate nearly four sizes of Camalots. Link Cams aren't lighter than other SLCDs, but offer a huge size range in one or two pieces. Of course, you'll only have two pieces to place rather than the three or four you might carry with hexes or Tricams. Some climbers opt to carry more Link Cams, but this comes with a weight penalty.

Planning and Prediction

So how do we know whether to add Tricams, hexes, Link Cams, or just carry doubles in particular sizes of SLCDs? Proper planning. You need to know which pieces are the most valuable, given the route you're climbing. Does the crux pitch require doubles or even triples of the same size? Do you need to conserve a critical piece for the crux, one that

is unique on your rack? Typically these are larger cams, but it could be anything from a tiny Ball Nut or cam to a Big Bro or even pins.

Typically we don't carry doubles in our largest pieces because of the weight penalty. If we place a large piece early on a pitch but then need it higher for the crux, we're out of luck! Hopefully we've researched our route, though, and if we need a 5 Camalot somewhere, we make sure we have it when it counts. On the flip side, consider a climbing area like Indian Creek, Utah. We might carry four, five, or even six of the same-size cam for a pitch. A bit of planning will help you decide on your rack.

More commonly the rock offers a variety of placements. By taking advantage of opportunities to place less-common sizes on a pitch—and the use of natural features like chockstones, horns, and threads—you can expand the usefulness of your rack without expanding its size or weight.

To do this well you need not only a good inventory of what you have, but also an idea of what you are likely to need. This last part, having an idea of what you need, is a prediction based on viewing the pitch along with the information you gathered in planning. Keep in mind, too, because you are predicting, you have to consider the chances for error. Error becomes more likely if you have incomplete or unreliable beta, or if you have a poor view of the terrain above. While climbing, you

Online Prep from Pros:
The Mountain Conditions Report

The Mountain Conditions Report (MCR) provides conditions reports from professional mountain guides throughout the United States and Canada. It's a great addition to the community and should help everyone from guides to first-time climbers plan and prepare. You can find it at mountain conditions.com.

In addition to the MCR, guidebooks, and word of mouth, the web has greatly improved access to route information. Much of the beta we find online proves helpful, but beware—a significant amount of stuff posted is useless at best, dangerous at worst! Don't consider online forums quite as authoritative as a guidebook . . . and for that matter, guidebooks can be inaccurate, too. Plan and prepare, but leave yourself a little margin for error, too.

should reassess as you get better views. This, as mentioned above, requires good terrain assessment skills and is something that needs to be worked on.

Back Cleaning

More of an option than a skill, back cleaning offers us the opportunity to conserve critical pieces on a climb by reaching down and cleaning pieces after having placed solid pieces above. This needs to be considered carefully, though. It can slow you down and add unnecessary risk, but it might just as easily be the key to protecting yourself.

Most often, we would back clean a piece to use it in another place. This might be planned or unplanned, but whatever the situation, make sure you're safe. If you're lowering to the piece you'll clean, consider adding a second piece up high. By back cleaning you're removing protection from the pitch, so if the top piece fails, you could be setting yourself up for an enormous fall.

Also ask yourself why you're back cleaning. If you brought the light-and-fast rack, would carrying a duplicate piece be faster than taking the time to lower, retrieve, and reclimb the section? Maybe back cleaning isn't the answer.

Fast and Accurate Placements

Next time you're hanging at the crag, waiting for a belay or a burn on your route, grab some gear and practice placing pieces quickly and accurately. Ideally you can look at a crack or placement and pick the right nut or cam on the first go. Race your buddies to see who can build a three-piece anchor the fastest. Bet beers on it. However you hone your skills, having an expert eye and identifying the right piece—both right in front of you and 25 feet above—is a critical skill for solid leading. Practice!

On the other hand, carrying two size 5 cams up a 2,000-foot route sounds like a total drag. Imagine a pitch that starts off wide, then narrows, then goes wide again—maybe planning and decisively back cleaning the 5 is the way to go. Expert planning and terrain identification will be key in that event. Judgment, practice, and planning will make the difference.

Slings, Carabiners, and Accessories

This is one aspect of the rack that is often an afterthought. Versatility, bulk, and ease of use are all things that become more and more critical as approaches, descents, and routes get longer. Your planning and prep will determine how many locking carabiners, cordelettes, regular carabiners, and quickdraws you need.

For traditional climbing quickdraws, we prefer Dyneema shoulder-length slings set up as alpine draws. We also carry three to five $^{11}/_{16}$ nylon slings. These can be carried over your shoulder (old school) or doubled up and twisted to have them clipped to your side. If the descent includes multi-pitch rappels, a double-length nylon sling acts as a nice extension/leash for your rappel rig. Include a locking carabiner to clove-hitch into your anchor, and another two to go with your belay device so you can use it in the self-locking/guide mode. Finally, if you hang your cordelettes on a locker, the leader will have a spare.

DRAWBACKS OF SPORT DRAWS

On longer routes and in the mountains, we usually avoid dog-bone/sport-climbing quickdraws. Although great for clipping bolts and less likely to tangle when racked, they're less versatile than alpine draws. Making quickdraws from shoulder-length Dyneema slings allows you to have three lengths: one-third length when in the alpine draw, half-length, and full-length. Sport draws rack nicely, particularly the superlight and compact ones, but they're fixed length, making them less appropriate on long, varied routes like you'll find in the mountains and in places like Red Rock.

Two followers in parallel mode can run into problems with sport quickdraws, too. In a parallel system the first follower will likely be unclipping from protection as she climbs, leaving the cleaning to the second follower. When the first follower unclips her rope, she needs to be able to rotate the carabiner so the gate faces toward her—this prevents her rope from being on the spine side of the carabiner and "trapped" under the second follower's rope.

Rope-side carabiners on a sport draw often have a rubber "stopper" to keep them from rotating and potentially unclipping—awesome when we're whipping on sport routes, but with two followers the stopper keeps the first follower from being able to rotate the rope-side biner and free her rope. While manageable for a more experienced follower, a stiff sport draw requires more fiddling if the first follower's rope gets trapped. Some guides elect to clip the fixed biner on the gear, but if the bolt-side biner has been notched by repeated falls, this can damage the rope or the biner can hang up and become cross-loaded.

In the end, unless guiding a multi-pitch sport route in a party of two or cragging, sport quickdraws are less useful in the alpine and/or when guiding two clients.

1. The follower has unclipped her rope from the carabiner, but she's now trapped under the piece. PHILBRICK PHOTOGRAPHY

2. In this photo the follower has rotated the carabiner so the gate faces up, so when she unclips, her rope is on top and free. Sport draws make rotating the rope-side carabiner awkward if not impossible with one hand.
PHILBRICK PHOTOGRAPHY

Anchor Materials: When to Use Cordelettes

The recreational party of two should consider whether or not to carry specific anchor-building material like cordelettes. We know, heresy! If they're leading in blocks, cordelettes may be a good idea. Having a simple place for the second to clip in when block-leading can make transitions more efficient. For the party that is swinging leads, though, cordelettes are more a convenience than an essential tool for efficiency and security.

The Classic Cordelette System

For guides, block-leading parties, and groups of three using a parallel system, the typical modern anchor made with dedicated anchor-building material is what we'll be using.

So what do you carry? The classic cordelette is 5m (15.5 feet) of 7mm (9/32 inch) cord. That is the original cordelette in the USA. What is becoming more popular is 5m of tech cord, usually 5.5mm, or even a quadruple-length Dyneema sewn sling. This is far less bulky and easier to carry. Some use that lower bulk to carry a longer piece. We feel that slings can make up for a shorter cord and be far more versatile.

No matter how long a cordelette you carry (within reason), you'll end up someday with it being too short. You'll need to learn how to use slings to extend a cord that comes up short. Use that skill a bit more often, and you'll end up with a small, light, low-bulk system that offers great versatility. (See chapter 4 for more information.)

Over the years the Prusik has proven itself useful, too—usually as a third-hand backup on rappels, or when you need to haul or ascend a rope to retrieve a stuck rappel rope. They're indispensable for rescue on rock and snow as well. As we'll see in our rappel transitions, there are times when a second belay device is useful, either a GriGri style or a GiGi device, depending on whether you are using a single rope or a double rope in a party of two or three.

Using the Rope

We'll often use the rope in place of a cordelette (or a double-length sling) when we're swapping leads on a climb. Rope-built anchors vary in style, but some can distribute the load like a quad, while others act more like a pre-equalized cordelette. Most of the common ones have a masterpoint, allowing the leader to belay her second off it. Think about the team's progression, though—if the follower will lead the next pitch, then all flows easily. If the current

Planning for Success

by John Morrone

John Morrone COURTESY JOHN MORRONE

I'd never hooked an ice tool as an undercling on a loose-looking block before, but then again I'd never heard a guide repeat "watch me" either. So as a guided second on a fun birthday climb with the author, "Coppo," I was pretty sure today was just gonna be a fun and no-stress November outing on the east face of Longs Peak.

Step high into the thin, shattered ice under a chockstone with my right foot and my right-tool undercling; stem far left onto a small crystal on the left wall of the chimney with my left crampon tip. Now move out, then scrape the left tool awkwardly back far right above the block in a wide moss- and mud-filled crack. Steel tip PLEASE don't shift on that crystal; stand up left and levitate the right foot back above the chockstone.

Hmm, this must be why he built the anchor with minimal slack in the not-so-comfortable corner below, and a directional piece of pro is right above my nose now! A bit of balanced pro cleaning, and two more steps to a high-five at the belay. Plenty of daylight left to finish the climb, rap off, and hike back to tree line before dark. Yet another case of planning and thinking in advance, adding observations and reassessing with the current and changing conditions, appropriate protection and solid decision making by the guide, all in pursuit of a safe adventure.

Great fun days in the mountains don't just happen. They are planned. Sure, you can drag out of a hungover morning and just head out to bag a peak or do a climb, but do it often enough and your luck will run out. A major "adventure," a fiasco, a near miss, stumbling home in the dark, or a SPOT signal rescue will eventually happen. Going out in the mountains 52 weekends a year with a 98 percent luck rate will catch up to you before long.

When I go out with the instructors and students in Colorado Mountain Club trips, we don't just end up whited out in a blizzard or on a loaded slope wondering what went wrong. Reviewing weather forecasts and snowpack conditions for several days in advance, planning reasonable routes for the conditions and the participants, noting observation and decision-point locations, planning options and bailout possibilities, and keeping options in place for snowpack or condition changes are all done in advance. Getting together and making sure all are on board at the onset; modifying plans because some folks are tired or have a cold, someone forgot a critical piece of gear, or slower travel conditions (or better conditions) occur; observing that no issues are occurring; and keeping everyone in communication cannot be underestimated for safe mountain travel. Going out with just your best buds or "Han Solo" allows more freedom, but can also get you into bigger trouble without appropriate information, planning, and observations.

Some days don't require as much vigilance and reassessment, but even average outings can quickly turn into fiascos with late starts, changing weather, losing the route (or actually getting "lost"), unanticipated delays, snow/route conditions being other than anticipated or changing rapidly, gear issues, blister repairs, and a myriad of other possibilities.

As explained in this book, we can all be better and safer by following methods from guiding: Planning, observing, decision points, reassessing as needed, and appropriate decision making for you and your group are all requirements if you want to grow old while enjoying safer, more enjoyable, and more successful travel in the mountains.

—John Morrone learned to climb with drilled-out hexes and ski in leather mountaineering boots and Silvretta cable bindings. Since then he's become a school director for the Colorado Mountain Club, an instructor for the American Institute of Avalanche Research and Education, and a serious fun hog. He lives in Steamboat Springs, Colorado.

leader will lead the next pitch, then she must break down her rope anchor when she leaves the belay. That leaves no place to anchor her second when he arrives at the stance.

The recreational party of three can use the rope, too. If the team is using caterpillar technique while swinging leads, the middle person can leave the anchor to climb the next pitch prior to the leader of the previous pitch. In this case the middle climber can simply clip the masterpoint to anchor while at the belay, then lead the next pitch when the time comes.

Climbing in parallel mode dramatically ups the complexity for the team, so much so we'll avoid diving into the topic!

RESCUE FROM A ROPE-BUILT ANCHOR (UH OH!)

One last thing needs to be mentioned about rope-built anchors. In the event of a self-rescue of a second, the process will be made far more difficult with a rope anchor. For a leader to get into a counterbalance rappel to perform a pickoff of his second, he will need to fashion a masterpoint anchor that isn't made with the rope. Doable, but it will take time and possibly more gear. Given the low likelihood of having to transition into a counterbalance rappel, a rescue shouldn't deter you from using the rope as your anchor—but you should definitely consider how you'd deal with the situation before defaulting to rope-built anchors.

Hauling off a rope anchor doesn't present any unusual difficulties beyond the normal ones. Make sure the anchor is up to the task, use just as much mechanical advantage as you need and no more—and then get the job done.

A GUIDE'S DAY OFF AND THE CORDELETTE

Guides have found cordelettes highly useful, and we attribute the popularity of that system in part to this. People at the cliff and clients learning to climb notice guides building anchors with cordelettes, and so incorporate them into their practice. Indeed, it would be strange for guides to teach something they don't use in their own climbing.

The rope, however, offers a strong, dynamic alternative as an anchor material, but using it requires practice and an understanding of the system. It's a worthy technique to know, and it's kind of cool *not* to look like a guide all the time. At least one of us loves to leave the work tools behind when he's out climbing for fun!

A Sample Trad Rack

Here's an example of a foundational traditional rack:

Group Gear

2 each Black Diamond Stopper 3 through 9, racked on one keynose carabiner

1 each Black Diamond Stopper 10 through 13, racked on one keynose carabiner

1 each CAMP Tricam .25 through 1.5, racked on one keynose carabiner

1 each Black Diamond X4 .1 through .3, racked on one carabiner

1 each Black Diamond Camalot .4 through 3, each with its own carabiner

8 Dyneema shoulder-length slings set up as alpine draws

4 nylon ¹¹⁄₁₆ shoulder-length slings with one carabiner each

2 5m × 5.5mm tech-cord cordelettes, both hanging on one locker carabiner

4 free regular carabiners

Individual Gear

1 Petzl Reverso or ATC Guide belay device with two locking carabiners (one compact and one HMS/larger)

1 free locking carabiner

1 nylon, or nylon-Dyneema combination, double-length sewn sling

1 Prusik (tied-off nylon, 5mm or a dedicated material like Sterling's Hollow Block, etc.)

1 keynose non-locking carabiner to hang the double-length and Prusik

With the foundation in place, the team can add larger cams if the route has wide sections, add doubles for routes with cracks of consistent sizes, replace the Tricams with SLCDs, or add more Tricams. You could reduce the list if the route has bolted anchors and a lot of fixed protection. You'll need to add more quickdraws or slings if the route has particularly long pitches or pitches that require a higher density of protection.

We used a specific company's equipment for simplicity, but you could carry the same size range of any company's gear that you prefer. By our count, the total number of regular carabiners is thirty-five and the total number of lockers is four for the leader.

If the route is more alpine in nature, with only short steps of fifth-class and lots of third- and fourth-class, you can start with this rack and begin to pare it down. The alpine-style rack varies much more depending upon objective, so it could range from this foundational rack to a single set of Stoppers, the Tricams, four alpine draws, two nylon slings, and the anchor/rappel kit, or even less.

CHAPTER 3

Leader Protection

We now head into the vertical, beginning with leader protection as an element in what we call the "fall-protection system." Rather than conceptualize the leader's protection as separate from the bottom anchor and the next belay (and even the eventual rappel or descent), we propose seeing these as components in an overall system. This system protects the leader and follower(s) during their time in the mountains.

Building the Fall-Protection System

Plenty has been written about how to place cams, nuts, pitons, and bolts. Add to that the titles on anchoring, and you've got quite a library going. Although individual gear placement and how to combine that equipment into anchors are both basic and critical skills, little has been written about how those parts work together to form an overall fall-protection system. We'll leave other titles to handle gear placements and basic anchoring, and introduce the more holistic concept of an overall system here.

Gear Fundamentals

When we place gear, we rate or judge its quality with three main criteria:

1. The strength of the piece (primary pull)
2. The security of the piece (secondary pull)
3. Ease of removal for the second

Most of us rank strength as our top priority in a gear placement, but if the cam or nut easily dislodges with a secondary pull (sideways, outward,

or upward), its strength is negated. As far as ease of removal goes, it might not seem too important at first, but on longer routes if you or your partner lose a piece or two to getting them stuck or "fixed," you may compromise your ability to protect subsequent pitches. Clients struggling with sticky gear waste a tremendous amount of energy. Placing easy-to-remove gear becomes even more critical when guiding.

Consider also the time it takes to remove a piece. If it takes an average of 30 seconds extra per piece, that adds up to significant losses on a long route. Take two parties on identical routes, for example, one with tricky gear and the other with simple-to-clean pieces. If we estimate ten pieces per pitch, at 30 seconds extra per piece, then that's 5 minutes extra per pitch. On a ten-pitch route, you are starting to look at nearly an hour of time lost.

The interface between anchors, protection, and the rope that runs through the system is complex and variable. As the leader climbs upward, the rope snakes its way through the protection system and remains slack until the leader falls. At this moment it tightens, and anywhere the rope bends through protection, an angle forms—introducing a secondary pull to the system.

The Secondary Pull

Secondary-pull angles generally face sideways, or occasionally and more seriously, upward. Since removable ("clean") protection can be removed by hand, it is sometimes susceptible to dislodging when pulled outward or upward. And not just the top piece in the system—intermediate pieces can pull out with sideways or upward forces. We call these secondary pulls, as most of the time we focus on the expected primary, or downward, pull. Secondary pulls can dramatically reduce the security and effectiveness of your fall-protection system, so let's dive into some detail about them and how to account for them.

A rope running plumb line from leader down to belayer results in no secondary pull whatsoever. Any deviation in the rope's path, however, can result in a secondary pull. This could be a belayer standing far back from the cliff (the rope runs down from the leader, through his first piece and outward, toward the belayer), or any time the rope wanders left or right to find a gear placement or a 'draw on a bolt.

As most of you know, a runner, sling, or quickdraw on a piece can dramatically reduce the potential for a secondary pull by straightening out the path of the rope, or just reducing the chances the natural upward snaking of the rope through gear (as the leader climbs) pulls a piece up and out.

STRENGTH VS. SECURITY

Most books focus more on placing pieces for strength and less on the security of a placement. We feel this is an appropriate way to learn the basics. Once the climber understands how to place strong,

reasonably secure pieces, he must begin to better understand how, where, and why to make pieces more secure. Too often we see leaders make mistakes in this part of the system, resulting in compromised fall protection.

The other, more advanced skill of ease-of-removal may appear to contradict security. At times this is certainly the case, but there are other instances when security actually helps in ease of removal (more on this in a bit).

In summary—and this is very important—ease of removal cannot compromise necessary security, and security cannot compromise necessary strength.

ANTICIPATING FORCES IN SECONDARY PULLS

Depending upon the nature of the climb and protection opportunities, secondary pulls can be difficult to predict. Pulls can change during a pitch, or change temporarily depending upon the leader's position. For example, if a leader were to put a piece of protection in and then climb to the right, the piece would get a slight pull to the right. Once higher, if the leader traversed back to a stance above the piece, it would get no secondary pull. If the leader continued her traverse to the left, the piece would then get a leftward pull. As soon as the leader placed another piece, the secondary pull would

Heads Up on Tagger!

Visitors to Eldorado Canyon State Park, outside Boulder, Colorado, may remember a climb called *Tagger*, 5.10. Many give the route an R rating because of its left-trending first pitch. A thin—barely fingers—crack traverses beneath a roof to the left and offers few positive nut placements. Over the years there have been many groundfalls here, mostly because less-experienced leaders do not accurately anticipate and mitigate the secondary pulls placed on pieces. Modern micro-cams make the pitch much less serious, but every summer *Tagger* surprises another climber or two. The culprit? Focusing on strength over security and failing to build an overall system that accounts for secondary pulls. Heads up!

come from that direction. This in reality is a rare case, but not unprecedented.

As a rule of thumb, the secondary pull generally comes from the direction of the next piece in the system. Knowing this gives us a clue in predicting where the secondary pull will come from and how strong it will be.

If we can predict the location of the next piece of protection, we can predict the direction of the secondary pull. Once we know the direction, we then need to visualize the angle the rope will go through the carabiner on the piece. This involves seeing where the climb goes *after* the piece. Most of the time this angle will be between 90 (an abrupt turn one direction or another) and 180 degrees (a straight line, no turn at all). The closer the change of direction is to 90 degrees, the stronger the secondary pull.

The leader experiences the secondary pull as rope drag during her lead. Rope drag on its own can certainly dislodge pieces. It's typically a fall, though, that results in a violent "zippering" of numerous pieces on a pitch.

We then ask ourselves, where does the rope come from? If the rope is coming from below, the secondary pull will be sideways and down. If the rope is coming horizontally across the cliff, the pull will be sideways and upward. The secondary pull typically bisects the angle at the carabiner where the rope connects to the sling, piece, or quickdraw.

Because the rope line changes direction at the bottom piece, it creates a secondary pull upward and leftward. The leader must anticipate this and place the piece so it can withstand the secondary pull.

PHILBRICK PHOTOGRAPHY

Outward secondary pulls are often unanticipated by climbers. Remember any angle in the rope creates a secondary pull—the rope going left or right after a piece is pretty obvious to most people, but the rope changing angle inward (toward the cliff) or outward (away from the cliff) often goes unnoticed. It's an easy thing to miss, as we're beneath an overhang or steepening pitch and focused on the hard climbing ahead, not the secondary pulls in our system.

Imagine a climb that starts on low-angle terrain, but then gets steep. The last piece on the low-angled section and/or the first piece on the steep section will get a substantial outward/upward pull. Which piece gets that force is usually the one closest to the transition in angle. If they are roughly the same distance from the transition, both the last piece in the low-angled section and the first piece in the steep section will get an upward/outward pull.

This can happen when we belay on the ground or on a sizable ledge. Visualize a belayer standing 8 feet away from the base of a pitch—the rope leaves his belay device, travels to the wall, through the carabiner on the first piece, then upward into the rest of the system. The rope changes angle at the first piece, so the secondary pull (outward and upward) will be toward the midpoint of the angle. This scenario risks failure of the entire fall-protection system, otherwise known as . . . zippering the pitch.

We've seen this scenario zipper a number of pieces, luckily usually just a few, before a cam or well-placed nut arrests the failure. If the first piece in these systems had been placed securely enough to resist that upward/outward pull, the rest of the protection would have been protected and remained in the rock.

Having the belayer set up closer to the wall would also reduce or eliminate the upward/outward secondary pull. Ideally the belayer would stand directly below the climber's first piece, so no angle whatsoever existed.

Off the ground and on the cliff, this scenario can be less obvious, but if you keep your eye out for steepening sections and keep the rope line in mind, you'll catch these critical direction changes and angles.

Mitigating Secondary Pulls

To deal with the secondary pull, we have three strategies:

1. Add a sling to minimize the rope angle to, or as close to, 180 degrees as possible.
2. Make the piece resistant to the secondary pull through its placement.
3. Use an opposition system to make the piece omnidirectional.

We recommend adding a sling (usually a shoulder-length, but occasionally even a double-length), even if it doesn't completely eliminate the secondary pull. It will partially mitigate the pull, while correspondingly reducing friction (rope drag) through the carabiner. The leader will appreciate this as he gets higher on the pitch, but less rope drag/friction in the system means more rope is "in service" should a fall occur—meaning more rope to absorb energy, which lowers the fall factor. A lower fall factor usually results in lower chances of pulling a piece.

CHOOSING THE RIGHT LENGTH OF SLING OR QUICKDRAW

Climbers often fail to choose the right length sling or 'draw. For this section we'll use the term *sling* to include all lengths of sewn slings and quickdraws. Choosing a sling that is too short, or not using one where you should, can cause three types of problems:

1. The friction or drag between the rope and the carabiner effectively adds rope weight to the leader that in the worst case can cause the leader to fall.
2. Rope drag can also increase the force subsequent pieces will have to hold in a fall. This

is due to the friction caused by the rope drag reducing the amount of force the rope receives below the offending protection point or points, thereby reducing the ability of the rope to stretch and absorb the shock. Looked at another way, it is as if the friction at the piece where the rope drag originates is acting like a belay device. This effectively reduces the amount of rope holding the fall and increases the fall factor.

3. The sideways or upward pull of the rope pulls out or displaces the piece.

Because traditional routes seldom take straight lines up cliffs, protection can make the rope "zig-zag" up a cliff. It is this zigzagging that causes the problem of rope friction on the carabiners. We use slings to straighten the path of the rope, which in turn reduces or eliminate the friction.

To understand how much force secondary pulls put on our protection, let's look at how the angle formed at the carabiner-rope point generates force. This is the same process that increases force on our anchors, but instead of loading the junction of the two tangents and determining the force on the outer points of the tangent, we will be loading the outer points and seeing how it affects the junction. This means that acute angles formed by the rope as it goes through protection will put more force on the piece.

A 90-degree angle creates forces 1.33 times greater on the protection than the force applied on the individual leg. This could be 1.33 times the force of a fall or 1.33 times the rope weight being pulled by the leader. This force will be pulling the protection sideways and/or upward. The direction it pulls the piece will be the direction that bisects the angle formed by the rope. If the angle becomes acute and is between 0 and 70 degrees, the force sideways on the protection is approximately double.

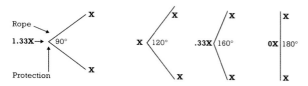

These numbers vary due to friction and other factors, but serve as a guide as to how rope drag is created. Don't worry about particular numbers—just know that a sharp, acute angle will dramatically increase rope drag and secondary pulls! The point is: Create as obtuse an angle as possible, preferably 180 degrees (or to put it another way, a straight line in the rope). In this configuration, there will be no secondary pull on the piece.

One solution would be to put a long sling (a 2-foot sling is our standard "long" sling) on every piece of protection. This does make some sense, and there is no doubt that because many people begin leading on sport routes, where bolts are placed mostly in line, the shorter quickdraw is overused in modern traditional climbing. The problem with placing too long a sling is the extended length of a fall. For every foot of sling that is added to a piece of protection, the fall lengthens by 2 feet. For this reason it is nice to put the appropriate-length sling on a piece to mitigate secondary pulls—no longer and no shorter.

So how do we determine what the right-length sling is? Imagine you're at a stance and you've just placed a good cam. Now you need to determine whether or not to extend it and by how much. Look down at your *previous* piece and then predict where your *next* piece will be—draw a line between those two placements. You should choose a sling that extends your *current* placement so that the rope-side carabiner reaches that imaginary line.

If the imaginary line runs through rock, we need to redraw the line to the point on the rock the rope will run over. In other words, this point on the rock acts in effect as the *next* piece of protection. Overhangs present this problem, as does protection placed at the back of a ledge. Ideally any sling placed on gear will allow the rope to run over the lip of the overhang with as little bend as possible. For ledges, the sling should be at least as long as the ledge is wide—if the leader is climbing directly above the placement. If he climbs diagonally off the ledge, the sling will need to be even longer.

This is particularly important because the rock, being rougher than a carabiner, will give you more rope drag than a carabiner. Also, if the rock is sharp at the lip of the overhang or edge of the ledge, it could cut or at least damage the rope in the event of a leader fall.

Not all the angles in every pitch can be eliminated with a sling. Sometimes large changes of direction in a pitch require that the rope will angle through a piece of protection—we can't avoid it. Traverses or large changes of angle from a low-angled section to steeper climbing will create situations that cannot be managed by just sling length. In those cases you'll need to employ another strategy to mitigate the secondary pull.

MITIGATING THE SECONDARY PULL: THE PLACEMENT ITSELF

Correctly identifying the direction and potential forces of the secondary pull allows you to place your piece in a way that minimizes the chances of it pulling out. Once the secondary pull is identified, placing your piece such that it can resist it allows you to have the peace of mind that the protection will be viable as you climb above it.

CRACKS AND FLAKES

Terrain helps us find a natural placement that resists a secondary pull. Cracks and flakes can be exploited advantageously with a little recognition and ingenuity.

A crack splitting a face trends upward, and its sides are the face of the rock itself—we often call these "splitter" cracks. If they're deeper, or the lip of the crack is featured, it offers points at which nuts, Tricams, and cams can be effectively "buried," meaning they're protected from being pulled upward, outward, or to the left or right.

Contrast that with a crack formed by a flake. Because a flake is usually a part of the face jutting out into space, the crack it forms is perpendicular to the face itself. For a right-facing flake, this means

A placement in this flake will naturally resist a leftward pull, while a placement in the crack is more likely to dislodge with the same pull.
PHILBRICK PHOTOGRAPHY

climbing to the left above it will naturally protect the placement from a secondary pull in that direction. If the climber moves to the right, the gear is naturally oriented to pull directly out and toward the secondary pull—not ideal!

A splitter or flake can be used to your advantage by accurately predicting the direction of the secondary pull, then placing gear such that the rock itself negates the pull. There are times, however, when we can't use the terrain to our advantage, so care must be given—most notably when our direction of climbing makes our pieces more vulnerable to the secondary pull. More on these situations below, when we discuss omnidirectional placements.

HORIZONTALS

Horizontal cracks offer natural protection from upward, downward, and often outward pulls. Left- or rightward pulls may still be a concern, though if the crack bottoms out, a cam placed against the back won't walk. Tricams and Stoppers offer the advantage of bending over the lip of the crack without dire consequences, though left-right secondary pulls can be a challenge to manage. Flexible-stem cams tend to be very secure in a horizontal, but can bend under hard falls.

OMNIDIRECTIONAL PIECES

We can use terrain, but also additional gear, to create an omnidirectional piece. Bolts and ice screws are omnidirectional, meaning secondary pulls don't affect them—they're almost always as strong in any direction as they are downward. This relaxes us when we lead above them because we never fear a bolt is going to pull out as we move left, right, or up above it. But what about gear placements?

Spring-loaded cams in a vertical crack can sometimes be omnidirectional, adding security.

The slight bump on the right, beside and above the outer red lobe, prevents the cam from walking into a less secure position.

PHILBRICK PHOTOGRAPHY

Cams will often rotate upward or "walk" in a vertical crack, which can make them difficult to remove. Climb anywhere with popular beginner routes, and you'll see these relic cams, stuck long ago and now weathered from the elements and other climbers trying to "booty" them. As long as the crack doesn't open up or widen above the cam, these placements can resist upward secondary pulls, offering some (imperfect) protection against zippering.

While cams may resist upward secondary pulls, rotating them into a non-ideal orientation (the stem sticking directly outward or even upward) makes them suboptimal when holding a fall. If we can keep a cam from walking, we have a much better placement in terms of security and strength. To achieve this, we need to look at the walls of the crack to see if we can spot a feature within the crack that prevents the cam from rotating upward. These are more common than you would think, especially in more featured cracks. If we can get the outermost lobe under this feature, this will prevent it from rotating and walking.

STOPPERS AND TRICAMS

Stoppers and Tricams can also resist secondary pulls, but as a general rule not nearly as well as a cam. Stoppers find purchase in the rock when grains and crystals gouge and scratch the surface. Some climbers even give their placements a solid tug to "set" it—we've all done it, especially when a particular nut is our "money piece" and having it dislodge would be dangerous.

In general, though, you should be able to visualize how strong the piece is, then set it relative to the secondary pull. Yarding on a piece that doesn't need it just makes it harder to remove. Setting stoppers requires a thoughtful loading, from a simple pull with no momentum to a hard jerk with a quick draw. Make it secure but remember only as much as is needed, or you'll end up just having a hard-to-remove piece.

This nut will resist an outward secondary pull.
PHILBRICK PHOTOGRAPHY

Placed in a more opened position, this Tricam will be easier to remove and is less likely to become fixed. PHILBRICK PHOTOGRAPHY

Often a tiny tweak or refinement to a Stopper or Tricam placement can make them fairly resistant to a secondary pull. Again, finding a tiny lip or constriction in a crack can help. Another strategy is to tilt the unit's top a little deeper into the crack, relative to its base. This orients the wire (or webbing in the case of a Tricam) at a slight angle, which allows it to flex a bit rather than just pulling up on the piece.

Tricams offer two placement types: active and passive. In the active mode we typically give them a good tug to set them, which helps keep them seated and secure. This is, of course, conditional upon choosing the right size for the crack.

In active mode the cam should be about halfway through its range, if not even more. Many climbers place too big a Tricam in the crack, so it's barely cammed. Put another way, it's "stuffed" into the placement. If you find yourself in this situation, be careful setting it. These stuffed Tricams end up fixed because rather than popping out of their cammed position when being cleaned, they tend to set too tightly on both sides. Tug hard on them, or even fall on them, and they become fixed gear. We probably see fixed pink Tricams more than any other piece.

Passively placed Tricams require a bit of care, as do nuts like the DMM Wallnut. Tricams have slightly less surface area than a traditional Stopper, and DMM Wallnuts have a groove vertically on the concave side of the nut. These pieces, if tugged too aggressively when setting, can get locked into their placements, making them very difficult if not impossible to clean. We've found that a steady, gradual pull downward sets them adequately, while a sharp tug tends to make them hard to remove—especially for clients and less-experienced climbers.

OPPOSITIONAL PIECES

Another technique to combat zippering is placing a piece specifically for an upward or outward pull. Imagine you have a good nut placement for a downward tug—it'll easily hold a fall, but only if the force pulls directly down. To secure this placement, you might rig a nut or a cam below it, but oriented in such a way that it resists an upward and outward pull. You could then connect these pieces with a sling, preferably clove-hitched to the upper piece to tension it and allow it to keep the upper piece slotted and secured.

Use gear placements in opposition to resist secondary pulls. We put the clove hitch on the piece that will hold the fall and the sling connects the pieces, creating an omnidirectional placement. PHILBRICK PHOTOGRAPHY

ANTICIPATION

To manage and mitigate secondary pulls, we must become expert at anticipating where the route goes and how our ropes will travel across and up the rock, and don't forget—we need to predict where our next placement will be, too. Terrain assessment is a skill that takes time to master and it's difficult to teach, let alone learn, within a book. Add to that reading a route, its sequences and gear placements, and you can see it's a subtle, demanding art.

Ultimately, managing secondary pulls requires you to know where you're going, where you're going to place gear, and how to calculate the angles created by the rope. With some practice you'll soon be connecting the dots in as straight a line as possible, and when it's not straight, you'll be dealing with the secondary pulls via gear placements and slings.

Ease of Removal

Security and strength come first when placing gear, but we should keep removal in mind, too. Especially for climbers looking to do long routes and guides maximizing their clients' enjoyment, wasting time and energy on stuck gear is a nonstarter. Cleaning gear from awkward stances or struggling to clean while hanging on with one arm can be nearly impossible for newer climbers and clients.

Protect yourself first and foremost, but if you can help it, make your followers' lives easier by placing from restful stances. Especially with inexperienced clients, placing at a stance with solid feet makes gear removal far easier. If they can use both hands, all the better. Coaching them to relax and reset the feet *before* they clean gear will help them save energy.

With cams, making sure they don't walk, even the tiniest bit, dramatically improves ease of removal, not to mention security. Those same lips and features on a crack that add security also help with cleaning by not allowing the cam to rotate or walk into a tricky spot. Adding a longer sling to a cam can make all the difference, too.

For Tricams, making sure that in active mode they are not too tightly placed will help when it comes time to clean them. Remember they should be placed from about halfway through their expansion range to larger. Also, placing Tricams when you have a nice stance and saving the SLCDs for the one-handed placements and removals will make it simpler.

For nuts and Tricams that are passively placed, exercise caution when setting them. Consider slightly longer slings on the piece rather than tugging on it to set it. At first, this will take time and you won't feel like you are gaining anything, but with practice the finesse will come naturally.

Strategy: Priorities and "Rules"

Leading more complicated routes, longer routes, and routes at our limit requires balancing options and making choices. Do we place an extra piece on the pitch and have less gear for the anchor? Do we clean a piece from a three-point anchor before leading the next pitch? Does a "perfect" anchor compromise our ability to protect the next lead?

Your rack and equipment are finite; this means you'll need to make some hard choices up there. One option is to bring so much gear you'll never have to compromise. Your first 10-mile approach, though, and you'll quickly discover the downside of this strategy. Many climbers apply "rules-based" decision making, hoping this will help them navigate the many variables in climbing and protecting themselves.

Expertise: Beyond the Rules

Expertise grows from a rigid sense of the rules into a more nuanced collection of guidelines. In this manner the more experienced, masterful climber can handle far more complex situations. Anchor building is where we see these rigid rules applied most fervently. Keep in mind, though, that a unique or complex situation may fall outside the parameters of the rules. If we follow, for example, the simple rules of anchor building, our basic understanding becomes incompetence when faced with an unusual anchor situation.

Sticking with the anchor example, this incompetence isn't necessarily the inability to build an adequate anchor. Rather, it's too little knowledge to manage a complex situation. Basic rules in a complex situation only provide a simple solution, which might not get the job done.

The competing priorities of reducing weight, increasing speed, climbing well, and taking care of oneself all demand attention. Expertise reveals itself in the solutions we devise to resolve the dilemmas and contradictions presented by these competing variables. Creating solutions with a rigid set of rules disregards the possibility of solving unique and complex problems with an advanced level of technique and application.

For example, after a long and demanding pitch, you may arrive at the belay with less gear than you'd like. You (and your partner!) will want a bomber anchor, but without a full range of protection you'll be forced to make compromises. Your anchor may be suboptimal. Is this acceptable? When the second arrives, do you rebuild it? If not, how can you justify and mitigate the risks of a suboptimal anchor? What if even with all the gear, you don't have the option to rebuild, due to a lack of gear choices, an old bolt anchor, or just a poor crack at the stance? Can you purposefully make a compromise at the anchor so you can better protect the next pitch? These questions require us to understand the interplay between the anchor and protection. By understanding that interplay we can manipulate the system such that we still have effective fall protection.

Expertise: A Holistic Solution

Let's look at a realistic situation that might occur through no fault of the climber. A leader finishes a lead, and finds that the anchor isn't "confidence inspiring." This anchor may be suboptimal because of poor bolts or it may be due to a crumbly crack at the only good stance. It may not even be a suboptimal anchor, but suppose there's a crux just above and the anchor position will make it awkward to catch a factor 2 fall.

In these cases, the best plan of action is for the leader to climb past the poor anchor, fire the crux moves to the next good piece of protection, then lower back to the anchor. Because there is so much rope out, any fall at the crux will be much softer and easier to catch when compared to the potential factor 2.

Once back at the marginal anchor, the leader can augment it by tying a big bight knot with the two strands coming from the piece of protection above and clipping that knot to the masterpoint. The double-stranded bight knot anchors the leader, and when he clips it to the masterpoint, he's secured by the good piece above and the marginal pieces in the lower anchor.

If the second will be leading the next pitch, the leader also clove-hitches in to the anchor, because when the lower climber becomes the new leader, the team can untie the bight knot and pull all the rope through the top piece, putting the new leader on a toprope for the initial moves.

In both systems the upper piece of protection is incorporated into the anchor. Once the second arrives, if he is going to lead the next pitch, the bight knot can be untied and the rope pulled through the upper piece till it comes tight to him. Now the new leader has a toprope for the section of concern. If the climber who led the last pitch will continue leading, the follower (or client) puts him on belay on the backside of the bight knot and now he has a toprope for his second trip through the crux section. We've used this

1. The first leader has clipped a top piece and lowered back to the belay, tied a double-stranded bight knot with the rope, and incorporated it into the anchor. Where you clip it into your anchor system depends upon the quality of the pieces, the material involved, and who will lead the next pitch. PHILBRICK PHOTOGRAPHY

2. This party will be swinging leads, with the new leader being in the plaid shirt. Note the previous leader has clove-hitched in because he will stay on the anchor. PHILBRICK PHOTOGRAPHY

Leader Protection **35**

3. *The previous leader has removed the double-stranded bight knot and will now pull all the team's rope through the upper piece, starting at the backside of his clove hitch. This will pull the rope tight against the new leader.*
PHILBRICK PHOTOGRAPHY

5. *The new leader cleans the plaquette and brings it with him. He starts up the pitch, effectively on a toprope through the high piece.*
PHILBRICK PHOTOGRAPHY

4. *The new leader takes a belay. Note that the previous leader takes the new leader's device off his harness and uses it. In this way, the new leader stays on the plaquette throughout this transition.* PHILBRICK PHOTOGRAPHY

approach on routes like *Bird on a Wire* in Joshua Tree and *Tits and Beer* on Looking Glass, in North Carolina—great routes with challenging climbing above a problematic stance, and this approach resolves the dilemma perfectly.

This example illustrates how understanding fall factors, the dynamic properties of the rope, and building an overall system of fall protection—rather than simply focusing on one piece at a crux—can help formulate creative solutions to the problems we continually face in climbing.

Difficult Problems

Let's look at more difficult problems for which there might not be any "good solutions," but nonetheless can be instructive to better understand the interplay of anchors, ropes, and gear in fall protection.

A party decides to link two pitches together, and the resulting mega-pitch ends up being longer than a rope length. (Moderate pitches without rope drag often present this option to climbers, whether on slabby or steeper, open terrain.) The leader finds himself 20 feet shy of the anchor after linking pitches and has three options:

1. The leader ties into his top/last piece(s), belays his partner to him, and then the stronger climber leads the 20 feet to the anchor.

2. The leader anchors into the top piece(s) and then belays his partner up to a piece of protection 20 or so feet above the old anchor. The follower then ties into that piece and puts the leader back on belay so he can finish the lead.

3. The climbers simul-climb a rope length apart until the leader reaches the anchor, builds an anchor, and puts his partner on belay.

In option 1, the team sets itself up for a potential factor 2 fall onto a single- or two-piece placement. This seems an unacceptable risk. The chances of ripping the anchor—and killing the whole team—shouldn't be accepted when other alternatives are available.

In options 2 and 3, the climbers keep as much protection between them as possible, as well as the full length of the rope in the pitch, greatly reducing potential forces should someone fall. The difference between these two options is that in 3, if the second falls the leader falls, too. This doubles the leader's chances of falling, especially if the second is tired or less skilled. If the terrain is well within the second's ability and he's aware of the risks, option 3 is less tedious and probably reasonable.

If the beginning of the pitch is difficult, or the leader does not wish to accept the risk of being pulled off by his partner, option 2 offers a better solution. In this scenario an entire rope separates the team, with a full pitch of gear placements between the climbers. Fall forces will be very small should the second fall, and the option takes a potential factor 2 off the table. Almost never would we consider belaying a second off a single piece of gear, but in this case it might be a viable, reasonable option.

Imagine another scenario, a rather common one, in which the leader finds herself having difficulty leading her pitch. She's the stronger climber within her team, but nevertheless she's thrutching up one of the crux pitches, more than 100 feet above the belay. She comes to a small ledge with a good crack, then some easy terrain, and finally a 6-foot crux just below the belay. She climbs a few feet up, gets a suboptimal piece, eyeballs the crux. She's considering it . . . but meanwhile the wind has begun to blow, clouds have grown on the horizon, and she realizes if her marginal piece blows, she'll hit the ledge below. Uh oh!

She wavers a bit and then decides she'd rather have her belayer nearby, take a rest, get some moral support for the hard climbing above. The belayer is the weaker climber, so having him lead the section isn't an option. She unclips from the marginal piece, downclimbs to the ledge, builds a bomber anchor, and brings up her second.

What her solution fails to take into account is the shock-absorbing capacity of the rope. If she blows the crux section with her belayer far below, she'll take a 12-foot fall on 100 feet of rope (perhaps a bit more with rope stretch—a consideration), for a fall factor of .12. If she takes the same fall with her belayer on the higher ledge, she'll take a 12-foot fall on 16 feet of rope, creating a fall factor of .75.

If the worry is the failure of the suboptimal placement and hitting the ledge, then she's set the system up to put more force onto that piece. Also, if the piece were to fail with her belayer on the higher ledge, not only will she hit the ledge, but she could fall past it. That could result in a very-hard-to-catch factor 2 fall. Her belayer could easily drop her, not to mention she risks pulling pieces in the anchor.

Fall-Line Management

As a leader places protection for a potential fall, he may also be developing a new fall line for his second. Creating a bad swing for the second can be a serious risk-management consideration. For any leader, there should be some concern how protection affects the second's fall; for the guide, it is a critical consideration.

If a leader were to climb a long, easy diagonal crack, then at the end of it place a piece, the second falling anywhere along that diagonal will swing until she's directly under that piece. That is their fall line, directly under the piece. If the same leader places gear along the diagonal crack, then the fall line for the second is directly under the next piece, making the swing less. We'll call this protecting the traverse. This is a classic system and requires that the leader place more gear.

In the simple case above, placing more gear lessens the swing, but sometimes placing less might straighten out a fall line for the second. Let's take the same situation, but after the diagonal the route

On a traversing pitch, the leader must protect before and after a crux, in addition to intermittent placements along the way. The pieces before a crux protect the leader; pieces after the crux protect the second.
PHILBRICK PHOTOGRAPHY

wanders the opposite way. So our leader does a 15-foot diagonal traverse to the right and then as he moves up, the route wanders back to the left. By not placing gear on the final feet of the traverse (or placing it but then back cleaning) *and* the terrain going up and left, the rope will take a nice straight line and the swing will not be as dramatic. This style of fall-line management is called the "high pivot point." The higher the pivot point above the second, the softer the swing will be.

All fall-line management combines some elements of both situations. Seeing the line and considering how the fall line will be for the second is an advanced leading technique. Guides need to be careful to not focus on a high pivot point so much that they end up putting themselves in jeopardy. A guide must always balance the risk of a runout with fall-line management for the second(s). On big routes a guide becoming incapacitated not only puts him at risk, but also puts his inexperienced clients at risk. Guide security is client security on big routes. It is easy for an experienced guide to take on too much risk, thinking himself impervious to falling on easy terrain.

1. Traverses don't always mean placing lots of gear. In this scenario, the leader placed pieces low in a crack, which means if his second falls while traversing, he'll take a nasty pendulum.

PHILBRICK PHOTOGRAPHY

We first need to recognize when the second might be at risk. One obvious clue is traversing, especially from difficult terrain onto easier terrain. Whenever you finish a section like this, evaluate the terrain for a possible swing.

The beauty of the high pivot point solution is that it reduces rope drag for the leader in most cases, and that can have a positive risk-management impact on him. This is especially true when using the parallel rope system. If the runout is too risky, or the guide doesn't notice the pivot point solution until after a section, perhaps a decisive and efficient back-cleaning decision is the best solution.

In a party of three, the team could climb caterpillar style and have the middle climber take a back-belay and strategically clean a couple pieces to give the last climber a high pivot.

The key to fall-line management is to think of the two methods as equivalent. Lots of leaders have been taught to "protect traverses." That phrase creates a bias toward the option of placing more protection over the high pivot point. If you can conceptualize the high pivot point in the same way you do managing rope drag or a secondary pull (see the "Choosing the Right Length of Sling or Quickdraw" section on page 28), it might be easier

2. If the leader decides he can forego a couple placements, or he back cleans, then he can establish a high pivot point, which gives his follower a much more effective belay as the follower traverses.

to recognize the two techniques as viable tools rather than one over the other.

In summary, the high pivot point becomes a risk-management problem for the leader if he elects to run it out to create it. If he back cleans to create the system, it becomes a time-management problem for the team. Weighing those two problems becomes a judgment call.

CHAPTER 4

Belay Anchors

Whole books have been devoted to the anchor. Friendly arguments over beers and passionate debates on web forums have generated a tremendous focus on this component of the fall-protection system. So much anchor information exists, it has displaced other important subjects and in many cases has led to confusion. We hope to add clarity to the topic, but to us this chapter is less important than others—not because anchors are unimportant, but because so much information on them already exists.

Common Myths about Belay Anchors

First let's look at some common myths about anchoring, and then we'll discuss each.

Myth 1: Three-point anchors are the most common.

Myth 2: The anchor is the most important part of the fall-protection system.

Myth 3: Redundancy at the anchor means it is twice as strong as a non-redundant anchor.

Myth 4: All anchors need to do the same thing, so they should be built to the same standard.

Myth 1: Three-point anchors are the most common.

We would agree that three-point anchors are the most common anchors when placing our own gear. However, if you take all multi-pitch climbing, even multi-pitch trad climbing, and look at how many

bolted anchors exist and how frequently we use trees or other natural anchors, you might find that the three-point anchor is much less common than people think. This myth does climbers a disservice in that it potentially overstates their competencies, when in fact anchor building may be a far less practiced skill. Many climbers have far less experience with anchors than they assume.

Question that assumption: Are you truly skilled at efficient, reliable anchor building? Maybe not! For most this may seem too basic a skill, but it is our experience teaching new guide candidates that some attention here is warranted. One problem we see is that masterpoints are often too low, which makes the anchor awkward to work with. It's also much more difficult to hold a leader fall in the event of a factor 2 fall.

Connecting three or even four pieces also challenges most climbers. Placements that are far apart or too numerous often leave the leader with the impression that her cordelette is too short. Cordelettes seem to get longer every year. We recommend carrying long slings that can ameliorate the above problems, while also being available for sundry other tasks during a climb. We strive to carry gear and material that fulfills as many uses as possible—why not apply this tactic to our bulky, heavy cordelettes?

Myth 2: The anchor is the most important part of the fall-protection system.

We don't suggest the anchor is unimportant, but it is a part of an entire fall-protection system made up of other equally important components. Leader protection failure is a common cause of accidents, as are rappelling or lowering off the end of a rope and poor belaying. Rappelling, lowering, belaying—these are all "fall-protection systems."

If you look at how often anchor failure causes accidents, it becomes clear it's not the hazard we assume it to be. This certainly does not mean we should be focused on leader protection or closing the system for rappels and belays at the expense of the anchor, but neither should we be so focused on the anchor at the expense of those other components.

Build anchors as we've learned to do—securely, efficiently, with some redundancy, but without overbuilding them. This saves gear for the next pitch and potentially improves your overall *system* rather than just the anchor on its own. Too often experienced climbers use too much gear, or too much gear of a certain size, in the anchor, which puts the leader at a disadvantage for the next pitch. We often see climbers carry an excessively large rack to compensate for an overbuilt anchor, too—not a huge penalty on a short route or a route with a short crux, but for longer efforts, the extra weight can be an enormous disadvantage.

Myth 3: Redundancy at the anchor means it is twice as strong as a non-redundant anchor.

In fact, a non-redundant anchor can be stronger than a redundant one. Take, for instance, a cordelette placed around a tree. As an anchor we would then tie a knot to make the cord redundant, but we also have the option of just basketing it around the tree. With a knot in the system, you see that should any strand break or cut, the entire anchor does not fail. In the basketed one, you can see that if one strand were to break, cut, or fail, the entire anchor would fail. So it is clear the knotted one is redundant, while the basketed one is not.

Now, we know that any knot tied into cord will weaken it. So how could the knotted/redundant one be stronger? The simple answer is that it is not stronger in tensile strength.

From here things start to get really confusing. We know from testing that if we pull the knotted cord to failure, it will be weaker than a basketed cord. But if we do a drop test, we might see some differences. Why? Because when the knot tightens, it adds dynamics/shock absorption to the system. We know from testing at DMM in Wales that nylon behaves this way, while Spectra does not—knotted Spectra does not seem to add any dynamic component to the system. We are guessing here, but it seems that Spectra's inherent "slipperiness," or lack of friction when running over itself, means that the knot tightens quickly and doesn't generate much in the way of heat. That means the knotted Spectra isn't as dynamic. (For simplicity's sake, we use Spectra and Dyneema interchangeably throughout the book.)

In short, we might be making compromises in strength in the pursuit of redundancy. This might not be a huge problem, but if you do the same comparative analysis with the classic pre-equalized cordelette system and the magic X/crossed sling system, you'll see the prejudice we have for redundancy over strength.

Bottom line, we need to evaluate the demands placed on each anchor we build. Modern testing has shown that most of our methods for equalizing anchors (pre-equalized cordelettes in particular) do *not* equalize effectively, so putting knots into our cordelettes and webbing may only be weakening our materials, without achieving significant overall strength in our anchors. Speed and simplicity (you're at risk of being benighted or beneath seracs on an alpine route, for example) can also deemphasize the need for redundancy. In instances like these, a non-redundant anchor might not be the end of the world—in fact, it might be the smart choice.

Too many times we see climbers and new guide candidates overly concerned with redundancy and to get redundancy they expose themselves to other hazards or carry too much equipment or burn time to solve the problem. In serious, complicated terrain, choices like these are critical to managing diverse hazards and keeping moving.

Myth 4: All anchors need to do the same thing, so they should be built to the same standard.

To discuss this myth we need to first delve into what anchors do. In the most general sense, they keep us from falling off the mountain. But who is the "us" in our definition?

Most of the time, climbing is a team sport, and like all team sports, there are positions. Our teams have three positions: belayer, second, and leader. Next we have to ask, how much energy can each position put onto the anchor? If a belayer is leaning back on the anchor, the amount of weight on that anchor is minimal. It's less than body weight, in fact, because of the amount of weight on the belayer's feet. Even at a hanging stance, it will be less than body weight because much of the climber's weight still rests on the feet, and the friction of the body against the wall reduces the weight even further.

For the following climber, or second, forces can be higher because some slack will be in the system and the initial rope stretch adds some momentum to any fall. Generally a second's fall can be as high as double body weight. Neither of these forces are really high, but the second putting 400-plus pounds on the anchor is not insignificant.

What about the leader? In most leader falls the anchor feels nothing at all and all the force is concentrated on the top piece of protection. But if a leader comes off at the beginning of a pitch, without any protection in, the anchor must hold a factor 2 fall. Even if the leader used the anchor as his or her first piece of protection, forces decrease on the belayer and climber but that first clip creates mechanical advantage that takes the force and theoretically doubles it (it's acting as a 2:1 pulley). In reality, the friction of the pulley/carabiner means

you multiply by 1.6/1.7. Either way, clipped or not, the forces in a leader fall far exceed the other two.

How does this factor into the myth? In some situations, as when the belay is on a ledge large enough that the leader can't take a factor 2 fall or there's good gear immediately available above the anchor, it might be smarter to build a minimalist anchor. If other factors like weather or time trump the "security" of an overbuilt anchor, the "less secure" anchor may actually be the better call.

Advanced Anchor Situations

Let's cover some anchor systems that might be helpful in advanced or complex situations.

It helps to have a process to analyze the strengths and weaknesses of an anchor in a particular situation. No anchor can be perfect; therefore, we need to know what aspect or function of the anchor is compromised, then make decisions to mitigate those compromises. We can also modify other parts of our fall-protection system to address these compromises.

The list below offers an acronym to help you remember a set of criteria with which to analyze anchors. We call this the NERDSS analysis:

1. **No Extension**: If one of the pieces were to fail, the anchor does not extend, thereby keeping the belayer stationary. Movement of the belayer, particularly if he's pulled off the belay ledge, can severely compromise his ability to hold a factor 2 fall. Shock loading and peak forces are less of a concern here, as the belayer should be attached to the anchor with the dynamic rope. Should the belayer choose to attach himself with a static/semi-static leash, a high-force shock load becomes a serious concern.

2. **Redundancy**: More than one anchor element (gear, material, etc.) must fail before the whole anchor fails. As we said above, there isn't a direct correlation between strength and redundancy. It is still something worth considering, though,

and any anchor analysis should. Bottom line, if your anchor isn't redundant, you should know it and have a reason to justify it.

3. **D**istributed: If there is to be more than one piece in our anchor, we want the force generated by a fall to be distributed among the pieces. We use the combined strength of those pieces rather than having one backing up the other. When joining pieces and distributing forces, we do not want to unwittingly amplify those forces by having large angles in the "legs" of our connection system (more on this below).

4. **S**implicity: How quickly can we build and break down the anchor? How simple is it, and does it allow climbers to easily check key elements?

5. **S**trength: The system, placements, and materials we use must be appropriately strong.

We must start by realizing that without a perfect anchor, our job becomes making the best compromises given our situation. The techniques we cover below are best described as a "system of anchoring." This system will solve most problems on multi-pitch climbs, but it is not exclusive. In other words, many valid anchoring techniques exist, and just because we don't cover them doesn't mean they're less worthy or applicable. The reason we do not cover them is to simplify the anchoring process and reduce duplication. These are the systems we use daily in our work and recreation. We find these systems to be versatile, and we seldom need to stray from them.

Single-Point Belay Anchors

The single-point belay anchor may seem like too large a compromise, but in many areas they're the most commonly used ones. On crags in forested terrain, single trees often provide solid anchors both on and at the top of the cliff.

Single-point anchors can be used if we feel the need to belay a short section of third/fourth-class terrain to check a slip. We could use a single nut or cam, along with a stance, to belay a climber off our belay loop. In this section we'll focus on the more robust single-point anchors needed for fifth-class rock.

By definition, a single-point anchor cannot be redundant, therefore we must be very comfortable with it if we are to employ one in fifth-class terrain. As mentioned above, the most common single-point anchor is a very stout tree. Other examples can be large boulders, a thread, and large horns. All must be inspected carefully, but horns and boulders seem to be the most common single-point anchors misjudged in the field. Pound on them, tap them with an ice axe, push them with your feet to test—but be aware they sometimes fail. Don't rain a rock down on your buddy if something gives way!

Although the anchor itself may be a single point, we can rig the sling or cord we use in a redundant manner. This is especially important with horns and boulders, as they may have sharp sides that could cut the material we place around them.

RIGGING MATERIAL ON A SINGLE-POINT ANCHOR

There are three common ways climbers place sling or cord around these type of objects:

1. Girth hitch
2. Placing a loop around the object and clipping the ends of that loop together with a carabiner (often called basketing)
3. Placing a sewn sling or tied cord around the object and tying the end loops together with a figure eight or overhand knot (the classic cordelette style)

Let's run through our NERDSS analysis for the girth-hitched single-point anchor. The "no extension" analysis becomes moot, because with only one point on which to anchor, there's nothing to fail and extend. When we analyze the girth hitch for redundancy, we ask, if the sling were to break or cut at any one spot, would the whole system fail? We can quickly see that the girth hitch lacks redundancy. When analyzing distribution, again we have a moot point because we are talking about a single point. When we do a strength analysis of the girth hitch, we see that only two strands of the cord or sling hold the force. This means that each strand of cord or sling needs to hold half the force that is placed on the anchor.

When we place a loop around the rock or tree and clip the ends of that loop together with a carabiner (basketing), four strands hold the force, which puts only one-quarter of the force on each strand This is a stronger arrangement than the girth hitch, but this system too lacks redundancy, because should any strand break or cut, the whole system fails.

Looping a cord or sling around an object, then tying it off with a figure eight or overhand, yields the strength of four strands, but we've also weakened the material because of the knot. However, if any strand were to break or cut, the system remains intact. While slightly weaker, this system provides redundancy.

A girth-hitched cord puts the load on two strands of the material and offers no redundancy.
PHILBRICK PHOTOGRAPHY

Basketing a cordelette puts one-quarter of the load onto each strand. PHILBRICK PHOTOGRAPHY

Tying off the cordelette reduces the chances of triaxially loading the carabiner.
PHILBRICK PHOTOGRAPHY

Because of their simplicity, analyzing that very simplicity in single-point anchors becomes an academic exercise. One could argue tying off the figure eight or overhand takes slightly longer, but generally this is seconds and the real difference is marginal. The only exception to this might be at a hanging belay with wet slings—with cold, tired hands, removing the knot from a weighted Spectra sling can be a drag, especially for clients at the end of a long day. Consider this when guiding.

Given that the girth hitch has no real advantage over the other two systems and is weaker than the other alternatives, its use as an anchoring system is limited and in most cases should not be employed. It is included here for comparison purposes only.

When applying the NERDSS analysis as we evaluate our anchors, we need to avoid falling into the trap of assuming a redundant anchor is always better than a non-redundant anchor. As important, given our slings and materials are typically far stronger than we need, overemphasizing an anchor's strength can also lead us to a flawed analysis.

What we may perceive as a positive or a negative might not be so on second glance. For example, knots weaken material, but in nylon can actually add dynamic capacity to an anchor (improving strength). Redundancy guards against cutting, but forcing a knot into a sling might shorten it to the point where it multiplies forces on two horizontally spaced bolts, dramatically weakening the anchor.

Redundancy, of any anchor concept, is the most habitually applied, and at times it's overemphasized. From the example above, imagine a tree so large we can't tie off a cordelette when we wrap it. Do you not use the tree as an anchor or basket it? You basket it! When you do, however, your analysis should immediately remind you that the anchor isn't redundant, so we need to address the problems of non-redundant anchors.

We immediately consider the method used to join the ends of the sling or cord because it's rigged in a non-redundant configuration. These methods range from factory stitching to any number of knots; the most common ones are the water knot for sling material and the double fisherman's or the flat overhand for cord. In a non-redundant system, if these knots were tied incorrectly or became untied, the anchor fails.

After the junction knot failing, our concern returns to the sling or cord cutting. This is of importance when the single-point anchor is made of rock, either a large boulder or more likely a horn. Using rock as a single-point anchor generally triggers us to seriously consider using a redundant system.

Typically this means doubling a cord or sling, then knotting it. The bight knot not only delivers redundancy, but other benefits as well. In our basketed system above, the carabiner can easily end up cross-loaded and compromised. Having a bight knot creates a masterpoint, which guards against the carabiner shifting, or being cross- or triaxially loaded. We could add another carabiner or just pay extra attention to it.

Like most situations, you'll have to balance compromises. If, for example, a tree proved too large to double a cord or sling around, then a basketed system isn't necessarily inappropriate. You should check the junction knot, use good material, and pay extra attention to keeping the carabiners aligned correctly. In short, you're identifying the shortcomings of your solution but "making it work" in that particular situation—something we should be doing constantly when building anchors.

This is an advanced approach to anchor building. We challenge our assumptions and analyze our systems as we go. We move beyond rules-based decision making into applying judgment and expertise in the field, depending upon the situation at hand.

Two-Point Anchors

We typically build *at a minimum* two-point gear (nuts, cams, Tricams, etc.) anchors for our fifth-class climbing. Because we consider two-point anchors a minimum standard, we should therefore consider them somewhat uncommon. Two-point fixed anchors (bolts and pitons, for the most part), on the other hand, are quite common and standard.

Whether gear or fixed, let's look at four main systems for our two-point anchors.

1. Crossed sling (magic X)
2. The quad
3. The cordelette
4. Direct tie-in

THE CROSSED SLING (MAGIC X)

To tie the crossed sling, take a sling (usually shoulder-length, but occasionally a double-length) and clip it into two pieces. Pull down on one strand of the sling between the two pieces and twist it, then clip a locking carabiner into the loop formed by the twist and the other strand of the sling. You should check to make sure that the locking carabiner is clipped properly *through the twist and the other strand*. If it is not, should either of the pieces fail, the carabiner could slide off the sling, causing the anchor to fail entirely.

The crossed sling (magic X).
PHILBRICK PHOTOGRAPHY

Tied correctly, you'll notice that either of the pieces could fail and the anchor would remain intact, though it would extend several inches. While somewhat redundant (as far as the pieces are concerned), the crossed sling fails the "no extension" test.

Looking more closely at redundancy, we notice that if the sling were to get cut, the entire anchor fails. So this anchor is not entirely redundant.

Keep in mind, however, that most masterpoint anchor systems are technically non-redundant. We commonly use a single locking carabiner for our

Reversed and Opposed: Non-Lockers at the Anchor

A truly redundant masterpoint anchor employs two carabiners at its connection—typically two non-locking carabiners, gates reversed and opposed. We certainly don't suggest you abandon your single locker. On the contrary, we use a single locker almost universally as our connection to the anchor. The reversed-and-opposed non-lockers, though, seem to be a forgotten tool at the basic level, so we include it here. It's a tool every climber should know, as there will come a time, no doubt, when a team has run out of lockers. That said, rest assured using a single locker is fine and standard—just make sure it's locked. The whole shootin' match counts on it!

connection. We don't mean to suggest a single locking biner is unsafe, but we find it a notable detail given the (over)emphasis placed on redundancy.

Now check the distribution of the forces with the crossed sling. We can move side to side or up and down while hanging on the anchor. With the crossed sling, the locking carabiner slides and the sling adjusts to keep the forces distributed somewhat evenly, though not perfectly. The sliding action of the crossed sling becomes much less effective with high forces like those generated in a factor 2 fall. The sling appears to bind itself in the locking carabiner, reducing the distribution further.

When we analyze simplicity, the crossed sling is hard to beat, especially with bolts or gear placements close enough that we can use a standard shoulder-length runner.

Next we consider the strength of the crossed-sling system. We can see that each piece receives about one-half of the force, but because we have four strands taking the force in the sling, we are stressing each strand with only one-quarter of the force. So in our analysis of the crossed sling, we find it will extend and lacks redundancy, but it has a good distribution of forces and is a simple and a strong system.

In summary, with a crossed sling we need to make sure the junction knot or stitching is in good shape and the material itself is undamaged.

We should also verify the sling doesn't contact any sharp edges along its length.

THE QUAD

The quad has grown in popularity over the past few years. We find it most useful in ice climbing, so look for more information on it in that chapter.

It works exceptionally well on rock as well, particularly if most or all of the anchors are bolted. *Plaisir* routes—that is, "pleasure" routes that are long, bolted, and with two-bolt belays—make the perfect venue for having two quad-style anchors ready to go at the base of the route. No need to tie or untie them throughout the day; have them ready in your pack at the base and leave them built all day. Fast and efficient.

To tie a quad, start with a quadruple-length sling (most likely in Spectra/Dyneema to save on bulk and weight, but a cordelette works fine, too), fold it in half with a twist, and then fold again. Each time you fold it, you give it a half-twist, so the sling should now be in fourths. It should be about the length of a shoulder sling now. Tie an overhand about 4 to 6 inches from each end. Clip each of those loops into each bolt. At the center of the quad you should have four independent strands between the overhands. Clip your locking carabiner into two of the strands, leaving the other two for your plaquette and/or for your partner to clip into it.

Two-point quad. PHILBRICK PHOTOGRAPHY

The quad extends a bit if a piece fails. It's redundant and it distributes forces better than a crossed sling, as there's no webbing running over itself. In tests it scores the best in distribution/equalization compared with the other anchors. Its strength is as good as a classic cordelette. For simplicity it is a bit mixed. If you need to build it at the stance, it is similar or a bit more work than a classic cordelette setup. If you can keep it tied as you would in ice climbing or on a route that has all bolted anchors, it is very simple.

THE TWO-POINT TRADITIONAL CORDELETTE

To build the two-point cordelette anchor, you clip the cord into the pieces as a giant loop. You then pull down on the sling between the two pieces until you meet the strand hanging below (the bottom of the big loop), grab the two strands, and tie either a figure eight or an overhand knot.

When we check for extension, we find little or no movement of the belayer should a piece fail. With redundancy, we find that at least two strands of the cord need to be cut or break for it to fail. The cordelette distributes forces between the pieces, but only in one direction. In this sense, it is "pre-equalized," or equalized for only direction of pull. Our cord (or sling) must usually be longer than a shoulder-length runner, and because of this, it is quite a bit more tedious to break down and store.

A traditional two-point cordelette.
PHILBRICK PHOTOGRAPHY

Taken as a whole, the cordelette method proves relatively simple, but not quite as quick and clean as the crossed sling. In terms of strength, we're working with four strands of material, but we also knot the cord—therefore compromising the strength. As we mentioned in the section on myths, the balance of strength, redundancy, and dynamics becomes a complex calculation.

As long as we're working with 5.5mm tech cord, 6mm nylon cord, Dyneema sling material, or at least ⁹/₁₆-inch (15mm) nylon webbing, the cordelette system measures well within our needs for strength. The point here is that many confuse redundancy with strength, and that is not always the case. A redundant system like the cordelette may protect you from a poorly tied junction knot in the sling or cord, or a manufacturer's defect, but it does not necessarily create a system that has a higher tensile strength.

THE DIRECT TIE-IN

For the direct tie-in, we build our anchor with the rope. First, tie a small overhand on a bight close to your harness. (We do this to conserve enough rope to create a masterpoint once we've built the anchor. This knot is really just a placeholder for the moment.) Next, measure from your stance to the lowest piece of your anchor. To do this, clip your

rope into the lowest piece and stand at the stance. Pull the rope tight to you using the piece as a pulley. Grab the two strands going to the piece, and walk your hands up this to the piece. Unclip the rope from the piece, making sure not to lose the measurement. Add about 4 inches of rope to the measurement to accommodate the extra length the knot will take up.

Now tie a figure eight knot so that the loop of the knot is as long as the pieces are apart. Clip this knot into the lower piece. Take the backside rope from this knot and clove-hitch it to the second piece. Adjust this so that both pieces are weighted

1. Two-point direct tie-in. PHILBRICK PHOTOGRAPHY

2. Tie a small bight knot into your rope just in front of your tie-in. Measure the rope to the lowest piece. PHILBRICK PHOTOGRAPHY

3. Tie a figure eight on a bight, forming a loop long enough to create a small angle when clipping the next piece. PHILBRICK PHOTOGRAPHY

4. Take the backside of your figure eight and clove-hitch it to the upper piece.
PHILBRICK PHOTOGRAPHY

5. Once you've connected the rope to the two pieces, untie the bight knot in front of your harness and retie it just below the lowest piece. This is now your masterpoint.

when you lean back against your anchor. Next, undo the overhand on a bight you tied and tie another one as close to the figure eight as you can. This overhand becomes the masterpoint you'll use to belay your second.

Comparisons and Scenarios

Let's compare the four methods just described using the NERDSS analysis. To analyze an anchor, it is best to imagine yourself tied into and leaning back on the anchor.

When we do a NERDSS analysis on the direct tie-in, we find it similar to the cordelette in that it does not extend should a piece fail. As we check the direct tie-in for redundancy, we first notice that we have done away with the sling or cord of the previous three systems. Of note, we have also done away with our locking carabiner! Because we have taken out the potential weak link (of a cord or sling) and the locking carabiner, we consider the direct tie-in to be a superior system from a redundancy perspective, despite the fact that arguably it isn't redundant because we are using only one rope.

For us, this is a classic example of the superiority of more advanced analysis. Rigid protocol systems that "require" an anchor to be SRENE or ERNEST are useful when teaching the basics to relatively new climbers. When climbers progress to advanced systems and practice, analyzing systems rather than applying hard-and-fast rules yields more creative, more adaptive solutions.

Checking the direct tie-in for distribution yields similar results to the cordelette system. Both do a reasonable job of distributing forces between pieces, but only in a relatively narrow orientation. In terms of simplicity, the direct tie-in falls behind the other systems, especially for newer climbers. It can be confusing and challenging. As for strength, it's probably the best of all of them, given we're using only the dynamic climbing rope.

The following chart compares the analyses of the four two-point anchor systems:

	No Extension	Redundancy	Distribution	Strength*	Simplicity
Crossed sling	No	No	Good	Good	Simplest
Quad	No	Yes	Very good	Good	Can be if left tied
Cordelette	Yes	Yes	Limited	Good	More complicated
Direct tie-in	Yes	Yes	Limited	Excellent	Most complicated

*All four anchor systems are strong enough for multi-pitch climbing if the proper width or diameter cord or sling is used.

How does understanding these various systems help us in deciding which two-point anchor system to use in a situation? Considering some examples might help you make better decisions on the rock when the time comes.

First let's note that the quad and cordelette require a long, dedicated anchor sling or cord to build. This leaves the crossed sling or the direct tie-in as alternatives if you drop or lose your dedicated material. Between those two, the crossed sling has a masterpoint, so that can be important for a team block-leading or a guided team. Of course, we've already identified the compromises of the crossed sling, but by knowing those compromises we can manage them.

Let's look at an anchor that has two older bolts that look about the same and aren't very confidence inspiring. Do we want to make sure both are weighted as equally as possible so the force is distributed, or are we concerned with one failing and causing extension? If we feel they are roughly the same age and quality, one being substantially weaker is possible but not likely. If we have our anchor-building kit, then the quad starts to look good. It has the advantage of good distribution and redundancy, so it is superior to the crossed sling. Since the classic cordelette system doesn't distribute forces as well, it may create a weaker system by loading only one bolt.

How about a two-bolt anchor at which we have one new bolt and one rusty old bolt? We might be more concerned with extension, since we likely have a much weaker piece in the older bolt. If the belay is on a small ledge, that extension could be serious and make catching a factor 2 fall almost impossible. So now we lean to the cordelette or direct tie-in. Several variables factor into our decision when contemplating those two systems: simplicity, the availability of gear, and whether we are block-leading or not.

We could also look at the comfort of the stance on two good bolts. On a cordelette, two or three

The Master Carabiner

One challenge when using the crossed sling or Dyneema in a masterpoint is that the point at which you clip a carabiner can be very small if someone has already weighted it. Adding a large-volume carabiner as a "master biner," instead of a masterpoint in the material itself, helps make clipping in easy. Ideally use a large "HMS" or "pear" style carabiner, as testing has shown them stronger than a "D" style master biner when weighted by several climbers.

climbers hang from the same masterpoint, so if one climber leans in one direction, the others get pulled around. With the quad you can have two independent masterpoints, so climbers can move more freely and with less stressful shifting in the anchor. The quad therefore may be better for the comfort of the climbers.

Decisions and analyses like these may seem unwieldy at first, but over time you'll be able to make them quickly and almost unconsciously. As with any new system, incorporating it into our daily repertoire takes some time, but then becomes second nature.

Three-Point Anchors

Three-point anchors are the most common gear anchors and are mainly variations and combinations of the two-point anchors you already know. We will cover two types of three-point anchor systems and then look at combination anchors building on these:

1. Three-point traditional cordelette
2. Three-point quad
3. Two-point cordelette/crossed sling combination
4. Two-point quad/crossed sling combination
5. Two-point direct tie-in/crossed sling combination

Traditional three-point cordelette.
PHILBRICK PHOTOGRAPHY

THREE-POINT TRADITIONAL CORDELETTE

To tie this, take your cordelette and clip it into all three pieces. Then much like the two-point cord, pull down the single strand from between each piece, then grab the bottom strand and tie either a figure eight or an overhand. This loop becomes the masterpoint.

When we do the NERDSS analysis on the three-point cordelette, we find the same results as we had with the two-point setup—no extension, redundant, so-so distribution, good simplicity, and adequately strong.

THREE-POINT QUAD

To build a three-point quad, take a cordelette and clip it into the two smallest, or "weakest," pieces. Then, just like a two-point traditional cordelette, pull down the strands between the pieces and tie an overhand. Tie the knot as close to the pieces as you can to keep the angle between them acute.

Next take the bottom of the sling or cord, what you would tie off as the masterpoint in a two-point system, and clip that to the third piece. Pull down on the section of the cord between the two pieces that are combined and the third piece to get an approximation of the expected direction of forces on the anchor. Now unclip the cord/sling from the third piece and tie another overhand knot, and clip that loop back into the third piece. Ideally the two-point side of the sling is equalized on the two smallest/weakest pieces of gear, while the single side is on the strongest piece.

When we do the NERDSS analysis on the three-point quad, we find similar results to the two-point setup. The three-point quad, however, doesn't distribute the load quite as well between the two combined pieces, so its distribution is less effective with three pieces.

1. Three-point quad. Connect the first two pieces and tie an overhand below, being careful not to tie them off so closely it creates an obtuse angle. PHILBRICK PHOTOGRAPHY

2. Clip the hanging loop of material to the third piece. PHILBRICK PHOTOGRAPHY

3. Tie an overhand below the third piece.
PHILBRICK PHOTOGRAPHY

Combination Anchors

Now let's check out the combination anchors. To build these anchors we will take two pieces and combine them into one via a crossed sling. We then use the two-point cordelette, the two-point quad, or the direct tie-in to join the crossed sling with the remaining piece to form a three-point anchor.

When we analyze the combination cordelette and direct tie-in anchors, we discover that they distribute forces a bit better than the three-point cordelette, two-point cordelette, or two-point direct tie-in.

Look at the previous photos and visualize what would happen if the belayer leans to the opposite

side of the crossed sling. The two pieces connected by the crossed sling would take the weight. If the belayer leans to the other side, the single piece takes the weight. This means if you can predict the direction from which a secondary pull will come, you can build the anchor so that at least the two pieces will take that force. The quad/crossed-sling combination appears to do the better job at distributing the load.

We do not cover the three-point crossed sling anchors because due to the friction caused by the multiple twists in the material, this system does not distribute the load effectively. Given that the main reason to use this type of system is its ability to

Two-point cordelette plus the crossed sling.
PHILBRICK PHOTOGRAPHY

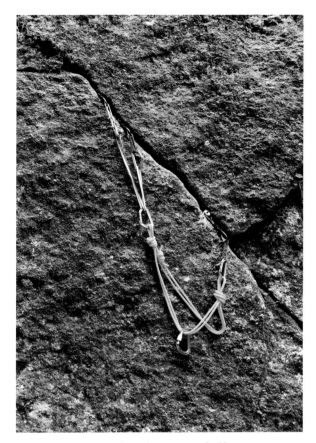

Two-point quad plus the crossed sling.
PHILBRICK PHOTOGRAPHY

Two-point direct tie-in plus the crossed sling.
PHILBRICK PHOTOGRAPHY

distribute forces, there is no advantage to the three-point crossed sling.

We also do not cover a combination crossed-sling anchor. The idea of having three pieces of gear and two slings come down to a non-redundant

system seems wasteful. In the rare circumstance you are without a long sling or cord (making a quad or classic cordelette impossible) and you need a masterpoint, perhaps it would be worth building a combination crossed-sling anchor.

In the following chart we compare three-point anchors:

	No Extension	Redundancy	Distribution	Strength*	Simplicity
Three-point cordelette	Yes	Yes	Limited	Good	Simple
Three-point quad	No	Yes	Good to very good	Good	More complicated
Two-point quad/ crossed sling combination	No	Yes	Very good	Good	More complicated
Two-point cordelette/ crossed sling combination	Yes	Yes	Good	Good	More complicated
Two-point direct tie-in/crossed sling combination	Yes	Yes	Good	Excellent	Very complicated

*All three-point systems are strong enough for multi-pitch climbing systems if proper-width slings or diameter cords are used.

As we get into anchors with more pieces, it is easier to get closer to a non-extending, redundant, distributed, strong system. Distribution and simplicity become the main variables. For most three-point anchors, what system you use becomes less important because with so many pieces and equipment to connect them, we can satisfy most concerns.

Notice when we use a combined system, the two pieces of the crossed sling act as one. That means at worst we should only be able to put half the force, and at best one-fourth the force, on those pieces. So, besides looking at where a secondary force might come from (and getting those pieces to mitigate it), we could also combine the two smallest or weakest pieces so they end up as a strong single piece within our anchor. In the end, simplicity and adapting the gear you have is where the art of the three-point anchor lies.

Four-or-More Point Anchor Systems

To build anchors with more than three pieces, you follow the same basic concepts as above. First,

cross-sling pieces until three points remain. When you're down to three points, do a three-point cordelette or quad system. You can also cross-sling pieces until two points remain and then choose between the two-point cordelette, the direct tie-in, or the quad.

We can assume anchors needing four or more pieces most likely consist of suboptimal pieces. Were the pieces bomber, three would be adequate. Suboptimal pieces mean distribution will be important. Also, by the time the anchor is fully built, the slings and other connections will drop the masterpoint down quite a bit. To use a given stance, you will need to get the pieces high and/or close together. If not, your masterpoint will be too low to have an effective anchor.

Angles and Their Effect on the Distribution of Force

No matter which anchor system you use, the angles between pieces demand your constant attention. Keep in mind we're concerned not only about angles between pieces, but also the angle created when we wrap sling or cord around a tree or horn. In short, any angle should be less than 90 degrees and the more acute, the better.

Any angle above 0 degrees increases forces somewhat, but once an angle exceeds 90 degrees, the forces will be multiplied significantly. For example, at 90 degrees a downward force of x becomes .75x at each piece—that's a 50 percent increase in forces! At 120 degrees the angle double forces on our anchor; at 160 degrees it increases forces on each leg three times, for a 6x increase on the whole anchor.

Force multiplication can occur even if the outermost strands of a three-point cordelette create the obtuse angle. Even though the middle strand of the cordelette may mitigate the problem, the chances that you will be able to get the three pieces working together to effectively distribute the force is slim. Angles are an important consideration in our anchors. Read up on them, as they are well covered in other books focusing on anchors.

Special Circumstances and Methods

To adapt these various anchor systems to the terrain and to the location of our gear placements, a couple skills will help. First we need to be able to effectively lengthen our cordelette and crossed slings if they are too short to join the pieces. Lengthening allows us to reduce an angle that is inappropriately large. Conversely, we'll need to shorten our cordelette and crossed slings in certain situations. This shortening allows us to have the masterpoint of the anchor at the right height so the belayer can take a proper stance to belay the leader or the second.

These two techniques run counter to one another, and compromises will be made. Refining these skills allows us to create the best anchor possible, even in awkward stances.

SHORTENING ANCHOR SYSTEMS

We commonly use three methods for shortening the cordelette. With the first, we simply double our cord and use it as we would normally, thereby shortening it by half. This works great and remains simple, though it's not adjustable—it's either full length or half.

In the second system, we tie an overhand knot in our cord and use the now-shortened loop to build the anchor. When using this technique, tie the overhand knot along the strands below the junction knot—in this way it keeps the junction knot out of your system and simplifies building it.

The overhand knot shortens one leg of the cordelette. PHILBRICK PHOTOGRAPHY

Another way to shorten the cordelette is instead of tying a figure eight knot at the bottom of the cord when pre-equalizing the rig, keep wrapping the excess before tying the cord off. Some climbers call this a figure nine or a BHK—big honkin' knot. Whatever you call it, it's a simple, quick means of taking up excess material and dialing the height of your masterpoint. It also makes the knot a bit easier to untie after weighting it, which makes it a nice option at a hanging belay or while wearing gloves.

You'll rarely need to shorten a crossed-sling anchor. Given the strengths and weaknesses of the crossed sling, it is primarily used on two bolts and it is done with a shoulder-length sling. This makes it exceptionally simple. When you are using a crossed sling as part of a combination anchor, you might need something longer than a shoulder-length, but shorter than a double-length. In this event, you could shorten a double-length by knotting one end of it (trap the sewn portion of the sling behind your knot to keep it from complicating the system). This is the second technique described above when shortening cordelettes.

There is a case when you might want to complicate the crossed sling, but it would not be just to shorten it (though it happens to do just that). This could happen when joining two suboptimal pieces and those pieces are far enough apart that you need a long sling. In that case you can use a crossed sling that has limiter knots tied into it. The limiter knots are overhands knots tied into each leg of the crossed sling. We call them limiter knots because they limit both the extension and the range that the crossed sling will slide to distribute the load.

With limiter knots tied into both legs as shown, a redundant system is created. Some find the analysis of the crossed sling with limiter knots so positive they use it on a regular basis. Most climbers and guides, though, find tying the crossed sling with limiter knots tedious and not as efficient at distributing the force compared to the quad. The quad's knots can be moved closer to the middle of

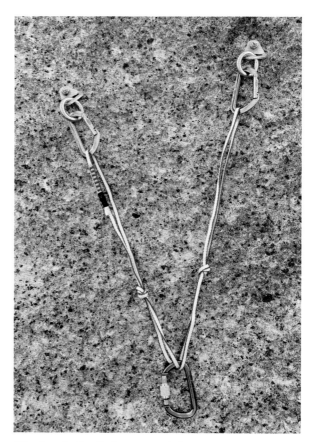

The knots limit the potential extension on the anchor. PHILBRICK PHOTOGRAPHY

the material to reduce the extension of that system if need be. The crossed sling with limiter knots is generally reserved for special circumstances, usually when two poor pieces are being combined in a three- or four-point combination anchor. For that reason, it is a good technique to know even if not used very often.

LENGTHENING ANCHOR SYSTEMS

The combination anchor in and of itself adds length to a system, because combining two pieces into one means you only need to join two pieces with your cord or quad.

Adding a sling effectively lengthens your cordelette. PHILBRICK PHOTOGRAPHY

We can also add a sling to a piece or a combination of pieces that is farther from the expected masterpoint to lengthen the cord or quad.

Anchors are an important component of the fall-protection system. The techniques outlined above give you some tools for constructing appropriate anchors. This overall system, along with the NERDSS analysis, should allow you to have an advanced understanding that adapts to terrain and individual placements on any given climb. At the least, it should give you a baseline from which to evaluate a system we did not cover. By applying this knowledge, you will be able to quickly and efficiently adapt to the variables you will take into consideration when deciding where and how to build a particular anchor in the field.

CHAPTER 5

Belaying

Belaying the Leader

Belaying the leader, as part of the fall-protection system, becomes complex due to one simple fact: The forces generated by a leader fall are transmitted to the belayer. This means the belayer must endure similar forces as those of the leader. These forces can be substantial, and if they catch a belayer by surprise, a hard fall can violently jostle him. Conversely if the belayer puts force into the rope, that force is transmitted to the leader. So our first two concerns of belaying the leader are:

1. The belayer getting smashed into the cliff while catching a fall

2. The belayer losing his balance and pulling the leader off

Before we get into specific solutions for these concerns, let's look at some of the basics common to most lead-belaying situations. We can use a device or a Munter hitch, just as when we belay a second. Unlike a second, though, we typically belay off our harness. In this application, we use the belay loop on our harness—almost all modern harnesses have them.

A few relics and superlight alpine harnesses do not. In the case of a relic, we recommend buying a new one! For any other harness without a belay loop, connect your belay device per the manufacturer's instructions.

Effectively anchoring the belayer solves the threat of having him smashed into the cliff in a high-force leader fall. We have two main techniques at our disposal:

1. Technical anchors: The use of the rope, slings, and nuts to create an anchor. This is what most people think when they hear "anchor."

2. Stance: This is an old-fashioned concept of anchoring. We use our stance more often than people think to solve at least one of our concerns for the belayer.

Belaying on the Ground

We define belaying on the ground as belaying in a spot where the leader cannot fall and pull the belayer off a cliff. That could be terra firma or just a ledge large enough that there is no potential for pulling the team off the mountain. Belaying on the ground removes the risk of a factor 2 fall, but we still must guard against a violent upward pull, as well as the belayer slipping, sliding, or falling and pulling the leader off mid-pitch.

If we position the belayer close to the wall and/or under the first piece of protection, this mitigates much of the risk of being pulled into the wall when catching a fall. The belayer's weight counteracts the upward pull to some degree. Were the belayer standing away from the base of the cliff or wall, the pull becomes more horizontal, which is more difficult and awkward to resist than an upward pull.

Imagine, for a moment, a high-force fall. With the belayer under the first piece, his weight counteracts the upward pull, giving a slightly dynamic catch without endangering himself or the leader, except in the circumstance of a ledge immediately below the leader. Now, if the belayer positioned himself 10 feet from the wall, that same fall becomes serious—instead of sagging into the weight of the fall and resisting the upward pull, he's now lurching or shuffling toward the wall, trying to resist the pull of the leader. Chances are he'll trip, greatly increasing the chance he'll let go of the brake strand. The leader falls farther and risks being dropped.

ABC—ANCHOR, BELAYER, CLIMBER

If we build a bottom anchor and anchor the belayer back, we mitigate much of this problem and keep the belayer back from the cliff. We need to line up the anchor and belayer with the first piece of protection, though, so that the anchor is effective.

Older climbers may remember the mnemonic ABC—Anchor, Belayer, and Climber. It applies here, but the force isn't necessarily toward the climber but toward the first piece of protection. We try to form a straight line from the anchor to the belay device to the first piece. Remember, though, whenever the belayer is back from the cliff with an anchor behind him, the first piece of protection must withstand an outward/upward pull to protect from zippering the pitch. This puts your entire protection system at risk should the first piece fail, so make sure it can withstand that secondary pull.

With the belayer anchored away from the cliff, should the leader fall early in the pitch, the rope going from the belayer to the cliff can act as a trip line, flipping a leader upside down dangerously close to the ground. For these reasons, this system is not recommended. It should only be used when the belayer is substantially smaller and/or inexperienced, like kids, and no bottom anchors closer to the cliff are available.

The bottom anchor, whether away from the cliff or close to it, reduces the chance of our belayer slamming into the cliff, but it doesn't protect the leader from being pulled off. Though rare, leaders have been hurt or at least surprised when their belayer slips or falls and in doing so, pulls down hard on the rope. Serious effort should be made to

position the belayer in a stance with solid, flat footing. Placing the belayer on a wobbly stance, a gravelly slab, or precarious perch invites having him pull the leader off. Beware!

Guides and experienced friends showing a newcomer how to climb will probably be on familiar, moderate terrain—and occasionally taking longer runouts. Being pulled off in these situations can be extremely serious. Consider anchoring the belayer in a spot he can't be pulled up, and one in which he can't pull you off.

GROUND ANCHORS

So we have to ask, why do leaders often feel like a beginner belayer needs to be anchored when belaying on the ground? It is pretty common for experienced belayers, even light ones, not to be anchored. Seldom do we see anchored belayers at a sport crag, yet falls are common and forces high due to the steep nature of the cliffs and the amount of rope holding the fall.

It seems, though, that when an experienced leader takes out a beginner climber, many feel the need to anchor him down. It often seems like a rule-based decision, something you're supposed to do, but no one ever really does—but since we have a new climber we'll "go by the book." We offer this rule: If you are teaching something you don't do in your own practice, you are either doing something wrong or teaching something wrong; either way it's wrong.

So let's try to clear up this murky situation. Experienced climbers and belayers intuitively know from experience the amount of force the leader will generate in a fall. If a leader is close to a bolt on a sport climb, the belayer will allow a little more slack in the system or prepare to unweight a bit to give the leader a softer catch. Conversely if the leader has a bit of a runout going, the belayer will be more braced and if a fall does occur, be ready to add force on his side by "dropping" onto the rope to resist the force. By adding some momentum on his side of

The anchor, the belay device, and the climber line up, "ABC." PHILBRICK PHOTOGRAPHY

hedge a bit if he does not react with the proper skill or timing. Of course, if you are having a new climber belay you on your project, don't expect a soft catch on his first day out. That skill is pretty advanced for a belayer and takes time to develop.

Pulling the Leader Off—Strategies for Preventing It

A solid ground anchor won't necessarily prevent a belayer from pulling the leader off. If you have decided to anchor a new belayer down, make sure you put him in a good spot, one in which he can stand comfortably. Next, if he's new to climbing, tell him about your concerns as a leader. He can't be careful about something for which he doesn't know to watch.

Finally, consider whether the chances of your falling are greater than the chances of your being pulled off. If the terrain at the base is so steep or slippery that even a careful belayer might give you an inadvertent tug, consider anchoring him from above. Just treat the ground like it is a pitch up and have the anchor above the belayer.

With an anchor above the belayer, how do we protect him from the upward force? The first thought is to anchor him both from above and below. Many aspirant guides have put their instructors in that situation, and it doesn't feel like a very rewarding experience. A more elegant solution would be better.

One possible solution combines a bottom anchor with a comfortable seated position. A seated position greatly reduces the chance of pulling a leader off. It should be comfortable, though.

Using an anchor above the belayer, then asking her to lean back against it with a foot braced in front, works well, too. We like this approach in low-angled terrain, not necessarily at a large base area or typical sport crag. This also mimics a typical belay stance on a multi-pitch route, which makes it a great strategy when prepping people for longer, bigger routes. Even if you are leading to set up a toprope, once down you can go through the calls

the equation, the belayer can better resist the force. Experienced belayers, particularly at sport crags, have little fear of being pulled up a bit and hanging on the rope once the fall is over.

Whatever the case, catching a fall is athletic and requires some technique. It isn't necessarily automatic or intuitive. Teaching someone how to belay, particularly in a sport-climbing setting, requires more than just a pronouncement to "never let go of the brake hand." Good belaying requires solid technique and athleticism, and it takes time to learn.

By anchoring someone down, we can give him the experience of feeling the force of the fall, but

After scrambling up to a stance, the team anchors the belayer from above even though there's no chance of a factor 2. She uses a braced stance to protect herself from being pulled into the cliff, and the high anchor protects the leader from being pulled off if she loses her balance.

and the process of how to come off the anchor on a multi-pitch climb. If you are actually starting a multi-pitch climb and your belayer is standing on flat ground, this allows him to practice coming off the anchor and go through the calls and the process.

Anchoring a belayer on the ground is usually reserved for beginners, something more experienced climbers set up. A very light, experienced belayer may decide to anchor himself down if he feels the catch will be too difficult given the weight, length of fall, and/or the steepness of the cliff. Whatever the case, in every situation both the belayer and the leader need to feel that the force of the fall and the hazards it creates are dealt with adequately.

Belaying on the Cliff

When we say that we are belaying on the cliff, we mean any stance at which the belayer can be pulled off the cliff should the leader fall without any protection in. In these cases, the belayer must be anchored from above with an anchor strong enough to withstand the impact of a factor 2 fall. Belaying on the cliff and belaying on the ground share the same two main concerns:

1. The belayer smashing into the cliff while catching a fall

2. The belayer losing his or her balance and pulling the leader off

We also add a third problem when off the ground:

3. Positioning the belayer so he or she can hold a factor 2 fall

Because we need to have the belayer anchored from above, we can easily solve concern number 2. For the anchor to be effective in keeping the belayer from pulling the leader off, the belayer's tie-in must be adjusted properly so that the belayer is tight and leaning back.

To prevent the belayer from smashing into the cliff, we are often limited to using stance. On most belay ledges, the terrain doesn't allow for an anchor *behind* the belayer. A high anchor allows our belayer to lean back against it, with a foot braced to help make the stance more secure.

With a braced position and an average-size climber, we seldom need to place an upward-pull piece for the belayer. Certain special situations, however, require protecting the belayer from smashing into the cliff and getting pulled violently.

Tension on Your Tie-In or Tether

We've seen guides teach students to keep tension on their tether or tie-in anytime they're at an anchor. With the popularity of non-dynamic tethers like the Personal Anchor System (PAS), this can be a good habit for newer climbers. It's less important when tying in via the rope, because of its dynamic capacity. Keeping tension on one's tether teaches new climbers to avoid allowing slack in their connections to the anchor, greatly reducing the likelihood of a high-force fall that could result in injuries.

ANCHOR FAILURE?

We know a lead fall can apply substantial force onto our belayer, and we've already discussed techniques to protect the belayer from that force when on the ground. Once on the cliff, many shift that focus to protecting the anchor; we feel this misprioritizes the problem.

We are still in a situation in which a violent pull could smash the belayer into the cliff with enough force to cause him to lose control of the brake. If we focus on protecting the anchor, but allow the belayer to still be pulled violently upward or inward, he could still lose control. Imagine a fall so violent the belayer gets yarded upward a meter. Perhaps the anchor remains intact, but a belayer—inexperienced or otherwise—moving that much, and perhaps without warning, really risks him losing control. If we can protect the belayer from being displaced, though, this protects him, the anchor, *and* the leader.

Having said this, there is one important detail that can affect the anchor. As we explore the complexities of belaying the leader on a cliff, we will at times suggest that the leader use the anchor, or a piece in the anchor, as her first piece of protection. When a leader does this, she needs to take into consideration all the secondary-pull problems we discussed in the protection section.

Of particular importance is the potential for an outward pull. Since climbers prefer ledges on which to belay and we suggest the belayer lean back and brace against the cliff, this can mean there will be a change in direction at the point where the leader clips the anchor. This change is often from lower angle to steeper, putting an upward/outward pull on the anchor. How much force this secondary pull places on the anchor will depend on the angle of the change.

Whether this change in angle exists or how severe it is will depend on the size of the ledge, height of the anchor, steepness of the start of the pitch, and the length of the quickdraw or sling the leader uses. The important takeaway is that if the leader clips the anchor as a piece of protection, then all the considerations of the secondary pull need to be considered. All this boils down to the question: Can the anchor or the individual piece withstand that secondary pull?

PROTECTING THE BELAYER

As we said: With a braced position and an average-size climber, we seldom need to place an upward-pull piece for the belayer. But there are special situations when we do need to protect the belayer from smashing into the cliff and getting pulled violently.

To make a plan to protect the belayer, we first need to realistically assess the direction the belayer will get pulled. If we ask a belayer to point toward the first clip, chances are he won't point directly upward. More than likely he'll point up and in—in our experience it's usually as accurate to describe that pull as "inward" as much as "upward." This is the reason a good braced stance works.

This being the age of the Internet, however, we've all seen dramatic footage of belayers getting pulled violently in "tests" on YouTube. Yes, they're dramatic and concerning. As a matter of fact, if you ever find yourself on a vertical-to-overhanging cliff, at a hanging belay with a climber leading above you, as depicted in many of those videos, we consider it a special case.

Keep in mind, we've said that *in most cases* bracing works, but this certainly doesn't mean always. Let's get back to some of those special cases that will require a more technical solution to protecting the belayer.

Special Belay Situations

Guides or adults taking kids climbing need to be concerned about a violent fall resulting in an injury to a child-belayer, or just as bad, that belayer dropping the adult. A substantial difference in weight (or experience) between adult climbers poses the same risks. If the terrain itself prevents a belayer from taking a braced stance—an awkward ledge or a hanging belay, for example—we need to seriously consider managing for upward pulls.

Protecting the integrity of the anchor, as we've discussed, is pretty easy, so our real concern becomes an upward pull violently displacing the belayer such that she is injured or drops her brake hand and loses control of the belay. In short, we need to focus on holding the belayer down and/or taking the force off of her.

But how? Our first thought might be to place an upward-pull piece near the feet of the belayer and attaching it to her. Unfortunately, with that setup you can actually accelerate the belayer's trajectory into the cliff after an upward pull. Imagine the belayer standing 2 to 3 feet away from the cliff. A leader fall tugs her upward and the piece protects her from going up, but it now acts as a pivot, transmitting the upward pull into an *inward* pull toward the cliff. Instead of yarding upward, she smashes inwards toward the cliff, risking an injury or loss of control.

We're not saying a piece positioned by the belayer's feet is a bad idea. Rather, if we put a piece in this way, we need to position the belayer leaning against the cliff. When we set the belayer up this way, we coach her to have one shoulder against the cliff and make sure her brake hand is on the *outside* so she can activate the brake. Of course, if we could get a piece below and behind her, that would be ideal. This proves to be rare since in most belays mid-cliff, the only thing behind the belayer is air. If that opportunity presents itself, though, you should utilize it.

Placing a piece low and coaching the belayer to lean against the wall helps mitigate risks for kids or small and/or inexperienced belayers when others might be able to manage the situation with just a braced stance. What about more complex scenarios where even an experienced belayer may want to be anchored down?

Let's look at a scenario in which a belayer is positioned below an overhang and the leader gets a first piece at the lip. For the belayer the force won't be upward and inward; it will be upward and outward. The belayer now has no way of bracing, as the pull is no longer toward the cliff, but outward and behind. In this case a piece placed near the feet of the belayer will easily line up with the pull.

We could invent endless scenarios to consider. The big takeaway, though, is that you need to protect the belayer from a pull toward the first piece, wherever that is. If you're using a technical anchor rather than a braced stance, the ABC—Anchor, Belayer, Climber—principle applies. The anchor must line up with the belay device of the belayer and the climber.

An upward-pull piece and the belayer leaning against the cliff works if there's a large weight discrepancy within the team. In the photo, the belayer has stepped back a bit to help show the sling position. In practice, she should have her feet just past the piece, so she can't get tugged out of position by a leader fall. PHILBRICK PHOTOGRAPHY

DIRECT BELAYING

Another solution when we want to anchor the belayer is to simply remove the chances of placing high forces on him. Guides and some climbers over the past few years have begun experimenting with belaying the leader directly off the anchor. This means the belayer feels little or no force when the anchor arrests a fall. Essentially we're anchoring the belay and leaving the belayer out of the system to some degree.

Now, we do need to be very concerned about the anchor's ability to withstand an upward pull. Bolts and ice screws lend themselves to direct belaying, and can also work on gear anchors in horizontal cracks. We can make a vertical crack work, but it adds complexity to the system. In the three types of anchors mentioned (bolts, screws, appropriate gear), not much has to change as far as the anchor building.

The techniques, rigging, and systems are all somewhat new to most guides and climbers. We expect manufacturers and inventive climbers will refine direct belaying in the coming years, so for simplicity's sake we'll cover the basics. However the system evolves, just keep direct belaying in mind any time a high-force fall risks the integrity of the belay or the belayer's security.

Let's focus on the bolted anchor to start. (This functions identically to the two-screw anchor as well.) The anchoring system we'll use is the classic cordelette with one small change. What we are going to do is change the junction knot of the cord into a bight knot. To do this, we take the ends of the cord and put them together, then fold them back on themselves and tie an overhand on a bight. This creates a double-loop bight. We clip this knot into one of the bolts with a locking carabiner. Next we clip one of the strands into the other bolt, pull down the strand from between the bolts, grab the other strand, and tie off the masterpoint as usual.

The belayer has her belay carabiner in a double-stranded bight knot formed by the sling. This maintains adequate strength for the potentially higher forces of a lead fall. PHILBRICK PHOTOGRAPHY

To belay a leader, place a locking carabiner on the double-loop bight and place a Munter on this carabiner. The belayer holds the brake strand of the Munter with his brake hand and feeds rope to the leader with the other. Ideally the Munter is not too high to facilitate feeding, so as not to "short" the leader as she climbs. We use a double-strand loop at the Munter attachment to add strength and redundancy, as this will be the section of cordelette "catching" the fall.

You've probably already noticed that a single bolt (or ice screw) will take the forces of a lead fall. Keep in mind, though, that the belayer's weight is on the bottom of the masterpoint attached to the bolt, so some of the upward pull will be resisted by that weight. The belayer may get pulled a bit upward, but only a few inches before the bolt (or screw) and Munter arrest the fall. The second protection point backs the whole system up. As you can see, the integrity of the protection points is critical.

This rigging has one main weakness—the factor 2 fall. In the case of a factor 2, the main bolt takes the entire force and should it fail, the anchor would extend quite a bit before loading the second bolt. Other systems reduce extension, but also lose all distribution of forces at the masterpoint. It's a trade-off. Whatever you choose to do, the factor 2 needs to be considered. Is the primary bolt (or screw) bomber? Can the leader avoid a factor 2? We should always avoid a factor 2 fall—don't get us wrong! If you're direct belaying, however, you need to ask yourself, how likely are the chances of one?

If the prospect of a factor 2 seems likely or too sketchy, we need to use a classic cordelette with distributed load at the masterpoint. Simply build it as you normally would, then attach an upward-pull piece from below. Belay off the masterpoint with a Munter as described above. Two bolts or screws now protect against the factor 2, while a single piece (and the belayer's weight) resists the upward pull.

Another rigging for the direct belay. The belayer sets up the Munter on a locking carabiner on the cordelette's masterpoint. An upward-pull piece connects directly to the masterpoint with a long sling and when combined with the belayer's weight makes a two-point anchor for an upward pull. By using the masterpoint for the direct belay, any factor 2 fall will be held by both bolts instead of one. Contrast this system with the rigging in the previous photo.

PHILBRICK PHOTOGRAPHY

Often the presence of a two-bolt anchor indicates there are no viable cracks for gear, making the above scenario somewhat unrealistic. Routes equipped in *plaisir* style will occasionally have cracks beside nice, new bolts, though. Keep the option in the back of your mind, just in case.

Belaying the leader, no matter how you do it, requires skill and training. When teaching people, instruct them to lean back on the anchor, brace a foot, and remain ready to catch a fall. If a belayer, due to size or experience level, can't do that, consider more training and/or your objective. You might also create a technical solution to help them give a reliable belay. Terrain and available gear will dictate what you can do. Keep in mind, if you find yourself building technical systems a lot, you might want to reevaluate your process for teaching friends and/or clients to belay.

Protecting against the Factor 2

As we mentioned earlier, this factor 2 is so serious that it should be avoided at almost any cost. It's not unusual for climbers with decades of experience to have never taken or caught a factor 2. As it should be! Having said that, we should still put effective systems in place should a factor 2 occur.

Let's imagine a belayer on a small ledge anchored and his leader has climbed a few feet up the pitch. If the leader falls, she will fall past the belayer and the resulting force on the belayer will be downward. This will twist the belayer around so he will be mostly facing down and will twist into the classic Anchor, Belayer, Climber orientation, or ABC. This will happen almost instantaneously and with a lot of force.

A low anchor in this scenario will allow the belayer to be pulled down and into the ledge—violently, too. This will be an awkward, severe fall. Point being—build your anchors high. This protects the belayer from being whipped around and "pile-drivered" into the ledge.

Now consider the belayer's brake hand. If the leader climbs directly above him, she could fall to either side. If she were to fall on the same side as her belayer's brake, it will make the fall even more difficult to arrest. A fall on the opposite side will twist the belayer with his brake hand uphill and the rope running across his body and down—a better braking position.

Inelegant Insurance: The Catastrophe Knot

Imagine a scenario in which the anchor is too low and a direct belay is inappropriate, and the leader could take a factor 2 fall. In this situation, consider tying a catastrophe knot in the brake strand. Estimate how much rope the leader needs to make it to her first good placement, then add a couple feet just to be sure, and tie a bight knot in the rope. Should the leader fall and you lose control of the rope, the knot will jam into your device and arrest the fall. Not particularly elegant, but better than watching your partner deck!

1. A low masterpoint risks the belayer being pulled down in a fall, making the odds of catching a factor 2 slim.
PHILBRICK PHOTOGRAPHY

2. Clipping a draw might seem like a solution, but then the belayer risks being pulled into the quickdraw and/or pinching his hand and losing control of the belay.
PHILBRICK PHOTOGRAPHY

3. The catastrophe knot . . . prevents a catastrophe by jamming against the device.
PHILBRICK PHOTOGRAPHY

Many climbers seeing this will suggest clipping into a piece of the anchor as a piece of protection. This guarantees the belayer will receive an upward/inward pull so the rope will not pin the brake hand down as it does on a downward pull.

This is a great solution for this problem, but creates some new ones. Great debates have taken place as to where to clip if the leader wants to use the anchor as his first piece. Some would even argue whether any part of the anchor should be used this way. Debates like this occur because of the variables, which include how high or low the masterpoint of anchor is, how high the highest piece of the anchor is, and the size of ledge.

If you understand the arguments for and against the various methods, you can make the best decision for the situation. Before we get into the variables, though, let's look at the forces involved. Namely, how the dynamic property of the rope and the pulley effect on a clipped anchor piece interact.

1. Heads up . . . Without clipping the anchor, the team risks a factor 2 until the leader clips the piece of protection. PHILBRICK PHOTOGRAPHY

2. The leader falls past his belayer and takes a factor 2. The force spins her into an awkward position, with her brake hand downhill.

3. Clipping the anchor prevents a factor 2, which is especially dangerous if the climber falls on the same side as the belayer's brake hand. PHILBRICK PHOTOGRAPHY

THE ROPE, PULLEY EFFECT, AND VARIABLES TO CONSIDER

When the leader clips the anchor, he will shorten his fall while keeping the same amount of rope catching it. This lowers the fall factor, which means lower forces—but remember, that top piece is now a 2:1 pulley, which multiplies the forces. Because the pulley is a carabiner, there is a fair amount of friction, so instead of multiplying the force by 2, we generally multiply the force by 1.6 to 1.7.

So, imagine the leader is 10 feet above his belayer. The leader clipped the anchor as he started the pitch; that clip is 5 feet above his belayer. In this case the leader will take a 10-foot fall on 10 feet of rope, for a factor 1 fall. Because the leader clipped a

piece in the anchor, the fall forces will be multiplied by the pulley effect.

Exactly which is a higher force—a factor 2 or a factor 1 multiplied by the pulley effect—depends on so many variables, it is hard to say. What we do know is the leader falls only half the distance, so that means he is less likely to get hurt. The belayer also catches the fall with upward/inward pull, making it much easier to hold. So far so good!

What if we change a few things? Again, we'll have the protection 5 feet above the belayer, but this time the leader will be 20 feet above the belayer, or 15 feet above the protection. Now we have a 30-foot fall on 20 feet of rope, for a fall factor of 1.5—a significant increase in force from the first fall, and the forces are multiplied. As we can see, clipping the anchor becomes a two-edged sword and it has less benefit from a force perspective as the leader gets farther away.

The takeaway, then: Clipping the anchor does not preclude placing a secure first piece as soon as possible. Clipping the anchor doesn't replace the critical first piece; it just allows you to get that piece with more security.

So where do we clip? The masterpoint seems the obvious place. We've built a stout, reliable anchor, so why would we clip only one piece of it? The masterpoint was designed, in large part, to withstand a factor 2. Clip there, right?

If only it were that simple! What if our masterpoint is a bit low? What if we have a good, high piece in the anchor? We'd prefer to clip the masterpoint, but if the belayer's hand is too close, he could get pulled into it, pinch it, and lose control of the brake. In that case, we'd clip the highest, best piece in the anchor. It's an imperfect compromise, but one that needs to be made.

Is there a time when not clipping the anchor at all is a good idea? For us, we will save the gear this requires if the climbing is very, very easy above the anchor to get to where we will place our first piece, or if the ledge we are leaving is so big that if we fell before we placed our first piece, we wouldn't be able to fall past it.

As of this writing we are very curious on how lead belaying will advance. Will belaying off anchors become the norm with new techniques, anchor designs, and devices developed to deal with the problems that are associated with it? Will new ropes come out that will be more dynamic? We're not sure, but we feel this is one aspect of climbing that is due for advancement. Climbers are heading into steeper, more difficult lines where longer falls are reasonable because there is less to hit and many of those climbers are light. Watch for innovation in this space.

Belaying the Second(s)

This aspect of the fall protection system has seen some substantial changes over the last decade or so. Big improvements have been made in anchor systems, but we think the changes in belaying the second have had more of an impact on how climbers move through terrain.

Arguably, the advent of the masterpoint-style anchor started the revolution in belaying the second. Climbers made the move from placing their belay devices on their harnesses to hanging them from the anchor only in the last 15 years or so. This change, along with some new devices, led to belaying two seconds simultaneously (parallel style) as standard practice. Thinner, lighter ropes made leading with two ropes more feasible, too.

At this point belaying the second, or seconds, off the anchor is so standard, climbers risk losing some of the other techniques and their applications. We rarely see a team of three using caterpillar technique, climbers redirecting their belays of seconds, or belaying seconds directly off their harnesses. In many ways this is a good thing, but losing these old skills means that in certain circumstances climbers are not using the best technique. Or worse, they're using one of these old techniques and not building them correctly.

Let's list and define second-belay techniques:

1. Belaying off the anchor. This appears to be the most common technique used in fifth-class climbing today. Using devices like the Black Diamond ATC Guide, Petzl Reverso, or GriGri on the anchor is widespread at multi-pitch crags and ice climbs. The Munter hitch, which was one of the first techniques used for belaying a second off the anchor, is still widely considered required knowledge in the event a climber drops or forgets a belay device.

2. Belaying directly off the harness. The most classic belay technique, it harkens back to hip/body

belays. In this system the climber places a belay device or Munter hitch on the belay loop of her harness. Rigged this way, the belayer gets a downward pull in the event of a fall. With a good stance or a solid seated position, a belayer can use her position as if it were a piece in the anchor. That is, she can hold some, most, or all the force generated by a falling second. If she can't resist all the force, she moves forward and the anchor begins to assist. Commonly used on easier terrain, it's still very important in an alpine setting, whether on snow, rock, or ice.

3. Redirected belay. This belayer appears to be lead-belaying, but the strand comes off his harness, up to the anchor, through a carabiner, and *down* to the second climber. The belayer receives a pull upward and inward should the second fall. In the past, climbers chose this belay on small stances when the discomfort of belaying off the harness might also compromise the belay. By redirecting the force through the anchor, the belayer could brace against the cliff as when lead belaying. Of note, the redirected belay multiplies forces on the anchor due to the pulley effect.

If you were to do a time line of belaying in most areas of the United States, you'd likely see a progression from body belays to devices on the harness followed by the redirect then to belaying directly off the anchor, with overlaps in the techniques along the way. It seems like the Europeans adopted belaying off the anchor more quickly, but international climbing history in rope techniques are very difficult to generalize due to the parochial nature of the techniques. Much more information gets exchanged now, but often things will get lost in translation. It appears the belaying of the second has been one of the most progressive techniques in climbing.

So for the most part we'll be clipping a self-braking or assisted-braking device onto the anchor to belay our second(s). This style of belay offers improved security (when done correctly) and confidence. It makes catching a second almost automatic.

Like all techniques that are "automatic," "secure," and "assisted," though, they can lead to a lack of focus—and that can cause serious problems. Most devices have inherent weaknesses, and some of these are caused by how we use a specific device in certain situations. It'd be nearly impossible to address each device, its strength and weaknesses, how each can fail, and common misapplications of each, but we will discuss a few of the more popular ones.

Most climbing hardware functions more or less similarly—carabiners, quickdraws, crampons, etc.—but "guide-style" belay devices vary significantly. Add to this the fact that many of these devices can also be used to belay leaders or seconds off the harness, either directly or as a redirected belay, and you'll see that reading manufacturers' instructions on how to use these devices is very important. We will attempt to cover the bigger picture and common problems for most of these devices, *but this should never replace the instructions for any particular device.*

Assisted Braking and Plaquettes

We use two main types of devices on the anchor. We'll call these:

1. Assisted brakes: These include the Petzl GriGri, Trango Vergo, and Edelrid Eddy.

2. Plaquette style: These include the Petzl Reverso, Black Diamond ATC Guide, Edelrid Mega Jul, DMM Pivot, Kong GiGi, CAMP Ovo, and Mammut Alpine Smart.

The assisted-braking devices require you to keep a hand on the brake strand. They are also designed for one rope so the challenges of managing two ropes with two seconds don't occur, but the flip side is, they don't allow you to simultaneously belay two seconds. These brakes tend to be easier to pull rope through, making them popular with guides climbing with one client. At first the work it takes to pull rope through a plaquette seems pretty easy, but over a season of climbing, the overuse injuries to the elbows, wrists, and shoulders make the assisted devices popular among some guides.

The best way to think about the assisted devices is they will brake for you so long as you initiate the braking with a little friction on the brake strand. Once the fall is stopped, little or no force is required of the brake hand with these devices.

Because these devices won't belay two seconds, most guides leave them at home when working in the multi-pitch environment with two clients.

Assisted brakes are often used to belay the leader as well. In that configuration, if a belayer is pulled into a quickdraw, the assist may not engage. This becomes an issue when the leader has clipped the anchor as her first piece and there's a chance the belayer could be pulled up and into that piece. Most assisted brakes have a cam-like device attached to a handle. If the cam can't engage because it's jammed into something (like a quickdraw or a feature on the cliff), the device may not function. This can happen lead-belaying or belaying a second. Leaders must be careful how a GriGri, Vergo, or Eddy hangs on the anchor, because if the device is loaded against the rock when a second falls, the device may not lock and arrest the fall.

When belaying seconds, plaquettes are by far the most popular option for guides and group leaders. Some manufacturers call the plaquette-style devices "self-braking." You'll notice we used *plaquette* instead of *self-braking* in categorizing the devices. Although *assisted braking* is used widely, the term *self-braking* is not. Some devices straddle the line between the two; devices like the Alpine Smart and Mega Jul act like assisted brakes when belaying a leader and a plaquette while belaying a second. Since we are focused on second belays, it is listed with the plaquette devices.

FAILURE SCENARIOS IN PLAQUETTES

This leads to the big question: Can I let go of my brake hand with the plaquette-style device? Technically the answer is no, but all the plaquettes are designed to belay two seconds and when you do that, it is nearly impossible to not accidentally drop

a strand while taking in rope. So in effect, we use them as if they are self-braking, but no manufacturer that we know of suggests you should let go of the brake hand. Why?

To be honest, it is for better reasons than just liability. There are times when they won't self-brake, and if you have not secured the rope before letting go in those situations, they will not stop a fall. Knowing when this is likely to happen is important so you can be extra vigilant. Here are two situations in which all the plaquettes we listed can fail to self-brake:

1. When belaying two seconds if both ropes exit the device parallel one another, the plaquettes work great, but if one strand gets pulled at an angle from the other, the device may not lock on one of the ropes. Different ropes and situations affect the angle at which the plaquette fails, so we hesitate to put a number on the failure mode. All we can say is, they can fail at relatively acute angles.

2. If the climber/load strand is clipped through a carabiner *above* the plaquette, it will probably not arrest the second falling.

3. The device and its blocking carabiner must be able to move and rotate freely into its braking position. If the device and/or the blocking carabiner are pinched or jammed into the rock or a crack, it may not brake properly.

4. Finally, at least three of the plaquette devices, when used with a single rope, can fail to brake in a fall if the carabiner in the back is not clipped in a specific orientation (see below). This failure could happen with some of the other devices as well if a very skinny rope is used. By skinny we mean a rope not rated as a single; that is, a half or twin rope (these are typically 8.5mm or less). Climbers will sometimes use these ropes on high-altitude or alpine routes, or alpine outings with just a bit of rock and mostly snow.

These are the four ways we know of in which plaquettes fail, but there may be other scenarios we don't know or can't anticipate. Below we'll discuss techniques to avoid plaquette failure, but bottom line, keep a focus on the brake strands and know the device you're using.

PROTECTING AGAINST PLAQUETTE FAILURE

When are these failure modes most likely to occur?

Any time we are belaying two followers, their ropes will pull parallel on the plaquette as long as the ropes are both clipped into the last piece of protection of the pitch. Once the first follower unclips his rope from that last piece, if he has to traverse to

the belay, he will be exposed to a pendulum. Should he fall in that section, his rope will now exit the plaquette directly down, while the other follower's strand will exit the plaquette and go toward the last piece of gear.

In short, if the two seconds' ropes exit the plaquette in a nonparallel orientation, the plaquette may not lock up. Again, this is so dependent on rope diameters and the particular brand of plaquette, it is impossible to give a hard-and-fast rule, but you should know: If the ropes exit the plaquette at different angles, you must be vigilant in managing the brake strands.

Luckily there is a simple fix for this problem. First, identify that the situation exists and be doubly

The first follower has unclipped the last piece before the belay. Should both climbers fall in these positions, their ropes will exit the plaquette at different angles and the device will not lock up.

Failure . . . or Lower?

One man's failure is another man's lower. The very reason a plaquette fails in scenario 2 is an opportunity for a smooth, controlled lower—with a couple caveats. As we said, if you clip the load strand to a carabiner above the plaquette, the device won't brake . . . and if it won't brake, it becomes a lowering method. As with any lowering method, you need to strongly consider whether a third-hand backup is appropriate.

We call this technique the load strand direct (LSD) lower, and you'll see it later in the book. We find the LSD offers a little less friction than a Munter hitch on the same rope. If we're setting it up as a lower, we tie an overhand in the brake strand and clip it to our belay loop with a locking carabiner. This backs the system up should we lose control of the brake strand or something go wrong. Once we're in control of the brake strand—or our friction-hitch backup has engaged—we unclip the overhand from our harness and continue the lower.

The LSD lower built with a third-hand backup. PHILBRICK PHOTOGRAPHY

vigilant as the climbers arrive at the belay. When the first climber reaches the anchor, the belayer should either hand him her brake strand to hold until the other climber arrives or tie a bight knot into the brake strand so it cannot pass through the device—a catastrophe knot. Once tied, the belayer can devote her attention fully to the remaining follower's strand.

In scenario 2, the plaquette fails if the climber's side of the rope, the load strand, is clipped to a carabiner (or anything else) above the plaquette. This is most likely to occur when the leader or second begins to clove-hitch his rope into a biner at the anchor. When tying a clove hitch, experienced climbers and guides usually do it one-handed by clipping the rope into a carabiner in two steps. Should the climber slip during this process, he would load his strand, but it would be redirected above the plaquette by the carabiner—even just a few millimeters can defeat the plaquette and result in an unchecked fall.

When you look at these first two weaknesses, you'll see they are most likely to occur as the seconds approach the belay. This is an important clue for the belayer to increase her vigilance as her seconds get closer.

Scenario 3 is quite manageable with a little forethought when building the belay. Simply make sure the plaquette hangs freely and can't be pulled into a crack or pod, jamming the device. On slabby terrain, make sure the device won't be blocked against the rock, inhibiting its ability to lock and catch the rope.

Finally, when using the Kong GiGi, the CAMP Ovo, and the Edelrid Mega Jul *with a single rope*, they must have the blocking carabiner clipped in such a way as to be impossible to rotate. The mechanism of failure for one rope in a plaquette is, as we said, possible with skinny ropes, like a single climber on a twin or thin single (less than *approximately* 9.4mm).

The GiGi and Ovo have large slots, through which it's easier to pull rope, compared to an ATC or Reverso. (The Mega Jul slots aren't quite as large, but its narrower sidewalls can allow a similar failure mode.) When belaying two strands of rope through these devices, you simply clip the blocking carabiner through both (as clearly indicated in the device's instructions). The two ropes prevent the carabiner from rotating 180 degrees and flipping.

With only one rope in the device, there's nothing to prevent the rope and blocking biner from being twisted 180 degrees. When rigged correctly, the climber/load strand of the rope is on top in the

To rig the Kong GiGi correctly with a single rope, the blocking carabiner must be clipped around the device itself.
PHILBRICK PHOTOGRAPHY

A Guide's Best Friend?

The Edelrid Mega Jul has made a splash within the guide community for its light weight and assisted-braking power when belaying a leader. It's less popular when used as a plaquette-style (like the ATC, Reverso, GiGi, and Ovo) device for belaying seconds, but we include it here because it's growing in popularity. (Mammut's Alpine Smart functions very similarly, though it's much bulkier and consequently not quite as popular.)

The Mega Jul offers braking assist when belaying a leader, which means guides and citizen-leaders have a bit more security built into their system when leading above a less-experienced climber or client. It's also becoming a go-to option with alpinists, when the possibility of rock- and icefall is greater. Users should recognize it can fail when used as a plaquette for belaying one second on a single rope—like the GiGi and Ovo. The fix is simple, though, and with the blocking biner oriented correctly, it's a perfectly fine tool for the job.

device, wraps over the top of the blocking biner, and exits the device on the bottom. Should the rope flip, the climber is suddenly on the bottom and this orientation offers *no braking whatsoever.*

Again, though, there's an easy fix—and it's indicated in the owner's manuals of all three devices. Simply clip the blocking carabiner into the rope behind the device and then back around the device and both strands coming out of it. Please see the photo for a clear indication of the correct orientation, as well as checking the owner's manual.

High-altitude alpinists and some weight-conscious climbers may choose to use a lone half- or twin-rope to belay a second. This is an unapproved use and presents numerous problems like cutting and excessive stretch. If you are pushing the limits of your equipment and using it outside of the manufacturer's specs, you should understand that it could behave in unusual ways. In terms of plaquettes, they may fail and the carabiner method described above may not work on many of the devices.

One problem with the rope flipping is it's possible to find older, outdated instructions online. Some of them include techniques no longer practiced; some of them are still current and appropriate. One

technique that some climbers still use is clipping the blocking carabiner into the carabiner from which the device hangs. Successfully using this requires the right blocking carabiner, but this system is finicky and tricky. If the back carabiner gets sideways and isn't large enough, the rope won't pinch on itself and lock. We don't recommend this fix when belaying a second on a single strand through a Mega Jul, GiGi, or Ovo, *despite many instructions still indicating this as a viable technique.*

Because the rope and carabiner used affect the performance of these devices, we recommend ample practice before "going live" in the field. In summary, using this rope system may seem so outside the norm that including it in this book may seem odd. As you will see later, the potential for using a single half or twin in an unplanned way exists, however, so knowing this weakness can be extremely important.

OLD SCHOOL AND NEW SCHOOL: THE MUNTER HITCH AND THE SELF-LOCKING MUNTER HITCH

And, of course, we have the Munter hitch. This hitch requires an active brake hand. If you let go at any time, the belay will fail. Even a belayer caught by surprise may get her hand pulled into the hitch with such force the pain will force her to let go. The brake hand not only initiates the braking, but is also an active part of the force required to stop a fall. Once the fall is stopped, the brake hand needs to hold tightly or the climber will be dropped. The brake hand must always be active in the holding of any force.

There is a technique to add a locking carabiner to the Munter to make it self-braking. This addition

Just like the Munter can stand in for a lead belay device, the auto-locking Munter offers an alternative to a plaquette.
PHILBRICK PHOTOGRAPHY

works well if you ever find yourself needing to belay two seconds and you've dropped (or forgotten) your device. In this instance, two auto-locking Munters can work. You will, however, need four locking carabiners.

You first build a Munter hitch and start taking in rope. You then clip another locking carabiner into the bottom, curved section of the Munter and the strand going to the second. As with so many of the techniques in this book, build and test this on the ground before committing to its use in the vertical.

SUMMARY

The nuanced nature of the brake hand with all these devices when belaying a second(s)—assisted braking or plaquette-style—is a problem. Assisted brakes are often so good that people treat them as some sort of "self-locking" device and let go of their brake hand. To their credit, many of these devices will often still stop a fall while hands-free. With plaquette devices, people with little understanding of the failure modes let go with too much nonchalance. In the end, remember you're protecting someone's life with your belay. You must arrest a fall regardless of the device or system, no excuses.

Belaying Directly off the Harness

We still teach and encourage another old-school system, belaying off the harness. It's important to know it. Belaying off your harness, or its ancestor, the hip belay, is very useful in alpine terrain, and you'll see it in the fourth-class section of this book. In some cases, climbers brace themselves behind a block or a short wall and belay. This is useful at the top of routes that end in a scramble. In this technique, their position is the anchor. In other cases, they build a quick anchor and the climber clips into it, along with a stance. How the belayer positions himself and/or which side the rope going back to the anchor is on are important elements of this system.

To make the decision of which belay method to use—the hip belay or a device off the waist—the key is how fast the climber will be moving. The hip belay takes in rope more quickly, so with a fast climber you're able to take in slack and give a better belay.

Without an anchor, the belayer's position must be very solid. He should be behind something, so that the force pulls him into a feature on the cliff. His foot should be braced, too. A seated belay helps to accomplish this.

If one foot is the main brace, the brake hand should be the opposite hand. So, if your left foot is the main brace, your right hand should be the brake. If you are standing and you are using a hip belay, consider clipping the rope going to the climber through a carabiner on your belay loop. This prevents the rope from getting pulled down your leg. Often terrain will keep the pull high enough, but make sure that during a fall the rope will run around your hip. In a seated position this

A properly arranged hip belay incorporating an anchored climber. Note the strand of rope going to the climber is on the same side as the belayer's anchor tie-in, and it's over the top of that tie-in. PHILBRICK PHOTOGRAPHY

With a belay device, we set up the anchor in the opposite configuration as the body belay. Note that the brake hand is on the same side as the belayer's anchor tie-in.
PHILBRICK PHOTOGRAPHY

isn't as important, but again make sure the rope doesn't slip below your butt.

When using a belay off the harness and incorporating an anchor, the anchor should be on the same side as the brake strand. If you're using a hip belay, the anchor should be on the opposite side as the brake hand.

Another detail to improve security involves running the strand going to the climber *over* the strand anchoring the belayer. This prevents the climber's strand slipping under the belayer and his belay failing. If you're lowering and worried about the friction of rope-over-rope, consider another technique. *Remember, the modern hip belay is for arresting a slip or low-angle fall, not for catching a fall in steep terrain or longer lowers.* Climbers "back in the day" held long falls with a hip belay, but a) they were tougher than us, b) they had leather gloves, and c) they even had leather patches on their bodies to protect themselves from the rope!

Our orientation changes a bit when belaying off the harness. Your brake hand should be the *same* side as the rope going to the anchor. If the rope going to the anchor is on your right side, your right hand should be the brake hand. Catching a fall will rotate you a bit, so if you're anchored on the right, you'll be rotated to the right . . . and you'll want your brake hand uphill. The rotation during the fall naturally helps you brake. Though a belay device supplies more holding power than a hip belay, hip belaying is still a technique for lower-force falls, arresting slips, or

slabby terrain—not the weight of a climber hanging in space.

Redirected Belay

We rarely see the redirected belay in use, but it still has applications. You rig your belay device as you would when lead belaying, clipped into your belay loop. We like the technique for a pitch that traverses into the belay stance with a high anchor. If the rope enters from the side with a high anchor, it's often beneficial to have the rope run through a high piece in the anchor to protect the second as she makes the final moves into the stance. We'll admit this is rare, but we have used it enough to mention it.

One pitch that comes to mind is the second pitch of *Dark Shadows*, in Red Rock. Many people link the first and second pitches, but whatever the case, after the short 5.7 corner, the climb traverses leftward and down to the anchor. Using a redirected belay here is not mandatory, but it makes having a high piece to protect the second much easier.

A redirected belay for two followers is cumbersome. A better strategy is to use a plaquette, but that's awkward, too. We consider it inappropriate to belay two seconds with an active brake hand; that is, a simple belay through your device off the waist. It's too much a compromise in security.

Another application for the redirected belay is a situation in which the belayer/guide wants to extend herself down to better see the second. We'll cover the details of that in chapter 7, under the section Seeing Your Client and Extended Anchors for Guides.

Ropes Systems: Double, Twin, Parallel, Caterpillar

Now that we've built an anchor, led a pitch, and found another belay spot, we must stop and ask—what rope system are we using? The terrain, objective, and party all dictate what system we use and when.

First we'll discuss a team of two, and then three, with considerations toward terrain mentioned here, but also throughout the book as we discuss glaciers, ice, and the alpine.

Single or Double Ropes for the Party of Two

Does a party of two use a single- or double-rope system? The main consideration is whether long rappels are required to descend. If that's the case, a double-rope system is obvious. Even if the descent on a long route is a walk-off or requires only 100-foot rappels, a party on a long route may still decide on a double system, as a hedge in case they cannot complete the route and need to bail.

You will see parties using half-rope systems on complex face climbs, to get more effective protection on wandering routes. As we mentioned in the rope section, this is likely going to require that the ropes are not alternately clipped as is recommended, but that two separate lines of protection are developed to reduce rope drag and sling use.

Many climbers on crags will use double-rope systems to facilitate rappels. Often a single rope will work, but it is more convenient to have two ropes for the rappels. That convenience needs to be tempered with the complexity and weight of using two twin or half ropes.

With a twin system, just treat both ropes as one in all aspects, including your clove hitch at the anchor. For the party of two, using a half-rope system can make things more complex. For this reason ropes rated both twin and half allow the party to separate the lines on the wandering pitches and keep the ropes together on the more straightforward ones.

One thing to be avoided is mixing the systems on one pitch. If you separate the ropes, keep them separate; if you are clipping both, commit to clipping both for the whole pitch. If you end up mixing the systems (and we don't recommend it except for one circumstance described in the ice chapter), you can get away with going from alternating clips (half-rope system) to clipping both (twin system). But "twin'ing" to then separating invites serious problems. If you've introduced any twists, they will catch on the first piece after beginning to alternate clips, causing severe rope drag and/or the displacement of the piece.

Alternately clipping the ropes in half-rope style also means the ropes take different lines up the cliff. One rope will most likely take a longer route up the cliff, which means in the event of a leader fall, the ropes will not stretch the same amount. The shorter, tensioned rope may pinch the other against a carabiner in the section where the ropes are twin'ed. This could cause rope damage in the form of a melted or "glazed" sheath.

Parties of Three— Parallel or Caterpillar?

In parties of three, the team will have two main choices of rope systems in fifth-class rock: parallel or caterpillar. End-roping will be reserved for fourth-class or very easy low-angle fifth-class pitches, approaches, and topping out low-angle features like domes. (More on end-roping in the alpine chapters.)

The length of route, experience levels of the seconds, difficulty, pitch lengths, and terrain configuration all help us decide between caterpillar and parallel systems.

Parallel System

In the parallel system, the leader climbs while trailing two ropes, each one attached to a second (we'll also use the term *follower* throughout the book). We recommend both of these ropes be rated as "single" by the UIAA. We frequently see guides overseas using half ropes, but that limits choices.

For example, should the team want to transition to caterpillar technique, this puts the leader in the position of leading on a lone half rope—not ideal because it increases risk for the leader and follower.

In the previous chapter we discussed failure modes in plaquettes. The blocking carabiner in plaquette devices, when used with a thin rope, can flip, causing the device to fail. A party of three using half- or twin-rope systems can expose itself to this

potential if it transitions to caterpillar mode for any reason (and thereby ends up climbing on single strands rather than two at once), particularly if they're less experienced and more focused on leader security rather than overall security of the team and belaying seconds.

When the leader climbs on two single ropes in rock, we recommend that she treat both ropes as if it were one. This makes it look very much like a twin-rope system; the critical difference, however, is that *she takes a belay on only one strand*. Using single ropes like a twin system (taking a belay on both ropes) significantly increases forces on protection during a fall. How? Two single ropes require more force to stretch, so in effect forces must be higher before they start working dynamically. Of course, if you are using a rope system that is rated for single, half, and twin, then the ropes can be used in any configuration, alone, alternated, clipped together, and belayed on one or two strands. In most cases, however, the rope is likely not rated that way and being belayed with only one is important.

At the anchor the leader can just tie a clove hitch with both ropes, but that can add twists. More commonly the leader will tie a clove hitch with the rope on which she took a belay, while passing the other rope through the locking carabiner on which she's anchored. This second rope isn't clove hitched; it's merely following the rope on which she took a belay to keep things neat and organized. This way both ropes stay together, simplifying the rope

Modern Magic: One Rope, Three Designations

Select manufacturers like Edelrid, Mammut, Beal, and Sterling offer ropes carrying all three designations—single, half, and twin. Brands indicate these designations with symbols not only in the literature provided with the ropes, but also on the little tag wrapped on each end of the rope. Know what type of rope you're using and its strengths and limitations. Having a rope certified in all three categories offers some cool advantages, too.

management, yet if the party wishes to transition or to stack their ropes separately to untwist them, one rope end can be freed easily.

Once the seconds are on belay, the typical scenario is for the first second to simply unclip from the anchor and start climbing while the second follower cleans the anchor. As the first second arrives at protection, he unclips his rope from each piece, with the second follower cleaning the pitch. This keeps the first second moving and maintains distance between the two followers, so the lower climber doesn't have to wait. Also, any protection protecting the seconds from a swing stays in place for both.

The leader clove-hitches the rope on which he took a belay, but not the other strand.
PHILBRICK PHOTOGRAPHY

TWISTS IN PARALLEL

Twists in parallel systems occur, no matter how careful you are. Often they are not as bad as they first appear. If a leader climbs a 120-foot pitch, she will pull up 80 feet of rope before putting her seconds on belay. As she pulls up rope, she may put a couple of twists in it. As an example, let's say she puts three or four right-hand twists in the rope as she pulls it up. Now she puts the ropes into her plaquette to belay. As she belays, no more twists can enter the system because the plaquette won't allow it: Each rope has its own slot in the plaquette and they're separated as they go into the stack.

Now the seconds approach the anchor. At times, the rope may appear twisted. Let's say there are three or four left-hand twists. This means overall, in the whole stack, there are no twists because the left-hand twists counter the right-hand twists put into the system when the leader pulled up the slack. If the team only took out the last twists by having the climbers step over them, the team would be, in fact, putting twists into the system. The punch line? Don't overreact to twists in the system as the seconds arrive at the anchor!

There is no question that apparent twists can cause difficulty. Sometimes they need to be removed just to make it easier or possible to belay and anchor the seconds. The important thing is first the ability to belay, so if you need to undo a few to make that happen by having someone step over or around the rope, go ahead. If the twists are not affecting the belay, though, you can leave them be.

When anchoring the seconds, all twists should remain in the pile of rope. The ropes between the seconds and their clove hitches should not be twisted. Once back in the pile (after the seconds are off belay and on their clove hitches), the twists and counter-twists may very well take care of themselves.

MANAGING ROPES IN PARALLEL

Occasionally the team will restack the ropes separately after the seconds arrive to clear any twists.

Tie in, Clip in

To facilitate untwisting and sorting ropes at the belay, when using parallel technique, consider *tying* into the rope on which you'll take a belay and *clipping* into the other rope with a light-weight locker that's hung *only* on the waist tie-in loop. Why? Should you need to untwist the ropes at some point, you simply unlock the biner, pop out the rope, untwist it, and drop the rope right back into the locker. Fast and easy.

Clipping the second rope into your harness allows you to unclip it and detangle your ropes more easily. PHILBRICK PHOTOGRAPHY

This would occur after the seconds have anchored with their clove hitches, and each second would stack his rope as the previous leader helps pull the ropes from the parallel stack. This makes it far easier to do. As the team nears the end of stacking, the leader unties from the end of rope that was simply passed through her clove-hitch carabiner. In general, this happens every three to five pitches, depending on twists and tangles. If you can, try to use larger ledges when untwisting the ropes.

We usually stack ropes together, or as one, when climbing in parallel style. Prior to leaving to lead a pitch, though, the ropes must be matched or evened out. Think about how the ropes usually get stacked: Seconds climb at different rates, so the ropes get taken in and stacked "unmatched," or unevenly. This means you need to even them out, so the ends leave the stack together for the next pitch, to avoid tangles and drama.

If we take an example of a leader doing a 120-foot pitch, when she pulls up the slack to put her seconds on belay, she pulls 80 feet together—it's the "leftover" rope at the last belay. Now the seconds start climbing. The first follower leaves the belay while the second follower cleans the anchor, so there's at least 20 to 40 feet when you'll take in the first follower's rope, while the second follower remains stationary. The second follower eventually starts climbing, but even then it's usually at a different rate than the first. Therefore, the 120 feet of rope to each follower comes into the leader's stack

Combining Clean and Dirty Stacks

Here's a tip to add the dirty stack to the clean. Once you've anchored in, pull the slack of both ropes up to your stance, creating a pile. This is a clean stack. Mark it by tying a BHK (big honkin' knot) on both strands and setting it down.

Now you put both followers on belay and belay as you normally would. This begins forming a dirty stack. As you stack more rope while the followers climb (provided you have time and can belay adequately), untie the BHK and take both strands, and pull rope from the dirty stack into the clean stack. Be careful to do this with both ropes matched. As you do this, you're transferring rope from the dirty stack to the clean, speeding up your transition when the seconds arrive. If you need to pause (you probably will), retie the BHK and keep the clean and dirty stacks distinct.

Again, maintain a good belay while doing this. Fast climbers may not allow you the time to do this, but it's a good trick for speeding up your transition once the followers have arrived.

uneven and mismatched. That's 240 feet ready and willing to tangle.

If the leader can keep those two piles (the "left-over" rope—the rope she pulls first, when getting ready to belay—and the second pile made while the followers are climbing) separate, she ends up with a 120-foot "dirty" (unmatched) stack and an 80-foot "clean" stack (ropes are matched). Once the seconds arrive, if the rope stacks can be combined, adding the 120-foot dirty stack to the 80-foot clean one, then the leader's ropes will pay out smoothly during the next lead.

If the same leader will be leading, the newly stacked pile can be flipped. Learning how to manage a clean and dirty stack can save time on short pitches, when a significant section of the ropes can be stacked cleanly as the leader pulls up rope. On long pitches it may not be worth creating a clean and dirty stack.

Flipping and/or feeding out from a dirty stack can be done, but expect tangles. With a team of three there are two people at the belay, so one person can manage the tangles ahead of the belayer. With inexperienced climbers, however, that task may be too much to ask under the stress of being

on a cliff and new to rope handling. If there's a doubt in your mind, set the belayers up with a clean stack. You'll thank yourself later.

PARALLEL LEAD TRANSITION

If a climbing party using parallel wants to swing leads, it can seem daunting or at least tedious to swap leaders. Since both ropes are stacked together, the team must make sure both ropes come off the top of the stack for the new leader/next pitch. Nightmarish rope tangles will occur if one strand comes off the top of the stack while the other comes off the bottom. Take our word for it!

Here's the transition for swapping leaders while climbing in parallel mode:

1. The leader arrives and builds an anchor, ties a clove hitch on each rope, and clips each separately into its own locking carabiner on the anchor.

2. The leader puts the seconds on belay, and while they are climbing, she unties from the end of one rope.

3. The second that is going to lead the next pitch should be the lower second (second follower).

Since that follower cleans the pitch, he's effectively racking for the next lead.

4. When the first second arrives at the anchor, he takes the rope the leader untied from and ties into it. *This new tie-in needs to be cross-checked by the leader.* This rope secures him because the leader clove-hitched it into the anchor in step 1.

5. The first second unties from the rope on which he was just belayed.

6. Upon arrival, the second follower ties into the rope the first second freed up. *This knot must be crossed-checked by the team.*

7. The new leader is now tied into the top ends of both ropes coming out of the dirty stack and is ready to lead.

This is a serious transition since two climbers now have new tie-ins. It is easy to cross-check these knots, though, because there is always a partner nearby. Be disciplined and cross-check these knots—it takes mere seconds and prevents a potentially catastrophic mistake.

Caterpillar

Caterpillar is a much more familiar technique. Although in some areas you'll see most parties of three using parallel, caterpillar is an older style and its use is more basic and understood. Caterpillar most resembles a party of two, only it is repeated for the third climber. Because the ropes come up separately and at separate times, it is easy to keep them separated, clean, and tangle-free.

When the leader gets to the end of a pitch, he ties a clove hitch and clips in with the only rope he has. As he belays the first second, the leader stacks the rope.

When the first second arrives, she ties a clove hitch into the rope on which she was belayed if the same person will be leading. If the lead will change to the second follower, she clove-hitches in with the rope she was trailing. Although not critical for an experienced party, the middle climber should be clove-hitched in with the rope the next leader is attached to. At this point if the leader did a nice job of stacking, the rope can be flipped if the same person will be leading. If the lead will change, then the rope is all set.

In a guided party, the importance of the middle climber being clove-hitched in with the same rope as the guide means the ropes for the clients will be color-coded. If the guide is tied to the blue rope (for example), the first follower will be belayed on the blue rope and trailing a red. Since the guide will be leading the next pitch, the middle climber should anchor in with the blue rope. When the second follower arrives, he only has the red rope so he will be clove-hitched into the anchor with red. When the blue leader leaves, the two seconds are now clove-hitched into the anchor with different-colored ropes.

This is important because it makes it easy for the first client to know which rope to unclip when it is his turn to climb. Detaching the wrong clove hitch from the anchor has deadly consequences because only the middle client is on belay when he leaves the anchor. Also of concern, in this scenario the guide and the first follower have the same-color clove hitch, so the guide needs to be vigilant when she unclips her clove hitch—*she must make doubly sure it is hers.*

For an experienced party swinging leads, the middle climber should clip in with the rope he is trailing, the red rope (in keeping with the example above). When the second follower arrives, he will stay on the plaquette, or assisted brake with a catastrophe knot in the brake strand, and should not clove-hitch in. Once the red leader is ready to leave, it is clear what rope to come off the anchor with because it is the one still in the belay device. Once the red leader leaves, the two seconds now have color-coded clove hitches. Other than color-coding, the seconds switching leaders is a very simple transition.

Pros and Cons of Caterpillar and Parallel

Parallel System Benefits

1. Speed is the biggest advantage. By moving both seconds at the same time, you can move a party of three almost as fast as a party of two.

2. Second's security. At the end of the pitch a leader puts both seconds on belay. Inexperienced seconds are less likely to make a mistake and come off the anchor prematurely.

3. Second's comfort. This is a very important aspect for guides or competent leaders. Because neither second needs to trail a rope, they do not have to deal with the rope weight. In caterpillar, the second follower most often cleans the pitch, so if you have an inexperienced person in the party, you'd prefer the more experienced person to be last. If that inexperienced climber is really light, in caterpillar they would need to trail a rope. Rope weight can exhaust and overwhelm a very light, inexperienced person.

4. Simplicity. Although not as pronounced as the other advantages, by treating both ropes as one you can simplify the rope management and reduce the potential for tangles compared to the caterpillar system. Don't discount how taxing it can be for a new climber to unclip the rope ahead and clip in the rope behind, as in caterpillar. Parallel removes that stress to his day.

Caterpillar Benefits

1. Leader's security. Since the leader trails two ropes in parallel mode, the rope weight is significant. Long pitches with a crux near the end can be next to impossible to lead. Caterpillar mitigates that.

2. Second's security. Because a belayer has to belay two seconds simultaneously in parallel, it's hard to keep up sometimes. This can cause slack to develop if one of the seconds out-climbs the rope. Also, because the focus of the belayer is on two people and two ropes, managing everything and maintaining the belay is more difficult.

3. Second's comfort. The first second in parallel has two ropes in front of him. Often it is hard for a second to keep one rope out of the way, let alone two. In a hand-or-larger crack, with deeply placed protection, if that second rope comes tight (the second followers falls, for example), it can pinch the higher climber's hand or knock him off the climb.

As you review these benefits, you see the need to balance security of the leader and security of the seconds. Especially for guides, the comfort differences for the seconds are also something to consider. We balance those things with the need for efficiency and speed, too. Being able to switch to and from caterpillar and parallel is important.

For guides, ensuring someone cannot make the mistake of unclipping out of sequence and falling an entire rope length is very comforting. That tips the balance to parallel in many situations. With more experienced clients the guide needs to be careful he isn't causing confusion by doing a transition without clearly explaining the difference between the systems. This is particularly true when going from parallel to caterpillar. After a number of pitches of both clients unclipping to start to climb, you can set up your clients to make a very serious error when they switch to caterpillar. *Be vigilant and give clear instructions.*

Stance Management

We constantly adapt our stance management to the numbers in our party and the rope system we're using at the moment. That said, there are commonalities in our techniques. We'll try to call out specific techniques for specific situations along the way, but you'll discover once your stance management improves, it will help with all your climbing.

Guiding presents its own challenges, because oftentimes your guests will not be able to quickly or safely resolve rope tangles or problems on their own. This puts the responsibility squarely on the guide's shoulders. She needs to recognize stance management not only as a risk-management consideration for herself and the guests, but also as a means to simplify and de-stress the guests' time in the hills.

Keeping the Ropes from Tangling in a Party of Three

When climbing in a party of three, stance and rope management become critical skills. At best, tangling the ropes can cause frustration and be a waste of time. At worst, a tangle can be a serious risk-management problem. It isn't unheard of for climbers to "unrope" on ledges they would normally stay roped up for to undo a tangle.

You can also imagine moving into a crux, just as your seconds yell, "There's something wrong with the ropes!" Most times things turn out all right, but the increase in risk is unnecessary, especially as just a little vigilance will prevent tangles.

All tangles are made; ropes do not tangle on their own. Any climbing party must take responsibility for their ropes and the management of them. That's good news—it means you can control most rope tangles!

Clipping into the Anchor

So, when clipping into the anchor, look at how your rope gets there. Is it over a strand it should be under? Or is it under a strand it should be over? Taking a direct line into the anchor isn't always correct; sometimes it is important to go over or under a strand of rope in the system. The first step in competently managing your ropes is making a conscious choice of where to clip in.

Workspace

Next, give yourself a sizable workspace. Tight workspaces make it harder to do good stance management, and we know poor stance management leads to tangles. The anchor's location relative to your stance is the definition of your workspace. Make it as large as possible by having a high anchor. Don't be afraid of being slightly more than an arm's length from your anchor. We are amazed at how tight people put themselves to their anchors! Although you might feel more secure with your anchor close by, there is nothing that makes the anchor stronger when you are closer to it.

Once you implement these two ideas, you can begin to look at specific techniques to keep ropes straight and feeding out smoothly.

Management Tips

Here are several tips that can be helpful:

1. Order your stance the way people will leave rather than how they arrive. If you are leaving the stance rightward, the leader of the next pitch should be to the right side of the stance, then the first follower, and the second follower farthest to the left.

2. When in caterpillar, begin to organize the first rope for the next pitch when the first follower arrives. You can always put the second follower on belay right away so he can begin to dismantle his anchor, but make sure the first rope is organized before the second follower arrives at the stance.

3. In a party of three, you have two ropes and four ends. Each climber needs one end with which to secure himself, which means there is always one end that can be freed. Make sure your ropes are organized and clean before the free end leaves the ledge. In a parallel system, that free end is on the leader; in caterpillar, it is on the middle climber (first follower).

4. If you are guiding or leading an inexperienced group, you need to make sure the ropes are not tangled before you lead out. An inexperienced second may unclip or untie something critical without realizing it if unsupervised. As an experienced climber it may be hard to imagine someone doing that, but the stress and performance anxiety new climbers feel can cause otherwise very intelligent people to do seemingly foolish things. Do whatever you must to make sure your ropes are not tangled before you leave the stance.

5. If you are leading out in parallel (remember you have the free end), or you are leading an inexperienced group, look down once you are 10 to 15 feet up the next pitch. Often this perspective allows you to see potential tangles while you are close enough to do something about it.

6. When guiding or when leading an inexperienced team, there will be times when keeping the climbers in the order they will leave the belay won't work. Usually the guide will want to watch both seconds to coach or give encouragement. Although the guide will be out of sequence on a stance, it is important that the seconds are still in the right order, so the first follower can leave the stance cleanly.

STANCE MANAGEMENT SCENARIO, CATERPILLAR

Let's imagine a scenario to highlight a few techniques. We're on a route, with a guided team of three, climbing in caterpillar mode. The route has a left-to-right traverse. The guide wants to watch the clients by staying to the left, but the next pitch exits to the right on the ledge.

When the first follower arrives, he stands to the right of the guide and anchors in. We will assume the client is right-handed and wants to use his right hand as his brake hand when he belays on the next pitch. When the first follower ties in, he will place his locking carabiner to the right of the guide's carabiner and tie a clove hitch going under the guide's strand coming off of her clove hitch leading to the stack of rope. The follower's tie-in will split the upside-down V shape formed by the two ropes hanging from the guide's clove hitch. One strand attaches the guide to the anchor, and the other is what we'll call the "backside of the clove." The first follower's clove hitch is under the backside.

1. Stance management caterpillar. The first client (dark blue shirt) arrives from the guide's left side. The guide (white helmet) wants to remain on the left to get a good view of the second client. This means the first client will move to her right. Remember in the end the guide will be exiting right and wants the first client to belay her using his right hand as his brake hand. PHILBRICK PHOTOGRAPHY

2. The follower clips in through the upside-down V formed in the guide's rope. This allows the guide to lead out right and sets the client up for a right-handed brake. PHILBRICK PHOTOGRAPHY

3. The second client arrives and will clove-hitch in beside the plaquette. Note that the backside of the guide's clove hitch goes over the first client's tie-in at this point and to his right, setting him up for a right-handed brake on the next pitch.
PHILBRICK PHOTOGRAPHY

4. The first client (solid blue shirt) has put the guide on belay and she has stepped around him to the right. Notice he can belay with his right hand and the rope is set up to feed smoothly.
PHILBRICK PHOTOGRAPHY

2. The second client arrives at the belay. The guide clove-hitches him in immediately beside the plaquette. PHILBRICK PHOTOGRAPHY

1. Stance management caterpillar opposite side. The first client arrives from the guide's right side in this scenario. The guide wants to remain on the right so she can see the second client. This means the first will move to her left. Remember, though, the client wants to belay with his right hand for the next pitch, so in this orientation he does not need to clip in under the backside of the guide's clove hitch. It's a subtle detail, but one that sets up the client for a more comfortable belay, and it gives the guide more security because her client can deliver a more effective belay. PHILBRICK PHOTOGRAPHY

3. The first client puts the guide on belay and the guide clips her strand of the rope through a quickdraw on the anchor. She then steps behind her belay and he passes her rope over his head, allowing her to lead out with the ropes running smoothly. PHILBRICK PHOTOGRAPHY

Though the guide is out of order for the next pitch, she prefers this so she can coach and see the second follower on the remainder of his pitch. The guide stays in the middle when the second follower arrives. The second follower places his carabiner to the left of the two carabiners (the guide's and the first follower's) already on the masterpoint and he clove-hitches into it. The ropes should now be organized so that the guide can depart to the right for the next pitch and the first follower can belay with his right hand.

What visually complicates station management while clipping seconds in is the belay device on the anchor. Focus on the clove hitch and the strand of rope between the guide and her clove hitch. As the followers approach the stance, if the guide ducks under the ropes between the clients and the belay device, she will likely need to pass the brake strand over her head when she cleans the belay device.

To illustrate the point, imagine the pitch traverses the opposite way (from the right to left). When the first client arrives, there is no need for his rope to go under the guide's backside strand for the client to belay right-handed. Likewise, if you flip-flop these two processes, you can set up for a left-handed belayer. The key here is recognizing where the first follower should clip in when he arrives at the stance. This means identifying which direction the guide will leave and making a conscious choice about the clip-in.

Caterpillar is by far the hardest to keep straight. Each rope is separate and needs to stay that way. If there is a tangle once the guide leaves, the second follower will not be in your control—*you'll only be able to directly protect the first follower with a belay.* That means if for some reason the second follower unclips (or someone inadvertently unclips him), he could fall the entire rope length. Note that in parallel system both seconds go onto belay simultaneously, so it will be easier for them to undo any tangles.

STANCE MANAGEMENT SCENARIO, PARALLEL

Because the clients climb simultaneously in parallel, usually both arrive before the guide ties them in—this allows her to be strategic when clipping them in. Our goal in parallel system is to allow either second to begin the next pitch while the other remains clipped in. This way the first follower can get started and out of the way before the second follower unclips from the anchor. This can be important on small stances.

Let's revisit the scenario described above, but this time in parallel system. When the guide arrives, she clove-hitches in with one rope and simply clips the other rope through the same locking carabiner. The guide now pulls up both ropes and puts both seconds on belay. If she's managed her ropes correctly, either second can leave the belay and the other can remain clipped in. More on this below and in ensuing pages.

While the first follower climbs, the guide can position herself wherever she likes, which makes staying in sight and offering coaching easier. When the first client arrives, the guide has a choice where to put the client and where to place herself. On traversing pitches the guide may choose to stay in a better position to see the second follower, especially if there's hard climbing just before the belay. If not, she may decide to just shuffle over and lose sight of the second follower for a short time. If she does need to see the final section of the pitch—as the guide did in the previous, caterpillar scenario—she will have the first follower step around her so she can remain in visual contact with the second follower. The guide ends up in the middle once the second follower arrives.

The parallel system simplifies stance management if the guide remains in the middle. As the first follower arrives, the guide ties a catastrophe knot on his brake strand and puts him to her right. When the second follower arrives, the guide places him to her left. The guide clips the second follower's locking carabiner to the left of her locker on the masterpoint and the right client (first follower) to the right of her carabiner.

In this case it's most efficient to clip in the second follower first. Recall we put a catastrophe knot in the first follower's rope, so clipping in the second follower first saves us putting a catastrophe knot in his strand. Not a huge detail, but it saves a step and a few seconds.

Once the second follower is secured, the guide unties the catastrophe knot and gets the first follower clipped in. Now the guide can grab the ropes coming off of the clients' clove hitches and restack the ropes. As far as who belays the leader on the next pitch, the client on the left could use his right hand or the client on the right could use his left—provided the rope stack remains between the two of them.

There will be situations in which it is easier to have both clients to one side of the guide. Whenever the guide is to one side of the clients, she can use a simple technique to ensure either client can leave the belay stance first. The guide anchors the client farthest away first, using a clove hitch. Next the guide takes the rope coming from that clove hitch to the pile of rope (here's the "backside of the clove" again; you'll see this term many more times in the book) and lifts it up. Now the guide ties the client closest to her into the anchor with a clove, making sure this client's rope goes under the backside of the outside client's clove hitch.

If the clients are to the right of the guide, they will be forced to belay left-handed. If the guide takes all the backside strands (her two and one from each client) and has the nearest client put them over his head, the ropes will come from the middle, allowing for a right-handed belay by one of the clients.

Art Mooney, an experienced mountain guide and an Instructor Team member for the AMGA, coined the mnemonic "outside, inside, under" to help students remember the order in which to do this. (Thanks, Art!)

For the recreational party, keeping ropes organized will increase efficiency, but if there is a small tangle, it usually isn't too serious and can be managed by experienced seconds. Remember, in caterpillar mode there is one strand on the middle/first follower that can be untied without consequence, but the second follower (last climber) must remain clipped in at the belay. No one is belaying him from above yet! In parallel both seconds can unclip their clove hitches since both will be on belay. With experienced people this usually makes it easy to undo simple to moderate tangles. So while parallel technique may seem more complicated—moving two ropes at once, etc.—it is often more forgiving of rope tangles.

For the guide or a more experienced climber taking out newer climbers, stance-management skills are worth practicing. It isn't just for efficiency; it's a risk-management tool. With that responsibility you should never leave a stance hoping it will all work out. You must be sure, for your clients' and friends' sakes . . . and for yours.

1. Stance management parallel. The guide belayed her clients on the plaquette and will put them to her right when they arrive at the stance. The inside client (gray rope) ties a catastrophe knot in his brake strand. The outside client (orange rope) clove-hitches in on the right side of the quad. PHILBRICK PHOTOGRAPHY

2. The inside client (gray rope) clove-hitches in under the backside of the outside client's clove hitch. This ensures both ropes will feed easily up the cliff and that either client can leave the belay first. Put another way, neither client's rope is trapped under the other's as long as the guide clips them in "outside, inside, under."
PHILBRICK PHOTOGRAPHY

3. The guide is now set up to lead and her ropes will feed smoothly off the stack. If her inside client is left-handed, he can belay with his left hand. If he's right-handed, it's ideal if the guide can get the leader's brake strand on the client's right—which she does in the next photo.
PHILBRICK PHOTOGRAPHY

4. The inside client passes both clients' backsides and the guide's backsides—so, four strands of rope total—over his head. This accomplishes two things. First, it puts the brake strand for the lead belay onto the client's right side, setting him up to deliver a better, more secure belay. Second, it keeps the ropes organized so that either client can leave the stance first. In other words, neither client's rope will be trapped under the other's.
PHILBRICK PHOTOGRAPHY

TRANSITION TO AND FROM CATERPILLAR AND PARALLEL

The transitions to and from parallel and caterpillar are pretty simple. Separating the ropes will prove to be the most time-consuming part when going from parallel to caterpillar.

Caterpillar to Parallel

1. Leader arrives and clove-hitches in and belays the first second.

2. When the first second arrives at the anchor, she clove hitches in with the rope going to the leader. If there is going to be a lead change, she uses the rope she's trailing. If the team is block-leading or it is a guided party, the middle climber clove-hitches in with the rope on which she had just been belayed.

3. When the last climber (second follower) arrives, if he is not going to be the leader, he clove-hitches in. If he will be, he ties a catastrophe knot on the brake strand and begins to collect gear from the previous leader. *Tip*: He should rack the gear he just cleaned from the pitch, as he wants it on the next lead.

4. The first second unties from the free end and hands it to the climber going to lead the next pitch.

5. The climber leading the next pitch ties into the end of the rope that the first second freed up and leads out.

5. The leader leaves the belay with the inside client belaying, using his right hand as the brake hand. The outside client can help feed rope. PHILBRICK PHOTOGRAPHY

If the middle climber were to become the leader, there is really no transition since they are already attached to an end of both ropes, though she'll need to flip the second rope stack to get her end on top.

Parallel to Caterpillar

1. When the leader arrives, he clove-hitches into the anchor. If the leader wants to become the middle climber, or if he is staying in the lead, he should clove-hitch in with the rope going to the new leader or the one on which he wishes to lead. If he's continuing to lead, like a guide would, the rope on which he wants to lead goes to the climber he wants as the middle climber.

2. When the first second arrives, she clove hitches in.

3. When the second follower arrives, he clove-hitches in. Where the first follower and second follower are located on the stance is determined by the order of the next pitch.

4. The leader unties from the free end.

5. Working from where the rope with the free end is attached to the anchor, the leader stacks that rope. If the team is careful, as they pull that rope from the combined stack it should come out cleanly, leaving the other rope well stacked.

6. The new middle climber ties into the free end.

The recreational party has many options available. The leader thinking through which rope he will free up based upon who will lead next can put him in the middle or as the last climber. If he is the last climber, the ropes will not be color-coded at the anchor for the next pitch. This isn't serious, just a detail. For the guide, which rope he frees up will determine who will be the first follower.

A special concern for the guided party is the fact the clients will be climbing one at a time. If the clients have grown used to coming off the anchor at the same time, as they do in a parallel system, *the*

guide needs to make sure the clients understand the new (caterpillar) system. As a guide, if you do not communicate well and you leave the clients confused, you are increasing the chances of the second follower coming off the anchor too soon—which could easily end in tragedy.

Seeing Your Client and Extended Anchors for Guides

An excellent tool when extending anchors is the double-stranded bight knot. Imagine you just finished leading a pitch to the top of a cliff. Once you top out, you walk around a tree and return to the top of the cliff, where you just topped out. You pick a comfortable belay spot, from which you can see your climber. Now, grab both strands of the rope coming down from the tree (one leads to you, the other down the cliff to your follower) and tie them into an overhand on a bight.

The two-stranded loop/bight knot you've created can function as a masterpoint. The bight knot also secures you; by tying it you've tied yourself off, provided you clip a carabiner to the two-stranded bight knot—which will probably be your locking carabiner and belay device in guide mode.

Guides often go to great lengths to position themselves at a belay such that they can see clients as much as possible. This is generally a good habit, since it is hard to coach or provide encouragement when you can't see the clients. In many cases, when you can't see your client or your partner, it is also hard to communicate. This can lead to risk-management problems. Some guides use family service radios on routes with long pitches and/or noisy backgrounds like streams, highways, or the wind. If you can see, you can at least communicate by pointing or using agreed-upon hand signals, etc.

Guides can keep visual contact by extending themselves from their anchors to maintain sight lines. In some situations this works well; in others it becomes very difficult. The problem is getting

Visual contact with followers and clients helps with coaching and communication. The leader extended using a double-stranded bight knot—a great application in this setting. Once the follower arrived at the belay, the leader had a friction-hitch pre-rigged on the rope to protect him as he moves above the belay. As he went by, she clove-hitched a locker to his rope so he can secure himself when he reaches the anchor. PHILBRICK PHOTOGRAPHY

the client(s) up to the anchor once they reach the guide's stance.

Whenever you consider extending, first ask yourself if you can simply build an anchor where you want to be. Breaking up routes differently than the first ascensionists or what a guidebook suggests is the best way to solve this problem. Before you build an anchor, look up the next pitch. How far you can see is how far you can go while maintaining visual contact with your client(s). Looking at the terrain configuration gives you clues about your sight lines and potential belay spots.

Many guides assume doing short pitches will increase their ability to see. That is often correct, but occasionally extending a pitch delivers a better sight line. If a pitch starts off steep then lessens in angle, belaying on the lower-angled terrain means the guide won't have a view of her clients. That means the guide needs to belay immediately after the change in angle to see her clients. Conversely, if the pitch starts out low-angled then gets steeper, chances are she can do a long pitch and still see her clients.

Cliffs unfortunately don't always cooperate, though. If a pitch starts steep, goes lower-angled, then steep again, sometimes a pitch ending on the final steeper section will have good sight lines. But if it starts low-angled, then goes steep, then back to low-angled, that means the guide would be out of sight. Add to that corners or overhangs, and you get the complex nature of the problem.

Techniques to Get Clients to the Anchor

Our analysis helps us realize that extending the belay most often happens when the terrain is lower-angled. This may pose no extra problems if the terrain is so easy the guide deems it reasonable to have her clients walk/scramble unprotected above where she has belayed. A large, flat ledge, for example, may allow the guide to extend to the edge of the steep climbing, but when the clients arrive they can safely walk to the anchor.

If the terrain is steeper than a walk, more of a mellow scramble, a guide may employ a fall-protection system that is less than what is required for steep exposed terrain, but offers some security. Let's look at a system like that for two people.

1. When the guide arrives at the belay, she builds the anchor, clips a locking carabiner into it, and clips her ropes into the locker like protection.

2. She scrambles down to a spot with good visibility, then ties a big bight knot into the ropes. This big bight knot will have four strands when she's trailing two ropes, as in parallel technique—two ropes doubled—with two followers. (It will be two strands with only one follower and one rope.)

3. She puts her clients on belay using that big bight knot as the masterpoint.

4. When the clients arrive, she puts two Prusiks on the ropes leading to her anchor and clips each of the clients to one of the Prusiks.

5. Now she ties a clove hitch onto a locker on each client's rope.

6. The clients scramble up one at a time, sliding the Prusik up the rope. As they do this, the guide keeps them on belay and feeds out rope. When they get to the anchor, each clips his locker with the clove hitch onto the masterpoint.

7. Once both clients are up at the anchor, each pulls up and stacks his rope at his feet. (This separates and detangles the ropes when using parallel mode, which always helps with rope management.)

8. The guide goes up protecting herself with a friction hitch on the ropes.

9. Once at the anchor, she clove-hitches into the strand of rope coming off of one of the client's clove hitches and going into the pile of rope. This is the backside of one of the client's clove hitches.

10. The guide cleans up the Prusiks and the extended anchor, then gets ready to lead off.

This technique can be executed in caterpillar, parallel, or with just one client, with slight modifications. If you are in parallel mode, when the guide clips the anchor for the extension, both ropes should get clipped. The big bight knot can be tied into only one rope, however, should the guide want to put one rope away—in the event she wants to begin end-roping because the terrain is mellowing up, for example. The reason is if only one rope is clipped as the guide descends, one rope gets slack as the other is pulling up. That mismatched pull off of the pile of rope at the lower anchor can cause tangles for the clients; it is better if both ropes move together.

With this system the guide needs to feel comfortable with a Prusik being used to protect the scramble. If not, it is likely best not to extend. More complex systems have been used to protect more difficult extensions, but they don't work as well in reality as in theory.

EXTENDING IN DIFFICULT TERRAIN

The only viable method for extensions in difficult terrain works well for one client, possibly two in caterpillar mode, but with some back and forth on the guide's part. This method employs a redirected belay so that the client can be belayed all the way to the anchor. (The guide belays off her waist and redirects the rope through a locking carabiner on the anchor and the rope travels down to the client. This is the same technique described in the section on belaying the second in the belay chapter.)

If the guide attaches a locking carabiner with a clove hitch to the client's rope as he goes by, the client can have a secure tie-in at the anchor, too. Once the client secures his clove hitch to the anchor, the backside is now fixed and the guide can flip her belay device into self-locking mode and belay herself back to the anchor. If you do not know how to flip a plaquette device into self-locking mode, revisit the tools section at the beginning of the book.

Guides' Use of the Climbing Calls

As recreational climbers, we use calls to communicate with our partner at a distance. In that situation our calls state a fact about an action we have taken, and we expect our partner to react accordingly.

For instance, when we say "off belay" it is because we have anchored ourselves in some way. We then expect our partner to remove the rope from his belay device. If our partner begins to break down the anchor after taking us off, we might consider it inappropriate, but we do not have to take responsibility for his actions and therefore we are not too concerned. He can judge whether or not he's comfortable cleaning part of the anchor, etc.

In a guided situation, if our client, either through confusion or intentionally, begins to break down the anchor, it is our responsibility. A guide needs to reassess how and why we use the climbing calls. In effect, when we use a call we are requesting that our client do a specific task. The task we ask of them probably has a direct impact on their safety.

In short, our calls as guides ask our client to do something specific rather than tell them we did something. It's an important distinction.

For instance, when we say "off belay" it is because we want our client to remove the rope from the belay device, not because we have anchored ourselves. This change is subtle, but can have a great impact on our ability to manage the risks associated with our client's transition from belaying to climbing—especially when the client is unreliable, exhausted, or overwhelmed.

Using Calls to Our Advantage When Guiding

Here are some examples of how a guide can use the calls in ways to better manage the risks for his clients. There are two main situations in which we use calls and at least one special situation.

The two main situations are: first, when we can see our client; and second, when we cannot. We often go to some lengths to see our clients. If that's the case, we should make the most of it.

If our new belay stance is in sight of the client, then if when we anchor ourselves and immediately yell "off belay," our back is to our client. In that situation we lose the opportunity to watch our client during a critical phase of this transition. You will often hear stories of a guide looking down to see his client inappropriately unclipping from the anchor. This can happen even with experienced clients, particularly if they haven't climbed for some time.

We suggest building your anchor, organizing yourself, and only then yelling "off belay." At this moment you can focus completely on your client. Once you are off and you are confident your client is not going to unclip from the anchor, you

Cloving-In on an Extension

If a leader wants to lower himself down the cliff to belay his second on a redirect, he can build an anchor, hang two locking carabiners on it, and clip his rope through *both* lockers. He then grabs the rope *between* the lockers, clips it to a locker on his belay loop, and descends (lowering or downclimbing) to his chosen spot.

Once there he clove-hitches the rope to the locking carabiner on his belay loop. He doublechecks it and goes off belay. He's now secured by the clove hitch. The guide pulls the second's rope through the locking carabiner on the anchor (this is now the redirect), and when the rope comes tight, he puts his follower on belay and brings him up.

1. The guide is set up and can now lower or downclimb to his belay spot.
PHILBRICK PHOTOGRAPHY

2. Once the guide descends to his chosen stance, he clove-hitches the backside of his lead rope into his belay loop, securing himself. PHILBRICK PHOTOGRAPHY

3. The guide puts his second on belay and brings him up. PHILBRICK PHOTOGRAPHY

can pull up the rope while giving your client an occasional glance.

In recreational climbing you typically pull the rope up until your partner says "that's me." At that point you turn away from your partner to work at the anchor, putting him on belay in a reasonable time frame.

With a client that you can see, we suggest when there is approximately 10 feet of rope left, put it in the belay device, then pull the remaining rope up until your client says "that's me." At this point you can wait to see if the client goes for the anchor prematurely. If not, you can say "on belay, climb" and your client can then disassemble the anchor. Remember, with an inexperienced client you may want to keep your eye on him to make sure he doesn't untie from the rope at this point!

If you cannot see your client and you are concerned he will make a mistake and unclip inappropriately, try this: Once you've clove-hitched in, don't give a call; instead, start pulling up the rope slowly. When your client yells that you do not have much rope left, put the rope through your belay device and yell, "Off belay!" Now you have your client reasonably protected from a mistake and you can proceed with the calls normally.

If after a few pitches of being in sight of your client he has performed well with the calls, you may decide to rely on your client's ability to perform the transition unsupervised. The key here is that before your client must do something critical without supervision, you should instruct him and test him for understanding. The above methods, when used in the proper context, can afford the client some supervised practice. Once he has satisfactorily passed your test, you can give him the responsibility of performing the transition from belaying to climbing unsupervised.

Some may say that a testing system on the ground is sufficient. We wouldn't necessarily disagree with that, but you need to take into account the stress (or excitement!) new climbers feel when on their first couple multi-pitch climbs. That stress can return to a climber who has had a long hiatus from the sport as well. These techniques, as well as choosing easily supervised routes, will help you teach and train your clients, as well as manage risks better.

CHAPTER 8

Transitions

A transition simply means a change—from one direction to another, one mode of travel to another, one technical system to another, and so on. Whether skiing or climbing, transitions offer us the opportunity to speed up our day through efficiency. Clumsy transitions can just as easily benight us through bumbling, though, so let's take the opportunity to dial some common ones and get us home in time for dinner!

Before we dive in, let's define a few technical transitions most often used in the alpine and rock disciplines. Keep in mind, some of these can just as easily be applied on skis any time the rope comes out.

Roped transitions can be:

1. A change in direction; rappelling being the most common, but we sometimes move from rappelling to climbing.

2. A change in technique. For instance, when a party of three climbing one at a time (caterpillar style) changes to parallel.

3. A change of leader.

4. A change in terrain. This might occur when going from fifth-class climbing to third- or fourth-class, when the party may want to travel with some of the rope coiled off.

5. A change in anchor. Again, rappelling comes to mind, but so does leading in blocks.

Some transitions can be more complex than others, but all tend to share this important characteristic: The party isn't moving. And as the old saying goes, if the rope isn't moving, you're losing time.

If we can shorten transition times, we can make gains in efficiency without incurring risk due to trying to climb faster. We can also get a bunch more climbing done in a day and that's the point, right?

Traditional Tools for Transitions

For complex transitions, climbers have traditionally used leashes or a Personal Anchor System (PAS). Climbers often use a sewn sling of some length and material to improvise a leash, though cordelettes serve the purpose, too. Several manufacturers make the PAS-style systems. These improve upon the improvised leash by linking small, individually sewn loops to create a stronger, more readily adjustable system, though the PAS itself is used only as a leash, while the improvised sling can be deconstructed and used in myriad other applications.

Leash, tether, or PAS, all of these systems detach everyone from the rope by first replacing it with the leash. Then the climbers build a new system and reconnect themselves to the rope. Simple and straightforward, many climbers use this strategy at transitions, but when we analyze it we discover that we often break down parts of the original tie-in and anchor, only to rebuild it minutes later. Leashes and PASs are also non-dynamic, increasing our risk of injury and potential failure when relying solely on them, without the dynamic rope as part of our anchor system.

The leash-PAS system has its place, as we'll see, but newer tools can simultaneously speed up our transitions while increasing our security, too. Win-win.

New Tools for Transitions

In large part we will employ the rope whenever possible for these modern transitions. By using the rope in ways we haven't, we create new tools that offer distinct advantages.

First, the rope offers dynamic stretch, greatly lowering forces on our anchors and perhaps more important, our bodies. Second, using the rope simplifies our techniques and leaves more material on our harnesses. Once we've practiced and incorporated these tools, they will speed us up as well, improving security and yielding more pitches for the motivated climber.

Here is the list of new tools:

1. The backside of the rope from your clove hitch or anchor knot—here's our backside of the clove again. Clove hitches and all bight knots have two sides. If you tie into an anchor with the rope via a clove hitch (recommended) or a bight knot, one side of the rope connects you to the anchor, but hanging from the back of that clove hitch is another side of the rope that is full strength. It can be quite adjustable, too, if a climber attaches to it with another clove hitch on her belay loop, effectively creating a dynamic leash. The resulting leash is stronger, faster to build, and far more adjustable than any improvised leash or PAS.

2. The rope-end equation. By this we mean knowing how many ends of the rope you have at your disposal, and if you have an extra end, knowing where it is. In a party of two climbers with only one rope, you have two people and two ends. In a party of three, you generally have two ropes and four ends, so there is a free end somewhere. In caterpillar style the middle climber has the extra end, but in parallel style the leader has it. Given people also climb with double- or twin-rope systems, you can see

thinking about your extra ends may help solve problems when it comes time to rappel or put away one of the ropes.

3. A more complete understanding of how the rope provides security. For most climbers being secure means being tied directly to an anchor. If we are competent with the rope system, though, we should also have some manner of protection when exposed to a falling hazard—leading, for example. Although some distance may be traveled in a leader fall, in the end the fall should be arrested if the system is built correctly. Seconds should have even more security.

So, we need to analyze how the rope works and name the tools. This will allow us to be more creative in securing ourselves during transitions. Here is a list of ways the rope secures us:

Direct anchoring. Clove-hitching directly to the anchor falls in this category, as does using a leash/PAS.

Friction anchoring. Included in this category are Munter hitches, mechanical ascenders (like Micro Traxions and Tiblocs), and friction hitches. Friction hitches and mechanical ascenders are generally considered not as reliable and may need additional security, particularly in steep terrain.

Belay devices also use friction, sometimes so completely they mimic hitches or knots. When in guide mode, devices like the Petzl Reverso and the Black Diamond ATC Guide, for instance, have so much friction they act almost like a clove hitch (brake hand or catastrophe knot still required). When rappelling and lead-belaying, the brake hand must hold some of the force with these devices. That is, there's no internal mechanism that locks off—like a cam in the case of a GriGri or Micro Traxion.

Counterbalance anchoring. We often pair this technique with friction anchoring. For instance, a leader fall ends up in a counterbalance with a belayer using a friction device. The leader fall in the end looks nearly identical to a bottom-belayed toprope system.

This counterbalance system can be used with short sections of rope as well. For example, two climbers attached to a rope 15 feet apart on either side of an alpine ridge, or around a horn or tree, functions as a counterbalanced anchor. If the short section of rope is clipped through a piece of gear or an anchor, this is also a counterbalance. (If the climbers attach the shortened rope to an anchor with a clove hitch, they've both directly anchored and one is on the backside of the clove hitch!)

Leashes. This is the most common form of direct anchoring when *not* using the rope. We mention it again because since we now have so many anchoring methods using advanced rope systems, we don't want to think of traditional leashes as wrong or sketchy. Simply because modern tools decrease the use of the leash doesn't mean leashes and PASs don't have their place—sometimes they're still the best method of anchoring.

Technical Descents—Rappels, Belayed Rappels, and Lowers

The preceding section introduced the most common tools and strategies for the modern system of transitions. We introduce other techniques throughout the book, but those generally appear in particular applications in more specialized situations.

To get started using some of these common ones, we feel rappelling offers the most applicable environment. Of course, we use *rappel* loosely; a better, more descriptive term is *technical descent* because we include belayed rappels and lowers here. So, for technical descents we have two other tools we'll use:

1. The extended rappel with a friction-hitch backup. This is becoming very common and is arguably no longer an advanced technique. Many

climbers already rappel this way, but for clarity we described it here.

The length of the extension may vary, but most commonly we use one of two systems. First, girth hitched: a shoulder-length runner girth hitched to your harness's tie-in points with a locker and rappel device clipped to it. Once the rope is in the rappel device, you tie a friction hitch (most commonly an autoblock) onto the brake strand and that is clipped into your belay loop.

Second, basketed: a shoulder-length (24 inch or 60 centimeter) sling passed through your harness's belay loop, with both ends clipped to a locking carabiner, which is connected to a rappel device. Keep in mind a basketed sling, if unclipped from

The standard rappel extension using a shoulder-length sling, which allows for a third-hand backup clipped to the belay loop.
PHILBRICK PHOTOGRAPHY

the carabiner, will slide out of the belay loop. We use this most commonly in the self-rescue section.

2. Fireman's belay. The fireman's belay has become fairly standard, but we'll mention it here for clarity. The first person to rappel typically anchors in at the next stance or comes off rappel in a safe spot. Once she calls up to the second rappeller, she can hold the ends of the ropes and should the person descending lose control, she can pull down on the ropes, locking off the rappeller's device.

Rappelling offers us a great topic with which to introduce and discuss these transitions. Advanced climbers and beginning guides have all rapped thousands of times, so it's a familiar component to their climbing.

Basic Rappelling, New and Old

Let's first look at a simple and common rappel transition and see how these new tools simplify the process. The example we use is two climbers with one rope, setting up a rappel.

Typically the leader finishes his pitch, ties into the anchor, and belays the second with a plaquette. Once the second arrives, the two climbers leash in and untie. Because the climbers do not want to drop the rope, they leave the leader's original clove hitch and likely the second's rope through a plaquette at the anchor. This means four locking carabiners at the anchor, the two leashes, the original clove hitch, and the belay device.

At this point the climbers pass one rope end through the anchor and place a stopper knot into both ends. Next they pull the rope through the anchor to the midpoint and one climber attaches himself to a rappel device, while the other climber waits for the first to rap and then get off rappel. The second climber then places his rappel device on the rope, cleans the gear on the anchor, and rappels.

Now let's perform the same rappel using a new system. The leader climbs and belays, as above. The follower climbs the pitch, but unlike our "usual way" of anchoring upon arriving, she cloves into the backside of the leader's clove hitch with a locker at her belay loop. She then unties and feeds her end through the anchor while the leader cleans the belay device. Once the middle of the rope arrives at the anchor, both climbers place their devices on the rappel ropes with the leader's device below the second's. They both attach themselves to their devices with extended rappel leashes, and the first rappeller uses a friction-hitch backup. They double-check each other's leashes and devices, then the second detaches the backside clove from her harness and the leader unclips his clove hitch. The leader now rappels while the second cleans any part of the anchor system they built (an equalized cord or sling, etc.).

BREAK IT DOWN

Let's first analyze how the new system uses the tools mentioned above, and then we can look at the strengths and weaknesses of each system. We know by the rope-end equation that there are no extra ends in a party of two with one rope, so we have to find the most convenient end to free up. In this case, since the leader is already anchored with a clove hitch, it means we have the second tool at our disposal: the backside of the clove hitch. The backside allows the climbers to untie the second's rope and free up his end.

The climbers can thread the end through the anchor until the mid-mark. Now the rope is rigged for the rappel, so we can see that with a new mind-set toward security, the climbers can now anchor themselves via an extended leash and a friction-hitch backup *on the rope*. At no point are the climbers anchored without the rope in the system.

The first rappeller could even forego a leash if she wanted, though this complicates the use of a backup friction hitch (we typically only do this on a short rappel with little hazard of losing control of the rope). The second rappeller, however, must use an extension/leash to connect to his device so as not to be pinned and awkwardly jostled by the first rappeller as she descends. Guides commonly do this, and it is described as "pre-rigging" the rappel for the clients.

By using the tools of the rope-end equation, the backside of the clove hitch, and a broader perspective of being anchored, we discover a new way to perform this common transition.

The next thing we need to do is compare the two methods from an efficiency and risk-management perspective. For efficiency we can look at how many clips are made and how much the climbers clutter the anchor. In both respects the new system has fewer clips and the anchor is far cleaner.

The new system requires three clips:

1. The clip of the second to the backside
2. The clip of the leader to the rappel device
3. The clip of the second to the rappel device

The old system requires four:

1. The clip of the second to the anchor with a leash
2. The clip of the leader to the anchor with a leash
3. The clip of the leader to the rappel device
4. The clip of the second to the rappel device

As far as clutter at the anchor, it is pretty clear the old system can have up to four carabiners at the anchor at one point, the two leashes, the belay device, and the clove hitch. The new system never has more than two biners, the clove hitch, and the belay device.

Now let's analyze the risk management. We know being clipped into an anchor with a leash or sling compromises our safety because those materials are static—they don't stretch and absorb energy. The new system never makes that compromise, as both climbers are always attached to the anchor with a section of the rope. Any time a leash is used, it is attached to a rappel device, which in turn is on the rope. In short, the climbers always have the dynamic, comfortable protection of the rope in their system.

The climbers have more safety built into their system via the rope, but they've also greatly reduced their potential for human error. Before rappelling, the climbers can check each other, thereby *doubling* their chances of catching an error before it's catastrophic. Between climbers of equal ability, this is a dramatic improvement, but for a team in which one member is more experienced, this is arguably many times safer than simply letting the second climber go on rappel without supervision or a second set of eyes to catch a mistake.

So we have a dynamic connection to our anchors and we've doubled our potential to catch an error, with fewer clips and far less clutter. Great! We're not done yet, though.

Another strength of the new system is that the leader, by going first as suggested, never unties from the end of the rope. This increases security in a few ways. First, because the second rappeller's device is pre-rigged on the rope, the rope is locked into the rappel anchor. It can't slide one direction or another, which means only one stopper knot is needed at the ends of the ropes to prevent the first rappeller from going off the end—but he's remained tied in through this whole transition, saving the time and effort of untying and retying a stopper knot. The climbers drop the second's free end of the rope without a knot in it, meaning it's far less likely to get snagged on the way down—another potential time savings, especially in a place like Red Rock or Eldo, where stuck ropes are common.

With this new system, the first rappeller down does need to consider the rope ends once she's at the new anchor, so we recommend threading the unknotted side through the anchor and tying a stopper knot (thereby securing the rope, too, once the team pulls it).

Pen and Tape

For less than twenty bucks, you should be able to buy a 100-foot tape measure and laundry pen. This will allow you to do two things: first, make sure your new rope is the length it's supposed to be, and second, make sure the middle mark is indeed the middle of the rope. Measure a new rope, or any rope that you're unsure of the location of the middle, with your tape measure and then mark it. Keep the middle mark visible, and it'll save you time and hassle, and it's safer, too.

One minor weakness of the new system is the need for an accurate, reliable middle mark. Without it, guessing where the middle is and getting it wrong could leave you short of the next anchor or the ground due to the aforementioned locking of the system by the pre-rigged rappel device of the second rappeller. We can easily mitigate this problem, however, with a three-dollar laundry pen and some diligence. Keep the middle of your rope clearly marked and accurate!

HYBRID SYSTEMS

Of course, hybrids of the two systems exist. For instance, instead of using the backside of the clove hitch, the second could just leash into the anchor to free that end of rope. Or the leader could have leashed in upon arrival at the anchor and the second could have been left on the belay device upon his arrival at the anchor. The climbers could place a catastrophe knot on the brake strand, thereby freeing up the leader's end of the rope. This would make the second climber the first rappeller.

These hybrids illustrate the power of this new way of thinking and the reason we consider them advanced. As problems get more complex and/or more climbers are included (parties of three), solutions to problems abound, but not coordinating with your climbing partner(s) can lead to confusion. In the case of a guide, there is a clear leader in the process of a transition. In a less formal or a recreational setting, climbers often work at anchors without clear leadership, and this is when protocol and standardization may be helpful.

The old system may make it appear that leadership in transition isn't essential, but we believe that is a false premise, particularly when situations get difficult because of external pressures (daylight or weather, for example) or because of the complexity of the transition. So, in a party of equals, leadership needs to be present, if for no other reason than streamlining procedures and "getting everybody on the same page." For a guide or citizen leader who already has leadership responsibilities, the new systems deliver greater efficiency, security, and simplicity—valuable benefits when one already has lots to think about.

More Transitions, Step by Step

Let's move into more complex transitions, involving more ropes, more climbers, and both the potential for greater gains in efficiency but problems, too. We encourage you to practice some of these with short sections of rope at the rock gym or at an improvised anchor in your garage or basement.

More Rappelling

Let's start with a step-by-step process of the situation described above. Two climbers, one rope, and setting up a rappel:

1. The leader arrives at the anchor and clove-hitches herself in, then belays the second.

Less Is More

by Sean Smith

Sean Smith COURTESY SEAN SMITH

I can recall at least one moment at every stage of my guide training where a new technique left me in awe. It wasn't always something incredibly complex, either. Instead, it was usually something brilliantly simple, a technique that was clean and elegant. A sense of frustration often accompanied these moments—why hadn't I figured that out myself?!

This was far from what I'd expected. I had always been a gear nerd. If it was new and fancy, I wanted it. The more complicated the technique, the more I wanted to really have it down. If it involved a Munter hitch, I was hooked. One of the initial draws I'd had toward guiding was the rumors of secret knowledge of rigging and rope work.

Then, a few years ago I took a clinic with Marc and Rob on self-rescue, with "beyond the basics" even in the title, so of course I jumped on it. It was being taught at the annual guides' meeting, so I was expecting the rope work equivalent of building a particle collider. Instead, I was presented with a major paradigm shift as transitions and techniques were pared down to the bare minimum. Watching Marc teach got me thinking about changing my whole approach to moving faster, and with each lesson I was moving fancy devices from my pack to the storage closet.

Months later on my rock-guide course, while practicing short-roping and short-pitching with an IFMGA-licensed instructor, it was my turn to "guide." I thought back to the clinic every time my instructor's suggestions included a statement like "just do this." His vast experience cut out every unnecessary step, in transitions, in movement, in maneuvers I thought I'd dialed years ago.

Since my first adventures in the mountains, I had always been looking for improvements in my climbing. I read every book I could get my hands on, pored over tech tips, and studied every example of "light and fast" to be found. However, I could never fully go over the edge, I kept the rack full, the rope out and belay on; I just couldn't start cutting down on safety, couldn't accept risks I didn't think were necessary.

After that clinic, however, I started questioning things. In fact, the question I was asking changed. It was no longer "What else could I have done here?" but "Was all of that necessary?" I began to see more of the lightness, not just weight in gear, but weight in methodology. More so, I was learning how to use the rope and locking carabiners to do almost everything I needed. The rack got lighter. I moved faster.

Since that clinic and my time on AMGA courses, I've spent many days in the field working alone, working alongside other guides, and climbing with friends—always looking at what my colleagues and I were doing, and asking the questions. I'm fully hooked now, committed to this new approach.

With some practice I've found many ways to apply this new philosophy. Where all of this really comes together, though, is being with a guest on a summit, or at the top of a route they didn't think we'd have time to do. Most things have gotten easier, gone faster. Cleaner systems mean I've given more concise instructions, lowering stress for me and the client, decreasing the chances of an error. This leaves more time to savor the views, more time on the summit, and a few more bites of food and sips of water. At the end of the day, there's room for more smiles, and more happy hours!

I now rarely look at gear releases with the same fervor. What excites me about advances in climbing now is seeing the gears turn in the head of another guide I'm training with, wondering what's next.

—Sean Smith is a Front Range transplant, total climbing nerd, and Apprentice Rock Guide pursuing higher certification in all three disciplines.

2. The second arrives and puts a clove hitch into the rope coming off the backside of the leader's clove hitch and clips that into his harness.

3. The second unties from his end of the rope, while the leader cleans the belay device she used to belay the second.

4. The second feeds the free end through the ring(s) at the rappel anchor until the middle of the rope arrives at the ring(s).

5. Both the leader and the second put their devices on the rappel ropes with the leader's below the second's.

6. Both climbers clip into their rappel devices with an extension and the leader places a friction-hitch backup on the ropes.

7. The leader descends to the ground or the next anchor and after securing herself, gives a fireman's belay to the second.

We've already analyzed this transition above. The remaining transitions will have an analysis below each step-by-step description when warranted.

TWO PEOPLE USING A DOUBLE-ROPE SYSTEM SETTING UP A RAPPEL

1. The leader arrives at the anchor and anchors in with both ropes—each with its own clove hitch on either two separate locking carabiners or two cloves on one large carabiner. He belays the second as normal.

2. The second arrives and places her rappel device onto the backsides of the clove hitches and uses an extension/friction-hitch system to clip into her device.

3. The second takes herself off belay.

4. The leader takes his belay/rappel device and places it above the second's device on the backsides of the clove hitches and clips into it with an extension.

Two separate clove hitches built in a single locking carabiner. A large-volume carabiner works best for this technique.

5. The second begins to rappel.

6. While the second rappels, the leader unties from the ends of the ropes, passes one end through the rings, and joins the rope ends together using his preferred joining knot.

7. Once the second is off rappel, the leader unclips the clove hitches and rappels. (See the discussion below for the order.)

In this case we see how rappelling on the backsides of the clove hitches offers the most efficient means of getting on rappel and starting to move down the cliff. Because we know there are four ends and each climber has two, it becomes obvious the leader's ends should be the ends fed through the rap rings (they're already anchored). The second stays tied in to the ends, so she never risks rappelling off of them.

This makes the second the logical person to rappel first, because her ends are going to be on top of the stack and they'll easily feed down the cliff. The leader's ends are already anchored and will be easily fed through the rap rings. The second has to attach first because the leader's device is being used to belay her. That quick transfer from a friction anchoring system (belaying) to a friction anchoring system of rappelling with a friction-hitch backup seems logical.

We also want the leader to get his device free and on the rappel so he can use it as his security while the second rappels. Once he's on a rappel extension, it allows him to untie and join the ropes through the rap rings. Because the second never unties from the ends, there is no way to rappel off the ends of the ropes. If the rappel is long, however, the ropes may kink, requiring the second to untie from the ends. She'll have to make that call, depending on conditions. Should she choose to untie, she should knot one end to prevent going off the ends. (Remember, the clove hitches above her fix the ropes so they can't slide either direction, so one knot below her would save her if she lost control.)

In step 7 we referred to a process for unclipping the clove hitches and joining the rope through the anchor. We describe this process in the following sidebar; it will repeat often, so we are calling it the "backside rap-feed."

The Backside Rap-Feed

If he's used two separate carabiners, the leader has a choice which clove hitch he unclips first. If both clove hitches rest in the same carabiner, the rope end of the clove hitch nearest the gate of the locking carabiner passes through the rings first. If you used separate carabiners, either rope end can be passed through the ring(s), but the clove hitch you remove first should be the one on the rope that you fed first.

After you've fed the ropes through the rings and connected them with the junction knot of your choice, you unclip the clove hitch on the rope that was fed through the rings. We do this for security. Why? Because when the first clove hitch is untied, there's slack generated—but the leader is still on the second clove hitch. He can't fall any distance. The leader can feed the slack through his rappel device, so his device is now tight against the junction knot which is jammed against the rings. When he takes out the second clove hitch, he's tight on the rappel device, so the slack in the other rope is non-consequential.

One downside of this transition is that the junction knot and the rope being threaded through the rings is not double-checked by the first rappeller. Knowing this, the second rappeller should exercise additional vigilance. Check and check again!

1. The follower has rappelled and now the leader needs to join the ropes through the rings. He's untied from the orange rope and will next untie from the red. Keep in mind he's secured by his rappel device at this point. PHILBRICK PHOTOGRAPHY

2. He has untied from both ends of the rope and now joins them through the rings with the junction knot of his choice. We prefer the flat overhand for joining ropes for a rappel.
PHILBRICK PHOTOGRAPHY

3. Because he fed the orange rope first, he needs to unclip the orange clove hitch first. This is important because the junction knot protects him, as it will jam against the rings if he loads the rope.
PHILBRICK PHOTOGRAPHY

4. The junction knot is tight against the rings. He can now unclip the red rope. His friction-hitch backup grabs the orange rope, preventing him from a slip at this point. He feeds the slack in the red rope through his device and starts rappelling.
PHILBRICK PHOTOGRAPHY

5. The leader rappels. Glory and beers await below. PHILBRICK PHOTOGRAPHY

THREE PEOPLE, TWO ROPES, USING CATERPILLAR TECHNIQUE (SPEED TECHNIQUE*)

1. The leader arrives at the end of the pitch, cloves in, and belays as normal.

2. The second arrives and clove-hitches into the anchor with the rope he is trailing.

3. The leader takes the second off belay and begins to belay the third climber.

4. The second places his rappel device onto the backside of the leader's clove hitch and clips into it with an extension and friction-hitch backup.

5. When the third climber arrives, he places a rappel device on the backside of the second's clove hitch using an extension and friction-hitch backup.

6. The second now unties from the rope he trailed (the one to the clove hitch). At the same time, the leader takes the third climber off belay and places her rappel device onto both ropes coming off the backsides of the cloves (both her clove hitch and the second's clove hitch).

7. Both the second and third climbers begin to rappel.

8. While the two climbers rappel, the leader unties from her end of the rope and performs a backside rap-feed and starts rappelling.

*The speed variations require a climber to rappel on a single strand of rope. Read on to learn a couple techniques to increase friction and control when rappelling on a single strand.

1. Three people caterpillar to rappel (speed technique). The first follower arrives (yellow helmet) and clove-hitches into the anchor with the rope he's trailing. He attaches a rappel device onto the backside of the leader's clove.

PHILBRICK PHOTOGRAPHY

2. *While the second follower is climbing, the first follower connects to his rappel device with an extension. He puts a friction-hitch backup on the rope and a catastrophe knot below that (red rope). The second follower arrives (gray helmet) and places her device on the backside of the first follower's clove hitch (on the orange rope). The first follower can then untie from his end of the orange rope.* PHILBRICK PHOTOGRAPHY

3. *The second follower attaches herself to her rappel device with an extension and puts her friction-hitch backup on the rope below it, with a catastrophe knot below that. The leader takes the second follower off belay.*
PHILBRICK PHOTOGRAPHY

4. *The leader (blue helmet) places her rappel device on the backsides of the clove hitches of both ropes (orange and red). She attaches to it with an extension.* PHILBRICK PHOTOGRAPHY

5. While the followers rappel, the leader performs a backside rap-feed. PHILBRICK PHOTOGRAPHY

THREE PEOPLE, TWO ROPES, USING CATERPILLAR TECHNIQUE (REGULAR TECHNIQUE)

1. The leader arrives at the end of the pitch, cloves in, and belays as normal.

2. The second arrives and cloves-hitches into the anchor with the rope he is trailing.

3. The leader takes the second off belay and begins to belay the third climber.

4. While the leader belays the third climber, the second climber puts his rappel device on the backsides of his clove hitch and the leader's clove hitch. He connects with an extension.

5. When the third climber arrives, he places a rappel device on the ropes below the second's, using an extension and friction-hitch backup.

6. The second now unties from both the ropes. At the same time, the leader takes the third climber off belay and places her rappel device onto both ropes above the second's.

7. The third climber begins to rappel.

8. Once the third climber is off rappel, the second climber rappels.

9. While the second climber rappels, the leader unties from the end of the rope and performs a backside rap-feed and starts rappelling.

ANALYSIS

Because the transitions above are quite similar, we need only perform one analysis of them.

Again, we use the backside of the clove hitch quite a bit. What makes this different from the previous transition is the rope-end equation. With three people and two ropes, only one person has an extra end—the second, or middle, climber. By using that extra end to clove in (something not normally done if the party were to continue upward), the second climber ends up fixing the second rope (the rope he's trailing).

With both ropes fixed, the party moves into its rappels. In the speed technique, it would initially appear that the second climber could place his rappel device onto either rope, but he's still attached to the opposite end of the leader's rope so it makes sense that he rappel down that rope.

Once the second climber puts on his rappel device and friction-hitch backup, it would appear reasonable for them to untie. We recommend he does not, however; the reason is to simplify the choice of rope for the third climber. If the second climber unties before the third climber chooses which rope to put his rappel device on, the third climber might mistakenly put his device on the short strand. This may seem unlikely, but on a larger ledge where the climbers are tied in long, this could have fatal consequences. We see no real enhancement in efficiency by having the second climber untie immediately, so staying tied in until the third climber has built his rappel rig seems prudent.

As for the differences between the two systems, the party will need to determine whether it's worth the speed to have two rappellers descend simultaneously. The system doesn't have the weaknesses of the common simul-rappels used by some climbers because both strands are fixed.

Some considerations exist, however: On ice, for example, could the second rappeller knock icicles down on the first? Does the rappel angle to one side at all, and if yes, could the first rappeller slip and "floss" the higher rappeller off? Things to think about and consider in the field.

Whatever the challenges, if any, there will be more going on with two rappellers moving simultaneously, and that may create some confusion.

THREE PEOPLE, TWO ROPES, USING PARALLEL TECHNIQUE (SPEED TECHNIQUE)

1. The leader arrives at the anchor and cloves in with both ropes, each with its own clove hitch, on either separate lockers or one large one. She belays the seconds through a plaquette in guide mode.

2. When the first follower arrives, he places his device on the backside of the leader's clove hitch on the same rope he's tied into, and clips into it with an extension and friction-hitch backup.

3. When the third climber arrives, he puts a device on the backside of the leader's clove hitch on the same rope he's tied into, and clips into it with an extension and friction-hitch backup.

4. The leader now takes both the second and third climbers off belay and places her belay device on the two strands coming off the backsides of their clove hitches, and clips into it with an extension.

5. While the two climbers are rappelling, the leader unties from the end of the rope, passes one end through the rings, and joins the rope ends using her preferred knot.

6. Once the second and third climbers go off rappel, the leader adds a friction-hitch backup and completes the backside rap-feed and starts rappelling.

THREE PEOPLE, TWO ROPES, USING PARALLEL TECHNIQUE (REGULAR TECHNIQUE)

1. The leader arrives at the anchor and cloves in with both ropes, each with its own clove hitch, on either separate lockers or one large one. She belays the seconds through a plaquette in guide mode.

2. When the followers arrive, they place their devices on the backsides of both of the leader's clove hitches and clip into it with extensions. The first rappeller places a friction-hitch backup on his brake strands. The second rappeller unties from his end of the rope.

3. The leader takes both the second and third climbers off belay and places her belay/rappel device on the two strands coming off the backsides of his clove hitches and clips into it with an extension.

4. Third climber rappels.

5. When the third climber gets off rappel, the second climber begins his rappel backed up with either a fireman's belay or a friction-hitch backup he places on the ropes.

6. While the climbers rappel, the leader performs a backside rap-feed.

1. Three people parallel to rappel (regular technique). The followers have arrived at the stance and the leader leaves them on the plaquette. If warranted, the leader can place a catastrophe knot on the brake strands.

3. The leader takes them off belay, cleans the plaquette, and will now place his rappel device onto the backsides of his clove, above the followers' devices, and clips into it with an extension.

2. Both followers place their rappel devices on the backsides of the leader's clove hitches, and the lower (first) rappeller puts a friction-hitch backup on her brake strands.

4. While the second rappeller descends, the leader performs a backside rap-feed.

Hopefully by this point of the book you've taken out a rope or two and rehearsed these transitions . . . or you're one of the blessed few that can learn these techniques simply by reading through them!

Although these transitions differ radically from the traditional systems most of us learned years ago, the modern transitions resemble each other in very fundamental ways. The big difference with the speed version of this last transition is that the ropes may be twisted together in such a way as to make the two climbers rappelling simultaneously work pretty hard to straighten them out. This may be particularly acute in terrain that is broken and brushy.

Guide and Citizen Leader Techniques

We present the following transitions for guides and citizen leaders working with less-experienced climbers, guests, or students. Guides and leaders have tremendous responsibilities heaped upon them by working with folks who may not yet have the tools to mitigate hazard, or even the awareness of what those hazards are.

Sending a paying client or very new climber down to an anchor before the guide is often inappropriate. It requires the new climber build and clip into an anchor unsupervised. In those situations, the most experienced climber should go down first, after making sure his guests are secure at the anchor above, they're correctly pre-rigged to rappel, and lastly, they understand how to rappel. This system is generally called the "pre-rigged rappel." You noticed several of these in the above transitions.

Belayed Rappel

Another strategy that guides (for clarity, we may sometimes drop the phrases "citizen leaders," "group leaders," or "more experienced climbers") can use is the top-belayed rappel, during which the guide uses one strand of a rope to belay a student while she rappels on the other strand. This strategy is best used when going to the ground, an unquestionably secure ledge, or any situation with no anchor necessary at the bottom. The top-belayed rappel puts the guide in a better position to coach and avoids the nearly unsolvable problem of a student or beginner climber getting something stuck in the rappel device during a pre-rigged rappel (think clothing, hair, or an errant sling). (We say "nearly unsolvable" because the guide could always ascend the ropes, but if a body part like hair or skin gets caught, ascending the rope on steep terrain would be excruciating for the victim.)

The belayed rappel solves the above problem, but it's not without its own risks. Arguably the most common rappelling accident is rappelling off the end of the rope. A belayed rappel doesn't do a very good job of protecting against that. As you can imagine, the belay rope would be loose enough to allow the student/client to control his descent. If the rappel strand is a bit shorter and doesn't reach the ground, either because that strand is shorter or some of the rope is being occupied by the anchor system above, the rappeller can go off the end. With a loose belay and the stretch in 90 to 100 feet of rope (one strand of a doubled 60m rope), it is likely the belay wouldn't come tight in time to catch a climber going off the other strand. A knot in the end of the rope could be used, but you will see when we cover the transitions that in some circumstances we'll want to pull that end up to the belay and it could get caught.

Another way to solve this problem is to change the belay to a lower for the last 20 feet. To do this requires that you just stop feeding slack until the belay rope comes taut, and then lower the student/client the rest of the way.

Belayed rappels can also be difficult and/or uncomfortable for the student because of the limited friction when rappelling on a single strand. A heavy student or a rappel on very steep terrain on one strand can be difficult to control. Again, the belayer can take some weight with the belay, as we might to protect the bottom of the rappel. This may not be necessary initially because the weight of the rope hanging down the cliff helps to create friction, but once the rappeller gets halfway down the rope, the weight diminishes and the rappel becomes more difficult to control.

Increasing the friction in the student's rappel device can solve much of this problem.

Assuming the student is rappelling on a Reverso or ATC Guide, the guide can clip a biner to the device's "ear" and clip that to the student's belay loop. Adding a second carabiner to the rappel rig can help, too—simply add a second biner through the rope and to the belay loop, exactly like the

Clipping the ear back to the rappeller's belay loop increases friction. No locker necessary.

PHILBRICK PHOTOGRAPHY

usual setup. The additional width of the carabiner exaggerates the angle at which the rope enters the device, increasing friction.

Lowering

Guides and citizen leaders also have lowering as a reasonable option, in certain situations. Lowering effectively doubles the length of the rope; because a guide can use the full length of the rope when lowering (she doesn't have to double it to retrieve it), she has far more range in lowering someone past an obstacle, like a sketchy downclimb.

For example, imagine a low-snow year at your favorite ice crag. A 100-foot rappel gets you to a reasonable ledge, but with a 20-foot downclimb. It's easy enough for you, the star sender of the group, but your less-experienced buddy could fall and get seriously injured. A single 60m rope won't make it past the downclimb when doubled for rappelling, but if you choose to lower your friend, you can easily lower him past the downclimb to safety. Once he's safe and sound at the descent trail, you pull rope back up, center it, rappel, and (carefully!) downclimb what is for you a manageable section.

Lowering longer distances can be problematic with sight lines and difficult communication. A party also needs to recognize that the rope moving with the climber below can be hazardous if any loose rock is present. In these situations, lowering may increase hazard rather than solve problems. Any time a guide considers lowering, he asks himself, "What's the rope moving over? An edge? Loose rock?"

There are situations, however, where a longer lower offers advantages. We rarely see recreational climbers, and to some degree beginning mountain guides, employ lowering as a useful technique. If you haven't added lowering to your toolbox, we suggest you reconsider and keep your eyes open to situations in which it can be not only helpful, but safer.

For example, lowering doesn't require the team to throw or lower a rope into position. Descending into a popular climbing area, you can imagine how much less stressful this might be for you and the parties below (provided there's no loose rock to dislodge). By lowering, you can better thread the needle getting your ropes down. Of course, it doesn't solve the problem of pulling your ropes to retrieve them, but it can derail miscommunications between parties of climbers when you don't have a clear view of the cliff.

Just make sure you're solving a communication problem rather than creating another one. Radios can help, if you're concerned about verbal communication. Knowing you'll have a clear line-of-sight is often enough to make things workable. Having a plan with clear, distinct calls or rope signals helps, too.

A windy day might also encourage you to lower a climber. By lowering your partner, you are less likely to have your rope get blown around and stuck in an inconvenient place. Again, think Red Rock or in the alpine, where a rope stuck 25 meters to the side could turn into a tricky situation.

Double Up on Devices

For the citizen leader and the guide it is very useful to have two belay/rappel devices for many of the transitions below. You can consider this the burden of responsibility! All kidding aside, many guides prefer to use a device with bigger slots to belay seconds, the Kong GiGi or the CAMP Ovo being the two most popular examples. For less than 60 grams, these offer far less friction when taking in rope when compared to a traditional device like the Reverso or ATC Guide. Many a guide has avoided tendinitis in the elbow because of the GiGi and Ovo.

That said, some guides prefer to rappel on an ATC Guide or Reverso so they often have two devices with them, and this offers some advantages in certain transitions.

Pre-Rigged Transitions

Although the pre-rigged rappel most resembles a recreational system, the transitions are often more complex than a belayed rappel or a lower. While counterintuitive, this begins to make sense once we dive into the transitions themselves.

In a transition to a pre-rigged rap, the entire system needs to be changed, whereas in a belayed rappel or a lower there are major parts of the system you used to climb that can be incorporated into the descent system, saving time and hassle. In short, a belay already exists so half the belayed rappel is already built, and if going into a lower, elements of the existing belay system can be used for that, too.

ONE LEADER WITH ONE STUDENT USING ONE ROPE TO SET UP A RAPPEL

This is the classic pre-rigged rappel, as described above. In this system the leader goes down first after she and the second check each other's extensions, rappel devices, and backup. This provides greater security, and not just for the less-experienced climber—the leader also benefits from a second set of eyes on her system. A fireman's belay, provided by the leader, also increases security for the student.

LEADER AND STUDENT USING A DOUBLE-ROPE SYSTEM TO SET UP A RAPPEL (LEADER WITH A SINGLE DEVICE)

1. The leader arrives at the anchor and anchors in with both ropes. She can tie a single clove into both ropes in this instance.

2. The second arrives and takes both strands coming off the backsides of the leader's cloves and clove-hitches into them.

3. The second unties from the ends of both of his ropes, while the leader cleans the belay device she was using to belay the second.

4. One end of the freed ropes is fed through the ring(s) and tied to the other end using the junction knot of choice.

5. Both the leader and the second put their devices on the rappel ropes with the leader's below the second's.

6. Both climbers clip into the rappel devices with extensions and the leader places a friction-hitch backup on.

7. The leader unties the clove hitch from the anchor and cleans the anchor. The second unclips from the clove hitch on his belay loop. The team flips the stack or coils and throws them down the cliff.

8. The leader descends to the ground or the next anchor and after securing herself, gives a fireman's belay to her second.

LEADER AND STUDENT USING A DOUBLE-ROPE SYSTEM TO SET UP A RAPPEL (LEADER HAS TWO DEVICES)

1. Leader arrives at the anchor and anchors in with both ropes (they can both be on the same locking carabiner or two separate carabiners).

2. The leader places his rappel device on the backsides of the clove hitches and clips into it with an extension and a friction-hitch backup.

3. The leader removes the clove hitches using the backside rap-feed.

4. Once the second clove hitch is removed, the leader ties a double-stranded bight knot above his device. This bight knot takes up rope so the follower can get on rappel when she arrives at the stance. The knot could roll and untie if loaded, so the leader clips a carabiner into it while the follower climbs.

5. The leader adjusts his device and ties a compact double-stranded bight knot directly below his rappel device but above the friction-hitch backup.

6. This bight knot can now be used as a masterpoint and the leader belays the follower off of this masterpoint.

The leader is already on rappel with a BHK below his device. He belays using the BHK as his masterpoint. PHILBRICK PHOTOGRAPHY

7. The follower arrives and places her rappel device above the leader's device and clips into it with a leash.

8. The leader takes the follower off belay, while she unties from the ropes.

9. The leader puts a stopper knot on one of the ends, cleans the masterpoint bight knot, and rappels.

10. Once the leader is off rappel, the follower then rappels as the leader gives a fireman's belay.

We continue to see how these tools increase speed and security, and offer options that traditional systems might not. In the first option, your student is with you as you build the rappel and the process is nearly identical to the single-rope system. In the second example, the rappel is already built before the student arrives, increasing the efficiency and comfort, especially at a small stance.

So now the leader has to prioritize her goals. Is it speed and efficiency? Is the stance comfortable and therefore conducive to teaching? Is it cramped and therefore better to have things prepped so the team spends as little time as possible at the stance? These and other considerations must be made on the fly and these techniques adapted as the leader or team sees fit.

THREE PEOPLE, TWO ROPES, USING CATERPILLAR TECHNIQUE

1. The leader arrives at the end of the pitch, clove-hitches in, and belays as normal.

2. The second arrives and puts a clove hitch into the rope coming off the backside of the leader's clove hitch to secure himself. The leader then puts the third climber on belay.

3. The second unties from both the ends tied into his harness. The leader takes the two ends the second has untied and freed up, passes one of the ends through the rings, and ties the ends together using the junction knot of her choice.

4. While the leader belays the third climber, the second climber places his rappel device on the rappel ropes and clips into it with an extension.

5. When the third climber arrives, he places his rappel device on the rappel ropes above the second climber's and clips into it with an extension.

6. The leader takes the third climber off belay and places her device on the rappel ropes below the second's device and clips into it with an extension and friction-hitch backup.

7. The second climber now unclips from the clove hitch on his harness (the backside of the leader's clove hitch).

8. The leader unclips her clove hitch from the anchor and cleans any part of the anchor she originally built.

9. The third climber unties from the end of his rope.

10. The leader rappels and once in position, fireman-belays the second climber and then the third.

This transition seems very complex, but because much of the work to build the rappel occurs when the first client arrives at the belay, it actually plays out far simpler than the description appears.

To analyze this, the main thing to look at is the rope-end equation. When the leader arrives she only has one rope, so not much can be done. When the second climber arrives, however, he brings up two more rope ends. Once they can free these two ends up (by having the second climber attach himself to the backside of the leader's clove hitch), they can build a rappel.

This is where things get a little tricky. Once the second climber unties from the rope he's trailing, there is the slight chance of dropping it. Probably not catastrophic, but it would be rather embarrassing and tedious to retrieve. That's why the team puts the third climber on belay—it guarantees the

rope cannot be dropped. To keep security high, it's best practice to join the ropes *before* the third climber removes his clove hitch at the belay below and begins climbing. This keeps the systems closed in the miniscule chance the belay device fails for some reason.

When a leader is dealing with two lesser-experienced climbers, it's always a bit confusing, especially on an awkward stance. For that reason we have the second climber build his rappel, but stay attached to the backside of the leader's clove hitch. In the event the leader (who will have some focus on the third climber) misses an error in the second climber's rappel setup, the second climber is backed up with his clove.

Another benefit of the second going on rappel is it clearly identifies the rap ropes. This makes it easy for the third climber to go directly on rappel, but the rappel isn't being relied on for security—yet. Once the third climber arrives, the leader can focus completely on the rappel setups. She can double-check everything before the third climber goes off belay, and before the leader and second remove their clove hitches. Again, a second set of eyes greatly reduces the chances of a high-consequence mistake.

Also of note, the leader doesn't need to untie, protecting her from rappelling off the ends of the rope.

THREE PEOPLE, TWO ROPES, USING PARALLEL TECHNIQUE (LEADER HAS TWO DEVICES)

1. Leader arrives at the anchor and anchors in with both ropes, each with its own clove hitch (they can both be on the same locking carabiner or two separate biners).

2. The leader places his rappel device on the backside of the clove hitches and clips into it with an extension and friction-hitch backup.

3. The leader performs a backside rap-feed and in doing so removes the clove hitches.

4. Once the second clove hitch is removed, the leader ties a small double-stranded bight knot a little below the anchor (clips a carabiner through it so it can't roll). He then adjusts his device so he's comfortable and ties another double-stranded bight knot directly below his rappel device, but above the friction-hitch backup.

5. The leader uses the lower bight knot as the masterpoint and then belays both the second and third climbers off of this.

6. Once the second and third climbers arrive at the anchor, the leader unties the unused double-stranded bight knot. This will create enough slack for the second and third climbers to put their rappel devices on the ropes above the leader's device.

7. The second and third climbers place their rappel devices on the ropes and clip into them with extensions.

8. After double-checking the rappel systems, the leader takes the second and third climbers off belay, unties the bight knot he was using as a masterpoint, and has the second and third climbers untie from the ends of the ropes.

9. The leader places a stopper on one or both of the ends of the ropes, throws them down the cliff, and rappels. He gives a fireman's belay to the next rappellers.

Belayed Rappel Transitions

Now let's look at transitions in which a leader or guide can offer a top-belayed rappel for a student or client.

BELAYED RAPPEL WITH ONE LEADER, ONE STUDENT, AND ONE ROPE

1. The leader arrives at the anchor and uses a leash to anchor himself (this leash will become his rappel extension in step 9).

2. The leader belays the second climber up to the belay and then puts a catastrophe knot in the brake strand.

3. The leader unties from the end of the rope, feeds it through the ring(s) until it reaches the middle of the rope, and then tosses the end down the cliff.

4. The leader takes the rappel ropes just below the rings and ties a small double-stranded bight knot; this will be used as a masterpoint.

5. The leader takes the brake strand of the follower's rope and ties a Munter hitch onto the new masterpoint.

6. The second climber places a rappel device onto the rope hanging down the cliff.

7. After checking the rappel and double-checking the Munter, the leader takes the second climber out of the original belay device and removes the catastrophe knot.

8. The second climber rappels while the leader backs up the rappel with a (slightly) loose belay.

9. Once the second climber is down, the leader removes the Munter, unties the bight knot, places his rappel device on the rappel ropes and clips into it with his extension, and adds friction-hitch backup.

10. The leader then unclips from the anchor and rappels.

This transition is fairly complex relative to the number of people and having only one rope. The rope-end equation works against us: With one rope for two climbers, we only have two ends. Since one end has to hang down the cliff for the eventual rappel strand and one needs to be the belay strand, the leader needs to free up his rope end by leashing in.

Another complexity is that the rappel strand must be fixed. We do this by tying the double-stranded bight knot, which also functions as a masterpoint. This means only the leader's leash uses the original anchor. The double-stranded bight knot (and masterpoint) reduces congestion and fixes the rappel rope.

BELAYED RAPPEL WITH ONE LEADER AND ONE STUDENT, USING DOUBLE ROPES

This transition is relatively rare. Earlier in the chapter we warned of the problems of a heavy climber rappelling on a single strand or someone rappelling on steep terrain on a single (skinny) strand. When that single strand is also a half or twin rope, this problem is even more acute. This may be something reserved for slab/low-angled terrain only.

1. Leader arrives at the anchor and anchors in with both ropes, each with its own clove hitch (they can both be on the same locking carabiner or two separate biners).

2. The follower arrives and anchors in with only one rope using a Munter mule overhand.

3. The follower unties from the end of the rope with which she is not anchored.

4. The leader now has to separate the ropes. The leader restacks the rope with the free end, starting from the backside of his clove hitch. If done carefully the leader may not need to restack the belay rope.

5. Once the ropes are separated, the team throws the free end down the cliff.

6. The follower places a rappel device on the rope hanging down the cliff.

7. The leader unties the mule overhand knot and belays the follower down the rappel.

8. Once the follower is down, the leader takes her off belay. At this point both ropes are hanging down the cliff from the leader's clove hitches. The leader places a device on the ropes hanging down the cliff and attaches to it with an extension and a friction-hitch backup. He unties from his ends and performs a backside rap-feed.

THREE PEOPLE, TWO ROPES, USING CATERPILLAR TECHNIQUE FOR TWO BELAYED RAPPELS

1. Leader arrives at the end of the pitch, clove-hitches in, and belays as normal.

2. The first follower arrives and anchors herself using the trail rope. Instead of using a clove hitch, however, she should use a Munter mule overhand.

3. At this point the first follower unties from the rope on which she was belayed. The team tosses that end down the cliff (provided it won't get in the way of the third climber when he climbs the pitch).

4. The leader puts the third climber on belay and brings him up.

5. When the third climber gets to the anchor, the leader ties a Munter on the brake strand and clips it into the anchor.

6. The third climber places a rappel device on the rope hanging down the cliff.

7. The leader takes the third climber's rope out of the plaquette so that he can belay with the Munter hitch while the third climber rappels. The leader should give clear direction to the third climber to untie and take the knot completely out once he reaches the ground and no longer has a falling hazard.

8. The leader pulls up the free end of the yellow belay rope (*not* the blue rappel rope) left when the third climber untied. When he has this end, he ties a clove hitch about 4 or 5 feet from the end and attaches it to the anchor.

9. The second climber places her rappel device on the backside of the leader's clove (this is the blue rope in the photo).

10. The leader undoes the mule overhand knot and belays the second climber down the rappel.

11. Once the second climber reaches the ground, the leader takes her off belay. At this point both ropes are hanging down the cliff, both from clove hitches. One of those clove hitches is also the leader's anchor. The leader places a device on the ropes hanging down the cliff and attaches to it with an extension and performs a backside rap-feed.

1. Three people caterpillar technique to belayed rappels. The leader belays the first follower on a plaquette on the blue rope.

2. The first follower anchors in on the trail rope with a Munter mule overhand, then she unties from the blue rope and drops the end down the cliff.

3. The third climber (second follower) arrives and places his rappel device on the backside of the leader's clove hitch on the blue rope. The leader ties a Munter onto the third climber's brake strand. This is the yellow rope, the one on which the leader belayed him up the pitch.

4. The third climber rappels to the ground and unties, removing the figure eight completely. The leader pulls up this free end. (This is the yellow rope on which he just belayed the third climber.) The leader clove-hitches the end he pulls up to the anchor. This closes the system for the belay for the next rappeller.

5. The second rappeller places her device on the backside of the leader's clove hitch (blue rope). The leader unblocks the Munter and belays her as she rappels.

6. The second rappeller reaches the ground. The leader takes her off belay. Both ropes now hang down the cliff from clove hitches. He puts his rappel device on the backsides of those clove hitches and performs a backside rap-feed.

Analyzing this transition, we again see how the rope-end equation steers us in a particular direction. Since the leader's rope is fixed and securing him, that rope only has one end to work with, so it makes sense to use that rope as the rappel strand. Since the trail rope is attached to both the second and third climbers, it makes sense to use that rope as the belay strand. The first climber down has to untie when he reaches the ground so that the leader can belay the next climber down.

Keep in mind, if the leader were concerned about that first client straying into a falling hazard at the base, he would have to make sure that climber was disciplined and recognized the hazard of wandering from the safe landing area.

For any situation in which the leader wants to prevent the climbers from straying too far from the landing zone, or for students who might not reliably follow instructions (kids or in case of a language barrier, for example), below is a variation that keeps both climbers tied into an end once they finish their rappels. This gives the leader more peace of mind, as well as control over the descending climbers.

THREE PEOPLE, TWO ROPES, USING CATERPILLAR TECHNIQUE (SECURITY VARIATION)

1. Leader arrives at the end of the pitch, clove-hitches in, and belays as normal.

2. The second climber arrives and ties into the anchor using the rope on which he was belayed. Instead of using a clove hitch, however, he should use a Munter mule overhand.

3. The leader puts the third climber on belay and brings him up.

4. The third climber arrives and ties into the anchor with a clove hitch using the rope on which he was belayed.

5. When the third climber is secure, the second climber unties from the rope he trailed up and tosses it down the cliff.

6. The second climber places a rappel device on the rope hanging down the cliff.

7. The leader undoes the mule knot and belays the second climber down the rappel. The leader should give clear direction to him to take the rappel device completely off the rope once he is

down—*but the rappeller remains tied in to the strand on which the leader belayed him.*

8. The leader pulls up the rope the second climber rappelled on, ties a clove hitch about 4 or 5 feet from the end, and attaches it to the anchor.

9. The third climber now places his rappel device on the rope hanging down the cliff (this is the rope the second climber is still tied into).

10. The leader puts the third climber on belay and belays him as he rappels.

11. Once the third climber reaches the ground, the leader takes him off belay. At this point both ropes are hanging down the cliff from clove hitches. One of these clove hitches is also the leader's anchor. The leader now places a device on the ropes hanging down the cliff and attaches to it with an extension and a friction-hitch backup. She performs a backside rap-feed.

In the previous transition the leader belays each climber on different ropes. This allows the leader to keep them tied in to their ends while on the ground. While this doesn't offer total security, it does imply that the climbers aren't to wander off or leave the landing zone until the guide arrives. To do this transition efficiently, it just so happened we reversed the order of the rappellers.

THREE PEOPLE, PARALLEL TECHNIQUE

1. The leader arrives at the anchor and anchors in with both ropes, each with its own clove hitch (they can both be on the same locking carabiner or two separate biners).

2. The first climber arrives and places a rappel device on the backside of the leader's clove hitch *on the rope that is tied into the other climber.* Below that rappel device, the leader ties a bight knot to secure the climber.

3. The first climber unties from her end of the rope.

4. The second climber arrives and anchors in with a Munter mule overhand knot.

5. The leader cleans the belay device.

6. The leader now has to separate the ropes. The leader restacks the rope with the free end, starting from the backside of his clove hitch. If done carefully the leader may not need to restack the belay rope.

7. Once the ropes are separated, the free end is tossed down the cliff.

8. The second climber places a rappel device on the rope hanging down the cliff.

9. The leader unties the Munter mule overhand and belays the second climber while she rappels. The leader should give clear direction to her to take her rappel device completely off the rope once she's down *but to stay tied in.*

10. The leader now pulls up the rope the second climber rappelled on and ties a small bight knot into it. The leader clips the bight knot into the first climber's belay loop.

11. The leader now puts the first climber on belay with the rope he just attached to the climber.

12. The bight knot that was tied below the first climber's rappel device is untied and she begins to rappel.

13. Once the climber is down, the leader takes her off belay. At this point both ropes are hanging down the cliff from the leader's clove hitches. The leader now places a device on the ropes hanging down the cliff and attaches to it with an extension and a friction-hitch backup, and performs a backside rap-feed and rappels.

Lowering Transitions

Lowering transitions are some of the simplest we use. When we belay a climber up the cliff, we typically reverse the process to lower her—simple. Once we lower a climber, we have a rope hanging down the cliff, so often a guide will then do a belayed rappel for the second descending climber. This offers at least one of the climbers a chance to rappel, which is usually more rewarding and comfortable. In the end, the transition is the same and we can take advantage of never having to throw a rope down the cliff—a nice bonus in high winds or rope-catching terrain.

By the same token, lowering requires vigilance. Loose rock or poor sight lines can increase hazard, so make sure a lower is appropriate before choosing it.

ONE LEADER, ONE STUDENT, ONE ROPE SETTING UP A LOWER

1. Leader arrives at the anchor, anchors as usual, and belays the second.
2. When the second arrives, the leader sets up an LSD (load strand direct) lower or uses a Munter hitch to lower the second. While building the lower, the leader may want to have the second attach himself to the backside of the leader's clove hitch for increased security.
3. The leader puts a friction-hitch backup on the brake strand and lowers the climber.
4. Once the second is down, the leader needs to leash into the anchor and untie from the end of the rope. If the second unties, the leader should instruct him to leave a knot in the rope end.
5. The leader passes the end of the rope through the ring(s) and ties a stopper knot, then pulls the rope through the rings to the midpoint.
6. The leader places a rappel device on the ropes and clips into it with an extension and friction-hitch backup, unclips her leash from the anchor, and rappels.

LEADER AND ONE STUDENT, A DOUBLE-ROPE SYSTEM SETTING UP A LOWER

1. The leader arrives at the anchor and anchors in with both ropes, each with its own clove hitch (they can both be on the same locking carabiner or two separate biners).
2. When the second arrives, the leader sets up an LSD lower or uses a Munter hitch to lower the second. While building the lower, the leader may want to have the second attach himself to the backside of the leader's clove hitch for increased security.
3. The leader puts a friction-hitch backup on the brake strand and has the second unclip from the backside of the clove hitch, and then lowers the climber.
4. Once the second is down, the leader disassembles the lower, then places a rappel device on the backsides of the clove hitches and connects to it with an extension and a friction-hitch backup. She performs a backside rap-feed and rappels.

THREE PEOPLE, TWO ROPES, USING CATERPILLAR TECHNIQUE: LOWER INTO A BELAYED RAPPEL

1. The leader arrives at the end of the pitch, clove-hitches in, and belays as normal.
2. The second climber arrives and ties into the anchor using the rope on which he was belayed. Instead of using a clove hitch, however, he uses a Munter mule overhand.
3. The leader now puts the third climber on belay and brings her up.
4. The third climber arrives and ties into the anchor with a Munter mule overhand, using the rope on which she was belayed.
5. When the third climber is secure, the second climber unties from the rope he trailed up. The leader takes this end and ties a clove hitch 4 to 5 feet from the end and clips it to the anchor.
6. The leader puts a friction-hitch backup on the brake strand of the second climber's Munter mule overhand, undoes the mule, and then lowers the second climber.
7. The third climber now places a rappel device on the rope hanging down the cliff. This is the rope that the second climber was just lowered on.
8. The leader undoes the third climber's Munter mule overhand and belays the third climber as she rappels.
9. Once the third climber reaches the ground, the leader takes her off belay. At this point both ropes are hanging down the cliff, both from clove hitches. One of those is also the leader's anchor. The leader now places a device on the ropes hanging down the cliff and attaches to it

with an extension and friction-hitch backup. He performs a backside rap-feed and rappels.

The lowering transition described above is actually a lower into to a belayed rappel. In step 7 you can see we have the third climber place her rappel device on the rope hanging down the cliff. If for some reason she doesn't rappel, the leader should place a friction-hitch backup on the brake strand of her Munter mule overhand, undo the knot, and then lower her.

With very little change the leader could choose to lower the third climber first, then have the second climber do a belayed rappel as well. This can be an important choice if the guide or citizen leader has one person who is more nervous or a less-experienced climber.

THREE PEOPLE, PARALLEL TECHNIQUE, LOWER TO A BELAYED RAPPEL

1. The leader arrives at the anchor and anchors in with both ropes, each with its own clove hitch (they can both be on the same locking carabiner or two separate biners).

2. The first climber arrives and places his rappel device on the backside of the leader's clove hitch that is tied into the second climber's rope. Below that rappel device the leader ties a catastrophe knot to secure the first climber.

3. The first climber unties from the end of the rope.

4. The second climber arrives and anchors in with a Munter mule overhand knot.

5. The leader cleans the belay device.

6. The leader now has to separate the ropes. The leader restacks the one rope with the free end starting from the backside of her clove hitch. If done carefully, the leader may not need to restack the belay rope.

7. Once the ropes are separated, a bight knot is tied into the free end and clipped into the first climber's harness.

8. The leader places a friction hitch onto the brake strand of the Munter mule overhand, unties it, and then lowers the second climber.

9. The leader now puts the first climber on belay with the rope she clipped to him in step 7.

10. The first climber unties the bight knot below his rappel device (step 2) and begins to rappel.

11. Once the climber is down, the leader takes him off belay. At this point both ropes are hanging down the cliff from the leader's clove hitches. The leader places a rappel device on the ropes and attaches to it with an extension and friction-hitch backup. She performs a backside rap-feed and rappels.

This lower is nearly identical to the parallel rope belayed rappel, but by lowering one climber there is no need to toss a rope or pull one up.

Conclusions

Transitions offer us the opportunity to speed up our climbing, improve security, and lower our stress—win, win, win. While many of these transitions may seem cumbersome at first, just remember the first time you practiced self-rescue, learned a haul system, or climbed as a party of three. Sure, it probably *was* slower the first time or two, but eventually you mastered the technique and now you have it comfortably stashed in your toolbox. These transitions can and will be the same for you.

Grab a couple of like-minded friends, rig a couple anchors on the back porch, and then go back and forth, swapping transitions. Next time you're out and you've got an extra few minutes to spare, incorporate some of these into your day. We recommend practicing them first on the ground, then on the cliff—but when you've got time to spare, no crowds, and the sun is shining. Eventually, it will be thundering in the distance and the sun will be setting . . . and it's just these times that buttoned-up transitions will make your climbing smoother, faster, and safer. Get on it!

CHAPTER 9

Alpine Rock: Approaches, Descents, and Variable Terrain

The alpine challenges us with wildly varying terrain, calling on all our skills as well as our abilities to transition between styles and techniques in fluid, efficient ways. We've focused largely on pure rock climbing—meaning fifth-class climbing—until now. Alpine climbing usually means long sections of third- and fourth-class terrain, in addition to the steeper pitches. It's potentially some of the most satisfying climbing we do, because we get to apply so many different skills on a single route.

Third- and fourth-class rock with steps of fifth-class is some of the hardest terrain to move through efficiently and still have reasonable fall protection. You need to be flexible in how you use the rope, and you'll need to employ tactics that are best described as "old-fashioned." Old-fashioned or not, this strategy will often utilize terrain features for anchors and protection. Using this approach, we will also shorten the rope so the team can move together in certain terrain, then lengthen it again to pitch-out and belay other sections. To do this a team must refine two distinct skills:

1. Rope handling so the team can quickly and securely coil off the rope and then uncoil it as the terrain gets easier or harder.

2. Have good terrain assessment skills so they can see when terrain is getting easier or harder early enough to adapt their rope systems. They'll also need to see natural features that can be used with the rope to protect the party.

It's this second skill involving terrain assessment that's impossible to improve without practice and training in varied terrain. Certainly a book can help, but rope systems are much easier to learn from a book and practice on small crags or even ground practice. The only thing that improves terrain recognition and assessment is . . . going out and doing it.

Terrain Recognition and Type

So what are we looking for in the terrain? What are some terrain clues that give us hints as to what to look for? To start, let's break down alpine terrain into three distinct types: slabs, ridges, and broken faces.

Slabs

Slabs are in some ways the easiest to identify and manage, since they are smooth and have few features; the best way to deal with them is like a simplified fifth-class rock pitch. There will be times when you reach a section you might approach like a broken face, but often slabs in the alpine can be pitched with the full length of your rope. The only reason you would go shorter is because of communication. If the slab is not fifth-class, simplifying the anchors and minimizing the protection will increase the speed and efficiency.

Keeping the Flow

by Emilie Drinkwater

Emilie Drinkwater COURTESY EMILIE DRINKWATER

I guided the Grand Teton for the first time on an impossibly dark, moonless night with only a speckling of stars illuminating the universe. Young and fit, my client, Lee, was utterly attentive to detail. A great person to climb with for his natural skill and ability, but also a terrible person to climb with because, somehow, he was always ready to go before me.

We left camp at 3:30 a.m. and had no trouble keeping a quick pace through the steep talus. I remember thinking, *This is good, we'll never have to worry about parties above us; we'll never have to worry about waiting in line at the rappel.* But as we approached the first section of easy fifth-class climbing, my headlamp faded and then gave up altogether. I pretended that this wasn't a horrifying moment and dug out my tiny backup headlamp . . . which did little more than prove that I had a tiny backup headlamp.

With only the faint glow of a single LED and at least an hour until the first dusky gleam of day, navigating the unfamiliar terrain was suddenly a far more daunting task. There was another guided team just ahead of us, and I immediately decided I needed to keep up. I hastily removed all of my Kiwi coils and, stretching every last bit of rope, reached an awkward stance below their follower. And with that hasty decision, I admittedly lost my rhythm.

The micro topography on the Grand Teton is far more complex than you might ever guess from a distance. As with most alpine terrain, a volatile mix of kitty litter granite, loose rock, and teetering boulders throws you off your game, not to mention lots of other people.

I called down to Lee, telling him that he could climb, but we were too far apart and my voice was carried away with the wind. Then I tried to peer over the edge but I didn't have enough rope to extend to where I might see him. I tugged at the rope, annoyed by our lack of communication. A line of head-lamps now rapidly approached from below.

Eventually Lee arrived, and rather than coil back in to move together, I took off, hoping to stay close behind the lead team. Again, I stretched my rope as far as it would allow, this time dragging it through rubble, sending loose rock down a gully at climbers below. Lee again arrived at the anchor, informing me that parties were stacking up just below us. The climbing above appeared to be easy third- and fourth-class, so I restacked my rope and put my coils back on. But in the course of this slow transition, the team ahead was long gone. Meanwhile, several recreational parties caught up to us, and now we were all racing for the top, vying for position on one of the most popular routes in the Tetons.

Somewhere along the way the sky began to lighten and I found my rhythm again. With most of the rope in Kiwi coils and the remainder in my hand, it became much easier to move efficiently through variable terrain, dropping my hand coils to climb short bulges of rock, then picking them up again to protect Lee through the same moves. Anticipating the terrain ahead and maintaining constant communi-cation allowed us to move far more efficiently than my previous strategy of long-pitching everything and hoping for the best.

We arrived at the summit amidst a crowd of people celebrating a beautiful, windless morning high above the plains of Jackson Hole and Yellowstone National Park. It was clear that we would not only wait in line for the rappels below, but that we would have a steady stream of parties both above and below us for the remainder of our climb.

Since that first climb on the Grand, I've subsequently guided the peak more than thirty times. With good use of large and small features, I rarely use much of the gear I carry along and the rope simply maintains pace. This depth of experience—gained through countless pitches, small errors, and many summits—has taught me that efficient movement in variable terrain doesn't actually mean moving fast. Rather, it means methodical movement and calculated planning . . . and fresh batteries in your headlamp!

—Emilie Drinkwater is an AMGA/IFMGA Mountain Guide based in Salt Lake City but will go wherever there's work.

A classic slab. PHILBRICK PHOTOGRAPHY

Terrain will not be a huge help for protection on slabs, but anywhere it can be used will be a plus. For the most part, you will be using cams and nuts, just fewer of them and with a minimalist strategy that maximizes the usefulness of each placement.

Of course, terrain assessment also includes route-finding. Anywhere you can find terrain that blocks or minimizes a fall, it allows the team to use less (or no) gear, which increases speed. This idea of a large ledge or some kind of feature that acts like a small wall between you and a fall is called "fencing."

Fencing and route-finding naturally follow from excellent terrain assessment—recognizing the easier

Fencing uses terrain to protect against a fall. In this shot the team faces a fall to the left as well as one in front of the climbers. The natural groove guards against the fall to the left so the guide can focus on managing the falling hazard ahead.

line or noticing features that protect you from a fall—and this in turns means a team can forego pausing to place gear, set anchors, or even just eyeball the next section of terrain. Keep in mind, this takes years to master and must be approached with humility. When in doubt, slow down, consider placing a piece, but always strive to perfect your assessment, route-finding, and fencing skills.

Ridges

Ridges are the antithesis of slabs. They offer ample natural protection features, and even a ridge itself can function as bomber protection. Imagine two climbers on either side of a low-angled ridge, but one that drops away steeply on either side. The team has 15 to 20 feet of rope connecting them. In this situation the ridge acts as a piece of protection because the climbers are effectively counterbalanced over it.

Ridges like the Matthes Crest Traverse in the Sierra, the West Ridge of Forbidden in the North Cascades, the North Ridge of Black Peak, and the West Ridge of Cutthroat on Washington Pass all come to mind where sections can be protected this

The western Alps offer some of the most dramatic ridge climbing in the world. The climbers here are traversing the Aiguille d'Entrèves, above Courmayeur. Ample natural protection in the form of horns and counterbalance positions makes this fun and often highly protectable terrain.

way. Little to no gear, the rope shortened, and the team moving steadily over exposed, exciting terrain.

Seldom will you want to deviate from the ridge itself. Staying on the ridge crest offers the protection of counterbalancing as described above, but you'll also discover more horns and better rock on the crest. Think about it—the crest is the crest because the rock has resisted weather and erosion better than the material around it, so now it's still jutting into the sky while everything else has fallen into the valley or eroded away.

Avoid dropping off the ridge as much as possible. Certainly there will be times to do this, but good beta and expert terrain assessment will let you know when to bypass a gendarme or drop off the crest. Notice when you choose to do so, suddenly it feels like a traversing pitch on a face climb, and that means pendulum potential, and that means placing gear. The team slows down immediately!

As rock quality deteriorates, too, you'll have to climb more slowly and carefully. Think twice before embarking on a route strategy that leaves the crest.

The guide secures the two clients by counterbalancing them over a ridge. The gent in the green jacket protects his partner in red. Should one fall, the other's weight and position protects him.

HORNS

Don't discount the advantages offered by having horns along a ridge crest. By flipping your rope to the far side of the horn, it immediately offers you protection and a running terrain belay. As you weave along the rough top of a ridge, you'll find yourself moving from one side to the other. Every time you move to the right side, it's ideal if your partner moves to the left, but in reality that won't always be the case.

Find a solid horn, though, and the team remains protected, even if the climbers happen to both be on the same side of the ridge.

Horns can also be used as anchors and belays. In effect, standing next to a horn and pulling in rope is the original way climbers "belayed off the anchor." No doubt you'll occasionally need cams, nuts, and pitons, but the fewer you have to place, the quicker and more efficiently you'll climb.

By looping the rope around a horn or feature, the guide protects both climbers against a fall, as well as himself.

Once in a while we need no fall protection on a ridge, but that's a minority of the time. We generally have potential for three fall lines when ridge climbing—one on each side and then down the ridge itself if it's steep enough.

By far, ridges are where you will channel the famous climbers of yore and where you often feel most in touch with the terrain, as you use it to solve the very problems the ridge throws at you. A good ridge climb delivers some of the most classic terrain in the mountains.

Broken Faces

Broken faces can act like slabs and ridges. We include gullies and couloirs in this section, although for the most part we avoid these in a summer alpine environment due to rockfall. A good example of a classic couloir-type feature is the *Fisher Chimneys* on Mount Shuksan, in Washington. On faces, the type and nature of the rock largely determine whether you will be relying on terrain belays and protection or using more cams and nuts.

A face dotted with horns and just the right amount of "featuring" can be as fun and satisfying as any ridge climb. Take away too many features, add a little loose rock or sand, and suddenly the face becomes frustrating and frightening, even more so in descent. Unfortunately, this happens more frequently than we'd like, but when faces are good, they are *good*.

Route-finding helps tremendously on wandering, unobvious faces. Sussing out the "right line" keeps movement straightforward and decreases the need for placing supplemental protection. Some of our favorite "broken face" climbs are Mix Up peak in the Cascades, the upper summit section of Triumph, the *East Ledges* descent on Forbidden, and the mountaineers descent of the *Spiral Route* on Notchtop, in Rocky Mountain National Park.

Open terrain and the lack of natural protection make broken faces sometimes hard to protect. The climber has negotiated the lower, fourth-class approach to **Moon Goddess Arête** *in the Sierra, on* **Temple Crag. Now the real climbing begins.**

Rappelling or Downclimbing?

Newcomers to alpine climbing often rappel when they could downclimb. Whether through inexperience or fatigue, rappelling seems the easier, safer option. Typically, though, downclimbing is faster and with some precaution, safer because a team doesn't risk getting its rope stuck or chopped. Good research and expert terrain recognition will help a team know when to rap and when to downclimb. Make a conscious choice, though; don't just reflexively rap when you might be able to find a reasonable descent on foot.

Descending

Ridge, face, or slab, descending is probably the most difficult movement to manage. Rappelling will not always be an option, so downclimbing becomes important. We have found on guide courses that watching someone descend offers an easy way to assess his skill level in the mountains. The sense of commitment, fear of the unknown, and movement skill of downclimbing all conspire to create a stressful situation.

Descending efficiently means just steadily picking away at the terrain. Less-experienced people often succumb to frustration and tedium, so it's important to remind oneself that descending is almost always more difficult than ascending. This leads some people to rappel when a downclimbable option exists. While rappelling might feel less stressful, often rap routes are steeper and potentially very difficult to climb. Should a rope get stuck, that puts the team in a tough spot. Do you attempt to climb the rap route (often with a small alpine rack), ascend the rope, leave the rope, downclimb?

Of course, these three categories are broad and general, but they give you an idea of the flavor of different terrain and potential approaches to them. Many routes will combine all three styles, so a flexible rope system, utilized by an organized team with excellent terrain-assessment skills, is what's required to move efficiently.

A solid, competent team will move smoothly over terrain where a less skilled or a disorganized team will seem to be standing still. Seeing terrain is a skill that needs to be developed and not something a book can really help with. What we can do is describe the rope systems and the big picture of where they might fit in on your next climb.

Rope Systems

What rope to bring? It's an important question. To start, we recommend a single-rope system. We sometimes use UIAA double-rope systems like twin or half ropes, but we find them more complex and unwieldy to carry coiled off when on third- and fourth-class sections. If a route demands a long rappel, carrying a UIAA single and a skinny UIAA twin or half rope in a pack weighs nearly the same as a set of twins or halves, but delivers the simplicity (not to mention durability) of a single-rope system.

Most of you have already asked yourselves—*what about a thin pull cord?* While this saves a tiny bit of weight when compared to a twin rope, we still advise against it when on rock. If your rappel gets stuck, you may find yourself needing to lead on the cord you pull to solve the problem—your pull cord. As of this writing, at least one manufacturer (Edelrid) offers a pull cord that can be doubled and led on in a pinch—perhaps worth it on less-featured

One Long or Two Short?

Occasionally in the mountains a team of two or three can bring two shorter ropes, two 30s or two 40s, for example. Doing so allows them to leave one stashed for the up but deploy both for the down, when a longer rappel may appear. This strategy allows them to not only keep rope management simple on the climb and execute longer rappels, but also divide the weight between the climbers.

rock, but in the alpine, where stuck ropes are more common, using a dedicated pull cord might be cutting your margin too thin.

Third- and Fourth-Class into Fifth

In varied terrain two climbers will be traveling a good portion of the time with 30 or 40 feet of rope between them. This will seem a lot like glacier mode with a few changes. The team will be traveling like this for the third- and fourth-class sections, but it will need to transition into fifth-class mode efficiently when the time comes.

The length of the fifth-class sections helps determine the length of rope needed. On slabs, a team can stretch out a 200-foot (60m) rope and still maintain good visual and/or verbal communication. On more broken terrain in the mountains, where wind, hats, and hoods can limit your ability to communicate, pitches tend to be shorter. In broken terrain, we often have more choice in belay stances as well. Typically we see mountain pitches that are no more than 130 feet (40m).

Mountain routes with simple descents and no rappels can be done with a 40-meter rope. Of course, this limits retreat options. If you must descend partway up the route, due to weather or another problem, 20-meter rappels can be unrealistic.

Many climbers opt for a 200-foot (60m) rope, allowing the team to rappel 100 feet. We've found we bring longer ropes because of descents, but seldom use more than 130 feet on the way up, the exception being long slab sections.

We need to mention only one other consideration: Longer ropes prove very useful and sometimes necessary on long alpine-ice sections and for glacier travel. If your rock route also has that type of terrain (think the Pointe Lachenal above Chamonix or on Mount Shuksan), then the 200-foot rope may be prudent.

Transitions from Third- and Fourth-Class to Fifth-Class

For the following transitions we will assume a party of two, with a 200-foot (60m) rope. Our first order of business is to store the rope somehow. We know we are likely to use 130 feet (40m) of the rope and might use the last 70 feet (20m). The first skill the party needs to master is coiling and tying off the rope.

You might notice that after tying off our Kiwi coils, we place a clove hitch onto the belay loop of the harness. We feel that for rock this is important, given the forces and serious nature of a fall in most cases. It will also aid in certain transitions.

OTHER MEANS OF STASHING THE ROPE

We often stash excess rope in our pack, because it's more comfortable. Hot days, or carrying a longer rope, make this a nice option. The leader or the second can both do this. It does make accessing the extra rope more difficult, though. If the team anticipates needing the additional rope at some point, the second should tie into the end—or better yet, already be tied in—prior to detaching the clove hitch.

IFMGA mountain guide Joey Thompson with tied-off coils and a clove hitch in front of them.

1. *Storing rope in a pack then coiling off. The excess rope is in the guide's pack. The rope exits the pack and goes to a clove hitch on the belay loop. Notice how the guide traps the strand with his sternum strap and hip belt to keep things neat.*

2. *From the clove hitch you pass the rope behind your neck and down to your hand. Your hand should be at the top of your belay loop.*

3. Form tight coils by wrapping the rope around your hand and neck. Try to keep your hand in the same position so your coils are all the same length.

4. To tie off the coils, pass a bight of rope through your belay loop. Reach your free hand behind your coils and pull the bight through, capturing all the coils. You do not capture the original strand coming from the pack.

5. With the bight, tie an overhand around the strand going to the client and cinch it tight. The guide will add a clove hitch in front of his overhand before moving.

When stashing rope and then connecting to the shortened section with a clove, we need to carefully consider security. If we're carrying coils, our tie-off backs up the clove hitch, but with rope stashed, our connection might be the lone clove hitch. In this instance, we strongly recommend connecting with two lockers.

LENGTHS OF ROPE

Now that we have covered coiling off and securing the shortened rope, we need to cover who carries how much rope. There is good reason for the leader and second to carry different amounts, and block-leading sections avoids the team constantly adjusting lengths, etc. Terrain that varies between third-, fourth-, and fifth-class makes distinguishing where one pitch begins and ends a difficult task. We recommend switching leads at logical resting spots, preferably where a significant break in the terrain presents no fall hazard.

Consider two main issues when dividing the rope: First, keep the leader's load as light as possible for fifth-class sections, and second, simplify transitions as much as possible. The leader should climb fifth-class sections without rope coiled off on her body. This not only makes it less likely she'll fall, but also connects her at the end of the rope—an important detail when the possibility of a leader fall exists.

So, in most third- and fourth-class terrain, we suggest the leader carry just about half the rope, with 30 to 40 feet (9m to 12m) between the climbers. The second carries the remainder of the rope in Kiwi coils while the team moves together using terrain and gear for protection.

Third- and Fourth-Class into Fifth

When the leader reaches a section of fifth-class that she feels must be pitched out, she then executes this transition:

1. The leader stops and builds an appropriate anchor, clips into it with a clove hitch, and either belays the second off her harness (incorporating a stance) or off the anchor, depending on the circumstance and quality of the anchor.

2. When the second arrives, a decision must be made. If the pitch looks long, the climbers might need the rope the second is carrying, so anchoring the second with the rope should be avoided and the team must use a leash. If the pitch looks to be 130 feet (40m) or less, the second anchors with the rope.

Converting a Munter to a Clove

If the leader belays a second for a short section and anticipates cloving-in the follower when he arrives at the belay, consider converting his Munter to a clove.

How? First, put the rope leading to the follower in a locking carabiner hanging on the anchor. Second, build a Munter on the brake side of the rope—*you must build the Munter on the rope in the carabiner, not in the air.* Next, belay the second to you, taking in slack. Last, when the second arrives, you simply repeat the second step—that is, build *another* Munter on the brake strand of the rope (not in the air), drop it into the locker, then cinch it tight—*voila,* the two Munters atop one another become a clove hitch. One tail of the clove will remain inside the locking carabiner, which might be unsightly but does not affect the security or holding power of the clove. Quick, fast, easy.

3. The leader uncoils the rope on her body, keeping the clove hitch on her belay loop intact until she's on belay.

4. The second puts the leader on belay, and then the leader removes her clove hitches (from the anchor and her belay loop).

5. If during the pitch the leader needs more rope, the belayer can uncoil some from his supply. If he's anchored with the rope, he must transfer to a leash to free up coils off his body.

This transition is simple, and if the rope on the second isn't needed, it will simplify the transition back to moving together. The rope lengths described require that the leader carry more rope than the second while climbing on easier terrain, but allows the leader to climb carrying no rope while leading the more difficult fifth-class sections. Once the fifth-class pitch or pitches are complete and it is time to move together again, another transition must take place.

Transitioning Back to Third- or Fourth-Class Terrain (Second Did Not Drop Coils)

This is the transition when the second *did not* need to uncoil any rope:

1. The leader finishes the fifth-class climbing at an anchor (or builds it) and anchors in with a clove hitch like a normal rock climb.

2. The leader belays the second off the anchor like any other rock pitch.

3. When the second arrives, he clove-hitches in.

4. The leader now attaches herself with a clove hitch on her belay loop to the backside of the second's clove.

5. She unclips her clove hitch from the anchor, and coils and ties off the rope. She adds a clove hitch on her belay loop in front of her coils, 30 to 40 feet from her second.

6. If necessary (depending upon the terrain), the second puts the leader on belay until she runs out of rope, then he cleans the anchor and begins moving with her.

To Leash or Not to Leash in the Alpine

Again, the above transition assumes the second did *not* untie and drop coils from his body. When the second *does* have to uncoil and drop rope, the transition becomes more tedious, especially if the party uses the rope as its dynamic connections to the anchor. If the climbers choose not to use the rope

The Leash

In alpine rock we see value in these systems and we understand their usefulness. What gives us pause is how the use of leashes can become a crutch. Now, having said that, we also acknowledge we could be wrong. There may be a day when no climber will do any type of climbing without a leash system. If that ends up being the case, this book may then be all but obsolete.

That said, our stand remains the same. The rope offers the strongest, most adjustable, most dynamic leash. While we aren't strictly opposed to a dedicated leash system, we fear a reflexive default to them overtakes your ability to solve problems with a rope, and in most cases the habit makes you less efficient and cluttered.

Time will tell if our attitude is correct or if it is just a Luddite argument. In the meantime, this book will suggest leashes where appropriate and tend toward using nylon slings as improvised leashes when necessary.

as their tethers, each team member can use a leash of some sort.

Since most of the transitions in this book are done without leashes, it seems appropriate to talk a bit more about them as they relate to the alpine rock realm.

The leash can be a powerful tool in recreational alpine rock. The fact that each climber carries rope (as coils on the body) means it is hard to consistently use the backside of one of the climber's clove hitches to free up rope (the ends are behind each climber's coils).

We try to avoid the use of leashes mainly because we strive to reduce the amount of equipment we carry in the mountains. Given the weight of our packs (especially on multiday adventures), the lengths of approaches and descents, and the lengths of the routes we do, we are keenly aware of the weight and bulk of our equipment. A leash that is semipermanently attached to our harness sometimes feels like just more stuff, and it clutters an already crowded waist area.

We also try to minimize the use of a leash to reduce the number of times we are attached to the anchor with a static connection.

Finally, we find that in most cases using the rope is more efficient, and in the few rare cases when it isn't, it doesn't justify a semipermanent leash system. Unfortunately, alpine rock is one of the main areas where we find leashes most useful, or at least the most tempting place to use them.

So the question is, do you carry a semipermanent attached leash in this type of terrain when climbing recreationally? For some of us, the answer is usually no. Those in this camp will suggest that the few times a leash is useful or even necessary, a nylon runner will suffice and it's much more versatile than a dedicated leash system.

DEDICATED LEASH SYSTEMS

For others, the answer is the opposite and they climb with a dedicated leash affixed to their harness. These climbers use systems like the Purcell Prusik that is often tied in directly to the harness, or a tether of individual loops, like those sold by Metolius (Personal Anchor System) or Sterling (Chain Reactor). Also newer and getting good reviews are adjustable leashes like the Petzl Connect.

Whatever the case, a team needs to know its system and preferences so it can move fluidly during transitions. Thinking back to the above transition, if both coils have been undone for the fifth-class section, then when the leader arrives she leashes into the anchor and belays the second as normal. The second then leashes in when he arrives and both climbers coil off until there is 30 to 40 feet of rope between them, and then continue climbing.

The biggest problem you will encounter with the above system is if the leader wishes to belay the second off her waist using a secure stance enhanced by a quick anchor, the leash may not be long enough or adjustable enough to put the leader in the proper stance. In that case the leader:

1. Clove-hitches into the anchor and belays off her harness.

2. Once the second arrives, he clove-hitches into the anchor.

3. The leader ties off the device on her harness, removes her clove hitch at the anchor, and coils off to just about mid-rope.

4. Once the leader has coiled off, the second puts her on belay and the leader cleans the device from her harness and begins climbing.

5. Once the leader is 30 or so feet away, the belayer clove-hitches the rope to the leader onto his belay loop and takes the leader off belay.

6. The second now cleans the anchor, coils off, and begins to climb.

As you can see, using the rope to anchor complicates and makes this transition a bit more tedious. The nice thing about using the rope is the space it will allow the party to use, and that may speed up the coiling process.

Parties of Three

The recreational party of three in this type of terrain has its limitations. Moving smoothly with a party this large is often difficult. Of course, on a modest objective, it may be reasonable for two experienced climbers to bring a third, less-experienced climber along. We are not saying on larger routes it is impossible or even imprudent; what we are saying is that it can be difficult and may significantly slow your progress if the team isn't well coordinated. The advantage to this might be on a glacier approach.

Bottom line, if you are looking at doing long, complex routes as a party of three, you should train a bit and practice your rope transitions.

Choosing Ropes for a Party of Three

Choosing ropes for a party of three is a bit untraditional. One 200-foot (60m) rope will limit the team to 100-foot (30m) fifth-class pitches (leader ties into the middle of the rope and belays one climber on each end) or require climbers to move together on fifth-class terrain if the leader needs 120 feet of rope to climb a pitch. In this case the two seconds would be climbing together for a bit during the pitch—not ideal.

We suggest considering two 130-foot (40m) ropes or if the fifth-class pitches are longer, two 165-foot (50m) ropes. If the route has lots of slabby climbing, however, using one 200-foot (60m) rope may be the best option. Experience and judgment will dictate the right rope choice.

Slabby Routes in a Party of Three

Slabby sections, while rare, do exist, just usually not in true alpine terrain. Where slab routes more often appear is on regular rock climbs with easy slab sections with harder climbing above or below. There are routes in Yosemite (particularly in Tuolumne) or in Red Rock that end in easy slabs. Popular routes on Whitehorse (in New Hampshire) like the *Standard Route*, *Sea of Holds*, or *Wedge* can start with easy slab.

In some cases the route might be relatively easy the entire way, an example being the First Flatiron above Boulder. This route is commonly soloed by experienced locals and it ends with a third- to fourth-class ridge, with a couple steps of fifth, for a few hundred feet. Someone not wanting to solo it, however, may feel climbing it in traditional caterpillar style, or parallel style in a party of three, seems over the top. For these folks, there must be some middle ground between soloing and the tedious system typically used by a party of three on fifth-class terrain.

END-ROPING

We recommend experimenting with a style similar to that used in alpine snow or ice. If the seconds are roughly 10 to 15 feet (3 or 4m) apart, that leaves a usable 170 to 180 feet of rope on which to lead. You recognize this system already: It's end-roping.

To put it into action, one second ties into the end of the rope while the other is clipped into a cow's tail (with a locker and non-locking carabiner, or just one triple-action Gridlock-style carabiner like the Black Diamond GridLock Magnetron).

The efficiency comes from the fact that both seconds can climb at the same time but the leader will have the rope drag of one rope rather than two. On a slab that alone can make a huge difference. The party will also have the benefit of only having to manage one rope at the stance, simplifying that aspect of the ascent. This system works great on a slabby route or section, but if the pitches get just a bit steeper or more difficult, it can take the fun out of climbing. Learning its limitations and using this system only on easy slabby climbs is important.

On lower-angled terrain, such as the upper steps of Boulder's First Flatiron (pictured here), end-roping two climbers can keep a party moving quickly.

We anchor the seconds at the belay with two main methods. The easiest and simplest is to tie a clove hitch just above the cow's-tail climber and clip it to the anchor. Now the two climbers can lean back on the rope standing on the slab. If the bottom climber needs to adjust upward a little to get a better stance, a simple bight knot can be tied between the seconds to take up the slack that is needed. There is no need to clip that bight knot into anything; it just simply eats up the necessary slack.

Another alternative is to tie a clove in between the two seconds and clip that to the anchor, so one is on the backside of the other's.

What should be avoided as much as possible is for each second to have his own clove hitch at the anchor. If the terrain is sufficiently steep and serious that they each need their own clove, this rope system should be reconsidered because it is likely not appropriate.

A SECOND, SPARE ROPE

In the above system we've been discussing climbing as a party of three with one rope, but if you are approaching harder climbing, or coming from harder climbing, then one of the followers may be carrying a second rope. The team simply stashes the rope for the mellower, slabby sections and then employs the second rope in steeper, more serious terrain.

Broken Faces and Ridges, Three Climbers

Now that we have discussed slabs, it's time to get into the more complex terrain of broken faces and ridges. We feel your best bet is to approach the three-person team quite a bit differently than the two-person team.

If there are significant sections of fifth-class climbing, the party should bring two ropes between 130 and 165 feet long (40 to 50m). When the party is moving together on third- and fourth-class terrain, the leader would not carry any rope. The middle climber would carry the spare rope (in a

pack), and the last climber would carry the coils. We suggest a little less rope between the climbers than we did with a party of two, so instead of 30 to 40 feet (9 to 12m), we propose 20 to 30 feet (6 to 9m) between each climber. That means the last climber has 70 to 125 feet (20 to 40m) depending on the rope length, etc.

The other significant change from a group of two, apart from how the rope is distributed, is how the transition takes place to leading and who in the party will lead. It will be cleaner if the last climber does the leading of the fifth-class sections. Parsing out the climb is a bit harder this way, so you'll need to think about where you'll change leaders. Here is how the transitions to fifth-class climbing can go. We discuss transitions in the three rope systems:

1. Parallel
2. End-roping
3. Caterpillar

THIRD- AND FOURTH-CLASS TO PARALLEL ROPE SYSTEM FOR A FIFTH-CLASS SECTION

1. The leader of the third- or fourth-class section builds an anchor, clove-hitches in, and belays the team to him.

2. Once the middle climber arrives, he attaches himself to the backside of the leader's clove hitch, unclips, and unties his cow's tail, then begins to prep the second rope. The leader can coach the third climber to pause while the middle climber unties his cow's tail, to avoid slack building up in the belay.

3. When the third climber arrives, she stays on the belay keeping the clove hitch on her harness intact and begins to uncoil and stack her rope.

4. The third/fourth-class leader puts the third climber on a lead belay. He may need to use the middle climber's device, or even the device of the third climber, if he used his device when

belaying the team, since it is still securing the third climber as she prepares to climb.

5. The third climber ties into the second rope, removes her clove hitch from her belay loop, cleans the belay device on the anchor (takes it if she had to give hers to the belayer), and begins to lead.

6. The middle climber ties into the other end of the extra rope as the leader leaves, but can remain anchored into the backside of the clove.

The parallel rope system is likely the best system to use. It allows the seconds to climb each with his own rope, so you don't have the problems associated with end-roping, yet both climbers can move at the same time. Given the nature of most alpine climbs, the problems associated with the parallel rope system—ropes complicating the climbing, ropes falling in a crack, etc.—are generally not present.

The transition back to third/fourth-class will seem a bit messy. That is the downside with the parallel system. Since the two ropes are together, separating them is often visually unaesthetic and a bit of a challenge at a cramped stance.

PARALLEL TO THIRD/FOURTH-CLASS

1. When the leader arrives, she clove-hitches into the anchor. This should be done with the rope that will be used on the third/fourth-class section. That means it is with the same rope as the leader of the next section. (At this moment, he is cleaning the pitch. It makes sense he is last up, since that is the cleaning position and he can effectively rack up while he follows the pitch.)

2. When the middle climber arrives, he clove-hitches in to the backside of the leader's clove on the anchor and unties from his end of the rope. The leader also unties from her end of the rope that will no longer be used.

3. The third climber is put on a lead belay as soon as possible when he arrives. The third climber

(second follower on the previous pitch) is the new leader.

4. As the third climber begins his lead, the second rope should be coiled and stored (by the climber not belaying).

5. Once the leader has gotten 20 or 30 feet up, the middle climber ties and clips into a cow's tail, unclips from the backside of the anchor clove hitch, takes the leader off belay, and starts climbing.

6. When the middle climber goes 20 to 30 feet, the last climber clove-hitches into the rope, comes off the anchor, coils off the rope, cleans the anchor, and begins to climb.

By getting the first climber leading out as soon as possible, we keep the stance as uncluttered as possible. The other advantage is that we can get good, accurate distances between the climbers since they clip into the rope as it gets stretched out. The team should consider cleaning some of the anchor, if appropriate, prior to the new leader leaving so he has as much of the equipment as possible.

THIRD/FOURTH-CLASS TO END-ROPING TRANSITION

1. The third/fourth-class leader builds an anchor, clove-hitches in, and belays the team either off the anchor or from his waist if appropriate.

2. Once the middle climber arrives, he attaches himself to the backside of the clove hitch on the anchor with a cow's tail, unclips, and unties the cow's tail he had been climbing on. He needs to make sure the new cow's tail is at an appropriate distance from his partner for climbing the upcoming fifth-class section.

3. When the third climber arrives, she stays on the belay and keeps the clove hitch on her harness intact, and begins to uncoil and stack her rope.

4. Once she uncoils the rope, one of the other climbers will put her on a lead belay; she cleans the belay she had been on and leads off.

End-roping is an aggressive technique that should be used sparingly. The terrain to use this should be fairly easy and low-angled for fifth-class climbing. In effect, it should almost be easy enough for the team to move together. This is the gray zone between the third- and fourth-class terrain on which the party feels pretty comfortable moving together and a real pitch of fifth-class. The transition is easier mainly because we do not need the second rope.

Besides the downsides of end-roping discussed in the rock section, in this application we are using a shorter rope, so the length available to the leader is closer to 100 feet (30m), which limits belay stance choices. This may end up causing the party to do more pitches and/or use suboptimal belay stances. If that is the case, the efficiency of the transition may be negated. In the end, this should be a seldom-used system, but not completely removed from your arsenal of choices.

The transition from end-roping back to third/fourth-class climbing is very similar to the transition back from parallel.

END-ROPING TO THIRD/FOURTH-CLASS

1. When the leader arrives, she clove-hitches into the anchor.

2. When the middle climber arrives, he clove-hitches into the backside of the leader's clove hitch on the anchor and unclips from his cowl's tail and unties it.

3. The third climber arrives at the belay, and one of the other climbers puts him on lead belay as soon as possible. The third climber up the last pitch becomes the new leader.

4. Once the new leader climbs 20 to 30 feet, the middle climber ties and clips into a cow's tail, unclips from the clove on the backside of the anchor clove hitch, takes the leader off belay, and starts climbing.

5. When the middle climber climbs 20 to 30 feet, the last climber clove-hitches into the rope,

comes off the anchor, coils off the rope, cleans the anchor, and begins to climb.

As you can see, this is nearly identical to the parallel transition but made simpler due to the lack of the second rope. The same consideration applies to taking some of the anchor out if appropriate so the new leader has as much of the equipment as possible.

THIRD/FOURTH-CLASS TRANSITION TO CATERPILLAR

1. The third/fourth-class leader builds an anchor, clove-hitches in, and belays the team.

2. Once the middle climber arrives, she attaches herself to the backside of the clove hitch on the anchor, unclips, and unties the cow's tail.

3. When the third climber arrives, he stays on the belay, keeps the clove hitch on his harness intact, and begins to uncoil and stack his section of rope. He ties into the end.

4. The third/fourth-class leader puts the third climber on lead belay and the new leader unclips his clove hitch (this was the one backing up his coils) and begins climbing.

5. While the leader is climbing, the middle climber ties into the second rope, anchors in with it, and unclips from the backside of the clove at the anchor.

6. When the leader finishes climbing, the leader of the third/fourth-class section ties into the other end of the spare rope and begins climbing once he is on belay from above.

Caterpillar technique is a viable system, but given its pros and cons discussed in the rock section of this book, it doesn't seem to be very useful. Again, it's not a system to ignore or forget, but this type of terrain highlights the caterpillar style's shortcomings. If we did face a pitch on which the rope drag of parallel system could be a factor, or we want to let a climber enjoy a pitch without another rope in the way, perhaps caterpillar becomes the go-to system.

The caterpillar transition back to third/fourth-class is not as easy as the end-roping transition, but it is visually less cluttered than with the parallel system. As you'll see, you can easily choose whether the climber that led the pitch leads off or the middle climber does.

CATERPILLAR TO THIRD/FOURTH-CLASS

1. When the leader arrives, he clove-hitches into the anchor and belays the middle climber.

2. When the middle climber arrives, she clove-hitches into the anchor with the rope on which she was just belayed.

3. The third climber is belayed up and clove-hitches into either of the backsides of the clove hitches. The rope he doesn't choose will be the new leader's rope.

4. The leader of the next section is put on belay and starts to climb.

5. Once the leader climbs 20 to 30 feet, the climber on the backside of the clove hitch ties and clips into a cow's tail, unclips from the clove on the backside of the anchor clove hitch, takes the leader off belay, and starts climbing.

6. When the middle climber goes 20 to 30 feet, the last climber clove-hitches into the rope, comes off the anchor, coils off the rope, cleans the anchor, and begins to climb.

Alternate Three-Person Systems

If the climb is easy and has very little fifth-class, having two ropes may seem excessive. In that case a single, 130-foot (40m) rope might be the best option. This can work where the route's difficulties are short and barely something you feel the need to pitch. With that system you will be end-roping the harder sections. Of course, this system limits rappels to 65 feet (20m). Good prep and planning will let you know if this is a disqualifier or not.

If the route is easy but there are rappels, you may find yourself needing a 200-foot (60m) rope.

In this case you may have enough rope to parallel or caterpillar, as well as end-rope. Of course, your pitch lengths are limited to less than 100 feet (30m). For some this tempts people to consider a 230-foot (70m) rope; we, however, think at that point the two-rope system previously described makes more sense.

Many climbers, however, don't own two 130-foot (40m) ropes, especially given the current ubiquity and popularity of the 200-foot (60m) rope. Whatever your situation, knowing how to do these transitions with one rope is worth exploring.

ONE LONG ROPE INSTEAD OF TWO SHORT

With a longer rope, splitting it up when climbing (so two people can carry a section) makes sense, but also makes the transitions a bit more tedious. Again, as with two people, we will not have an end easily accessible to work with. If in reality the team is built of equivalently skilled climbers, we can solve some of the tediousness by having the middle person cow's-tailed to the middle of the rope with the end climbers 20 to 30 feet (6 to 9m) on either side, carrying the remainder of the rope coiled off. By doing that the middle person is then perfectly situated to lead a section on a parallel rope system or be the second person on the caterpillar.

THIRD/FOURTH-CLASS TO PARALLEL WITH ONE ROPE

1. The leader builds an anchor and puts a Munter hitch on a locker on the anchor. This counterbalances him with his followers. He uncoils his rope and keeps the clove hitch on his waist tied, so it attaches him to the Munter. Once the rope is uncoiled, he ties into the free end and then clove-hitches into the anchor with the section of rope coming from the figure eight knot on his harness.

2. He unclips the clove hitch on his waist (that was in front of his coils) and belays the party to him on the Munter he built in step 1.

3. When the middle climber arrives, the leader flips his Munter into a clove hitch. The middle climber is secured and goes off belay.

4. The middle climber belays the third climber in. When he arrives he stays on belay and keeps his clove hitch clipped on his belay loop and uncoils his rope. Once the rope is uncoiled, he ties into the end and clove-hitches in with the section of the rope coming from his figure eight knot. He goes off belay and unclips the clove at his belay loop.

5. The middle person now takes a belay, unclips her clove, and leads out. One note: The middle climber's rope attachment may need to be beefed up. She is likely clipped into a cow's tail. Adding another carabiner (third) or, if you know the middle person will be leading, tying in at the outset may be preferable.

2. Start by passing the bight through your harness tie-in points, then through the first overhand. PHILBRICK PHOTOGRAPHY

1. Cow's Tail tie in. The rethreaded overhand makes a great knot with which to tie in to the middle of the rope. In this photo the additional overhand creates a cow's tail.
PHILBRICK PHOTOGRAPHY

3. Rethread the overhand and cinch tight. You can clip the resulting loop off for additional security. PHILBRICK PHOTOGRAPHY

Adjusting the Clove

Y ou'll notice in these transitions that the climbers coil off excess rope behind their clove hitches (farther up the rope). Unless you're the luckiest person on the planet, it's rare the excess rope will coil up into perfectly matched coils—it seems there's always one too-long or too-short coil left. Because the climbers have a clove hitch connecting them to the rope/anchor, they can always take in or out a bit of rope, making their coiling easy and neat.

As you can see, we have the middle person leading the fifth-class terrain. In a party of three, it makes sense to have the leader of the third/ fourth-class section and the middle climber on the rope be the more experienced climbers. This order requires the last climber be the inexperienced team member (assuming there's a discrepancy in skill among the team). Keep in mind, this puts the last climber in a position to clean any gear placed on the easy climbing. This shouldn't be too difficult, but it isn't as intuitive as placing the least experienced person in the middle where he just needs to clip through the protection.

The downside of the parallel system with only one 200-foot (60m) rope is the length of the pitch. It is uncanny how many pitches are 110 to 120 feet (33 to 35m) long, so the leader will often need to make compromises as to where he belays, or he'll be forced to move together with his two partners some distance away—at best an awkward process and at worst a dangerous cluster!

To solve that problem, the caterpillar technique can be used. With the caterpillar system the leader could move together with the second climber until the leader arrives at an appropriate belay stance. The leader can then ask the second to pause, construct a quick and solid anchor, then put the second on belay. The third begins climbing once the rope becomes tight.

Even better, the team adjusts the second climber's position on the rope, moving him off the middle. If the leader needs another 15 feet (5m) of rope, instead of having the second climber attached to the middle of the rope, the team moves him 15 feet (5m) toward the third climber. Of course, this means that the second and third climbers end up climbing simultaneously for 30 feet (10m).

So to do some quick math: If the pitch is 115 feet long and we bump the second climber 15 feet toward the third climber (who's on the end of a 200-foot rope), that leaves 85 feet between them. The leader climbs 115 feet, builds a belay, and begins bringing the second climber up. The second climber is almost at the belay when the rope comes tight to the third climber. The second pauses while the third cleans the belay, then they start moving again. They'll have to climb 30 feet simultaneously before the second arrives at the belay and secures himself.

Although this scenario isn't optimal, it's preferable (we feel) to two other obvious options: first, end-roping the pitch; and second, having the leader climb the last 30 feet of his pitch while simul-climbing with the second climber.

THIRD/FOURTH-CLASS TO CATERPILLAR WITH ONE ROPE

1. The leader builds an anchor and puts a Munter hitch on a locker on the anchor. This counterbalances her with her followers. She uncoils her rope and keeps the clove hitch on her waist tied, so it attaches her to the Munter. Once the rope

Keep the Belay Moving

It's worth discussing how the middle climber arrives and secures himself at the next stance after a fifth-class pitch and going into another fifth-class pitch. If, in fact, the second and third climbers did move together, a clean and efficient belay system that can keep the third person on belay and moving is what we want (a Munter or a plaquette). So, upon arrival the second climber leashes in and unclips from his cow's tail and unties the cow's tail so that the belayer can keep the rope moving without interruption.

The new leader climbs the next pitch, and when he arrives at the belay, he calls down to the middle climber and he reties his cow's tail, clips back in with two carabiners, and is ready to follow.

is uncoiled, she ties into the free end and then clove hitches into the anchor with the section of rope coming from the figure eight knot on her harness.

2. She now belays the party to her stance.

3. When the middle climber arrives, he leashes into the anchor and goes off belay. (He leashes in rather than clove-hitching in for a reason, as you'll see in step 6.)

4. The third climber is now belayed in. When he arrives, he stays on belay and keeps his clove hitch clipped on his belay loop and uncoils his rope. Once the rope is uncoiled, he ties into the end and clove-hitches in with a section of the rope coming from his figure eight knot. He goes off belay and unclips the clove at his belay loop.

5. Either the first climber or the third climber can now lead. If it is the third climber, there is no need for him to clove-hitch in; he would just be put on belay.

6. If the pitch is longer than 100 feet (30m), the middle person would unclip and untie his cow's tail, and the leader would continue to climb with little or no interruption. In that case, once the leader finishes the lead, the middle climber reties a cow's tail and gets ready to climb once he is on belay.

7. When the rope comes tight to the third climber, he cleans the anchor and climbs.

If another pitch of indeterminate length is going to be led, the second climber stays as he is. If the next pitch looks short (within 100 feet or 30m), or the party is going to be returning to third/fourth-class style, the second climber ties a cow's tail at the rope's midpoint and clips in there.

In this scenario the second climber can be, and arguably should be, the least skilled climber in the team (unlike in the parallel system). This is something that needs to be considered at the start of the route. Of course, hedging and putting the least skilled climber last can work in both transitions because the above transition could easily be modified to have the leader of the third/fourth-class section lead the fifth-class pitch. In that scenario we would occasionally switch out the middle climber and the leader so the two more-skilled climbers can lead in blocks.

CATERPILLAR TO THIRD/FOURTH-CLASS WITH ONE ROPE

1. The leader builds an anchor and clips in using a clove hitch.

2. When the second climber arrives, he leashes in and unclips and unties his cow's tail so that the third climber can stay on belay. This assumes the

pitch was longer than 100 feet (30m), so that the third climber was already climbing when the second climber arrived at the belay.

3. As the third climber is climbing, the second climber finds the midpoint of the rope, ties a cow's tail, and clips that into his harness.

4. When the third climber arrives, he clove-hitches into the backside of the leader's clove hitch on the anchor.

5. The third climber goes off belay and coils off to within 20 to 30 feet (7 to 10m) of the middle of the rope and leads out.

6. Once the leader is out of rope, the second climber starts climbing.

7. Once the second climber is 20 or 30 feet (7 or 10m) away, the third climber clove-hitches into the rope, unclips from the anchor, and coils off the rope.

But the Leash . . . It's So Easy!

WOW! If you just read through all that without pulling out some rope with friends and working through those systems, your head is likely spinning. You might be asking, how much easier would it be to just have everyone leash in? In theory it seems like it should be much easier, but in practice, with everyone tight to an anchor trying to sort out ropes, coiling, passing gear, etc., life quickly becomes difficult. So difficult, in fact, that many just don't leash in. Wait, let's get this straight: The leash is so easy people would rather just not be protected?!

That is a fundamental reason why we feel this book is necessary—the number of times we see climbers take on unnecessary risks because of the poor working conditions created by the cramped work space leashes lead to. There is a better way, and it works. You just need to familiarize yourself with alternate ways to protect yourself from the falling hazard, and in this case the backside of the clove hitch and the other rope techniques introduced here allow you that space and flexibility.

Of course, if you really can be unroped without having a significant falling hazard, there is no need for a leash or the backside systems. Using terrain to your advantage is key. Suffice to say that every terrain advantage you can use to simplify your transitions and give you room to work needs to be taken. But when there is a falling hazard, you should be able to have reasonable security when transitioning.

If you find yourself unclipping in exposed terrain and coiling your rope while thinking, *Well, this terrain is so easy I would solo, so it's all good,* flip the question around and ask yourself, *Would I solo while coiling off? Would I solo with so little focus on the falling hazard and with so many tripping hazards around?*

Complacency and familiarity are the enemies. Just because you've gotten away with it ten times, a thousand times, or even a million—you will eventually make a mistake. It's guaranteed. Can a backside solution, or even a leash, easily and quickly protect you from the one-in-a-million? Find a way to make the answer to that question *yes.*

If the last climber is the least skilled, a slight variation needs to be done so that the leader of the fifth-class section can continue to lead the third/fourth-class section.

The transitions to and from end-roping are the same as what was described with two shorter ropes, so we won't repeat those here.

Guiding Alpine Rock Terrain

In some ways guiding this terrain with one client is easier from a technical transition perspective than climbing recreationally. In most cases guides carry all the rope; this means the problems of distributing the rope between partners and not having an end accessible to work with is not an issue. Of course, the most convenient end to use remains with the client, but nonetheless it is available for use.

As far as rope lengths, not much is new here. There is a greater incentive not to bring more rope than is necessary, as the guide generally carries all the rope (as well as "group" gear like a med kit, repair kit, etc.).

Be careful, however, not to have too little rope. Often the extra rope we carry is for the descent. For that reason, guides will often bring a 200-foot (60m) rope and put 60 to 80 feet (18 to 25m) of rope into their packs. Think about it this way: We stash in the pack the rope we expect to use on the descent; we coil the rope we might need for occasional pitches on our body; and the rope connecting us to the guest(s) is what we'll use when moving together.

Short-Roping

As with recreational climbers, the guide tries to have terrain between himself and his client (as intermediate protection) while they're moving together. If there is one place where recreational climbers' techniques look the most like short-roping, it is in this terrain. If this isn't possible, the guide begins short-roping.

While the two approaches share similarities, some subtle and critical differences emerge. A guide will stop and do a quick belay (body, terrain, or Munter off the harness, for example) when terrain separates the guide and client. The guide then adjusts his position (to the other side of the terrain or another feature entirely) when the client moves into a position that is no longer protected by the initial feature. With a new feature between them, the guide speeds through the next section while protected.

The guide loops the rope over a horn to give a quick belay while clients move through an insecure section. As soon as they're safely past it, he can remove his rope and hand-coil as he approaches them.

Without a horn or boulder to use for protection, the guide stays close and keeps the rope barely tensioned with a hand belay. Should a client slip here, the short rope allows the guide to immediately react and keep the client upright.

This type of progression has the guide trying to keep the client moving steadily while the guide adjusts his pace, timing his moves to get the most out of the terrain. Ultimately if there are no useful terrain features, the guide will stay very close to the client, carrying coils in his hand and using tension on the rope to prevent a slip from becoming a fall. The guide keeps gentle tension in the rope so he can react immediately and pull the client into the terrain (and back into balance) if the client slips.

Yes, real short-roping is stressful, and good guides use it far less than most think. On ridges, a good guide can have terrain between himself and his client most of the time. It is on third-class faces with sandy and/or sloping ledges when short-roping as a guide gets very scary. Guides may start to pitch this terrain out, even when the movement seems easy. There are lots of guides who have short-roped on this type of terrain and were not pulled off, not because short-roping worked, but because clients didn't fall. Of course, that leads to another discussion entirely. (That is, making sure your client has the appropriate skill for the route you've chosen.)

For the guide who is short-roping and runs into a section he feels is too difficult to be assured his client won't fall (like the sandy, third-class terrain mentioned above), he can move above it and do a quick belay even if the anchor only involves a solid stance. Short-roping therefore requires that the guide is ready to check a slip at all times, and when he can't, to use a quick belay when the terrain gets harder.

Relatively easy but dangerously exposed terrain presents some risk, and in many cases a recreational party chooses to unrope and accept the risk individually rather than as a team. In guiding, the guide accepts the responsibility for himself and the client(s), and therefore it is inappropriate to unrope from them. For this reason guides must have the final say as to who gets to climb what route. Guides also decide unilaterally when to turn back.

Guides must exercise their best judgment and in serious terrain forget the pressures of goal-focused clients for the moment. After all, both the guide's and clients' lives depend on expert judgment. Clients' disappointments and squabbles over refunds can wait until the safety of the trailhead.

If you are a citizen leader, this terrain—low probability of an accident, but high consequence should one occur—can be very problematic. If you would unrope with a friend, then what do you do when leading a club group? Often it is the leader that picks the route, so he is making some informed decision that the new participant may not fully understand.

Naturally we can suggest the leader pitch it out, but why wouldn't a professional guide? Often the routes we are talking about don't allow for pitching given their length and commitment; time and weather pressure can provide risks as great as those a guide takes short-roping. We would hope that the club leader has a solid knowledge of a route and picks an objective he feels comfortable leading with a less-experienced partner. In some cases the club leader will have people so competent they will stick to purely recreational techniques described earlier. It isn't impossible to get training in short-roping so that the citizen leader can use that technique, but it takes time to learn and even with that it is easy to get rusty. We won't suggest that the citizen leader can't do it. It will require dedication to the training and keeping up the skill, however.

Having said that, excellent rope skills can allow you to move quickly and protect both you and others in places that, without the skills, would require taking on unreasonable risks. If you can't remove all risk, you should remove as much as you can.

Rope Systems for the Guide with Two Clients

First we need to discuss how the guide is climbing together with two clients. Unlike in recreational climbing where everyone is separated by 30 feet (9m) or so, the guide prefers to have the clients closer together, usually 7 to 10 feet (2 to 3m) apart. One client ties into the end while the second client ties into a cow's tail and clips in with two carabiners, one locking and one regular at a minimum, or a single triple-action gridlock model like the BD GridLock Magnetron.

While short-roping, the guide will want to have the two clients as close as possible, but will need to add distance for steeper sections. To facilitate this, the guide ties the first client in to the end of the rope, then adds a figure eight knot just in front of this client and clips that into his belay loop. The guide then ties a cow's tail for the second client so that the clients are close enough to be effectively short-roped. The figure eight (or Swiss Miss; see below) on the end client simply takes up rope and shortens the distance between the two clients.

If the climbing gets steeper and the distance becomes uncomfortable (the client at the end of the rope will have the next client's feet in his face), the guide will ask the lower client to unclip and untie the figure eight on a bight—this will add enough distance for the clients to be comfortably apart.

It is easy to train the client to retie the knot once being shorter becomes useful again (a traversing section, for example). For the most part the guide should use the longer spacing more than the shortened system because it allows the team to potentially have more terrain between members, but when purely short-roping, the guide wants there to be as little chance for slack to develop as possible, so adding the figure eight and shortening the distance becomes advantageous.

So how short are we talking? For doing a walking traverse across an exposed ledge, a guide will have her clients so close the rear client can just touch the person in front of him. When that short, if the figure eight on a bight is untied, it barely gives the clients the room they need on steep terrain.

Crossing an easy but wickedly exposed section in the Fisher Chimneys, Mount Shuksan.

The Swiss Miss

American guides call the Swiss method of shortening the "Swiss Miss" because our friend and colleague Caroline George helped popularize the technique. Caroline is a Swiss native, married to an American, and completed her IFMGA training in the United States. Thanks for the tip, Caroline!

Caroline George. COURTESY EDDIE BAUER

Guides in the United States typically use the figure eight to shorten the system, but another system gaining popularity is the Swiss Miss. Some guides prefer the Swiss Miss because it doesn't require a carabiner and can be faster once a client learns and practices it. To tie a Swiss Miss, the client simply passes a bight of rope through his belay loop, then an overhand around the strand connecting him to the next client (as you'd tie off coils). Should you experiment with the Swiss Miss, keep in mind that the knot *must* stay tied off. If it came undone, the resulting slack in the system will make any slip or fall much, much harder to arrest for the guide.

The figure eight knot takes up a bit more rope than an overhand, making the spacing better for a steep section. It's not necessary to use a locking carabiner in this instance, as the knot itself takes up the extra rope, not the carabiner. We only clip it off to keep it from dangling and bugging the client.

We've seen other shortening methods, but the two above keep it simple and take up about the same amount of rope.

Short-Pitching for the Guide

Having the back client set up with a figure eight shortening knot allows the guide to "short-pitch." This resembles end-roping, but we reserve it for steps of difficulty in third/fourth-class terrain that make the guide feel uncomfortable moving with his clients (difficult, exposed, and consequential terrain might do this).

In this case the guide may put the clients on either side of a ridge, loop the rope between them over a horn, or even clip the rope between the clients into a cam or nut the guide places. With the clients reasonably secure, the guide can move up 30 or so feet (9m) and do a quick belay on a horn or anchor himself with a piece along with a stance to belay. By having the clients reasonably close together, it is easy to secure them quickly using some form of counterbalance anchor.

This short-pitch skill is not as difficult to learn as short-roping and is something the citizen leader should use. Having said that, some training from a guide or another more experienced citizen leader will help. Being experienced in this terrain will give the leader the ability to anticipate difficulty, see quick anchor options, or find terrain features with which he can belay. These techniques are part of the lost art that makes this type of climbing so fun and challenging, and makes you feel close to the terrain.

The guide surmounts a small step of fifth-class in Eldorado Canyon, Boulder. Once at a stable stance, he runs the rope around a boulder to give a secure belay for his followers.

Rope Lengths When Guiding

When choosing a rope length, we employ the same decision process as in recreational climbing. We suggest two 130-foot (40m) ropes for parties of three. When using two ropes, having your client carry one is generally considered appropriate, but if it causes him to get fatigued, the party can suffer. Guides need to make that decision based on the fitness of the client as it relates to the length and difficulty of the route, while always remembering there is a cost to having the guide burdened with the weight and bulk of the extra rope.

Many guides will decide to use a single 200-foot (60m) rope, as many rappel descents are set up for that length. Obviously if there are occasional fifth-class sections, the guide will be less able to store rope in her pack without incurring the tediousness of removing it from, and replacing it before and after, each fifth-class section. Of course, putting away the second rope in the two-rope system isn't that much easier.

As we discussed in the recreational section, where the 200-foot (60m) rope impacts a party of three is on the fifth-class sections of the ascent. We keep saying it, but it is uncanny how often you will run into 120-foot (35m) pitches. So with one rope in the parallel system, you'll likely be forced to use suboptimal stances. The solution of moving together with two less-experienced climbers is even more unacceptable than doing that with competent partners.

Caterpillar style becomes more common when you have roughly 120 feet (35m) of rope between you and your first client, with 80 feet (25m) separating the two clients. This necessitates them climbing together for 30 feet (10m). The difference is that the middle climber needs to be attached to the rope prior to the guide leaving the stance. In our recreational transition we had the middle climber attach himself to the rope once the leader finished the lead—a luxury we can't afford in the guided realm, unless you have very competent, trustworthy clients. This means the leader will need to estimate fairly accurately the length of the pitch prior to leaving the stance.

In the guiding transition to caterpillar, you will notice it is pretty common to have the middle client leash in. Since this is likely a common transition, we suggest the middle client have a leash semipermanently attached to his harness.

GUIDE TRANSITION TO CATERPILLAR WITH TWO CLIENTS AND ONE ROPE

1. The guide builds an anchor and belays the two clients in. The guide may not decide to anchor before belaying the clients in since they are pretty close by.

2. The guide anchors the clients with a clove hitch tied above the middle client and clipped into the anchor.

3. The guide has the middle climber leash in and unclip, and then untie his cow's tail.

4. The guide adjusts the clove hitch on the anchor to take up the slack produced by untying the cow's tail. Next she ties a clove hitch into the backside of the clove on the anchor and clips that into her belay loop.

5. The guide uncoils the rope and frees any rope in her pack, and ties into the end.

6. The guide now has to decide how long the pitch is likely to be. We will assume that she thinks it is longer than half a rope length since she is using caterpillar. Once she makes that decision, she ties a cow's tail into the rope so it leaves her enough rope to lead the pitch. This distance depends on her assessment of the pitch length.

7. The guide goes on belay and leads off.

One thing to note is although a cow's tail is clipped into the middle climber in step 6, he stays on a leash as an anchor method. This greatly simplifies the rope management at the stance.

We should revisit what happens when the middle climber finishes the pitch and arrives at the anchor with another fifth-class pitch above. As in the recreational system, the middle climber leashes in, unclips from the cow's tail, and unties it. The guide continues to belay the last client. Once the section of rope where the cow's tail had been slides through the belay device, the guide ties a new cow's tail and the middle client clips it into his belay loop. We feel that the tediousness of doing this is less than rebuilding the belay, as the middle climber is likely already climbing. This way that whole system can be done with both clients completely secured—the last client on belay, and the middle client leashed in. The guide can focus on belaying and not be harried to complete the task.

Once the group finishes the fifth-class section, the transition back to third/fourth-class goes like this:

GUIDE TRANSITION CATERPILLAR TO THIRD/FOURTH-CLASS ON ONE ROPE

1. The guide arrives at the anchor and clove-hitches in.

2. When the middle climber arrives, he leashes in and unclips and unties his cow's tail.

3. When the last client arrives, he clove-hitches into the anchor.

4. The guide now ties a cow's tail into the back-side of the last client's clove hitch on the anchor and has the middle client clip into it. The guide needs to be precise with the cow's tail since this is the spacing the clients will have for the next section of third/fourth-class.

5. The middle client removes his leash from the anchor.

6. The guide ties a clove on the backside of the cow's tail and clips it into her belay loop.

7. The guide can now remove her original clove hitch on the anchor, store rope in her pack, coil off the rest, and begin to lead the third/fourth-class section.

As mentioned earlier, the guide must be precise when tying the middle client's cow's tail, particularly if the next section will have significant short-roping.

GUIDE TRANSITION THIRD/FOURTH-CLASS TO CATERPILLAR WITH TWO ROPES

The guide transition to caterpillar with two ropes should be rare. Time and efficiency are critical with two clients, and the nature of alpine routes seldom creates situations in which the parallel rope system has substantial negatives. Knowing this, the use of caterpillar seems unlikely.

If the guide and clients carry two ropes, the guide needs to take advantage of that extra weight and bulk, which usually means parallel style. You know as well as we do, however, never say never. We can imagine someone doing a long rock route with a middle section of third/fourth-class climbing, so here is that transition:

1. The guide builds an anchor and belays the two clients in. The guide may not decide to anchor before belaying the clients, since they are pretty close by.

2. When the middle client arrives, the guide grabs the rope between the clients, ties a clove hitch, and clips it into the anchor. The guide should try to have the first client to the outside of the stance so that the second client is standing between the guide and the first client.

3. The guide ties a clove hitch on the backside of the middle client's cow's tail and clips that to his belay loop.

4. The guide uncoils the rope on which he was climbing.

5. The guide uncoils the extra rope and stacks it between the clients.

6. The bottom end of that extra rope should get tied into the climber with the cow's tail. He then clove-hitches into the anchor with it, then unclips and unties his cow's tail.

7. The top end of the extra rope gets tied in to the other client.

8. The guide goes on belay, cleans the clove hitch off his belay loop, and leads out.

It is important for the guide to keep the ropes untangled. Once the middle client unclips and unties the cow's tail, the guide needs to get that slack sorted out before the other client ties into the top of the extra rope. This shouldn't be too difficult, but if the top end of the extra rope gets tied into prior to the slack getting sorted out, it could cause a tangle that will not be noticed until the guide is up the pitch.

You will notice that the guide did not clove-hitch into the anchor upon arrival. This is not unusual, since the clients are only 20 or 30 feet (9 or 12m) away. Once they arrive the guide will attach to the backside of the clients' clove hitch on the anchor. While the guide belays, his brake hand acts as a hand belay for himself as well.

In this last transition, however, we have the guide reaching between the clients to tie them in with a clove hitch on the anchor. This move could be considered aggressive with 20 to 30 feet (9 to 12m) of slack in the system. It is reasonable for the guide, prior to tying the clients in, to take the brake strand and tie a clove and clip it into his belay loop. This ultimately will be the backside of the cow's tail. The same thing can be done in the first transition when the middle client arrives, especially if the crowding increases the falling risk for the guide.

Finally, with this last transition we end up moving the second climber into the last (third) position. Since guides will often place the weaker client close to themselves, this means the weaker client will be required to clean the anchor and pitch. If both clients are of equivalent skill, this isn't a problem, but if the guide wishes to keep the second client in the second position, the transition becomes a bit more tedious.

GUIDE TRANSITION CATERPILLAR TO THIRD/FOURTH-CLASS WITH TWO ROPES

1. The guide arrives at the anchor and clove-hitches in.

2. When the first client arrives, he clips into the anchor with a clove hitch using the rope on which he was belayed.

3. When the second client arrives, the guide ties a cow's tail onto the backside of the first client's clove hitch and has the last client clip into it. The guide needs to be precise with the cow's tail since this is the spacing the clients will have for the next section of third/fourth-class.

4. The rope the first client trailed to the second can be untied from their harnesses and stored.

5. The guide ties a clove hitch on the backside of the cow's tail and clips that into her belay loop.

6. The guide removes her original clove hitch on the anchor, stores the spare rope, coils off the rope still in use, and begins leading the third/fourth-class section.

With this transition the clients are now back to their original order, with the last climber who cleaned the pitch returning to the middle position for the third/fourth-class section.

Parallel rope technique will be far more common when the guide has decided to bring two ropes. In fact, climbing parallel is the main reason a guide brings two ropes on a route.

The assessment is that there will be little to no end-roping terrain on which a single 200-foot (60m) rope is superior. The fifth-class sections will also be substantial enough that moving the clients through them at the same time will be not only faster, but more enjoyable, too.

With a single rope the guide can still have the clients follow parallel style, but doing that means the guide must belay within 100 feet (as the rope is halved to allow each client to follow on one end, with the guide tied into the middle). Being limited to 100-foot pitches presents a significant problem, one that shouldn't be underestimated. Not being able to find a place to belay within that distance puts the guide in a very difficult position.

GUIDE TRANSITION THIRD/FOURTH-CLASS TO PARALLEL WITH ONE ROPE

1. The guide builds an anchor and belays the two clients in. The guide may decide to not anchor before belaying the clients, as they are pretty close by.

2. When the first client arrives, the guide grabs the rope between the clients, ties a clove hitch, and clips it into the anchor. The guide should try to have the first client close to him with the second client to the outside.

3. The guide ties a clove hitch on the backside of the first client's cow's tail and clips that to his belay loop.

4. The guide uncoils the rope and frees his end. While he does that, he will be stacking the rope. When he sees the mid-mark, he should put it such that it can be easily found and then stack the other half in a different spot.

5. The first client is handed the end of the rope so she can tie in.

6. The first client clove-hitches into the anchor with her new tie-in and unclips and unties from the cow's tail.

7. The guide now ties or clips in to the middle point of the rope.

8. The guide goes on belay with one strand, unclips the clove hitch on his belay loop, and leads out.

Consider carefully the guide's attachment at the midpoint of the rope. Tying in is preferable, and we strongly recommend it. Clipping in could be used to speed things up if the guide feels there will only be one pitch and it is well within his movement

skill, but to be clear—the benefit of speed needs to be carefully weighed against the risk.

GUIDE TRANSITION PARALLEL TO THIRD/FOURTH-CLASS WITH ONE ROPE

1. The guide arrives at the anchor and clove-hitches in.

2. When both clients arrive at the anchor but are still on belay, the client that will be last on the third/fourth-class section gets clove-hitched into the anchor.

3. On the backside of the clove hitch, the guide ties a cow's tail and attaches the other client to it. The guide needs to be precise with the cow's tail since this is the spacing the clients will have for the next section of third/fourth-class.

4. The guide ties a clove hitch on the backside of the cow's tail and clips that to his belay loop.

5. The guide unclips his original clove hitch on the anchor, unties from the center point of the rope, and coils off. When he's ready, he unclips the clove from his belay loop and leads out.

GUIDE TRANSITION THIRD/FOURTH-CLASS TO PARALLEL WITH TWO ROPES

1. The guide builds an anchor and belays the two clients in. The guide may decide to not anchor before belaying the clients in since they are pretty close by.

2. When the first client arrives, the guide grabs the rope between the clients, ties a clove hitch, and clips it into the anchor. The guide should try to have the first client beside him with the second client to the outside.

3. The guide ties a clove hitch on the backside of the first client's cow's tail and clips that to his belay loop.

4. The guide uncoils the rope the party has been climbing on and stacks it.

A Second Now Saves a Minute Later

Time and time again we see climbers and guides attempt to speed up their days by rushing at belay stances. Whether it's completing a complex transition or just trying to start the next pitch, it seems like nine times out of ten, taking the extra minute to restack a rope saves minutes during the pitch. Snagged, tangled ropes, or forcing clients to step over/under each other when leaving the belay, eats up more time than avoiding the problem in the first place. Be a perfectionist when managing your belay stances!

5. The guide uncoils the second rope.

6. The first client ties into the bottom end of the second rope, then uses that rope to clove-hitch in to the anchor (supervised or double-checked by the guide).

7. The first client unclips and unties from the cow's tail.

8. The guide ties into the second rope, gets put on belay, unclips the clove hitch from his belay loop, and leads out.

Whether using one rope folded in half or two separate ropes, in parallel style it is important to organize your ropes. Stack them in reasonable places and make sure the ropes will feed off the stance well. Practice and perfect the parallel rope skills discussed in the rock-climbing section of this book. You have ample opportunity to keep your ropes organized, since you will be organizing your stance with free ends. In the case of the single-rope transition, the guide doesn't tie into the midpoint until the very end of the process.

In short, as you flake out and stack your ropes, use the free ends to your advantage—if there's a tangle, free it up *before* your clients tie in.

GUIDE TRANSITION PARALLEL TO THIRD/FOURTH-CLASS WITH TWO ROPES

1. The guide arrives at the anchor and clove-hitches in.

2. When both clients arrive at the anchor and are still on belay, the client that will be last on the third/fourth-class section clove-hitches into the anchor.

3. On the backside of this clove hitch, the guide ties a cow's tail and attaches the other client to it. The guide needs to be precise with the cow's tail since this is the spacing the clients will have for the next section of third/fourth-class.

4. The guide ties a clove hitch on the backside of the cow's tail and clips that to her belay loop.

5. The guide unclips her original clove hitch on the anchor and has the cow's-tail client untie from the end of his rope.

6. The guide unties from the end of the rope she will be putting away and coils it up.

7. The guide now coils off the rope the team will be using and leads out.

End-Roping

The final system the guide can employ is end-roping. Because the transition is so simple, it's tempting to overuse the method. A guide who is falling a bit behind on his or her time plan or a guide or leader who hasn't the skill to do a parallel or caterpillar transition quickly and cleanly may default to this technique.

End-roping involves significant hazard in steep, difficult terrain. If the last client falls, he will certainly pull the cow's-tail client off with significant force. This in and of itself can cause injury to the middle client. Add to that the potential for damaging the rope over a sharp edge, and you have a serious situation.

If the guide is using a thin UIAA single rope, edge problems become even more acute. Although the end-rope system has its place, such as on slabs or on very easy lower-angled terrain, we caution against using this on real fifth-class terrain. End-roping should be reserved for easy sections the guide feels uncomfortable short-roping, or the citizen leader cannot protect well with terrain.

GUIDE TRANSITION TO END-ROPING

1. The guide builds an anchor and belays the two clients in. The guide may decide to not anchor before belaying the clients in since they are pretty close by.

2. The guide anchors the clients with a clove hitch tied above the middle client and clipped into the anchor.

3. The guide ties a clove hitch into the backside of that clove hitch and clips it into her belay loop.

4. The guide uncoils the rope and gets put on belay.

5. Once on belay, the guide unclips the clove hitch on her belay loop and leads out. She tells the client with the shortening knot to unclip it and untie it.

Since only one rope is used in an end-rope system, there is only one transition (even if the guide has brought two ropes, the second rope will not be used). The big difference is how much rope the leader has to lead on.

Descents

Let's turn toward descents, and we'll start with the recreational party. As was mentioned at the start of this chapter, descents are difficult. Much of the descent in this type of terrain will be in the form of downclimbing. Often terrain that is quite simple to climb up is more intimidating and difficult to climb down, especially for less-experienced climbers.

It is one thing for the party to descend the same route as they ascended, as they will have previewed the entire route on the ascent. Descending from a hard route by an easier one that you have not done can be very intimidating and stressful. Take heart, though—although it may seem daunting, in most cases reversing a mistake while downclimbing tends to be easier than the opposite.

A rappel, however, marks the exception. A rappel can be much harder to reverse and may even be impossible after the rope is pulled.

Steady On

Careful, steady downclimbing with more focus on your movement and a little less on micro routefinding will be more efficient. If you find yourself staring down wondering where to go, make your best guess and give it a try. If it is too hard or doesn't look right, move back up and try an alternative. Once you have as much data as you can collect by looking down, all you're doing is burning time that would be better spent reversing a mistake you could make either way. So don't rush decisions, but don't agonize over the unknowable either.

For the recreational party the downclimbing can be much like the ascent. The first climber down may feel like she's being belayed, but remember that a fall on her part will create a serious fall for her partners above. When it's you on the hill, try not to let the rope give you the confidence to downclimb something for which you should take a proper belay. With very little effort the higher climber can do a quick belay around a horn or off his harness with a stance and terrain, or find a quick cam or nut placement. You can then scope the downclimb and even place gear so the higher climber has better protection as he downclimbs.

This leads to the logistics of who carries the gear. For the most part the lower climber needs the equipment so he can place it for the higher climber, but there will be occasions the upper climber may need to build a quick belay. Knowledge of the route will help, but when onsighting you might consider dividing the gear or giving the lower climber at least a range of pieces. On a route with lots of downclimbing, the time it takes to go down may be roughly the same as it took to go up the same route.

Time—Friend or Foe?

This leads us to another stressor for the descent: time. Time planning and focusing on efficiency on the way up can pay off here. At this point in the day, you are often too late to make up very much time. What you have for daylight/time is what you have; you shouldn't waste time or get sloppy with your efficiency, but trying to speed up to take back minutes may be far riskier on the descent than it would have been on the ascent.

For climbers at the end of a long route, fatigue, low blood sugar, and mild dehydration are all starting to peak as stressors. Slow, steady, relaxed—easy to say but far harder to do—keep reminding yourself and breathe. Remember, everyone gets down. You want to do it in control with the ability to celebrate the ascent.

If long, varied, complicated, interesting routes intrigue you, then practice your downclimbing. Learn how to face outward on third- and easy fourth-class terrain. Facing in seems less exposed but makes downclimbing third- and easy fourth-class feel much harder. It is hard to overemphasize the importance of this.

Rappels in Varied Terrain

Of course, certain routes and terrain require the rope as your main tool for descent. The rope facilitates everything from full rappels to hand lines to helping make downclimbing more secure. Because the transition to a rappel takes time, if we're going to rap, in most cases we take full advantage of them.

For instance, doing some difficult downclimbing to find there is a 15- to 20-foot (5- to 10m) section that needs to be rappelled at the bottom means that a rappel set up 70 or 80 feet (20 or 25m) earlier may have been more efficient. Conversely, once a rappel is built, the climbers should use that security as far as the rope takes them regardless of how easy the downclimbing is. Of course, the pull and retrieval need to be considered, but by getting as much out of every rappel you build, you end up making them more efficient.

Our roping-up system will remain about the same for a party of two. If only one rope is being used, the climber leading the descent should be carrying just over half the rope in a coil with 30 or so feet (9m) between the climbers, with the last climber carrying the rest in coils. The coiling off will stay the same with a tie-off of the coil, then a clove hitch to the belay loop.

As the team descends, the second climber needs to make sure there is terrain protecting him from a slip by his partner. If he can move faster than his partner, then on sketchy sections he can give her quick belays around horns or move into a stance and a quick belay off his harness.

If the team has two ropes on route, the lead climber should only carry a few (two or three) coils, but she should have the second rope or at least get it from the middle climber if the team is approaching a rappel.

As the lead climber arrives at the rappel, she will be setting up a large share of it. Often in this type of terrain the stances can be awkward and anchors uncomfortable. If only one person does the initial work and leaves her teammates at a more comfortable stance, there is more room and less confusion.

DOWNCLIMBING INTO RAPPEL TRANSITION FOR TWO PEOPLE

1. The lead climber arrives at the anchor and communicates to her partner to keep her belayed/secure while she works.

2. The lead climber now uncoils her rope and frees the end. While she does this, she stays clipped into the clove hitch on her belay loop. This keeps the belay from her partner active.

3. The leader feeds the end through the rappel to the middle mark, places her rappel device on the ropes, and clips a rappel extension to it.

4. The lead climber puts her partner on belay, unclips the clove hitch on her belay loop, and belays her partner over. She can use the anchor itself or if more convenient she can tie a small, double-stranded bight knot below her rappel device. This can both secure her and be used as a masterpoint for a belay.

5. When the second climber arrives, he places his rappel device below the leader's, uncoils the rope he is carrying, goes off belay, and begins his rappel.

In this situation the lead climber can carry a little more than half the rope so as to quickly build the rappel. By placing her rappel device on the rappel ropes, she locks the rope in. When the second climber comes over, he stays tied into the end for the rappel, so it is impossible for him to rappel off the end of the rope.

For three people the transition stays pretty much the same. If the team is using two ropes, the lead climber needs to have the second rope. Again, things stay pretty much the same, except after freeing her end, she would uncoil the other rope, and after passing her end through the rappel ring, she would tie the second rope to it to build the rappel.

When the middle climber gets to the anchor, he places his rappel device on the rope and clips an extension to it, then unclips his cow's tail. The leader continues to belay the last climber in. He arrives, sets up his rappel device, uncoils the rope he was carrying, and rappels. Again, by having the last climber rappel first, the knot he's tied in with protects him from rappelling off the end.

RAP ANCHORS

Seldom mentioned or discussed is the state of many rappel anchors in the alpine setting. Often rappels are slung horns or threads, maybe with an old nut and a couple of rap rings that may or may not be rated for climbing. As time goes on, climbers add slings and/or rings and the station becomes a nest of "tat." This strength-in-numbers approach can be ugly, but also comforting in a strange way.

Some climbers with the time and extra sling material will often cut away all the old material and rebuild the anchor. This service is appreciated and should be encouraged. For many, because of time or lack of expendable material, they will use what is there or maybe just add another sling. Even those with good intentions will only be able to fix up so many of these anchors on a descent. This means that alpine rappel anchors aren't always as confidence-inspiring as we would like.

A BACKUP PIECE

Since many climbers carry a limited rack of equipment in the alpine, they are reluctant to leave gear. In the end, if you really do not like the anchor, add a piece to it—it's not worth the risk! If you trust an anchor but feel that trust needs to be verified, adding a cam or nut as a backup makes perfect sense.

The backup piece shouldn't take any of the weight, but if possible come tight before a total failure takes place. Imagine a horn beginning to shift, but before failing completely the backup piece takes the weight of the system. Do your best with that strategy, always remembering the risk balance between that and time. Be creative, be decisive, and be efficient in adding this security, but whatever the situation—consider adding it.

A backup piece should take no weight of the rappel and only come tight if the initial anchor begins to fail. Tension your sling or cord accordingly.

THE THIRD HAND—A GOOD IDEA ON "BROKEN" TERRAIN?

While we generally recommend a backup (or third hand) when rappelling, on broken terrain the decision isn't quite as simple. Often the backup makes the rappel less than smooth. Many of us have probably been on a horn or anchor when a partner had a "bouncy" or jerky rappel—it's a bit disconcerting. With practice it is indeed possible to smooth out a backed-up rappel, but consider the risk-benefit equation of a rappel that isn't backed up.

Given that many of these rappels are 100 feet (30m) or less and on terrain that often has big ledges, backups may not be as necessary as you might think. We suggest making the use of a backup a conscious decision, not rote protocol or automatic. If you made a thoughtful decision to have one and are stuttering down, that's fine with us.

On the other hand, if you're nervous about your anchor and don't have any good options to reinforce it (yes, this happens; welcome to the alpine), you might want to revisit the idea that a rappel backup "always make you safer." Bouncing down a rappel with the rope into a tat anchor on a rounded horn might dramatically increase your risk. Weigh the risks and make a conscious choice.

When the party gets to the bottom of the rappel, there are two situations in which they'll find themselves: needing to do another rappel or transitioning back to third/fourth-class downclimbing. First let's discuss the transition to another rappel.

TRANSITIONING FROM A RAPPEL TO ANOTHER RAPPEL

The team can use the classic method in which each climber leashes in, then the team pulls the rope, feeds it, and rappels. In this scenario it's important to place knots in both ends of the rope.

The team could consider pre-rigging its rappel devices and clipping each member's extensions to them so that the devices can be cross-checked. If the climbers do this, there would only need to be one stopper knot, because remember with teammates above and already pre-rigged, the rope can't feed through the anchor.

Natural and Fixed Anchors

Remember to test all natural anchors; kicking is a good way to test them, but make sure not to lose your balance! Check slings even if there are a number of them. Rodents occasionally chew through them. Be vigilant and take a minute. It is easy to be complacent; after all, the last party rappelled from here and got away with it. What could go wrong? Sometimes we see anchors and focus on the transition, the weather, and the terrain—but remember to look closely at the anchor itself.

In this scenario the team feeds an end through the ring(s), ties a stopper knot, pulls the rope, and doesn't need to worry about pulling up the other end to tie a knot (if it had fallen cleanly down the next section). At that point everyone would place his or her device on the rope and cross-check their teammate(s). The first person then starts down.

Of course, it can get very crowded on the stance, and even with ample room, the anchor may be situated such that the leashes do not allow for the whole team to use it. If that is the case, the team can use the system below, described here for a team of three.

1. When the first rappeller gets down to the next rap station, he takes the end they'll pull and passes it through the rings, ties a bight knot, and clips it into his belay loop.

2. He pulls a little more rope through the ring, ties a clove hitch, and clips it into the anchor (if rappelling to a two-bolt station, for example, he builds an anchor on the bolts). He can now come off rappel.

3. As the next person rappels, the climber at the anchor pulls a little more rope through the ring and ties another bight knot.

4. When the next rappeller gets down, she clips her leash/rappel extension into new bight knot.

5. The last rappeller descends, and he also clips his leash/extension into the second/new bight knot.

6. The team pulls and feeds the rope through the rings and has everyone place their rappel devices on the rappel ropes and attach their extensions.

7. The two climbers that are clipped into the bight knot with leashes now remove them, the clove at the anchor is removed, and the rappeller that was clipped into the bight on his belay loop should descend first.

1. Two-person leashless rappel transition. The first rappeller arrives at the station, builds an anchor, threads the end he's going to pull, clips into it with a locker, and clove-hitches into the anchor. On the backside of the clove, he pre-rigs another locking carabiner on a clove hitch.
PHILBRICK PHOTOGRAPHY

2. When the second rappeller arrives, she clips into the pre-rigged clove hitch. The team pulls the rope and continues to feed it through the rap rings. PHILBRICK PHOTOGRAPHY

3. When they reach the middle mark (or the junction if rapping on two ropes), they place their devices on the ropes, then connect to them with extensions. The climber with the bight knot clipped to his harness should rappel first without unclipping so he's protected from going off the ends of the ropes. PHILBRICK PHOTOGRAPHY

4. The team cleans the anchor. The second rappeller drops the clove hitch from her harness so the first rappeller can start down.
PHILBRICK PHOTOGRAPHY

Easy Safeguard

Seems like every year in *Accidents in North American Mountaineering* we read five or so reports of accidents or fatalities involving rappelling off the ends of the rope. Simple safeguards like knotting the ends of the rope (or one end on a pre-rigged rappel) or remaining tied into the rope could save a few lives a year.

Get Moving on Rappel

Advanced climbers often do not wait till they have removed their rappel device from the rope before calling out "off rappel." Once the rappeller is down and will no longer need to weight the rappel rope, they call out. In fact, on long rappels where you might have limited communications due to the distance, the wind, a river, or a road, for example, the team can decide to have the next rappeller begin as soon as there is enough slack for him to move. Of course, the lower rappeller might just be on a ledge and they'll start rappelling again, but in the worst case the upper rappeller gets temporarily locked into place. If it is steep or on overhanging terrain, it might not be a good idea, but in most cases it isn't a problem. Regardless, there is no need to wait until you remove the rappel device to get the next rappeller moving.

This transition needs 6 to 7 feet (2m) of slack to work with at the new anchor, so it doesn't work on rope-stretching rappels. Consider the benefit, though: Everyone has a dynamic connection to the anchor, something that could be more important on many anchors found in alpine terrain. Another added bonus is the rappeller with the bight knot clipped to his harness has no chance of rappelling off the end of the ropes on the next rap.

Keep in mind the number of ropes strands coming from the anchor complicates the stance a bit. The team must make sure to put its rappel devices on the correct strands.

RAPPEL INTO THIRD/ FOURTH-CLASS TERRAIN

The next transition for the team will probably be back into third/fourth-class mode. In that case there will likely not be an anchor, so one may need to be built or a suitable horn must be found. If the landing is large enough, the team may feel no need to anchor.

Be careful with this calculation, though. When the team pulls the rope, it can bring down rocks and people may need to scramble out of the way. Without sufficient space to move, climbers have a terrible choice—risk a fall or being hit by rockfall. Being leashed in short may also hamper a climber's ability to dodge rocks. Consider these risks.

Another thing we see is climbers taking enormous risks when the rope gets caught off to the side, above exposed terrain. While tempting to retrieve it or adjust the angle of pull while unroped, it can also invite disaster. Especially at the end of a long route, the idea of roping up with the free end to retrieve the rest of the rope can seem tedious. Consider the consequences of a mishap when foregoing an anchor!

TWO-PERSON TRANSITION TO THIRD/ FOURTH-CLASS AFTER A RAPPEL

1. The first climber down the rappel builds a quick anchor and clove-hitches into it (remember, he's tied into the end of the rope, so uses the rope).

2. When the next rappeller gets down, he ties a clove hitch on the backside of the first rappeller's clove.

3. The team pulls the rope.

4. The second rappeller ties into the free end of the rope and coils off to just past the middle mark of the rope.

5. Once the rope is coiled off, he takes a belay from his partner and begins downclimbing.

6. Once the first climber down gets 30 or so feet (9m) away, the second climber clove-hitches into the rope, unclips from the anchor, coils off, and begins descending.

This sequence is very similar to the transition from fifth-class climbing to third/fourth-class. The team can add a bit of security here when the second rappeller clips into the rope, as he can clip the rope between himself and his partner into the anchor. This acts as a counterbalance anchor during the coiling-up process in the event one of the team members slips, is hit by rockfall, etc.

THREE-PERSON TRANSITION TO THIRD/FOURTH-CLASS AFTER A RAPPEL

1. The first climber down the rappel builds a quick anchor and clove-hitches into it (remember, he's tied into the end of the rope, so uses the rope).

2. When the next rappeller gets down, he ties a clove hitch on the backside of the first rappeller's clove.

3. The third climber comes down and ties a clove hitch on the backside of the second rappeller's clove.

4. The team pulls the rope.

5. The rappeller that came down last ties into the free end of the rope and coils off to just past the middle mark.

6. Once the roped is coiled, he takes a belay from a partner and begins downclimbing.

7. Once the first rappeller downclimbs 30 or so feet (9m), the second rappeller cow-tails into the rope, takes a belay from the last rappeller, unclips from anchor, and starts down.

8. Once the second rappeller downclimbs 30 or so feet (9m), the last climber clove-hitches into the rope, unclips from the anchor, coils off, and begins descending.

Gray Zone—Downclimb or Rappel

There will be times when you find yourself in the gray zone of downclimbing and rappelling. As we mentioned, the first person down can get a belay from above and place gear as she descends, allowing the top person to down "lead" the section. Another option is for the top climber to hook the rope over a horn and use it as a hand line to help herself downclimb and then "cowboy" flip it off the horn. This can work for very short sections. For most climbers, flipping a rope off of a rough horn when you're more than 10 feet (3m) away can be difficult. Some try to pull the end around it, like you would a rappel, but quickly find that the friction makes that impossible.

Of course, the last climber could leave a sling and a ring behind, which would allow for pulling the end, but if the team is going to the trouble of doing that, it would be best (as we suggest above) to use the full length of the rappel and take advantage of it.

Guiding Descents

Guiding descents can be stressful. There will be times you would love to be in front, finding the easiest, mellowest way down, but that leaves your clients in a very exposed position above you.

Route-finding from the back of the pack means your vision is limited. If you are descending the route you climbed, taking note of certain sections on the way up can be helpful. If you are onsighting the descent, the stress will be substantial. Guides will short-rope or use quick belays and do short pitches in this terrain. To route-find, they will want to be closer to their clients than a recreational party, which leads to many more quick belays so the guide can have a better view.

At times the guide will flip his team so he can be in the lead for sections. On traverses, flat sections of a ridge, or sections on which there is no falling hazard, the guide will want to lead. Upon arrival to a steep section, the guide needs to use terrain and position to flip the group again so he can belay clients down. Once the clients are down, the guide needs to consider securing the clients so he can downclimb.

As in the ascent, most guides choose to carry all the rope. Unlike on the ascent, if there are a number of rappels, putting part of the rope in the pack will make setting up the rappels and transitioning back to third/fourth-class mode tedious. This means after the first rappel on the descent, the guide will be carrying most of the rope as coils. This impacts the guide's freedom of movement and comfort. Good, organized, nearly perfect coils help with balance and decrease the likelihood of a fall.

If the guide has decided to bring two ropes, he'll have fewer coils on the body, but he'll need to carry the second rope in his pack. Occasionally the middle climber can carry the spare rope, but the leader or guide will want to grab the second rope before heading into a rappel if he will arrive at the station first.

At certain times a guide finds benefit in descending with two clients rather than one. On ridges the guide can have clients stand on each side of the crest, creating a counterbalanced anchor. Anytime a guide sees a horn, he can have his clients put the rope between them over it, creating another variety of counterbalanced anchor.

With a trained eye, guides can efficiently and seamlessly use the two clients as a counterbalance after a section of belayed downclimbing—as long as the terrain allows it with a tree, horn, or crest. When the guide has only one client, this natural counterbalancing isn't available, so he must look for other features for the client to wrap with successive loops of the rope. A horn or big, stable boulder suffices in this situation.

It's useful to keep in mind, as guides, when we downclimb to an unsecured client, we are effectively soloing while tied to another person. The stakes are high, and if there's one thing we can count on, we will eventually make a mistake.

Coaching a client to wrap a horn at his stance can save the day, just as the guide temporarily flipping his rope over horns on a downclimb can, too. Get good at spotting these and using them on the fly.

There is a technique to secure yourself and client for short downclimbs. Read on to discover it; it's known as the equivocation hitch.

Of course, as we saw on the ascent, a team of three does move more slowly. We'll have three people rappelling, so that takes more time and it is harder to purely short-rope two clients, so quick belays are more common. The guide must take advantage of the counterbalance anchor potential two clients provide, just to make up for some of those deficits.

Guided Descents: Lowers and Top-Belayed Rappels

When it comes to more technical descent options, the guide must go beyond just rappelling. The main reason for this is the nature of alpine rappel anchors. As we mentioned, alpine rappel anchors are not always as confidence-inspiring as we would like. This means, just like the recreational party, placing a backup that may be removed by the last rappeller (once the anchor has been tested) is a good idea.

Some anchors also need careful starts—a low anchor on a horn, for example. In both these cases having the guide rappel first, leaving her client to make a judgment about whether it is appropriate to remove the backup, is not prudent or professional. On low anchors or horns, the guide would rather not have serious outward pulls, so being able to coach someone as he goes over the edge is something a guide should be able to do.

For these reasons and others such as a nervous client, guides will use lowers and top-belayed rappels. In most cases this isn't as daunting as it would be in a pure rock environment. Most alpine rappels are 100 feet (30m) or less, so guides can often see their clients at the landing and with a little work usually hear them.

Where things get tricky is when the rappel ends at another rappel station that is exposed and the guide has not had the chance to preview the quality of the anchor, or it ends in a transition to third/fourth-class where there are no anchors. If these rappels are short, so that they end with enough slack that the falling hazard is not properly protected for the clients at the bottom, the guide has a significant dilemma.

Another common situation for guides is a rappel that requires a short downclimb to an area at which the clients can unrope. Recreational parties often down solo, but the guide can't simply hope her clients don't slip on a downclimb to safety. In this situation the guide may decide to lower her clients farther than 100 feet (30m) to the safe area and have them untie. She then rappels and downclimbs without having to do another transition with the clients for such a short section.

SHORT-ROPING TO TECHNICAL DESCENTS

All the transitions in this category start with one of two scenarios:

1. The guide arrives at the anchor first.
2. The client arrives at the anchor first.

If possible, it is nice for the guide to arrive at the anchor first; this gives the guide more room to work. There will be times, though, when the approach to the anchor requires the guide to be above the client(s)—an exposed slab to a rap anchor on a vertical wall, for example.

All the transitions we will discuss start from the point where the guide uncoils the rope. Getting to that point depends on who gets to the anchor first, so all the transitions start with one of the two sequences below.

Guide arrives at the anchor first:

1. The guide takes the clients' rappel devices with him and leaves the clients in a secure stance so that he cannot pull the clients off if he were to fall.

2. As he approaches the anchor, he ties a clove hitch into the rope coming from the backside of the client's cow's tail and clips it into his harness.

3. Once the guide reaches the anchor, the clients above provide his security. If he feels he needs more, he clips the rope between himself and the clients into the anchor with or without a clove hitch.

4. The guide uncoils and frees the rope.

Client(s) arrive at the anchor first:

1. The guide clove-hitches a locking carabiner to the rope between the clients.

2. The guide belays the clients to the anchor and has them clip into the anchor.

3. The guide downclimbs toward the anchor. As he gets closer, he ties a clove hitch into the rope coming from the clients cow's tail and clips into it to increase his security. (The guide may pull rope through the clove hitch to shorten the length of rope out as he gets closer, if it feels prudent.) Upon arrival at the anchor, the guide adjusts the clove hitch to be his anchor tether.

4. The guide uncoils and frees the rope.

In many cases the guide doesn't need to clip into the anchor at all to get the rope uncoiled because the clients are in line with the fall line and protecting him. If there is a traverse to the anchor, using it as a directional or actually using a clove at the anchor will be necessary. If at all possible, keeping the anchor clean makes the transition easier. Remember to check the anchor and if it is prudent, back it up.

In these transitions we assume the guide has not been able to preview the rappel. If this is really the case, the guide should use the mobility the rope provides or the adjustability of cloving-in to the anchor to get the best view of the terrain. In this way, he can make a good choice as to which technique he'll use.

A better view of the upcoming terrain increases the chances the guide will be able to lower or do

Pre-Rig an Anchor

When sending clients to an anchor first, a guide will often build a pre-rigged anchor on the rope between the clients, clove-hitched to a locking carabiner. When the clients arrive, they simply clip the locker into the anchor, lock it (and let the guide know they've done this), and they're protected. The rigging could be a pre-equalized sling with two carabiners ready for bolts or simply a locking carabiner on a clove hitch on the rope if there's a sling anchor in place on a tree or boulder.

a belayed rappel. If only one rappel is needed, the landing area must be assessed for safety. The guide must also evaluate the configuration of the terrain and the distance.

If the guide is not confident his rope will be long enough for a rappel, but the landing zone poses no falling hazard and there is none close by, the guide can lower one client down to the safe landing and check the distance via the rope. If the safe landing is more than a half-rope length down, the client can untie and the guide can lower the second client. Once both clients are down safely, the guide can do two rappels or more likely, do a rappel with a downclimb.

Taking the clients' devices is important so that the guide has the option to pre-rig a rappel prior to his clients getting there. This allows him to focus on the belay and get clients clipped into their devices, which should be blocked off when they arrive. Having to help clients get their devices onto the rope once they arrive makes their setup at the anchor more confusing just when they're closest to the edge and a secure belay most important. If the guide ends up lowering, having the clients' devices gives him more tools to work with, and at worst he'll have devices he doesn't need—no big deal.

GUIDE TRANSITION: PRE-RIGGED RAPPEL

If you want to do a pre-rigged rappel because you cannot see the landing or will be doing multiple rappels, continue into the next steps in the transition. Should the anchor need any backup pieces, you'll be leaving them in this case. Consider it an investment in your future and a community service!

1. The guide feeds the free end of the rope through the rappel ring(s), ties a stopper knot, then pulls until the middle of the rope.

2. The guide places her device on the rope and clips into it with a leash. She uses the longest leash with which she's comfortable rappelling; this is important if she arrives at the anchor first. A standard over-the-shoulder sling usually works well.

3. The guide places the clients' devices on the rope, above hers.

4. The guide blocks her device with a big bight knot.

5. If clients are already there, the guide asks them to clip into their devices, each with an extension; or if she arrives at the anchor first, she belays them over (using the big bight knot as a masterpoint) and has them clip into their devices with extensions when they arrive.

6. Once she and her clients are into their devices, the guide detaches her clove hitch on her belay loop and has the second client untie from the rope and the first client unclip and untie his cow's tail.

7. The guide rappels down and gives a fireman's belays to her clients.

For the guide with two ropes, this transition remains essentially the same. Instead of threading the rope to the middle mark, the guide uncoils the second rope and joins the ends after threading one through the rings.

One thing to consider is which end the guide puts through the rings. This determines which end the guide will pull after the rappel. In some cases it can simplify the transition back to third/fourth-class or make it more complex. This is a very advanced thought process and requires that you are fluent with the various transitions, but as you progress with your skills, making a conscious decision here rather than just passing an end through will lead to insight and help you progress to ever higher efficiency.

GUIDE TRANSITION: LOWER TO A TOP-BELAYED RAPPEL

Here's the transition if: The guide wants to lower the first client and then do a belayed rappel for the second. Or, the guide wants to lower both clients and he's confident it's within half a rope length, *and* the landing is safe enough; the clients can be somewhat unprotected.

1. The guide feeds the free end of the rope through the rappel ring(s) to the middle of the rope while stacking the rope. Note he does not toss the free end down the cliff.

2. The guide places his rappel device on the rope, clips into it with a leash, and blocks it with a big bight knot. He uses the longest leash with which he's comfortable rappelling. A standard shoulder-length sling usually works well.

3. With the free end of the rope, the guide sets up a lowering system (Munter, Super Munter, or a plaquette with a redirected brake strand) using the big bight knot as a masterpoint and blocks it off.

4. If the clients are already there, the guide ties or clips the cow's-tail client into the free end and has her detach from the cow's tail. If the clients are not there, he belays them to the anchor with a Munter hitch using the big bight knot as a masterpoint. Once the clients arrive, the guide ties or clips the cow's-tail client into the free end, detaches her from the cow's tail, and takes in the slack this produces.

5. The guide places a third-hand backup on the brake strand and lowers the end client.

6. Once this client is down, the guide unblocks the lower built in step 3 and lowers the cow's-tail client. Just to be clear, this is the client who came off the cow's tail and clipped into the free end of the rope that was set up to lower. (Note the cow's-tail client could also do a belayed rappel on the strand going down the cliff to the end client.)

7. Once the cow's-tail client is down and comfortable, the guide takes her off belay.

8. The guide disassembles the lowering/belay system, undoes the BHK, decides whether or not to use a friction-hitch backup, and rappels.

With two ropes, instead of feeding to the middle mark in step 1, the guide passes an end through and ties a junction knot with the second rope.

If the guide has only one client, he can toss the free end down the cliff and then lower or give a top-belayed rappel to his one client. No need to build the lower with the free end.

1. Short-roping to a lower/belayed rappel. The guide arrives first at an exposed anchor. His clients remain above in a secure stance so were the guide to fall, he can't pull them off. If there's still slack between him and the clients, once at the stance he can adjust the clove hitch on his harness to tighten himself up and protect himself against a fall. Now he's free to drop his coils and free up the rope.

2. The guide threads the free end of the rope until the middle mark and places a rappel device on the ropes.

3. He attaches himself to his device with an extension and blocks it with a double-stranded bight knot.

4. *He takes the free end of the rope (the one he threaded) and ties a Munter mule overhand into it about 2 meters from the end and attaches it to the double-stranded bight knot with a locking carabiner. On the same double-stranded bight knot he hangs a locking carabiner and belays his clients over using a Munter hitch.*

5. *In this close-up shot, you can see the guide's system. He is belaying his clients into the stance with a Munter on the yellow carabiner. He has built a Munter mule overhand on the blue carabiner on the same double-stranded bight knot. On the end of this strand he's tied an overhand on a bight, and he'll use this to secure the first client who arrives at the stance.*

6. The guide clips the first client who arrives (the cow's-tail client) into the bight knot on the blocked Munter mule overhand (this client is in the red helmet). This client unclips from the cow's tail and unties it for the guide. The guide keeps the second client (green helmet) on belay with a Munter. He adds a friction-hitch backup to the brake strand and lowers the client.

7. Once the first client is down, the guide disassembles the Munter (on the yellow carabiner) and friction-hitch backup. The remaining client puts a rappel device on the strand going down the cliff. The guide unblocks the Munter (on the blue carabiner) and provides a belay while the client rappels. When the client is down, the guide removes the double-stranded bight knot and rappels.

GUIDE TRANSITION TO A LONG LOWER

In alpine terrain, or even on rock routes, after a rappel we often face a short downclimb to a safe landing. We usually solo these downclimbing sections, as most recreational climbers do, but most of the time it's unacceptable for a client to downclimb the section without some protection.

If you're onsighting, this type of terrain can be challenging. Even determining the exact distance to a large, safe area can be tough. If you see a safe area where clients do not need to be secured, but it appears to be more than half a rope length away or farther than just one of your two ropes is long, you can use this transition.

1. If the clients have not arrived at the stance, the guide clips into the anchor with a leash, uncoils her rope, and unties from the end.

2. The guide takes the free end, passes it through the rappel rings, and feeds it through a plaquette. This is a plate with a redirected brake strand system, with the redirect being the rappel rings. The guide blocks this off.

3. The guide belays the clients over on a Munter. When they arrive, she clips or ties the cow's-tail client into the free end and has him detach from the cow's tail.

4. The guide ties the second client into the anchor by converting the Munter into a clove hitch. If the guide needs to extend to watch the lower, she clips into the backside of this client's tie-in with a clove hitch and removes her leash.

5. The guide lowers the first client down to the safe area.

6. Now the guide has a good measurement of the distance. If it's farther than a half-rope length, the guide asks the client to untie, then pulls the rope up.

7. When the guide has the free end at the stance, the second client clips or ties into it, and the guide sets up a lower on this strand. The client

unties from his original figure eight *and if the guide is on the backside of the client's clove hitch (as described in step 4 for improved viewing) the guide ties a stopper knot in that free end.* The guide lowers the second client and asks him to untie.

8. The guide places the mid-mark of her rope at the anchor, sets up the rappel, and descends.

If the clients are already at the stance, step 1 is not necessary since the guide is already secured to the anchor by being on the backside of the cow's-tail client (that rope is already clove-hitched into the anchor). When the guide transfers the cow's-tail client onto the lower, she may want to adjust her backside clove hitch on her belay loop to take in the slack that is produced by the untying of the cow's tail.

Conversely if the clients aren't already at the anchor and the guide must belay them in, she will need to leash in. If she feels the leash is too short to see and manage the lower, then once the cow's-tail client is transferred onto the lowering system, she flips the Munter with which she belayed the clients into a clove hitch. Now she clips into the backside of that and unclips her leash. This allows her to get into a good position to see the lower and manage the system.

If the landing is within a half-rope length, then instead of having the client at the bottom untie, he remains tied in. In this situation, the guide follows this process:

1. The guide puts the middle mark at the anchor, places her rappel device on the ropes, clips her leash into the device and adjusts it so that she has a view, blocks it off with a big bight knot, and unclips from the clove hitch at her waist if she was on the backside of a clove on the anchor.

2. Using the big bight knot as the masterpoint, the guide lowers the second client. Or, the second client rappels on the rope connected to the first client, with the guide giving him a belay on the other strand.

3. Once the second client is down, the guide undoes the big bight knot and rappels.

Most of the transitions change very little if you are using two shorter ropes rather than one long rope, as we have suggested when guiding two clients. In the transition above, the two-rope transition adds complexity, however. With two ropes, if you'd like to get farther than a rappel will get you, you'll need to pass the knot joining the ropes.

A KNOT-PASS WHEN LOWERING

Keep in mind, if you are using two 135-foot (or longer) ropes, you aren't as likely to need to go farther than this distance in a rappel. In the unlikely event you do want to lower your clients more than the 135 feet (40m), the client will probably be on easy ground—he should be able to easily stand up when it is time to pass the knot since it is terrain a recreational party would be able to downclimb. If this is the case, you should be able to just "pop" a knot through a Munter hitch while the rope is unweighted.

Using a "Munter pop" means you will need to change your system for lowering from the one described in the above transition. The reason you are using the redirected brake strand system is so you have a head start feeding the rings. In the case of two ropes, that is unnecessary, as you can just untie the junction knot and retie it through the rings. This means you can use a Munter hitch to lower, allowing you to pass the knot more simply.

Remember not to get too greedy with lowering when you're passing a knot. If it gets jammed on the way down, it will really complicate your life. The knot should only need to go a little way for the client to reach the safe zone. To fully appreciate the process of, and the hazards of, the knot pass, see chapter 12 on self-rescue. You'll also find more information about performing a weighted knot pass in that chapter.

A Knot-Pass in Patagonia: Rescue Application

by Angela Hawse

Angela Hawse. COURTESY ANGELA HAWSE

Ten years into guiding, and having climbed in the Himalaya and Alaska, I thought I'd seen it all. Not even close. On a personal climbing trip to Patagonia in the mid-90s, my partner Jim and I ended up saving another climber's life. The effort put just about every skill I'd learned into practice over an intense 35-hour period.

Jim and I had just climbed Guillaumet and returned to the ice cave bivouac at Paso Superior, where we debated descending to base camp with a team of Chileans. I had a gut feeling we should stay. So we did. It was the end of the season and most teams had packed it in, including Kurt Albert and Bernd Arnold after putting up *Royal Flush* on Fitzroy. The remaining folks on a route were an American and Chilean climbing Fitzroy via the *Franco-Argentina*. At the time no one carried radios and cell service was nonexistent.

At midnight my gut feeling turned into a nightmare when a very distraught Chilean appeared, shouting at the top of his lungs that a terrible accident had occurred. His partner had fallen 1,000 feet down 85-degree mixed terrain and was badly injured. Although we thought it incredible he could be alive, we jumped into our boots, grabbed our gear, and got the Chileans to descend to El Chaltén for help. Jim and I ran back up the glacier with the solo climber by headlamp at an adrenaline-filled pace. This guy had just downclimbed 1,000 feet of difficult terrain by headlamp after his partner plummeted past him with both ropes. He was really glad to find us at the ice caves.

Remarkably, when we got to the American—Mike, we later learned—he was still alive in a heap of struggling breaths and twisted ropes, perched on a 40-degree slope. We assessed his ABCs, identifying a bad head injury and a few minor breaks. He was responsive to pain, but remained unconscious.

We dug a platform, insulated him, assessed for other injuries, got him into a sleeping bag, and rechecked him through the night. We melted snow, took care of ourselves, and tried to reassure Mike he would survive.

To ourselves, however, we feared Mike wouldn't make it through the night. The sky eventually lightened and we could see the gravity of our situation. Hope for a helicopter rescue was gone. Snow started falling in earnest and we had to get off the slope, fast.

Jim and the Chilean packaged up Mike, stabilizing him as best they could. I built an anchor, tied two ropes together, and lowered the team down the slope, getting us 120 meters away from our precarious position. Although I used snow anchors commonly, I had only just learned the knot pass. As taught, I stacked the ropes so they'd run smoothly, pre-rigged the knot pass, and executed it flawlessly. When the rope came to the end, Jim secured the team while I downclimbed and re-rigged it for one more go. This got us off the slope quickly, with the threat of avalanche looming overhead.

Again the gravity of our situation became real as we attempted to pull a 200-plus-pound Mike across the glacier. We bumped to Plan C: Jim would dig a shelter for himself and Mike, while the Chilean and I would run for help, which we hoped was already on the way.

Almost back to Paso Superior, we found Arnold and Albert with the two Chileans and a Stokes litter and snow Skeds in tow. It was a huge relief. We attempted to communicate the situation in broken Spanish, some German, and English. Although this represents only a nickel version of the five-dollar story, after another several knot passes and a lot of effort and teamwork, we got Mike down and several years later we learned he'd made a full recovery.

These key takeaways have stuck with me: 1) listen to my instinct; 2) always be ready for a call to action; 3) maintain a high level of fitness; 4) first-aid skills matter; 5) think on my feet; 6) be decisive; 7) situational awareness will keep me alive; 8) there is no "I" in teamwork; 9) keep my skills sharp; and 10) never stop learning.

—*Angela Hawse is an IFMGA/AMGA Mountain Guide who has more fun than just about anyone.*

THE EQUIVOCATION HITCH

When managing variable terrain on the down, guides occasionally use what's known in American-English as the "equivocation hitch." Non-climbers might know this tool as the highwayman's hitch.

Guides use the equivocation hitch when faced with terrain involving short downclimbing sections of exposed fourth- or easy fifth-class. In most situations, the guide won't be able to have his clients place protection for him on the descent, making a "down lead" impossible. Carrying the entire rope as a coil can also lower the guide's movement skill, so downclimbing fifth-class terrain becomes riskier. Also, the guide may not be able to direct the clients to a suitable anchor or ledge where he feels comfortable having them wait without security.

So when faced with any of the above, the guide can belay around a feature (a tree, horn, or fixed anchor) and tie an equivocation hitch. This establishes a fixed hand (or rap) line, avoids an unprotected downclimb, and secures clients. Note that the guide's side of the hitch cannot be weighted during the downclimb or it will release the hitch—no falls!

Cowboys originally used the highwayman's/ equivocation hitch to tie a horse to a hitching post so the rider could undo the hitch from the saddle with an easy tug of the rope. Pretty slick, throwing a leg over a horse, tipping your hat to your crew, then gently pulling a strand of rope and riding into the sunset.

The equivocation can be tied several times, repeating the same hitch in sequence. Cowboys only tied the hitch once, but guides typically tie the hitch six or seven times in sequence for added security.

What's in a Name?

Piolets d'Or winner and IFMGA guide Vince Anderson popularized the term "equivocation hitch." A Chilean guide showed Anderson the hitch in 1994 but had trouble translating its name into English. Some folks jokingly called it the "Chilean death hitch" for a time, but eventually Americans settled on the name "equivocation hitch." When tying it, you go "back and forth," tying one side and then the other, like equivocating on a topic—hence the name.

1. Equivocation hitch. Pass a bight of rope around the horn or tree you'll be using. Reach through the bight and grab one strand of the rope on the other side of the tree (or horn).
PHILBRICK PHOTOGRAPHY

2. Pull the strand through to create a new bight.
PHILBRICK PHOTOGRAPHY

3. Take the other strand and pull it through the newly formed bight. This will form yet another bight. Notice the left hand in the photo grabs the newest bight, while the right hand switches strands and tensions the older bight.

PHILBRICK PHOTOGRAPHY

4. Repeat the process six or seven times.

PHILBRICK PHOTOGRAPHY

5. Make sure to finish the last hitch such that the client-side strand is fixed and not the release strand. **This is critical!** PHILBRICK PHOTOGRAPHY

6. Rappel or hand-line down the fixed strand to the client, making sure not to weight the release strand until you're ready and secured. Double-check before starting down that you have enough rope out to reach the client. This might require dropping coils. PHILBRICK PHOTOGRAPHY

So let's add a disclaimer: This hitch is a legitimate tool for guides or very experienced recreationalists. It is best used for sections of 20 to 30 feet (6 to 9m) that many would downclimb but are hard enough that a little extra security can make a big difference (a nervous client, rain-slicked rock, darkness, high-consequence terrain). If you find yourself rappelling a long distance on this hitch, you are likely misusing it.

Notice that once at the bottom, the guide pulls the free strand and this unties the hitch, bringing a bight of rope down the cliff. Now the team has a bight or loop of rope coming down, rather than a single strand. This feature of the equivocation means for a longer downclimb, it is more likely to get caught when pulled.

The beauty of this hitch is that it doesn't need a free end of the rope. The guide won't need to uncoil all the rope, untie from the end, thread it, and/or build a rappel anchor. The hitch protects his clients, too, at the landing zone. As we'll see, this will be an important function of the system for the guide.

When the guide ties it, he should also consider how the final bight travels around the horn. Are there any protrusions on the horn that will catch the bight? If so, can you pass the bight from the other side and mitigate the problem? Of course, you absolutely must make sure the horn is solid and robust enough that the rope won't slip off of it.

The word *equivocation* means to go back and forth, to avoid making a decision, hedging. The back-and-forth method to tying it, and because we use it as a hedge on a downclimb, makes equivocation the perfect name.

SHORT LOWER, TWO CLIENTS, INTO AN INSECURE STANCE

When the guide uses lowers and belayed rappels, some of them will be built in such a way as to protect her clients once down and before the guide arrives. This frees the guide to be the last at the

The guide belayed her client's downclimb into an insecure stance, then secured him with an equivocation hitch, making sure the hitches are on the outside of the feature and easy to release from below. She's put her rappel device on the fixed (client) strand of the hitch and will descend to him. Once at this stance, she'll secure him and herself on a new anchor and then release the hitch. From there she'll continue her descent as she sees fit based upon the terrain below.

anchor, should she want to back it up temporarily or get clients down quickly because the stance is uncomfortable or any other reason.

The final and arguably the most complex transition is lowering both clients (or first a lower and then a belayed rappel) to a landing not secure enough to leave clients unanchored. In most of these situations, you will just do a pre-rigged rappel; but there are times when you might want to descend last. A backed-up anchor you want to monitor, a rappel with an awkward or strenuous start, or a low anchor that can't tolerate an outward or upward pull are all situations in which you might need to remain at the top while the clients rap or you lower them.

If the lower is long and uses up most of the rope, a 29-meter descent with a 60-meter rope for instance, you do not need to go to any great lengths to protect your clients; by requiring them to stay tied in, they remain secured once down. If the lower is much shorter, though, you will need to change the transition to keep the clients secure at the landing.

1. If the clients have not arrived at the stance, the guide clips into the anchor with a leash, uncoils her rope, and unties from the end.

2. The guide takes the free end, passes it through the rappel rings, and feeds it through a plaquette. This is a plate with a redirected brake strand system, with the redirect being the rappel rings. The guide blocks this off.

3. The guide belays the clients over with a Munter. When they arrive, the guide clips or ties the cow's-tail client into the free end and has him detach from the cow's tail.

4. The guide ties the second client into the anchor by converting the Munter into a clove hitch. If the guide needs to extend to watch the lower, she clips into the backside of this client's tie-in with a clove hitch and removes her leash.

5. The guide lowers the first client down to the stance.

6. The guide feeds out a few extra feet of rope (about 3 feet) and blocks off the lower by placing a rappel device (she can use the client's device) on the rappel rope and clips into it with a leash.

7. The guide disassembles the plate with which she lowered the first client, repositions herself, and blocks off the device with a big bight knot.

8. The guide attaches a leash to the second client's harness and readies to lower him using the big bight knot as a masterpoint.

9. Before sending the client down, the guide has the client clip his leash into the *first client's* rope with a locker. The guide lowers him. (Read below to understand why.)

10. The guide disassembles the lowering system and unties the big bight knot and rappels.

If the guide has the second client rappel, the client uses an extension and once he arrives at the bottom, the guide makes sure he keeps the device on the rope and stays clipped into it.

By lowering the first client and then placing a rappel device on the ropes, the guide fixes the two strands—and note that the mid-mark will most likely *not* be at the anchor. The guide blocks the rope from feeding through the anchor with his rappel, therefore protecting the first client down. The client remains tied in on a now-fixed line.

The guide asks the second client to clip his tether to the first client's strand in step 9, above. When he arrives at the stance, his tether is attached to the shorter strand connected to the first client, so he is now protected as well. Should he fall, his tether will come tight at the first client's tie-in and prevent a catastrophe.

1. Short lower to an insecure stance. The guide arrives at the stance, builds an anchor, and leashes in.

2. After dropping his coils, the guide feeds the free end through the rings and builds a redirected lower on a plaquette. He adds a friction-hitch backup on the brake side and a catastrophe knot behind that.

3. The guide belays the two clients to his stance with a Munter on the anchor. When the first client arrives, the guide clips him into a locking carabiner on a bight knot on the redirected lower. This secures the cow's-tail client (he's to the right in the photo, in the green helmet). The client unclips from the cow's tail and unties it. The guide continues to belay the second client to the stance with the Munter. When the client arrives, the guide blocks the Munter with a mule overhand knot (this client is now on the left in the photo; the guide is in the middle). In the step-by-step description of this transition, we describe converting the Munter into a clove so that the guide could then use the backside of the clove to extend into a better position to see the landing zone. In the photos, the guide elects not to do this, and so rather than convert the Munter to a clove, he blocks it with a mule overhand. This simplifies the transition, but the Munter-clove conversion gives you an option should you need to extend.

4. The guide takes his client's rappel device and places it on the ropes at the anchor. This secures the client below because the ropes are now fixed at the anchor by virtue of the rappel device. The client below can't fall from his stance. The guide disassembles the redirected plaquette after putting on the rappel device. He can then transfer his leash onto the rappel device, and then blocks it off with a double-stranded bight knot. The guide places a third-hand backup on the brake strand of the Munter mule overhand, then unblocks the mule overhand and pulls slack through the backup. The guide asks the client to girth-hitch a shoulder-length sling to his belay loop and clip it to the other client's strand with a locking carabiner. The guide lowers the second client. Notice the guide doesn't use the double-stranded bight knot as a masterpoint for the second lower. Because he's already in a good position to see, he didn't extend on the client's backside of the clove, as the step-by-step instructions suggest. Instead, he uses the blocked-off Munter to lower. This simplifies the transition, but the guide needs to make sure the double-stranded bight knot blocking his rappel device doesn't roll and untie, so he clips a carabiner into it (an orange locker in the photo). After lowering the client, he cleans the second lowering system and the anchor, unties his double-stranded bight knot, and rappels.

TWO ROPES, LOWERING TWO CLIENTS INTO AN INSECURE STANCE

If you are using two ropes, it will change this transition substantially. You will have to lock the rappel in a different way and you will only be able to rappel one strand, since there will be a knot on one of the strands hanging down.

1. If the clients have not arrived at the stance, the guide clips into the anchor with a leash, uncoils his rope, and unties from the end.

2. The guide uncoils and stacks the second rope.

3. The guide joins the end of his rope to the end of the second rope coming from the bottom of the stack.

4. The guide takes the free end of the second rope, passes it through the rappel rings, and feeds it through a device. This is a plaquette with a redirected brake strand system, with the redirect being the rappel rings. The guide blocks this off.

5. The guide belays the clients over with a Munter. When they arrive, the guide clips or ties the cow's-tail client into the free end and has him detach from the cow's tail.

6. The guide ties the second client into the anchor by converting the Munter into a clove hitch. If the guide needs to extend to watch the lower, he clips into the backside of the second client's tie-in with a clove hitch and removes his leash.

7. The guide lowers the first client to the stance.

8. The guide feeds out a few extra feet of rope (about 3 feet) and blocks the lower by placing a bight knot on the rope behind the rings (the side opposite the client he just lowered), then clips a locker from that bight knot into the rope coming out the other side of the rings. (This is the same system Petzl recommends to use when rappelling with a GriGri.)

*Known as a **reepschnur** in German, we often call this the GriGri system because rappelling with a GriGri requires fixing one strand of the rope. The reepschnur/GriGri system does this for us, and we can apply the tool in various other situations. Here it allows the guide to rappel on one strand because the junction knot is in the other. Rather than pass a knot on rappel, the **reepschnur** simplifies this transition and secures the clients below.*

9. The guide disassembles the plate with which he lowered the first client. Now he puts his device back on the fixed single strand (going down to the client) in rappel mode and clips into it with his extension.

10. The guide adjusts his position so he can see and/or communicate with the clients, then ties a big bight knot with *both* ropes below his device. (He ties the bight knot in both strands and uses this as his new masterpoint. By tying a BHK in both strands, he belays off both ropes. If he tied a blocking knot only on the strand below his device, he'd technically be belaying on the *reepschnur*/GriGri system. We prefer to have weight on both ropes through the rings rather than relying on a jammed *reepschnur*/GriGri system for a belay.)

11. The guide places a leash on the second client and lowers him using the big bight knot as a masterpoint.

12. The guide asks the second client to simply clip his leash to the rope going down to the first client.

13. The guide disassembles the lowering system, unties the big bight knot, and rappels.

If the guide has the second client rappel, he uses an extension and once he arrives at the landing, the guide makes sure he keeps his device on the rope and remains clipped into it.

TECHNICAL DESCENTS TO SHORT-ROPING

After a rappel, getting back to short-rope mode can be pretty consistent and simple. If it takes place in an area where you and your clients must be secured at all times, it complicates the rope management but the transitions remain basically the same.

1. In the event neither client is tied into a rope, as is the case in a pre-rigged rappel, one of the clients ties in. If using two ropes, the guide must tie the client in on the end of the rope he will be pulling (this choice is determined by the location of his junction knot above).

2. The guide anchors this client with a clove hitch if security is required.

3. On the backside of the clove hitch, the guide ties a cow's tail and clips his other client into it. The distance here is important because this will be the distance the clients will be apart as they descend the next section.

4. The guide ties a clove hitch on the backside of the cow's tail and clips into it.

5. The guide pulls the ropes, coils off, coils and stashes the second rope (if using one), unclips from the clove hitch on the backside of the cow's tail, and begins short-roping.

CHAPTER 10

Glacier and Snow Travel

S now climbing, glacier travel, and ice climbing all differ from one another, but one common element distinguishes them from hiking, rock scrambling, and fifth-class rock climbing—the use of the tools.

We use ice axes, ice hammers, and crampons, which at first seem like necessary implements to make handholds and footholds for ourselves, but these tools have greater impact than that. In particular the ice axe and ice hammer fundamentally change how we approach this terrain because we can embed the pick or the shaft into the snow or ice to give us another means of fall protection. Indeed, the primary function of the ice axe when on snow and glaciers is fall protection. On flat glaciers we carry ice axes to arrest crevasse falls, while in snow climbing we use them for fall protection/self-arrest, before we deploy the rope to the same ends.

Crampons function differently. We use them not exactly as fall protection, but rather to create footholds virtually anywhere we want. Readily available and well-positioned footholds facilitate repetition in our climbing. We adapt our footwork when hiking, scrambling, or climbing fifth-class rock, changing the length of our stride, varying it from side to side, etc. With crampons, we can generally keep our stride more consistent, allowing for better pacing and easier movement, making this form of climbing more efficient and less strenuous.

Ice axes and crampons fundamentally impact how we approach climbing—our physical movement, our psychological approach, and our technical systems. Consider for a moment just the additional weight of the tools, crampons, our boots, and our

Crampons allow a climber to kick a steady, relaxed line up a slope. Compare this to hopping between boulders in a talus field or connecting awkwardly placed footholds on a rock climb, and you'll see why snow and ice movement can be more efficient and easier. The climber's ice axe also belays each of his movements, giving him reliable security on steep snow.

extra clothing in the alpine environment. Unless we are actively and consciously taking advantage of this gear, upward progress can become tedious, tiresome, and plain hard!

A rock climber with no experience on glaciers or snow might consider her rope system as the first line of defense against falling, when in fact her ice tools are. Failing to recognize the advantages her tools offer and foregoing the predictable, rhythmic footholds only her crampons can provide, ice and snow climbing suddenly becomes exponentially harder than it need be.

Snow

Snow climbing is more related to second-, third-, and maybe easy fourth-class climbing on rock than it is to fifth-class climbing. Occasionally we'll pitch out steeper sections on snow, but it's relatively rare. Even when we do use that system, the ice axe functions as our main fall protection.

Short-Roping

Of course, if you are climbing with someone new to the sport or guiding, you may want to use the rope to protect them if you feel they're incapable of self-arresting. For the guide this is where short-roping can be effective. For the recreational leader short-roping can be used, but it will require training and practice on the part of the leader and only one, perhaps two, less-experienced climbers behind the leader.

The Risk of "Rope Teams"

An overused technique, in our opinion, is having three, four, or even five climbers on a rope 20 to 30 feet apart on a snow slope. Climbers imagine if one person falls, the others can self-arrest and stop the fall. This might be useful if the entire team is good at self-arrest, but the leader doesn't feel comfortable trusting everyone with self-arrest individually. If the group is not truly competent with self-arrest, there is a good chance a fall will pull everyone off. Stack multiple rope teams on a slope, and you have a recipe for one team to "floss" everyone off, causing a catastrophe.

So if a group were quite competent and well practiced and tested in self-arrest, using the team-arrest system would be a good hedge, but to be clear—it is at the expense of risking the whole party falling off the mountain. *This hazard should not be underestimated—by roping together, each team member is now exposed to the risk of every other team member falling, multiplying the chances of an accident.*

Short-Roping: Limits

Short-roping can be a quick, efficient, and safer means of moving a party over moderate terrain, but it needs to be kept in context. By shortening the rope and offering a moving belay to a less-experienced climber or climbers, we offer insurance from a slip becoming a fall—no more. If a slip could mean immediately weighting the rope with full body weight, then short-roping becomes ineffective.

The guide or leader uses tension on the rope, her eyes, and/or her ears to sense when a climber has slipped. She'll then have a moment, relying on her solid stance and rope tension, to pull the climber back into balance, preventing a fall. If the terrain or the guide's ability don't allow for this, then short-roping is not an effective risk-management strategy.

To Belay or Not to Belay

We mentioned a leader pitching out a section on which team self-arrest or short-roping doesn't provide enough security. As the leader leads that pitch, though, does she take a belay? Obviously taking a belay offers some protection in the case of a fall, provided the leader places some gear (a screw, picket, or deadman) during the pitch. A belay, though, can also slow the leader down, especially with an inexperienced belayer. In rare cases an inattentive or inexpert belay has caused a fall, too, when the leader was abruptly stopped because the belayer couldn't feed rope quickly enough. Consider the pros and cons and make a conscious choice whether or not to take a belay on easy terrain, where an experienced climber can self-arrest.

Pitching It Out

A party with too many climbers to short-rope, or a team unfamiliar with the technique, needs to consider upping its security by pitching it out. The team leader or guide at this point can quickly climb a pitch; set a belay with a picket, screw, or axe; and then belay his followers up, all of them tied in 7 to 10 feet apart at the end of the rope.

Guides do this frequently when the number of their guests exceeds the guide's ability to short-rope safely. And as for tying in as a "team," remember: Self-arrest is for a climber to stop himself, not another climber, and certainly not a group of climbers. Team arrest only works when multiple people can self-arrest to stop another person.

Relying on Self-Arrest (in Lieu of a Belay)

Climbing snow un-roped is fast, fun, and efficient, but if you're relying on self-arrest, you need to be prepared. It may seem simple, but you need to have your ice axe in your hand, in the correct position. You need to be thinking about self-arrest; it needs to be in the forefront of your thoughts. In short, do not be complacent.

If you're leading less-experienced climbers on a snow slope on which more skilled climbers would be un-roped, you should probably feel comfortable not taking a belay. Self-arrest is a reasonable and proper technique, so in the event you forego a belay (see sidebar), relying on your self-arrest skills is a fine tactic if the conditions and terrain warrant it.

Let's imagine you're pitching out a long, moderate (for you) snow slope. Because you feel dialed and comfortable, you leave your climbers at a stance and run the rope out a full length. Once you near the end of the rope out, you can either use a picket or your ice axe as an anchor (or a screw if there's glacial ice exposed in places). What you use depends on how much force you expect and the quality of the snow.

Snow Anchors

Snow anchors require special attention when choosing one and building it. Here are three things to consider when deciding what type of anchor to use based on the forces you expect:

1. The number of people you will be belaying.

2. The angle of the slope.

3. The "slipperiness" of the snow. Hardness mainly determines how slippery the snow surface will be, but roughness and dirt can both add friction.

Snow hardness not only suggests how slippery the snow surface will be, but it also indicates how strong a picket or axe anchor will be. Usually depth creates strength in an anchor; that is, how deeply you bury an axe or picket determines the anchor's strength. Knowing this, it would make sense to just dig a T-slot-style anchor every time. T-slots take time, however, and can be overkill in certain situations.

To Slot or Not to Slot

Let's run through this a bit. Let's say you are on very hard snow and just finished leading a pitch—a T-slot might take quite a bit of time to build and you would have to chop vigorously. Of course, while you are doing that, you likely have a significant falling hazard. So now you have your axe in a position to chop, so getting into a self-arrest position becomes more difficult. While chopping, you are making fairly big, strenuous motions, and because the snow is hard, a slip will quickly accelerate into a fall that will probably be difficult to arrest.

If the leader is able to use a vertically placed picket or axe, the time and effort to build an anchor will be shorter, exposing her to the fall for a shorter period of time. She may still have to hammer or drive the picket in, but that will require less time and focus. Building a T-slot requires hitting at various angles and often from various positions. If the snow is softer, the amount of time will be reduced, the force you swing will be less, and due to the

softness of the snow, a fall won't accelerate as fast. Therefore, choosing the right anchor style means a balance between how strong it is and how much time and risk it takes to build.

The Mid-Clip Picket

Up until now we have been comparing pickets and ice axes either driven vertically with the attachment point at the top or a T-slot with the picket or axe oriented horizontally, with a midpoint attachment. The newer "mid-clip pickets" offer a substantial improvement over traditional models. Right now one company we're aware of makes a picket with a wire attached to the midpoint—Yates.

We believe the superiority of the mid-clip will eventually replace the top-clip picket in most cases. In essence, the mid-clip picket forms a vertical T-slot that relies somewhat on the surface strength, but it does so much less than a top-clip picket. Attached to the middle, the cable pulls more evenly across the length of the picket, so it's less likely to pivot and fail, but a few centimeters of melted snow on top affects the holding power much less than a top-clip. Another critical improvement is that as one loads the mid-clip picket and pulls it downslope, it tends to drive the picket deeper, improving its holding power. If you're in the market for a picket or two, we strongly recommend the mid-clip model by Yates.

To place a mid-clip picket, you pound it into the snow, estimating the appropriate uphill angle.

The climber helps seat the cable by scoring the snow with the pick of his axe—not the adze. We see people use the adze, but it produces a channel nearly as wide as the picket itself, which risks weakening the placement.

Angles and Such

A topic of much debate and discussion, let's consider the angle at which we drive our anchors. We discuss ice screws in the chapter on ice, so for now let's limit our thoughts to the most oft-employed snow anchor, the picket.

When driving a picket, we keep two factors in mind:

1. Without some kind of protractor, you're estimating the angle at which you're driving the picket.

2. The variability of snow makes holding power vary considerably.

While some fundamental rules of thumb exist, snow anchors are generally far more difficult to judge and assess than ice and rock anchors. We usually have a good idea about the snow and its strength (its holding power or "integrity") because we've just climbed a pitch of it. Keep in mind, though, if you've just led a steep, shady pitch to a sunny ridgeline, snow quality may change dramatically in a few meters. A good rule, however, is that the harder and more slippery the snow, the stronger the anchor. The converse is true, as well: The softer the snow, the weaker the anchor.

Keep in mind, we're lucky that usually on softer, weaker snow we're getting better foot placements and more purchase with our axe(s). While our anchor is probably weaker, we're probably less likely to fall, and if we do, accelerate more slowly. These considerations must be kept in mind, in addition to the skill of our followers, our own skill, and the probability of falling.

BUT THE ANGLE?!

But enough talk—at what angle should you place a vertically placed picket? The top needs to be tilted back such that the load on the picket drives it deeper into the snow. If the top tilts too far back, however, it can get pulled downward so the picket then points downhill and fails out the

bottom. If it tilts too far forward, the picket can pivot and pop out the top. In short, when placing a picket, try to put it at the angle at which it pulls against the most snow.

Things get complicated when the terrain changes abruptly within your pitch or descent—for example, when you are building a snow anchor on sloped or flat terrain to belay or anchor someone getting lowered or rappelling down a steep section. Another tricky situation would be someone climbing from vertical or overhanging terrain onto a flatter top-out. You might have already remarked, "This is usually the problem in a crevasse rescue." Exactly!

In a crack rescue, we're going from vertical to overhanging terrain (where the victim's hanging in space) to much flatter terrain where we've arrested the fall. Often this is a sun-baked slope. Other less common situations exist, but no matter the details, in these cases a snow anchor that is robustly built, if not overbuilt, seems prudent. Remember, too, if we're hauling in a rescue, our forces begin to increase on the anchor. In weak snow this demands careful construction to achieve a bomber anchor.

The Axe as Anchor

For snow climbing our main protection is the ice axe. If climbing ropeless isn't realistic, pitching may be useful in protecting less-experienced seconds or when short sections of ice or steeper firm snow will be encountered and protection can be placed. In reality, on most snow slopes the old-school saying of "the leader must not fall" is still very relevant.

Pitching becomes much more useful on multiday climbs where the team has large packs. If you know there will be significant exposed snow climbing, the team may make the decision to adjust its packs so that one of them will be significantly lighter. This "lead" pack affords the leader the freedom of movement, making him better able to protect himself with the axe while climbing. It also makes building anchors more efficient and lowers the risk. The second or seconds can carry more equipment because they will be able to more or less just hike up the pitch. Cleaning snow anchors is far easier than building them, too. This strategy will be discussed again in the section on alpine ice, where it is even more important to employ.

Descending Snow

In our opinion, descending snow is best done on skis! That being said, there will be times when you will find yourself needing to go down a snow slope without those tools. Again, simply downclimbing without a rope is reasonable, but just as the rope is employed going up, it can be used in much the same way down.

For a team with one highly skilled member, or if the team is using the lead-pack strategy mentioned above, having him belay the team, then downclimb, can reduce the risk for the group. The belayed climbers tie in as they would on the way up, with one climber at the end of the rope, then one or two others on cow's tails 10 or so feet apart. Of course, if the last climber falls while downclimbing, he is likely to pull the entire party off. Some suggest that once the team is down, the top climber unties, drops the rope, and downclimbs—in this way he doesn't expose the others to a potential fall. Obviously, if the fear of pulling the party off is real, then maybe the top climber is overestimating his ability. In other words, if this is a concern, perhaps the terrain is too hard for the climber doing the downclimbing. That means another strategy needs to be employed.

Another option is the belayed, downclimbing members placing one or two pickets as protection for the top climber. If that level of protection is needed, however, it may be faster and more secure to rappel. Rappelling requires anchors that typically need to be left behind. So doing three rappels would mean leaving three ice axes and/or pickets.

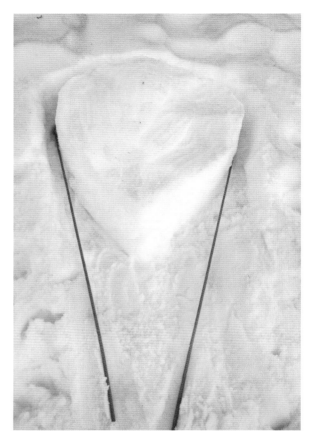

It's a bit of "garage science," but try to evaluate the snow's integrity and build a bollard big enough to be secure. Undercut the rear portion of it to guard against the rope being lifted up and off.

That is an option but may severely hamper progress farther down the mountain.

Fortunately, snow can be sculpted and is malleable, so anchors like the bollard can work. We can also bury things other than an axe or a picket; rocks can be used so long as their shape is such that a sling will stay on it. Of course, both of these have limitations—the bollard is time-consuming to build and rocks are not always available.

A Little Luck in Alaska

by Howie Schwartz

Howie Schwartz COURTESY HOWIE SCHWARTZ

Here's an old adage: "Good judgment comes from experience, and experience comes from bad judgment."

Technical skills do not replace good judgment in the mountains, but they may be helpful both to reduce risk and to respond effectively when things go awry. At any level of experience, some risk is unavoidable and bad things can happen. For those getting started in alpinism with relatively low levels of experience, some knowledge, awareness, and technical proficiency can be critical assets for survival and maximizing enjoyment of mountain endeavors. These same assets may sometimes get us into more trouble than we would like.

In my early 20s, I somehow got my first guiding job in the Wrangell–St. Elias National Park in Alaska, way before I knew much about how to guide. Before the start of the guiding season, I ventured one spring with two good friends to climb the highest peak in the Wrangell Mountains, Mount Blackburn. The North Ridge is a moderately technical Alaskan climb. We were exceedingly high in enthusiasm, middling in skills and knowledge, and fairly low in high-Alaskan mountain-climbing experience.

We skied our way up the massive glacier and onto the ridge. There we encountered a large transverse crevasse that barred our upward progress. We attempted to descend into the crevasse and climb up the other side, but the 30-foot overhanging wall above had faceted deeply and would not hold ice tools or screws, or even pickets.

It became apparent that we would have to either abandon our climb or risk a technical, 200-foot traverse on the east side of the ridge beneath a well-established and fully matured Alaskan-scale cornice. We knew we would be able to rappel the crevasse on the descent so we would not have to traverse under the cornice twice. The cornice overhung the slope we were on by more than 50 feet for most of the way. To this day, it is the spookiest place I have ever climbed. It took us over an hour to get completely across and back up to the ridgetop. I am still not fully sure what compelled us to take that glaring risk.

The climbing continued from there in spectacular form with beautiful alpine ice pitches in a grand Alaskan panorama. We used our developing skills to get ourselves high onto the mountain, where we were met by a storm. We spent an unplanned six days in a deteriorating and malfunctioning tent pitched wonkily inside a crevasse. We ran out of food and lost some important gear in high winds during a failed attempt to descend—a pack, part of the stove, and a sleeping bag. We learned a lot about how to go ultralight after that. Our collective general mountaineering skills and jovial spirit enabled us to survive, and even laugh about the situation a bit.

When the weather finally cleared, we were able to descend. The temperature was −40 degrees on a windless day and the lower ridge had accumulated 10 feet of fresh snow. We found ourselves descending through waist-deep snow across a narrowing ridge above the freshly loaded cornice on the right and a dangerous avalanche slope on the left. We decided to stretch out a 50m rope and travel with one person on each end and one in the middle—an unconventional and low-confidence plan. If one person fell off of the ridge in either direction, maybe at least one of the others could manage to jump the opposite way.

Two of us had just arrived safely at the belay on top of the crevasse where we would rappel when suddenly we felt the mountain quake violently. We could not see what had happened from our position. I went up to get a look and saw the unforgettable sight of a ridge missing a 50-foot-wide-by-70-foot-long section of snow, broken right at the edge of our track, with our rope descending into the abyss. Somehow, our third had taken a 70-foot swinging bungee jump alongside hundreds of tons of snow and ice, triggering a size 4 avalanche that traveled 6 miles. He had little more than a scratch and some soiled trousers to show for it.

Our improvised, last-ditch plan had somehow worked! Our pilot arrived to pick us up just in time to see one of us free-dangling off the ridgeline. Using practiced technical skills, we were able to successfully self-rescue, getting everyone back up to the ridge and down to our pickup location.

Close calls, near misses, and accidents can be fortunate or unfortunate opportunities to identify areas of expertise and judgment that we may be lacking in our mountain pursuits. This experience led me to very actively seek out more knowledge, mentors, training, and new experiences that would help me to better manage my risk and the risk of others, both personally and professionally. As a result, I became one of the first twenty American IFMGA Mountain Guides and an active member the AMGA Instructor Team.

Though technical proficiency cannot replace judgment, it might reduce the potential for, or the extent of, a bad situation as we aspire to grow from our mountain experiences.

—Howie Schwartz owns Sierra Mountain Guides in Bishop, California, where he lives with his wife, Karen, and son, Cosmo.

The Self-Cleaning Rap Anchor

One method not often used, but worth knowing, is the self-cleaning anchor. Few people know the technique and most climbers opt to downclimb, as rap anchors in snow present problems—the bollard can be time-consuming to build and rocks are sometimes hard to come by. The self-cleaning anchor, however, can be a better option than a sketchy downclimb, so practicing it a couple times is worth the effort.

To construct the self-cleaning anchor, we tie a short length of cord to the bottom of a vertical picket or axe, drive it vertically, then place another picket or axe in front of it horizontally. The rappel anchor is the top of the vertical piece. The two pieces are attached to each other at their tops via a shoulder-length sling. The idea is that after the rappel, a climber pulls down the side of the rope (more on this below) attached to a short length of cord (tied to the bottom of the vertically oriented tool). This ends up launching the vertical tool upward, pulling the horizontal piece out of its slot, and the whole anchor slides down the slope.

There are a number of ways to set this system up. With a single rope, you put the mid-mark at the anchor, then on the side you pull, tie a bight knot, and connect the cord to it. When rapping on two ropes joined with a junction knot, attach the cord to the rope you will pull. Lastly, you could use a pull cord with the rope attached to the anchor and the pull cord attached to the bottom of the vertical picket or tool.

The releasable anchor system works well, but the anchor can get stuck if it isn't built right or if an ice axe is used. There are times when the pick(s) will embed as the anchor slides down, in effect self-arresting, and because the cord is attached to the bottom of the axe, it won't dislodge. To avoid this you should use a picket or remove the pick of your axe and/or hammer if you can.

Although we use the term *rappel*, the climbers might find that just walking down using the rope as a hand line is more than enough to reduce the risk of a fall and speed up the descent. If the rope does get stuck because the anchor was built incorrectly, or a tool pick gets caught, going up is pretty simple so long as you have at least one axe with you. Since you can climb protecting yourself with the axe, you can always re-ascend, reset the anchor, and try again. This is one of the few applications in which the pull cord is ideal. If you are practiced with the removable snow-anchor systems, it often can be faster and more secure than just downclimbing.

1. There are two main techniques for the self-cleaning anchor. The first involves joining two mid-clip pickets. You start by passing the end of a thin pull cord through one of the bottom holes on the picket and then out the top hole. Connect the pull cord to the top hole via a bowline. Putting the knot at the top of the picket prevents it from sticking when trying to remove it.

2. Hammer the picket in, as you would to place it normally. After it's placed, slide it up and down in its hole; this helps with retrieval without significantly compromising the placement.

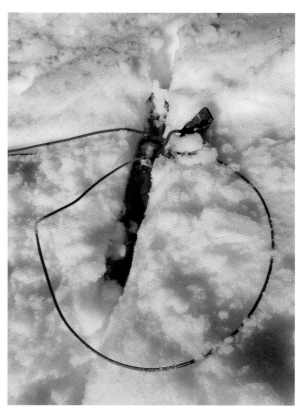

3. Place the second picket and clip its cable to the top of the vertically placed picket. Orient the second picket horizontally just downhill and in front of the vertically placed picket. The pull cord must exit the snow and run over the horizontally placed picket.

4. *Attach the rappel rope to the cable of the vertically placed picket with a locking carabiner. Gently move the vertically placed picket up and down, verifying it will pull upward when the time comes. Now rappel, keeping the end of the pull cord with you. Once down, pull down hard on the cord to get the vertically placed axe to displace the anchor.*

2. *Place the axe vertically with a picket placed horizontally and just downhill of the tool. Clip the picket's cable to the top of the ice axe. Make sure the cordelette runs over the picket.*

1. *To construct the ice-axe retrievable anchor, attach a cordelette to the base of the tool. If the knot at the base seems to stick in the snow, you can also feed the cord through the base and tie the cord to the top (as you did with the vertically placed picket in the first photo on page 210).*

3. *Feed the rappel rope around the shaft of the axe, with the middle mark on the axe. On either strand of the rope, tie a bight knot and clip the free end of the cordelette to a locking carabiner on it. After your rappel, you will pull the side of the rope with the bight knot on it, which pulls the cordelette down until it comes tight and pulls the ice axe out of the snow. This method is more prone to problems, as the pick of the axe can self-arrest in the snow, stranding your anchor above you.*

Glaciers

Snow and ice make up what we know as a glacier. For this reason, the decisions you make in those two mediums are generally appropriate when on a glacier in similar conditions. What the glacier has that is unique, and this is particularly important for snow-covered glaciers, are the crevasses.

If you find that the glacier is steep and melted out to the point you are climbing on ice, the crevasses should be obvious. On a snow-covered glacier steep enough to be concerned with a slip and a fall, you also need to be concerned about the crevasses. This can make choosing a rope system—long for protection against a crevasse fall, or short to protect a less-experienced climber or even pitched out—particularly difficult and especially consequential.

Ironically, it is often moderately angled, melted-out glaciers that can be very scary. With ice exposed, you might be on a very small slope that if it had a good runout, you'd feel comfortable just walking across, but if a huge crevasse waits below, it can be extremely threatening. Imagine four climbers strung horizontally across the slope, with a bottomless crack just below them. One member falls, and he'll probably take everyone in with him!

In short, with a snow-covered glacier you never know when you are exposed to crevasse fall; on an icy one you know all too well. For snowy glaciers steep enough (and/or with snow hard enough) to have a falling hazard, the crevasses are likely to be well bridged. Hard snow is usually strong snow. Nonetheless, there is still potential for a crevasse fall.

Bottom line, for glaciers you have to make an assessment: Are you more likely to fall down the glacier or into it? Once you answer that question, adjust your rope technique and climbing strategy accordingly. Long rope, short rope, pitched out? Make a careful decision and then execute it.

For all glaciers, route-finding is crucial; but for icy glaciers or steep, hard, snow-covered glaciers, it is often the primary risk-management tool. Since we have already covered how to protect ourselves from falling down a snow or ice slope, let's start looking at glaciers from the point of view of just having a crevasse-fall hazard. We will then look at situations during which we have both.

Glacier Route-Finding

Route-finding and terrain assessment present some of the hardest skills to master in the mountains. Teaching them in a book is an even greater challenge. We offer a couple points to help you start seeing the best line.

But what is the "best line"? On flat or low-angled glaciers where there is no falling

A Stuck, Retrievable Rap Anchor on a Glacier

A stuck, retrievable anchor on a glacier presents a real problem. Whether it was built incorrectly or the pick of the ice axe gets stuck, ascending the rope requires some thought. We suggest the following system, as it protects against a crevasse fall.

The climber who will remain at the bottom of the rappel ties into the rope.

The climber going up attaches a Prusik to the rope and slides it up as she ascends. If she falls into a crevasse, she will come tight to the climber below via the Prusik. Remember, this protects her in the event of a crevasse fall but does next to nothing in protecting her from a sliding fall down the glacier. There's a chance it might stop a slide, but she'll be relying on a partially removed or a fully removed anchor and stuck ice axe as an anchor!

hazard—only crevasse hazard—the best line avoids the most-crevassed sections. For steeper glaciers on which there is both a falling hazard *and* a crevasse-fall hazard, it means finding a route on which you can keep as direct (meaning straight up and down) a line as possible avoiding traverses, particularly those on steep terrain, above open crevasses.

Low-Angled Glaciers

Here are a few things to consider when navigating around crevasses on flat and low-angled glaciers:

1. Think of glaciers as flowing rivers and anywhere there could be turbulence, or "the river" speeds up, there is a higher likelihood of crevasses.

2. Turns on a glacier mean the ice on the inside of the turn is under compression and the ice on the outside is under tension. Depending on how sharp the turn is and the underlying bed surface, both edges can have crevasses—on the inside due to "turbulence" and on the outside due to tension or stretching. Oftentimes staying near the center may be your best option.

3. If two options exist when going around an obstacle (likely a crevasse but not always), try to pick the one that gives you the most flexibility. If one option tends to pin you to the edge versus moving toward the centerline, and both look equivalent, moving toward the center likely leaves you more options when you hit the next obstacle.

4. Utilize views whenever you can and, if possible, take a picture for reference. Once on the glacier your perspective may be limited and a picture may save you time.

5. Be decisive—sometimes you just have to pick a way. When two options around a crevasse/obstacle are possible and neither appears to have a greater chance of success, pick the one easiest to reverse and go find out if it works. Standing in one place agonizing over a choice that is unknowable only prolongs your ignorance.

Often you'll discover both would have worked and you just wasted time and mental energy.

6. Remember that the solution may be behind you. Reversing direction may seem like a huge waste of time, but indecision or forcing a solution rather than going back to try another option is the real time-waster. Going forward may feel more efficient, but going the right way is almost always the better solution. Error correct early.

7. There are unsolvable problems, particularly late in the season when bridges are melted out. Late-season glacier approaches may mean you don't get to do the route you want, and descents may be far more serious if you can't reverse the route you took to get there. Planning for alternatives is essential, and be careful to get good info if you are going to get yourself in a committed position.

Crevasse and *Falling Hazard*

Here are a few things to consider on steep glaciers that have both falling and crevasse hazard:

1. If it really is both steep enough to fall down and has crevasses, you will need to pitch it out.

2. Try to set yourselves up to climb straight up the fall line. Often you can get a good view of the steep section so you can line up with the straightest route.

3. Avoid traverses, particularly above crevasses, even if it seems to be more difficult to climb than traverse.

4. Anticipate crevasses when possible and try to make gradual diagonal pitches to get around obstacles rather than pinning yourself up against a crevasse and then traversing directly across.

5. If as a leader you do run into a hidden crevasse, consider reversing a bit and traversing around it so your seconds can take a more gradual line around it.

6. Even if it seems tedious, if you find yourself approaching a big crevasse with steep terrain above, anticipate the hazard and set a belay, then pitch it out. Trying to climb a short steep slope with a crevasse below while in traditional "long" glacier-travel mode is risky. On a short slope there will be no time to self-arrest, so pitching it out is the best option. Untying and soloing a short section may be safer than staying roped together, too, for a team of equally experienced climbers. *If soloing, you need to be confident there are no hidden crevasses.*

Roping Up for Traditional Glacier Travel

Roping up for glacier travel is unique in that we will not have an anchor to catch a fall. Up to this point we have advised you to resist the temptation to simul-climb in rock, snow, and ice, but on low-angled glaciers that is exactly what we will do.

It would be nice to have a reasonable alternative, but except for the rare circumstance, belaying is far too tedious for the distance we travel and the risk over that distance. Crossing thin or sketchy snow bridges makes an exception to this rule, but most of the time you'll just be walking up a consistent, low-angled hill.

Even with awesome views, a long, low-angled glacier can be mind-numbingly monotonous. This monotony is the first thing you need to battle because a surprise bridge collapse or crevasse fall requires you to be reasonably ready to self-arrest to stop the fall. This is even more important in teams of two, when only one person can stop the fall. In parties of three or four, you have more ballast on the team to arrest the fall.

Crevasse Rescue

What low-angled glaciers lack in physical difficulty to climb or descend, they more than make up for in technical difficulty if a crevasse rescue

is needed. Glaciers are often called easy hiking terrain—but that can quickly turn into the most difficult technical challenge that can occur in a typical climbing situation.

Many climbers consider rock self-rescue a technical challenge. Crevasse rescue may be shorter in that you usually only have to haul a victim 20 or so feet compared to descending two or three pitches of rock with an injured person. In crevasse rescue, however, you start from a point where you catch a fall without an anchored rope, and from that position you need to build an anchor and then perform the rescue.

Even to compare it to rock rescue is a stretch since rock rescue wouldn't be considered a typical climbing situation. Although we use the term *rescue*, hauling or ascending out of a crevasse is not considered to be the result of an accident—it is simply the reaction to a fall. So although glacier travel is something nearly anybody can do easily, catching a crevasse fall and extricating someone from a crevasse requires a high standard of technical skill.

Why can a rope team usually stop a crevasse fall, but often has no chance of arresting a fall on a steep snow slope? Generally speaking, crevasse falls occur on low-angled terrain without a falling hazard. On a flat slope or on soft snow, the arresting climber(s) don't risk sliding into the crack, so even if the climber(s) on top don't self-arrest, just their body weight slumped in the snow helps to catch the falling climber.

Imagine a climber falling into a crevasse downhill of his teammates—if the falling climber pull another teammate off her feet and toward the crevasse and she starts sliding, it's a far worse situation. Now the arresting climber(s) must stop a sliding fall and a crevasse fall—not good! This is why we must be cautious and lean toward pitching out anytime there is both crevasse *and* fall hazard on a glacier.

Luckily, though, the team usually has only to stop a crevasse fall. Arresting climbers are hopefully ready and can drop into a braced stance or self-arrest position. The bend of the rope going over and cutting into the lip of the crevasse aids the team through friction.

KNOTS AND FRICTION

In a party of two we don't have the ballast of several climbers dragging across the snow; we only have one person available to self-arrest and catch the fall. We do still have the 90-degree bend of the rope over the lip of the crevasse in our favor. The rope itself doesn't significantly slow the fall, but if we can enhance its friction, it can make a huge difference.

Because the rope often cuts into the lip of the crevasse, knots on the rope can add substantial friction. Knots slow down the fall, helping the victim's teammate to get into a solid position and catch the fall. Often the knots stop the fall entirely on their own, wedging in the slot cut by the rope at the lip of the crevasse.

Like many of our choices and solutions in alpinism, knots aren't without their problems, though. Knots in a rope between you and your partner will cause drag as you walk on a glacier; this can be very noticeable in the right snow conditions.

A trickier problem, knots create difficulties when ascending the rope and when hauling. Ascending a rope with knots in it can be tedious, but if the knots form loops (alpine butterflies) and are spaced such that you can reach from one to the next, then you can effectively aid between them to ascend the rope. This means that you should be conscientious when placing them in the rope.

Alternatively, you can always "jump" your friction hitch or ascender over the knots, which makes for a tedious ascent. Doable, but a pain.

Passing knots while hauling, although possible, is practically unfeasible. It's time-consuming and awkward, and if the victim has two or three knots in his end of the rope, it's usually the second or third knot that catches. This means that when the rescuer begins hauling, she might get the rope started, but if the knot closest to the victim pulled through the lip of the crevasse during the fall, it will probably get stuck when trying to haul it upward.

KNOTS IN THE ROPE . . . THEN WHAT?

Having knots in a rope means getting another strand or loop down to the climber in the crevasse. This at first may seem like a significant drawback to having knots, but in practice getting another strand or loop to the climber in the crevasse is often necessary even without knots.

When someone falls into a crevasse, it is likely that the rope will cut deeply into the lip. This means to ascend, the climber in the crevasse will have to surmount a significant overhang and to haul you'll need to chop a substantial amount of the lip away, swinging your axe dangerously close to a tensioned rope. Because of this we feel the advantages of knots in the rope for a party of two greatly outweigh the negatives.

In a party of three, however, knots are less necessary due to the ballast on the surface. Even though we recommend still planning to get a separate strand or loop to the victim, the drag generated by knots may be enough to tip the balance away from using them.

One exception is when one person greatly outweighs the other two. This is something a guide with younger rope mates needs to consider. Even a recreational team with a significant weight discrepancy should strongly consider knots between climbers in a party of three.

Roping Up

To rope up properly you need to consider how you and your team will attach yourselves to the rope and how to organize the spacing between members. Because we will need to be prepared to get another strand or a loop down to the climber in the crevasse, the climbers on the ends must carry some rope. That means no one is attached to the ends of the rope.

The easiest way to do that is to tie a bight knot like an overhand, or a figure eight, and clip it into you harness with carabiners (more on what type below). Of course, we could tie in directly with a triple loop bowline or an overhand/figure eight on a bight follow-through, but those could cause some significant problems if we find ourselves needing to detach from a weighted rope.

Since there is no anchor in the system, we need to be as versatile as possible, and not being able to free ourselves from a weighted rope would be imprudent. We've seen some people use a clove hitch as their attachment point, the argument being the biners will get loaded in their strongest (long) axis. Fair enough, but consider that you will probably not be able to get the carabiner out of the clove hitch once you've arrested a fall. You can probably unclip it from your harness, but the carabiner(s) will probably be stuck—which could become serious if you're short on gear, which we often are while traveling on a glacier.

Clipping In

We recommend a small overhand on a bight with two locking carabiners for the clip-in attachment on a glacier. You can also use a single, triple-action carabiner with a captured eye, like the BD Grid-Lock Magnetron. The captured eye prevents cross-loading, and the triple-action gate ensures it won't rattle open over the course of a long day.

Spacing and the Drop Loop

The roping-up process will differ depending on the number of people on the rope. By far the most difficult scenario is a party of two. With only two climbers, one person must hold the fall—a difficult feat in and of itself—but once the fall is held, that person must build an anchor, transfer the weight, possibly build a hauling system, and do the hauling. Because of this we will be setting up to use a drop-loop-style hauling system.

The drop loop adds efficiency by reducing the friction in the overall system. The drop loop is a 6:1 haul system that uses an anchored rope going down through a pulley/carabiner at the victim's harness, then back up to the anchor where a 3:1 haul system is built.

When not moving, the climber is suspended on two strands and the friction on the lip removes forces on the anchor. Once the haul begins, only one side of the loop moves, meaning that only half the friction needs to be overcome while the other half of the friction continues to aid the anchor.

If we were hauling on a single strand, when the climber was suspended in the crevasse, all the friction over the lip would reduce the forces on the anchor. When we hauled, however, all that friction would have to be overcome by the hauler and much of that force would go into the anchor.

In short, the drop loop is efficient because half the friction stays on the anchor side of the equation, meaning not only less force to overcome by the hauler, but also less force on the anchor (because it's being "assisted" by the remaining friction on the nonmoving half of the loop).

What the drop loop does require is the rescuer(s) having enough rope to reach the climber in the crevasse and come back up to the anchor. Remember, we're dropping a loop, so there needs to be twice as much rope available to do the haul. If the distance to the victim is 25 feet, the rescuer needs at least 50 feet of rope to effect a drop-loop system.

Oddly, as you will see, this means a party of two needs a longer rope than a party of three, and a party of three needs a longer rope than a party of four. This fact means that for pure glacier travel, a party of two carries more rope, so the temptation to not use the drop loop is strong. Despite that, as we said above, in a two-person team one person has to stop the fall, build the anchor, and then haul. Having the drop loop as an option is, in our estimation, very important in a climbing area where there aren't likely other climbers around to help. Think Asia and (most of) Alaska, rather than Chamonix and popular zones in the Cascades.

Because of the technical difficulty and the requisite knowledge required to pull off a haul of any type, many guides do not have their clients carry any rope. The idea is that if the guide falls in, the client wouldn't be able to stop the fall, build an anchor, transfer the weight of the victim onto the anchor, approach the edge of the crevasse, and build a haul.

Given what we have seen on guide exams, this conclusion is not without merit. This isn't an indictment of clients' inabilities. No, we mention it to illustrate the difficulty of crevasse rescue, *particularly in one-to-one situations*. The warning: Do not take crevasse rescue lightly. This is difficult stuff!

If the guide is carrying all the rope, she can more easily perform a drop loop. As you will see, having enough rope to build a drop-loop system, particularly for a party of two climbers, can be a problem. If the guide does carry all the rope, she needs to only rely on her client to stop and hold the fall. She can then ascend the rope to climb out. Guides may also feel comfortable because on a busier glacier other guided groups may be nearby to help, and typically these other groups will have plenty of rope to effect a rescue (see the "Team C" on page 223).

Virtually all guides carry two ice screws when traveling on a glacier. In the event of the guide falling in a crack, she can perhaps reach the sidewall of the crevasse and can aid out. For the recreational climber, having at least one ice screw each is a good idea; that way you may be able to anchor yourself to the sidewall, making the building of the rescue easier for your partners since they wouldn't have to hold your weight.

TWO-PERSON TEAMS

For the two-person team, each climber will have to carry enough spare rope to reach to his partner and back. Simply put, if a distance of 40 feet is used between climbers, each climber will have to carry 80 feet of rope. This means a total length of 200 feet will be necessary. If we add knots, however, we will shorten the distance between the two climbers, hence requiring the climbers to carry less rope.

We suggest three butterfly knots for each climber, starting 6 feet from the climber, 3 feet apart from each other. This keeps the knots closest to the climbers, which reduces rope drag on the section of rope between them. We like butterfly knots because they have a pronounced lip and they jam better than most other knots when pulled into snow. Having them 6 feet away from the victim increases the chances of the knots arresting the fall. Experience shows the first knot often slows the fall and allows the second knot to wedge or "catch" in the groove cut by the rope.

If we want our climbers to be about 40 feet apart, we have to add enough rope to account for the knots. Each knot requires about 2 feet, so with six knots we need to start with about 50 feet between the climbers, which is reduced to 38 feet once the knots are tied, giving each climber 75 feet of rope to carry.

THREE- AND FOUR-PERSON TEAMS

For three-person teams you will need to break up your rope into quarters. In other words, each end person will carry enough rope to reach the middle person. So if there is 40 feet between each person, the end people will be carrying 40 feet each. Ironically a rope 160 feet long will suffice for a party of three, while the group of two needs a 200-foot rope.

With four-person teams all the rope can be used up. If you want to be closer together, split the extra rope between the end people. For instance, if you wanted to be 40 feet apart with four people, you would need to use 120 feet of rope; if you were using a 160-foot rope, each end person would carry 20 feet of rope. For a 200-foot rope, the end people carry 40 feet each.

Setting Up a Haul

Once someone falls into a crevasse, one method to extricate the victim is to haul him or her out. We will start with a three-person team. In a two-person team we follow the same process, but it's more complicated because one person has to do all the work. In a four-person team the rescue is similar, except you have more people power.

The first thing you must do is stop the fall. The three climbers utilize the team-arrest technique. Once the team arrests the fall, the middle climber holds the victim using a solid self-arrest position while the third climber approaches the middle rescuer using her Prusik as a self-belay. The end climber then builds an anchor near the middle climber. After the third climber builds the anchor, the middle climber eases the victim's weight onto the anchor's masterpoint. The middle person then attaches another Prusik onto the rope between him and the end rescuer and attaches himself to it with a long sling, providing security for himself during the hauling.

The end rescuer can now go toward the edge of the crevasse protecting herself with her Prusik. Once there, she can check on the victim, clean the edge, pad it, uncoil the extra rope, extend her Prusik, and unclip from the rope, leaving only her extended Prusik as her attachment. She can now lower a loop down to the victim. It is important that she does not drop the end of the rope down the crevasse. At this point the victim can clip the loop into his harness with a locking carabiner.

THE HAUL

Now the rescuers are ready to set up the haul. First, a figure eight must be tied into the rope on which the rescuers have their Prusiks. This knot should be at least 15 to 20 feet away from the lip of the crevasse and in between the rescuers' Prusiks. Now the end coming up from the crevasse can be passed through a pulley/ratchet system on the new knot. The pulley/ratchet system can be anything from devices like a Micro Traxion, Ropeman, Tibloc, a carabiner-and-ascender combination, or a carabiner-Prusik combination. Some climbers use an Alpine clutch or Garda hitch. The rescuers then pass the rope through another pulley or carabiner attached to a Prusik below the ratchet.

Here is a step-by-step process for the hauling scenario with a party of three:

1. The team arrests the fall.

2. The climber at the end of the rope approaches the middle climber, using his Prusik as a self-belay.

3. He builds an anchor near the middle climber.

4. He clips the anchor into the middle climber's bight knot or into a clove hitch between himself and middle climber close to the middle climber's bight knot. The middle climber now shifts his position toward the crevasse/victim to weight the anchor.

5. The middle climber places a Prusik onto the rope between himself and his fellow rescuer and clips into it with a long sling.

6. The end climber approaches the crevasse still using his Prusik as a self-belay, communicates with the victim, and preps and pads the edge. (If the victim requires immediate help, he rappels to the victim at this point.)

7. He secures the end of the rope he was carrying onto his harness and drops a loop to the victim, and has the victim clip the loop into his harness with a locking carabiner. The end climber extends his friction hitch and unclips from his bight knot and unties it.

8. Either rescuer ties a bight knot into the rope that has their safety Prusiks on it about 15 to 20 feet away from the edge and between their Prusiks.

9. Either rescuer feeds the end of the rope through a progress-capture pulley on the new knot.

10. The middle climber places a tractor Prusik on the rope below the progress-capture pulley.

11. He passes the end of the rope through a carabiner or pulley on the tractor.

12. Both rescuers can now haul.

13. The end climber resets the tractor, and the middle climber manages the ratchet.

14. As the original rope that caught the fall gets slack, the rescuers tie a large bight into it to shorten it, securing the victim should there be a malfunction in the haul.

1. Three-person drop loop. Playing with fire! The climber in orange got too close to the crack and now he's gone inside. Because it's a team of three, they do not have knots in the rope and arresting the fall is easier with two climbers on top.

2. The end climber approaches the middle climber, belaying himself in on his waist Prusik.

3. The end climber first clips the cable of mid-clip picket to the middle climber's bight knot—not his belay loop. Once he's done this, he places the picket so that the cable is as tensioned as possible.

4. The middle climber gradually shifts toward the crevasse to transfer the load to the picket. While he does this he maintains a braced stance in case the picket fails. The end climber places another anchor—either a picket or a T-trenched axe—behind the first picket. He attaches the second anchor to the carabiner on the first anchor via a trucker's hitch. (The trucker's hitch is on the blue cordelette in the photo series.) In this way the team creates an equalized two-point anchor. Note the middle climber stays in a braced stance until the two-point is finished and loaded.

5. The end climber (green helmet) self-belays to the lip of the crevasse on his waist Prusik. Before the middle climber (red helmet) unclips from his bight knot, he places a Prusik on the rope going to the end climber—he must do this with a double-length runner or an extension to a short Prusik to allow himself to stand upright.

6. The end climber assesses the victim and decides whether he's rappelling to attach a drop loop to him or the victim can attach himself. In either case, he removes the stashed rope from his pack and connects the free end to himself so he can't drop it in the crevasse. He unclips and unties his bight knot, and is now only secured by his Prusik. The rescuer drops a loop to the victim with a locking carabiner on the end of the loop.

7. The end climber comes back toward the anchor and extends his Prusik, and either rescuer ties a bight knot into the rope between their two Prusiks.

8. The rescuers hang a progress-capture pulley on the bight knot and put the rope into the pulley. There are now three strands of rope going into the crevasse. One is tensioned; this is the victim's original strand on which the team arrested the fall. One strand has the bight knot the team built in step 8 (and in the previous photo). The third strand is where the team will place the tractor on the rope to create the 3:1. This will be a friction hitch or any rope-grab like a Tibloc. The rescuers pass the end of the rope through a carabiner on the tractor and begin hauling the victim.

Here is a step-by-step process for the hauling scenario with a party of two:

1. Arrest the fall.

2. Once the fall is arrested, if the team had knots in the rope (recommended) and if the rescuer has the weight of the victim on her, the rescuer should *slowly* creep a little toward the crevasse to see if a knot will catch. If she discovers a knot has already caught, or one catches as she moves toward the crevasse, she can reposition herself so the rope is taut. She must stay vigilant until she can build a bomber anchor, as a knot can pop and surprise a rescuer.

3. She builds a quick anchor and attaches it to her bight knot. In most summer snow, a Yates mid-clip picket usually works very well in this application.

4. The rescuer stays clipped into her bight knot, pulls out the extra rope, and attaches herself to it using a clove hitch. She can now unclip from the bight knot. Her new attachment (the clove hitch) extends her a bit so she can build a second anchor. Because the first anchor is a "quick" one, we want the rescuer to stay in the system and ready to take the weight of the victim (again) should the quick anchor begin to fail and the new clove hitch keeps her in the system.

5. Behind the quick anchor, she builds a more robust anchor (a T-slotted ice axe is common here).

6. Once the second anchor is built, she connects it to the locking biner on the quick anchor via a cordelette rigged with a trucker's hitch. The locking biner from the quick anchor is already clipped into the bight knot that came off her harness.

7. The rescuer places a Prusik on her rope and clips into it with an extension, unclips her clove, and belays herself to the lip of the crevasse with the Prusik.

8. Once at the lip, she checks her partner, then preps and pads the edge. (If the victim requires immediate help, she rappels to the victim at this point.)

9. The rescuer pulls the extra rope from her pack (or drops Kiwi coils), secures the end of the rope to her harness, and drops a loop to the victim and has him clip the loop into his harness.

10. Fifteen to 20 feet from the lip of the crevasse, the rescuer ties a bight knot onto the rope her Prusik is on, between her Prusik and the anchor.

11. She passes the end of the rope through a progress-capture pulley on the bight knot she just tied.

12. She places a tractor Prusik on the rope below the ratchet.

13. She passes the end of the rope through a carabiner or pulley on the tractor.

14. She begins the haul.

15. As the original rope that caught the fall gets slack, large bight knots can be tied into it to shorten it, securing the victim should there be a malfunction in the haul.

SPECIAL PROBLEMS

Two main problems can occur with the drop-loop system:

1. The loop is not long enough to reach the victim.

2. The victim is incapable of clipping the loop into his harness.

In the first case, the simple solution is to add a sling to the bottom of the loop. This effectively lengthens the loop twice as much as the sling is long. Once the victim has been hauled up enough to have the loop reach, it is often useful to transfer his weight to the now-shortened rope he was originally caught with. This allows you to then lower

When You Can't Rappel

If for some reason rappelling won't work, give this trick a try. Place a mechanical rope-grab onto the rope holding the victim so that it will slide down the rope. Connect the loop to the rope-grab and weight it (a stuff sack of snow works well) so it slides down to the victim's waist. When you pull on the drop loop, the rope-grab will lock up and you are able to pull the victim out of the crevasse. This trick won't work when the rope between the climbers is knotted, as is suggested in the two-person rigging, or if you can't reach below the lip to attach the rope-grab.

the loop down to him. We strongly recommend doing this because it can be very difficult to get the extended sling over the lip.

The second problem—an unconscious or incapacitated victim unable to clip into the loop—probably means rappelling down to the victim. This is the preferred method if there are first-aid considerations.

Rescuing Another Party

This book is not going to cover outside team rescue in most instances, but the crevasse situation is so unique that a process by which one team can help another needs to be covered. Two groups of friends or guides working together, or a couple of rope teams from the same club, is quite common on a glacier. Beyond that, you may be on a popular climb with other parties nearby. Especially on well-traveled routes, the chances of coming upon another party after a crevasse fall are pretty high. Having a quick, effective system with which to help seems prudent.

THE "TEAM C"

If you analyze the drop-loop system, you quickly see that the party arriving on the scene should be able to simply set up the drop-loop section (the "C," hence the name) while the victim's partners manage the belay on the victim's rope. Here is a step-by-step process for a team crevasse rescue:

1. Once a climber falls into a crevasse, the team arrests the fall, but does not begin building an anchor.

2. The party nearby has one of their end climbers carefully approach the edge, preferably crawling the last 5 or 6 feet to the edge to check on the victim.

3. At this point the climber preps and pads the lip, puts a Prusik on her rope if one isn't already there, takes out the extra rope, and clips the end to her belay loop with a locking carabiner.

4. The loop of rope is then lowered down to the victim and he clips it into his harness.

5. Now the rescuer unclips from her original bight-knot clip-in (*not* the new attachment from step 3), so she is only protected by the Prusik. Her team now starts to walk away from the crevasse, in effect hauling the victim up on a 2:1 system. This requires that she manages (releases) the Prusik so the rescuers can pull rope through it.

6. Once the rope that initially caught the victim gets loose, the climber at the lip frees it and puts it on the padded lip.

7. Now the victim's partners stand up and start to walk away from the crevasse, hauling on a 1:1 system in addition to the other team's 2:1.

During the haul the climber at the lip will feel a tug downward and could possibly get pulled into the crevasse. If that starts to happen, she should let go of the Prusik and that will stop the fall immediately. At first you'd expect the force to be significant on the climber at the lip, but if she takes a solid stance on one knee with a leg braced toward the crevasse, it is our experience in practice and in actual rescues that it is quite easy to hold the stance during the haul.

1. The team C. The team on the yellow rope arrests its teammate's fall. The team on the orange rope sends one of its end climbers to the lip of the crevasse to assess the victim's condition and set up the Team C.

2. The rescuer has approached the crevasse, placed a friction hitch on the rope (if he doesn't already have one on), taken out his extra rope, and lowered a loop to the victim with a locking carabiner on it. Note that rather than clip into the end of the rope, the rescuer lowered just enough rope for the victim to clip in, and then tied a bight knot and clipped it to his harness. All this does is shorten the distance the team must walk before engaging the haul. The rescuer can now unclip his original bight knot from his harness—the one on which he's been traveling on the glacier—and the team can begin the haul.

Self-Rescue/Ascending

After a fall, ascending out of the crevasse is a logical solution, but is more difficult than it may first appear. In the following discussion, we assume you've fallen into a crevasse while roped and you're ascending the rope on which you were traveling.

In many cases it may be hard to touch one of the walls of the crevasse, so you will be free hanging. You'll probably be wearing a pack, too, which can make it very difficult to stay upright. The other problem is getting over the lip of the crevasse if the rope has cut in substantially. Finally, the ascending needs to be done carefully and in a controlled manner, as you might not know what exactly you are anchored to. If you don't ascend the rope smoothly, you may cause some real problems for your partner or partners, who may be trying to build an anchor and transfer your weight onto that anchor.

All the same, if you can begin to ascend the rope on which you're hanging, you can shorten the haul your partner(s) will need to do or get over the lip before the haul can be set up. Ascending even a few feet might also prevent problems if your partner lacks the rope to complete a drop-loop haul. This is most likely in a party of two, so any help you can give your partner in that case will be valuable.

ORGANIZATION

Having your system ready and organized is important. A well-designed and practiced system will smooth out your ascent. The best way to set up is to use two ascending tools, either Prusiks (or a friction hitch of your choice) or mechanical rope-grabs like a Tibloc, Ropeman, or Micro Traxion.

The traditional ascension rig attaches the higher hitch/device to your waist and the lower one to your foot. This works best when using a friction hitch like a Prusik.

If you are using one or more rope-grab devices, particularly one that runs smoothly up the rope like the Micro Traxion, you can clip it directly to your waist and then have a foot loop on a friction hitch or rope-grab above it.

Quick Systems for Ascension

In an un-roped crevasse fall, especially if the most experienced team member is the victim, his teammates will probably elect to build an anchor, fix the rescue rope to it, and simply drop the line to the victim. At that point the victim will ascend the rope, hopefully to a well-padded lip and a quick escape.

Several systems exist for this scenario, from the relatively simple involving a climbing rope and Prusiks to new-school hauling rigs like Petzl's RAD (Rescue and Descent) System. Either approach involves building a solid anchor, then fixing the rope or system to that anchor, then throwing the free end to the victim in the hole. With the RAD System, partners on top haul the victim.

Particularly with the newer systems like the RAD, climbers and skiers should practice and test their skills *before* heading into the field. While lightweight and compact, these newer systems use thinner cords of different materials, which can be finicky once wet, frozen, or tangled. Practice up before relying on them.

Rigging the Rope-Grab

There are a number of rope-grabs out there and some may not be suitable when rigged at your waist. The one telltale sign is the cam should be spring-loaded; a passive device like the Tibloc is not appropriate at the waist. Check the manufacturer's recommendations and do some research before using a rope-grab off your belay loop.

SPEEDY, EFFICIENT ROPE ASCENSION

First we'll describe rigging a rope-grab device at your waist:

1. Once the fall has been arrested, place a locking biner and Micro Traxion, or similar device, on the rope a couple of inches above your tie-in or clip-in knot.

2. Set up a foot-loop friction hitch or rope-grab above that.

3. Place a foot-loop sling on the upper friction hitch or rope-grab. The length of this sling should be such that with the friction hitch or rope-grab at arm's length away when hanging, your leg is bent at 90 degrees.

4. To get started, place the foot loop just high enough that you can gain about 6 inches or so. Stand on the foot loop and clip the locking carabiner on the Micro Traxion into your belay loop on your harness.

5. Weight the Micro Traxion. At this point you should have a small loop of rope between your Micro Traxion and your clip-in knot. Take your pack off and clip it into this loop.

6. You can now begin ascending, sliding the foot loop as high as is comfortable, then standing in it. When you stand, your Micro Traxion should automatically slide up and your pack will move up only half the distance you do (because it's hanging on a loop).

Hanging your pack tensions the strand below your rope-grab. In this photo the climber's pack hangs from the Magnetron carabiner by his hip. This makes the ascension smoother and easier.
PHILBRICK PHOTOGRAPHY

The system described above has some real advantages and can be done very smoothly.

Nothing is perfect, though, and this ascension rig is no exception. While ascending, it is nice—even prudent—to clip into the rope every 10 feet, so if something goes wrong with your system, you won't fall as far. If you do this with this system, you will remove the weight the pack puts on the rope—this weight helps to keep the rope tensioned so the Micro Traxion slides up on its own as you stand on the foot loop. One practice lap with this system, and you'll quickly see how helpful the pack weight is. Also, instead of the pack moving up on a 2:1 system, it will be hanging below you, with you hauling it as you ascend.

We suggest ascending within 2 or 3 feet below the lip and clipping into the rope, then pulling your pack up and clipping it above your new clip-in but below the Micro Traxion. This is important due to the complexity of surmounting the lip. Until you get to the lip, the ascent should be straightforward and you shouldn't have had to go very much past that 10-foot distance. Stopping just before the lip to set this up is also a good time to relax, slow down, and assess the strategy of the next section. The lip will not be easy!

TRADITIONAL ASCENSION RIG

If you don't have a Micro Traxion or similar device, then using a traditional ascension rig is your next best choice. To use this system you'll need to have a sling or cord set up in advance so that your top rope-grab or friction hitch is within a comfortable arm's distance when you are hanging on it. Below that you need to set up a foot-loop friction hitch or rope-grab. The foot loop needs to be rigged so when hanging on the waist Prusik (or rope-grab) you can slide the foot-loop friction hitch (or rope-grab) up, to just below the one you're hanging on. Your leg should be bent around 90 degrees.

With this system you can keep your pack on, but if you like you can clip it into your rope as you did in the first system. Of course if you do, you will have the same problem clipping into the rope from time to time to protect yourself from a malfunction. We would recommend, as we did with the Micro Traxion ascent, that you at least clip in just before the lip.

PRUSIK AND ASCENSION CONSIDERATIONS

Often on a glacier we have suggested and will suggest that you protect yourself using a Prusik. We've mentioned doing this during the drop-loop rescue when the rescuer goes to check out the victim in the crevasse and in the three-person drop-loop scenario when the back rescuer moves up to build an anchor near the middle rescuer.

It would be tempting to use this Prusik (that is likely clipped short to your harness while traveling) as part of your ascent system. This would mean that the foot loop would be above the waist friction hitch. Why that doesn't work well is that when you stand on the foot loop, the rope below it hangs loose. You then have to slide the waist Prusik up the rope—far more difficult on a loose rope than on a tensioned rope. With the foot loop *below* the waist hitch, the rope is under tension and the hitch slides up much more smoothly and easily.

In the event of a fall, if you have a friction hitch pre-rigged on the rope, it should be pretty easy to unclip it from your harness. (It should be set up such that the rope takes the fall, not your hitch.) If you are using the Micro Traxion system, the hitch can be slid up to create the foot loop. With the traditional method, it can be modified with a short extension to be either your waist Prusik or your foot loop. If in the classic system you have a rope grab that is not appropriate for the Micro Traxion system (like a Tibloc, for example), then it should be connected to your waist, making it quicker and easier to push up while you're balanced on the foot loop.

Belaying across a Bridge—Teams of Two and Three

Crossing an obvious, sagging, spooky-looking bridge should put you on guard. Chances are you've already crossed some other sketchy bridges while roped and walking, but if you're looking at an exposed bridge, that means much of the snow on either side has already collapsed—heads up!

Stay vigilant when on a glacier; it's that simple. Stay especially vigilant if bridges are sagging and some have already fallen. It's real-world feedback that bridges are suspect.

If you are ascending and reach a bridge, the leader is likely to be able to cross without a belay. Why? Mostly because of gravity: Her rope team is in a strong position to hold the fall, being lower and having gravity on its side. Once the leader is across, however, the last person to cross is in a far more perilous position. The team now has gravity working *against* it. In this case a belay maybe prudent for the last team member.

If the team is going downhill, the leader should get the belay. The rest of the team crosses with the security of having at least one person downhill and in a good position from which to stop a crevasse fall. Of course, when we are talking about ascending or descending, we are talking about terrain low-angled enough or covered with snow soft enough that *no substantial sliding hazard exists.*

Things become more complex when the glacier is essentially flat. For a party of three, all the situations are pretty straightforward, as we'll see when we go through the transitions to belaying a bridge. In brief, parties of three have ballast that makes stopping most falls far easier.

A three-person team finds itself at a disadvantage, however, when two of the team are on steep terrain but the lead climber is below and falls into a crevasse. If one of the two climbers trying to stop the fall loses control, the remaining climber must now stop two victims—one in the crevasse and one

sliding down the snow slope. Smart money isn't on the lone climber at this point!

Generally speaking, though, a three-person team offers more security for crevasse falls and when crossing bridges.

The two-person team loses security without the extra ballast a third team member provides. Knowing this, when crossing bridges as a team of two, we're far more likely to stop, set an anchor, and belay with a traditional system.

Recall, too, that teams of two usually have knots in the rope, which complicates belaying (and hauling). To some, knots complicate the belay enough that they consider not using them; however, we see it differently. Given the likelihood of crossing hidden bridges, the knots offer enough security that the benefits outweigh the inconvenience of managing them while belaying.

Belaying a Bridge in a Party of Three, Ascending

First let's consider a party of three moving uphill, encountering a bridge, and belaying across. In this case the first and second climbers cross without a belay because of the advantage of their teammate(s) being downhill. The last climber will take a belay, though, because the first two climbers will be at risk of being pulled down and into the crack in the event of a fall. (We should mention here that if the steep terrain is significant in length, a transition to pitched climbing should be considered.)

1. When the last climber gets to the bridge, the leader and the second climber stop.

2. The leader takes a solid stance using his feet and/or incorporating a plunged ice axe.

3. The middle climber makes sure the rope to the leader is snug and takes a solid foot stance.

4. The middle climber puts the last climber on belay either by taking in the rope through a Prusik on her waist or using a belay device (or Munter).

5. When the last climber crosses the bridge, the leader and the middle climber begin moving forward. The middle climber simultaneously slides the Prusik along her rope until it comes tight to the third climber.

6. When there is no slack left, the third climber begins to move.

As you can see, we use the ballast of the two climbers as the anchor, making this very fast and efficient. If the bridge had collapsed, the middle climber could have held the fall quite easily with the assistance of the leader's tight rope. Once the pair arrests the fall, the top (former lead) climber comes down to the middle climber, sliding his Prusik along the rope to keep slack out of the system—protecting himself and backing up the middle climber's stance should she begin to slide toward the crevasse. The pair then effect a crevasse rescue as described earlier.

Belaying a Bridge in a Party of Three, Descending

For the party of three going downhill, the process is similar.

1. The first climber reaches the start of the bridge and stops.

2. The middle and last climbers descend a little farther than the bridge is long. While they do this, the middle person takes in the rope between herself and the first climber through the Prusik on her waist.

3. Once the middle climber and the last climber have moved down far enough to create enough slack for the first climber to cross, the middle climber belays the first climber across the bridge by feeding rope through the Prusik on her waist.

4. Once the first climber is across, the rest of the team can cross normally.

In this situation it may be prudent for the last climber to introduce some slack between himself and the middle climber as the middle climber crosses the bridge. The downhill climber will almost certainly be able to catch the middle climber should she fall in, but if the middle climber pulls the uphill (last) climber off his stance, he might slide down into the crevasse.

As the middle climber crosses, the downhill climber can turn and walk backward, as it's easier to keep slack out of the system and to watch the middle climber.

Party of Three on Flat Terrain

On flat terrain the party of three has lots of advantage, and it would be rare for them to feel the need to belay. If they do, it would primarily be for the middle person since it is hard for the other two climbers to easily work together. Who does the belaying—either the leader or the last climber—will be dependent on who is more capable at setting it up and any terrain features that would simplify it for either one.

1. The first climber crosses the bridge. When the second climber arrives at the edge of the bridge, either the first climber or the third climber begins setting up the anchor—it's a judgment call based on who's more experienced or in a better position to belay.

2. If the first climber is going to belay, she sets up right where she's standing. If the last climber is going to belay, he needs to move toward the middle climber while protecting himself with a Prusik. He must move forward a little farther than the bridge is long.

3. The belayer now sets up a quick anchor. We recommend a vertically placed mid-clip picket if the snow isn't too soft.

4. Once the picket is in, the belayer clips a locking carabiner into the anchor and into the loop of a Prusik on the rope.

5. Depending who is belaying, he or she takes in or feeds out rope through the Prusik.

6. Once the middle climber is across, the belayer cleans the anchor. If it was the lead climber, she removes the anchor and begins walking, protecting herself with the Prusik until the rope comes tight to the middle climber. If the third climber belayed, he removes the anchor and lets the middle climber keep walking while the rest of the rope runs through his Prusik.

7. The party then moves normally as the last climber crosses the bridge.

What is new in the above scenario is how we use the anchor to belay. We know we'll need to escape the belay in the event of a fall, and our attachment system can either make that escape easier or more difficult. Clipping the anchor to our belay loop would trap us between the Prusik and the anchor, making escape challenging, but by clipping the anchor into our Prusik—while we stay clipped into the Prusik, too—we create a two-point anchor system, the picket and us. With a little body English, we can easily loosen our locking carabiner and unclip in the event of a fall.

Belaying across a Bridge—Teams of Two

Because of the butterfly knots in the rope, the two-person transitions get tedious. The belayer needs to untie his knots to free up enough rope to belay, but then retie them when he crosses. This applies to both team members because they'll each belay the other. That's a lot of tying and untying at each transition, but maintaining security takes priority and we do it.

For teams of two the decision to belay becomes easier, because without two teammates on top, you need the extra security an anchored belay provides. So, in a sense it's an easier choice, but the execution presents problems. Knots in the rope mean lots of tying and untying.

TWO PEOPLE BELAYING A BRIDGE, MOVING UPHILL

Uphill and downhill bridges may benefit from the lower climber being assisted by gravity, but it's situation dependent. Traveling uphill is the simplest transition, so we will start with that.

1. The leader crosses the bridge and continues until the first of her partner's knots just reaches the start of the bridge.

2. The leader places an anchor—we recommend a mid-clip picket vertically placed if the snow is good enough—and clips her Prusik into the picket. She stays clipped into the Prusik as well.

3. As her partner moves forward, she takes in rope, removing her knots as they come along.

4. Just as she unties the last of her knots, her partner should be reaching the start of the bridge. The belayer will have about 14 feet of clear rope, which should be enough to belay her partner across the bridge without having to stop him to untie a knot (because her knots took up the same length of rope that her partner's did, and he stopped that distance before the bridge).

5. Once her partner is across the bridge, he stops and she removes the anchor.

6. The leader now moves forward, sliding the Prusik along; once she gets about 9 or so feet past the mid-mark, she'll tie a butterfly knot, 3 feet later another butterfly, then 3 feet after that another.

7. The leader keeps moving until she is out of rope and the party continues moving together.

We feel it is important for the belayer to have a clear rope while belaying her partner across the bridge. Having someone stop mid-bridge so that the belayer can untie a butterfly is unacceptable. By setting up the anchor just as the first of her partner's knots gets to the bridge, she can untie the knots on her end of the rope *before* her partner gets onto the bridge. This clears up her rope to give an uninterrupted belay while he crosses.

If you have placed your knots as we suggested in the roping-up section, you'll have about 38 feet between the climbers. Each climber will have the first knot 6 feet from his or her body, then another 3 feet later, and another 3 feet after that. The farthest knot on your half of the rope is therefore 12 feet away. That means there are 24 feet of rope with knots and 14 feet of clear rope in the middle. It is with those 14 feet we want to belay. If your bridge is longer than that, well, maybe you should look for another option!

The anchor system we use is identical to the anchor we used in the belay across a bridge with three people on flat terrain. Again, you don't want to complicate the rescue with a belay escape, but you don't want to have to build a monstrosity of an anchor for a quick belay. The system we describe allows you to use your stance and the picket together to hold a fall. It also functions as a quick anchor that can be backed up should we need to haul. (We used this system in the two-person drop loop described earlier.)

TWO-PERSON TEAM DESCENDING

If the two people are descending, then the system is similar.

1. The leader gets to the bridge and stops.

2. The uphill (second) climber moves forward, sliding his Prusik along to self-belay, all the while removing his butterfly knots.

3. Once the last knot is removed, he only needs to advance far enough to make sure he has enough rope to belay the leader across the bridge, likely not much farther than the last knot.

4. At that point he can build an anchor and belay his partner across the bridge using the Prusik-picket combination anchor.

5. Once the lead climber is comfortably across the bridge, she should stop.

6. The belayer now removes the anchor and moves forward using his Prusik as a self-belay. When he is about 9 feet from the mid-mark, he ties a butterfly knot. The leader then starts to move again—the second climber feeds out rope through his Prusik—but will stop in about 3 feet so that her partner can tie another butterfly knot. She then moves forward 3 feet and stops so that her partner can tie the third and final butterfly knot.

7. The leader continues to move downhill and the second climber starts to walk as soon the rope comes tight. He crosses the bridge and continues.

Although it sounds a bit complicated to retie the knots before the second climber goes across the bridge, it is prudent since the second climber will not be belayed, so the knots can really help. Of course, tying the knots should not expose the climber to a crevasse fall or force him onto the bridge prematurely. That will depend on how far across the bridge the first climber needs to go before she feels comfortable stopping. If the knots can't be tied into the rope prior to crossing the bridge, the team should either continue to cross the bridge as planned or the second climber should get belayed. That will depend on how steep the terrain is, how soft the snow is, and how comfortable they are with the bridge.

As with the three-person belay across the bridge, the most complicated scenario is crossing a bridge on flat terrain. This requires two anchors and the removal and replacement of all the knots. In the three-person system, we didn't need to remove knots and we only had to build one anchor.

TWO-PERSON BELAYED BRIDGE CROSSING, FLAT TERRAIN

1. The leader arrives at the start of the bridge and stops.

2. The back climber moves forward using a Prusik as a self-belay and removing the butterfly knots as she goes.

3. Once the last knot is removed, she only needs to advance far enough to make sure she has enough rope to belay the leader across the bridge, likely not much farther than the last knot.

4. She then builds an anchor and sets up a belay.

5. She belays the leader across the bridge.

6. Once the belayer runs out of rope, the leader stops.

7. The second climber now removes the anchor, and the leader and second move together until the second is at the start of the bridge.

8. The leader now self-belays back toward the bridge and removes his knots.

9. The leader now moves away from the bridge until the rope is tight and sets up an anchor and belays.

10. He belays the second across, and she stops when comfortably across it.

11. The leader then removes the anchor and starts to walk away, self-belaying with his Prusik and replacing knots in the rope—the first knot about 9 feet past the mid-mark and so on.

12. Once the leader has replaced his butterfly knots and runs out of rope, he stops.

13. The second climber now moves up, sliding her Prusik forward to the point where she needs to tie the butterfly 9 feet from the middle mark.

14. Once she ties that knot, the leader starts to walk forward. After about 3 feet the second ties another knot and then that process repeats. As soon as she ties the third knot and the rope comes tight, the team moves on as normal.

1. Two people belaying across a bridge. The leader arrives at the bridge and pauses.

2. The back climber uses his Prusik to move forward while removing the butterfly knots.

3. When he determines he has enough rope with which to belay the leader, he stops, builds an anchor, and connects it to his Prusik—not his belay loop. This connection is the red carabiner in the photo. By connecting the red carabiner to his Prusik, it becomes a two-point anchor (the picket and the climber). This is both more secure and also simplifies transferring the load should a crevasse fall occur.

4. The rear climber belays the leader across the bridge in a braced stance. He belays until he runs out of rope.

5. The leader has crossed the bridge and run out of rope. The team moves together until the rear climber arrives at the start of the bridge. The team stops.

6. The leader walks toward the bridge, self-belaying on his Prusik and removing his butterfly knots as he goes.

7. *The leader moves away from the bridge, feeding rope through his Prusik until he runs out of slack. He builds an anchor, clips it to his Prusik, and belays the second across the bridge.*

8. *Once the second is safely across the bridge, the leader removes the anchor and begins walking away, self-belaying through his Prusik and retying the butterfly knots at the appropriate locations.*

9. *Once the leader ties his butterfly knots and tensions the rope, he stops. The second moves forward from his position, self-belaying with his Prusik, to the location of the butterfly knot that will be farthest from himself. He ties it, then the leader starts to move forward and the second releases rope through his Prusik and ties the second and third butterfly knots in the appropriate places. Once the rope is tight, both climbers continue moving across the glacier.*

Maintaining Space during Transitions

We try to leave our excess rope stashed in our packs when performing these transitions. We do this to make sure we have enough rope to effect a rescue and to keep things simple. As soon as we go for our excess rope, we add complexity to the transition itself, but we also potentially complicate a rescue if we've used our extra rope to belay. Keep in mind that we need twice as much as rope available in the event our partner falls, because we'll use a drop-loop system to rescue him.

Having said that, if a bridge is long enough that we need that rope, you should deploy it and use it. It would be foolish for both of you to end up on the bridge or in a sketchy stance, only to have your excess rope in the pack. If you need it, use it, then problem-solve if a situation arises. It's more important to give an effective belay when your partner crosses a bridge than to avoid theoretical problems that may or may not come to pass.

Let's take a bird's-eye perspective for a moment, though. If you're on a bridge long enough and sketchy enough that you need most of your rope for a belay, it's time to consider whether or not you're in the right place and whether or not conditions permit traveling on this glacier. Don't force a route and risk an enormous bridge collapse because, remember, that person could take a huge pendulum into a crevasse wall. Rope or not, he's going to get jacked. Heads up!

Transitions from Glacier Mode to Pitching and Back

As we mentioned at the outset, there will be times when the glacier is so steep that moving together is no longer appropriate. It becomes impossible to protect against a crevasse fall, so pitching out increases the security.

The transition from glacier mode to pitched climbing can be quite simple if you feel comfortable not being secured by the rope during the transition. This is reasonable if a) you do the transition before you are at risk from the falling hazard, and b) you are as certain as possible you're not on a snow bridge. If that's the case, you can bring your team/partner to you by protecting him with your Prusik or by having him slide his Prusik as he approaches. Once all together you can break out the extra rope from your packs, tie into the ends (if there is a third climber, put him on a cow's tail 10 to 15 feet from the end), and begin leading up.

Unlike on a snow slope, however, it is prudent for the leader to take a belay. If the glacier has enough snow on it to feel comfortable for the leader to self-arrest, it is hard to be certain there are no crevasses lurking. And consider the opposite: If the glacier is snowless enough to know there are no crevasses, it is likely that it is icy enough to warrant a belay and some protection for the leader. Either way, the leader takes a belay.

Staying Protected throughout the Transition

The transition becomes tricky when the team wants to stay protected throughout. This could happen when crossing a crevasse below a steep section of the glacier. *Bergschrunds* pose the same situation. Often the leader will feel comfortable crossing the *bergschrund* in glacier mode because the slope is just starting to get steep and that uphill approach makes it pretty easy for her partner to catch a fall into the crack. Once across, however, the leader is now on pretty steep terrain and a fall into the bergschrund by her partner would be very difficult to hold, if not impossible.

Having neither climber tied into the end of the rope complicates things. Also, the leader is likely going to be belaying close to the upper edge of the crevasse or bergschrund, so rope management will need to be good so that a loop of rope doesn't end up hanging down into the crevasse and get caught on something.

Certain situations change the transition. For the first one, we'll assume you switch leaders once you go into pitched climbing. We'll cover more below.

Switching Leaders Going into Pitched Climbing

1. Once the leader gets across the crevasse and is comfortably above it, but before the next climber reaches the bottom edge of it, he builds an anchor.

2. The leader now takes his rope (between him and the next climber) and places a Munter hitch on the anchor.

3. The leader then takes out the rope from his pack, lap-coils it, and ties into the end.

4. He then anchors himself with a clove hitch using the rope he just tied into and hangs his lap coils across his new tie-in.

5. He then belays his partner(s) up to him.

6. If he has two partners, when the first climber gets to him, he ties into a cow's tail on the backside of the leader's clove hitch so that it will be appropriate spacing for the upcoming pitch.

7. The middle climber then unclips and unties the knot he had been clipped into, and the leader continues to belay the third climber off the Munter.

8. When the last climber arrives, he stays on belay or the Munter gets muled off. The last climber now takes out the extra rope.

9. As the third climber frees up extra rope from his pack, the leader adds it to his stack or coils he made with his extra rope and the rope he took in while belaying.

10. The last climber can then tie into the free end, grab any gear the others have, and begin climbing as the new leader.

*1. Transition from glacier mode to pitching. The leader has crossed a crevasse or **bergschrund** and stopped where he can belay the next teammate. He builds an anchor and clips into it with a **Munter hitch**, which counterbalance-protects him with his teammates.*

2. He takes the excess rope out of his pack and lap-coils it, and then ties into the end.

3. *He clove-hitches into the anchor (blue carabiner) and transfers the lap coils onto his tie-in. He can now unclip from his bight knot and remove the knot. Once he does this, he should maintain control of the brake strand.*

4. *The leader belays his climbers in and when the middle climber arrives, he attaches himself to the backside of the leader's clove hitch on a cow's tail (yellow and gray carabiners on his belay loop in the photo). The middle unclips his bight knot and unties it, allowing the leader to continue to belay the end climber into the stance.*

5. *The end climber (green helmet) has arrived and stays on belay on the Munter (orange locker on the anchor), takes out his excess rope, and lap-coils it. He finds the end and ties into it.*

6. *After he ties in, either climber puts him on a lead belay (in this case the climber in blue does so). The new leader transfers his lap coils to the coils made earlier. The leader unclips his bight knot, unties it, cleans the Munter off the anchor (blue carabiner), and prepares to lead out.*

7. *The new leader takes a deep breath and leads out.*

As we learned in the transitions chapter, some simple tools aid this transition, making it easier and giving the team more room to work.

When our leader first arrived at the anchor, he clipped into it with a Munter hitch and he was then counterbalanced with his team below. That allowed him to free up the rope he was carrying and tie into the end and anchor himself. Once that was done, the middle climber attached himself to the backside of the leader's clove hitch with a cow's tail. For the middle climber this becomes the attachment on which he will climb the next pitch.

Maintaining the Same Leader, Going into Pitched Climbing

If transitioning and the same person will remain leading (as a guide would), the transition is similar but a bit more tedious.

1. Once the leader gets across the crevasse and is comfortably above it, but before the next climber reaches the bottom edge of it, she builds an anchor.

2. The leader now takes her rope (between her and the next climber) and places a Munter hitch on the anchor.

3. She takes out the rope she has stored, lap-coils it, and ties into the end.

4. She anchors herself with a clove hitch using the rope she just tied into and hangs her lap coils across her new tie-in.

5. She belays her partner(s) up to her.

6. If she has two partners, when the first climber arrives, she clips him into a clove hitch tied on the backside of her clove hitch.

7. When the last climber arrives, she clips him into a clove on the backside of her clove hitch below the middle climber.

8. The back climber then frees up the rest of his rope and ties into the end of it. All the while, the leader adds the freed-up rope to her lap coils on her tie-in.

9. Once the last climber ties in, he clove-hitches into the anchor.

10. The middle climber then gets cow's-tailed into the backside of the last climber's clove hitch.

11. Both the last climber and the middle climber unclip from the backside of the leader's clove hitch.

12. The leader flips the lap coils onto the middle (most likely) or the last climber's rope.

13. The middle or third climber puts the leader on belay and she starts leading.

As you can see, this transition is a bit more tedious. The second and third climbers need to temporarily anchor themselves (steps 6 and 7) until the third climber can free up his end of the rope. The leader must also flip her lap coils. Most parties opt to anchor temporarily via improvised tethers (like a double-length sling), but we find that by using the backside of the leader's clove, the climbers have more room to work and it speeds things up.

A SHORT STEEP SECTION

One thing to note is if the steep, pitched climbing above the crevasse is short, it may be more efficient to keep one section of the extra rope stored. In a party of three with 40 feet between people, if they free up one section and the middle person reties 10 to 15 feet from the end person, the leader frees approximately 130 feet of rope on which to lead (assuming a 60m rope). In a party of two with 40 feet between the climbers, they free up 120 feet of rope by deploying one section of stored rope.

In a party of three of equally skilled teammates, it makes sense to have the first leader free up his rope. He's working alone at the top anchor and will have space to do so. When the new leader takes over, he'll have excess in his pack. If the pitch proves longer than the team estimated, it's a simpler transition to have the new leader deploy extra rope than having the two climbers behind do it—so, we elect to have the new leader leave the belay with extra rope rather than have the original leader keep his extra rope.

In the guiding scenario (the same person continues to lead), it's a bit more complex decision which rope you will free up. If the guide frees up her rope, it will make the transition back to glacier mode easier—since the guide will be quicker at putting the extra rope away—but if the extra rope is with the clients at the anchor, it is all but impossible to put it into service if the guide needs it. To get that rope into the system, the cow's-tail client (middle client) needs to unclip and then build a new cow's tail, not to mention leash in, etc. The end client would need to do a similar process.

Bottom line, it would be inappropriate to have clients do such a complex transition unassisted. So the guide must make a decision: If she decides to go short and have the clients keep the rope, she'll have to belay within 120 to 130 feet. If she wants to have the rope available, she will need to deal with a more tedious transition back to glacier mode.

Transitioning Back to Glacier Mode

The transition back to glacier mode needs to be thought out as well. Once you arrive onto terrain where the falling hazard no longer exists, it usually means the glacier is lower-angled or the snow has gotten softer. If the glacier has gotten lower-angled, it likely means that some kind of transition has taken place in the underlying bed surface of the glacier. That terrain change can stress the glacier ice, and crevasses must be expected. If the snow has gotten softer, the chances of a crevasse fall may not increase, but it's probably hidden and the softer snow also means any bridges may be weaker.

Whatever the case, surmounting a steep section and belaying your team into the anchor risks staging it on a hidden bridge. If you are reasonably certain there are no crevasses, this transition can be made simpler, as was the case when we transitioned into pitching. Remember, the reason the team was able to come together in the pitching transition,

though, was because they moved into the steep terrain already rigged in glacier mode. The team arrived where the ice was going from low-angled to steep, so they were in an area where the ice was compressed, meaning fewer crevasses. They were also in terrain that was more likely firm, so any bridges were probably stronger, too.

Balancing Fall Hazard vs. Crevasse Hazard

In a perfect world, we simply finish the steep climbing once the angle eases and we perform a relatively simple transition. It's the same transition a team uses when starting on the glacier—flat terrain and no crevasse hazard.

Most of the time, however, we don't have this luxury. We need to balance the fall hazard with the crevasse hazard. So as we move up the slope in pitching mode, we are always somewhat at risk of a crevasse fall. Every time the party comes together, it is in a high-consequence situation. That means throughout the pitching section we must continually assess the balance between the falling hazard and the crevasse hazard. As soon as we no longer see a falling hazard, we must transition back to glacier mode. In other words, once there is no benefit or little benefit to pitching, the risk we take to pitch out is no longer acceptable.

The team should transition where the risk of crevasse fall is lower. In many cases this means stopping before the angle eases, where there is still falling hazard but before the crevasse hazard begins. This transition requires an anchor at a crevasse-free spot, and the team then departs the anchor in glacier mode.

Transitioning Back from Pitching to Glacier Mode, Party of Three

1. The leader finishes the pitch, builds an anchor, and belays as normal.

2. As the seconds climb, the leader watches for the mid-mark on the rope.

To Lap-Coil . . . or Not?

You may notice at times we do not mention lap-coiling. In many cases the slope will be smooth enough that there will be no need to manage the rope; it is perfectly fine to allow it to hang down. If there are features in the snow like sastrugi or an open crevasse, though, the rope can fall and get snagged. In this case lap-coiling and dealing with it during transitions becomes necessary.

3. Once the leader has the mid-mark in his brake hand, he tells the seconds to stop, clips a clove hitch into the anchor before the mid-mark, and ties a bight knot at the mid-mark.

4. The leader continues belaying the climbers up to the anchor.

5. When the first climber arrives, he clips into the bight knot hanging from the clove hitch on the anchor, unclips from the cow's tail he used while pitching, and unties it.

6. The last climber then leads out, after taking any gear she might need from her partners.

7. Once the rope comes tight, the middle climber starts up.

8. Once the rope comes tight to the third climber, he starts up.

9. Once everyone reaches terrain without a falling hazard, the leader stops and belays the team toward her using a Prusik. Because the team is now above the falling hazard, she does not need to set an anchor.

10. When the middle climber is within 30 to 40 feet of the leader, the team should stop. The leader at this point ties a bight knot into the rope and clips it into her harness.

11. The back climber now belays himself using a Prusik in toward the middle climber. Once he gets within 30 to 40 feet of the middle climber, he ties a bight knot and clips it into his harness.

12. Now both the leader and the last climber can untie from the ends of the rope and store the excess rope.

You will notice that the climbers move together while some of the team remains on steep terrain. Shortly after the leader tops out, the middle climber starts, and the third climber begins once the middle climber tops out. This takes place at the top of a substantial falling hazard. The team must recognize this because this is a conscious risk taken to avoid all being exposed to a crevasse fall (by bunching up). The decision to do this must be made with a realistic appraisal of the team's experience and strength. A fall here would be catastrophic.

Two Climbers Transitioning from Pitching to Glacier Mode

The two-person team does a very similar transition, but the climbers will be 200 feet apart as they top out, so communications become more difficult. The other complication will be tying butterfly knots between the climbers. Here is that transition.

1. Once the leader tops out, he keeps walking back from the edge of the steep terrain.

2. When the leader runs out of rope, the second starts to climb.

3. Once the second tops out, the leader stops, places a Prusik on his rope, and belays the second toward himself.

4. The leader takes in rope till the mid-mark is about 9 feet away and tells his second to stop.

5. The leader then ties a butterfly knot into the rope between the mid-mark and his Prusik. While this is going on, the second places a Prusik on his rope.

6. The leader then walks away from the second, belaying himself with the Prusik, and places another butterfly 3 feet from the first, and then another 3 feet from that one.

7. The leader now goes 6 more feet and ties a bight knot, then clips it into his belay loop. He unties from the end of the rope and stores the extra rope.

8. The second moves forward to within 9 feet of the mid-mark and goes through the same process of putting knots in the rope, clipping into a bight knot, and storing the excess rope in his pack.

Transitioning from Pitching to Glacier Mode for the Guide or Citizen Leader

As the group nears the end of the steep terrain, the guide may suspect hidden crevasses where the glacier lessens in angle, at the rollover to flat terrain. If this is the case, the group must perform a transition to protect themselves.

For the club guide or citizen leader, giving her group responsibility to do the transitions described above doesn't seem overly aggressive, so long as the team has proper training and the climbers are not overly stressed. The same applies for the professional guide—if he has strong, reliable clients with solid technical skills.

If the clients or the club leaders' partners are tired, stressed, or aren't technically skilled, they must rig the glacier rope system for their clients before they leave the anchor. As we mentioned, guides often won't have their clients carry any rope on the glacier, so if the guide feels the need to pre-build the glacier system for the clients, the clients are likely not technically experienced enough to perform a drop-loop rescue—having them travel with extra rope doesn't serve much purpose. With that

in mind, the party performs the transition such that the guide carries all the extra rope.

THREE-PERSON TRANSITION FROM PITCHING TO GLACIER MODE FOR THE GUIDE

1. The guide finishes the pitch, builds an anchor, and belays as normal.

2. When the first client arrives, he leashes in.

3. The guide continues belaying the second client to the anchor.

4. The second client arrives and anchors in.

5. The leader measures out 30 to 40 feet of rope from the end client, ties a small bight knot, and has the first client clip into it for glacier travel (two carabiners, etc.).

6. The leader leads off.

7. Once the leader climbs past the difficulties, she stops 60-plus feet past the point where the falling hazard ends and belays (more on this below).

8. When the rope comes tight to the middle client, he starts up.

9. Once the rope comes tight to the third client, he starts up.

10. When both clients are off the steep terrain and when the middle client is 30 to 40 feet away, the guide has them stop.

11. The guide ties a bight knot into the rope and clips it into her harness, stashes the rest of the rope into her pack, and heads out with her team.

As you'll note, we have the middle client leash in so the guide can set up the spacing for glacier mode. The leash reduces confusion at the anchor when the middle client leaves. Using a backside system here may cause some real confusion as to what to unclip from when the middle client leaves the anchor.

In step 7 the guide belays. The belay may require an anchor like a picket, as when we belay across a bridge, or she might use a braced position using her Prusik. However she belays, she must feel confident in her ability to catch a slip. By using the Prusik, she is also protecting herself if she inadvertently stopped on a crevasse.

1:1 Guiding on a Glacier

When a guide has only one client on a glacier, it is likely that client will have a higher knowledge base. Should the guide fall into a crack, the client must be able to perform some basic tasks. This may be less important on a busy glacier where the guide can be assured other parties are nearby.

It is safe to say that in a 1:1 guiding ratio, the guide must seriously consider if the client has enough skill to deal with a crevasse fall. At the least, the client must hold the fall so that the guide can ascend her line out. For the guide, ascending out becomes more complex with knots in the rope. This makes it harder, but a guide needs to feel comfortable that if her client can stop the fall, she can get herself out.

Of course, it would be optimal if the client can build an anchor, transfer the load to it, safely get to the edge, and drop the extra rope into the crack. The guide will have a much easier climb out because the new strand won't be cut into the lip. If the client can perform at that level, then he should be able to tie a few butterfly knots and a bight knot with which to clip in, particularly with a guide supervising nearby. Knowing this, having the guide and client perform the same transition as suggested for the recreational party of two seems reasonable.

If the guide determines that it would be faster and cleaner to do some of the work for the client, the guide can perform a modified transition. This modified transition can be useful for the recreational team as well.

In the case of a two-person team—whether guided or not—a climber falling into a crevasse above the angle change would mean significant rope stretch since the party can be as far as 200 feet apart. In the three-person team, the distance between climbers is significantly shorter and so the problem isn't as severe.

There is an argument for one of the climbers in a two-person team to put some of the rope away and rig up for glacier mode at the anchor. When 1:1 guiding, the guide will help her client do exactly this, prior to leaving the belay.

If the guide doesn't want the client to carry any rope, she would do the same transition as the three-person team above, without having to deal with the middle client leashing in. The only addition is the guide may want to add butterfly knots to the client's end at the appropriate places.

If the guide wants to have the client carry rope, they follow this next transition.

TWO-PERSON TRANSITION FROM PITCHING TO GLACIER MODE

1. The guide finishes the pitch, builds an anchor, and belays as normal.

2. When the client arrives, the guide attaches him to the backside of her clove hitch.

3. The client unties from the end of the rope and begins to stuff it into his pack.

4. The guide finds the middle and starts to put butterfly knots into the rope. From the middle moving toward the client's end, the guide puts the first butterfly 9 feet from the mid-mark. The guide puts two more butterfly knots in, 3 feet apart, and then finally a small bight knot 6 feet from the last butterfly (the clip-in point).

5. The guide helps the client put his pack on, place a Prusik on his rope for glacier travel, organizes his system, and has him clip into the small bight knot for glacier mode (two locking carabiners).

6. The client clove-hitches into the anchor, unclips from the backside of the guide's clove hitch, and puts the guide on belay.

7. Once the leader climbs past the steep terrain, she stops 40-plus feet past the point where the falling hazard ends and belays.

8. When the rope comes tight to the client, he starts up.

9. When the client climbs past the falling hazard and arrives 40 feet from the guide, he stops.

10. The guide ties a bight knot into the rope and clips it into her harness, and stashes the rest of the rope into her pack.

11. The guide then belays herself with her Prusik toward her client and once she is about 9 feet away from the middle, ties a butterfly knot. She then moves away from her client, tying the next two butterfly knots 3 feet apart. Once she is out of rope, the team continues its climb.

Rope Types for Glacier Use

It is fitting we ended the previous section with some concern about rope stretch in a crevasse fall. Because of all the dynamic aspects to crevasse fall—climbers sliding on the snow surface and the rope bending over and cutting into the lip—it is becoming acceptable to use static rope. In fact, Petzl has conducted tests that suggest the spring/rebound nature of a dynamic rope actually makes it more difficult to stop a fall. Some of this information is new as of this writing so all the ramifications of it are not fully known, but the takeaway is that more and more people are using static ropes on glaciers.

Static Ropes(?)

Because static ropes do not require the kind of mass or material that dynamic ropes require, static cords

New Systems

It seems like another pre-rigged rescue or ascension kit hits the market every couple years. Petzl's RAD System and Mammut's RescYou ascender are both lightweight, compact systems, but we recommend practicing extensively with them before taking them into the field. Any super-specialized piece of equipment presents both solutions and challenges.

Edelrid's Rap Line II arrived on the US market in late spring of 2016. It remains to be seen how it's used in the field, but it's a potentially interesting advance. The Rap Line II uses three separate components—a nylon sheath, an aramid middle sheath, and a braided inner core—to act as a static cord to loads up to 7.2kN, but under great loads the aramid sheath "breaks" and the nylon interior cord offers a dynamic catch. It is *not* a certified dynamic or fall-rated rope at present, but when tested as a twin rope, it will hold two UIAA falls.

Maybe the perfect compromise on a glacier? The Rap Line II is intended for use as a tag/rap line, first and foremost. Engineers created the dynamic "backup" in case a climber needed to re-lead a section to retrieve his stuck dynamic rope. While glacier travel isn't its intended use, no doubt climbers and skiers will experiment with it due time. Worth watching.

tend to be much thinner. Using a tech cord can reduce rope diameters to as little as 5.5 mm!

As we said, the implications of this are still being sorted out. For instance, it is shown to be easier to stop a fall with a static rope, but in a two-person team we have been suggesting using a knotted rope. If the rope is 8mm or more, knots seem pretty effective, but what about in a 5.5mm rope? The main debate centers on roped-up glacier travel. Some consensus seems to be emerging that in un-roped travel (usually downhill skiing), thin static rope offers a lightweight, appropriate solution.

Conventional Cords, Static and Dynamic

Let's move past the super-skinny ropes for now and focus on a thicker 8mm-plus static rope. The first question we need to ask is, what about a steep section on a glacier that we would like to pitch? Using a static rope for a pitch provides very effective protection for the second(s), but a lead fall is an entirely different story. The question we need to answer is, what is our expectation of a lead fall on a steep section of snow on a glacier?

If we're pitching because we feel a team arrest won't work due to the steepness of a particular section, it doesn't necessarily mean a leader or more experienced climber can't individually self-arrest. The leader might be perfectly capable of self-arresting on a given slope. Knowing this, a team might be comfortable having a skilled leader lead a section on a static cord—assuming she can self-arrest were she to fall—and then provide adequate protection for less-skilled seconds. This is a judgment call, and one with potentially dire consequences should the leader take a fall on static cord.

Limits on Static

There is no question that a static rope limits what the party can do. Steep ice pitches on the glacier change the decision balance from static to dynamic, and, of course, if you are planning to do any rock pitches, this makes a static rope inappropriate.

Now this is where things get really interesting. What if two climbers are going to do some short rock pitches during a long route involving glacier travel as well? Well, if you are carrying, say, a 40m (120-foot) dynamic rope for the rock, then a very strong 40m, 5.5mm static might be appropriate if there is a rappel.

So if one person carries one of the ropes and is tied into the end of the other while their partner is clipped in about 40 feet away in glacier mode carrying the rest of that rope, then one team member has 120 feet of extra rope in their pack while the other has 80, and each carries enough to do a drop loop but one has a very light skinny rope.

The question becomes, which rope do the climbers use on the glacier and which goes in the pack? The old-schoolers might use the dynamic rope with knots, while the new-schoolers might use the skinny rope. The jury is still out whether it's easier, when in a team of two, to catch a fall on knotted skinny rope or on a conventional dynamic rope with knots. Time will tell.

Right now just be aware that skinny static ropes are being investigated and used in some cases. One last, important consideration: All your rope grabs will need to be specifically designed for skinny rope, and as far as we know, there is no material that is appropriate for a Prusik on a 5.5mm rope.

Bottom line, consider a static line on simple, relatively low-angled glaciers when pitching is rare, and start to look into the skinny version of the static for ski mountaineering.

Short-Roping on a Glacier

Because certified guides are trained and examined in the art of short-roping, they use that skill on a glacier when appropriate. Often a guide will have a considerable knowledge of the glacier on which he's working. That means he's seen the glacier in a wide variety of conditions and can be comfortable no crevasses (or very small ones) are in the area in which he will short-rope.

Significant falling hazard often renders crevasse hazards secondary. In those situations the recreational party may just decide to remain roped up in traditional glacier mode and simply not fall. A guide or experienced leader may deem the crevasse-fall hazard low enough and the fall-hazard significant enough that short-roping becomes the answer. Remember, though—*there is no benefit to short-roping when a team of equivalently skilled climbers are tied together on a rope.* Short-roping, by definition, suggests one climber is more skilled than her teammate(s) and further, that the leader has been trained in the application and technique.

So many may ask, why not pitch it out? The guide must ask that question as well. Short-roping becomes useful on traverses with significant falling hazard, when pitching is of little help. This happens when an open crevasse is a short distance below the team. Another situation suited to short-roping is a brief section of terrain with significant consequence, when most recreational parties would simply move through without any real concern.

The standard of care and of decision making for the guide is much higher than for the average team of climbers. Remember, the guide may have two or (watch out!) three climbers on her rope and those climbers may have just met a day or two before. The guide needs to understand that friends may accept the risks posed by the other climbers, but the guiding team has to accept that putting strangers together on a rope team requires a higher standard of risk management.

We are not going to get much beyond that as to when to short-rope on a glacier, since that decision requires high-level, professional training, but since we expect many aspiring guides will read this book (or at least we hope they do), we feel going over the technical transitions so that they can have a head start in their courses is appropriate. *We must emphasize that we see no useful purpose in doing these short-roping transitions on a glacier for the recreational party.*

As difficult as the decision to short-rope is, the transitions are simple. The fact that the guide is making the transition to short-roping means he feels there is little to no crevasse hazard and he's comfortable with the team coming together. In this situation, bringing in the group and changing the rope system should be easy.

What the guide must consider, however, is the transition back to glacier mode. Again, this may be simple because the guide feels comfortable about the lack of crevasse hazard, but that's not always the case. We mention in the pitching section the potential for crevasses to exist where the terrain goes from steeper to lower-angled, due to the tension of the ice over the convexity. In this case the guide will want to extend out quickly and over some distance as the party reaches lower-angled terrain. The rope systems we describe allow for this eventuality.

1:1 Short-Roping Transition

In a 1:1 situation, the transition to and from short-roping is very simple. When the guide decides to short-rope, she belays her client in using her Prusik. While she does this, she unties all the butterfly knots between her and her client. Once her client arrives, she coils off the rope and is finished.

When she decides to go back to glacier mode, she has her client stop and she uncoils the rope and belays herself out using the Prusik. As she moves, she ties butterfly knots in their appropriate places.

2:1 Short-Roping Transition

For the 2:1 transition, the guide belays the middle client into him with his Prusik, then asks the second client to belay himself in with his Prusik. As the second client approaches, the guide ties a bight knot behind the middle client, at the appropriate distance for short-roping. When the second client arrives, he clips into the new bight knot. The second client coils the excess rope and wears it on his body (no need to tie these off, as the bight knot closes the system). The guide coils the rope between himself and the middle client and ties off, as was done in the 1:1 transition, and begins short-roping.

To go back to glacier mode, the guide asks the clients to stop. The guide unties the knot securing his coils and starts walking away, protecting himself with a Prusik as he goes. Once out of rope, the last client unclips his bight knot (his attachment while being short-roped) and feeds out rope through his Prusik while the guide and middle client walk away, until all the coils are gone. The party moves together once the last climber is out of rope.

If the last climber is clipped into the rope in glacier mode (because the guide wanted him to be carrying some rope), it is important that during the transition this client unclips the appropriate bight knot. The bight knot for his attachment in glacier mode will have two lockers and only one for the short-roping clip-in point; differentiating should be easy but care should be taken to remind a less-experienced climber.

If the last client is tied in (rather than clipped), there is only one bight knot to unclip, so the situation is even simpler. Because we short-rope for only short sections, a single locker is usually appropriate (even more so if it's triple-action). Also, that single locker is made somewhat redundant via the Prusik on the rope directly behind the knot.

Descending

Descending on a glacier introduces a few variables to our transitions. While mostly similar to our transitions while climbing, we need to consider:

1. Crevasses in steep terrain, which we downclimb or rappel.

2. Steep terrain on which we walk while descending: A guide or very experienced climber with beginners will be conflicted whether to go first to route-find or last in an effort to provide more security against a fall from a teammate in the front.

We decide to rappel based on the same criteria when climbing steep snow, but the addition of crevasse hazard means just using the rope as a "hand line" may not be enough security. A rappel device, or at least sliding a Prusik along, improves security. A

Prusik, or an auto-assisted braking/rappelling device like a Mega Jul, offers the advantage of goings hands-free immediately after a crevasse fall, too.

As for who goes first as the party walks down, this decision will be highly terrain- and team-dependent. If the terrain is fairly low-angled and/or the snow is soft so that a fall will be easy to hold, then having the most experienced climber go first and route-find is likely best. As the terrain gets steeper, however, having the most capable climber above, ready to quickly arrest a fall, is likely best.

Flipping the team as the terrain changes also exposes the team to a bad situation (everyone lined up on a horizontal crevasse), so executing this maneuver with some finesse, and in a place where there is a low likelihood of a lurking crevasse, is important. The best way to do it is:

1. Have the back climber move forward sliding her Prusik on the rope while the team is stopped.

2. The back climber catches up to the middle climber and keeps going until she is fully extended again and near the lead climber.

3. Once there, the lead and the back climber can communicate and then the back climber leads off.

4. The previous lead climber now slides his Prusik as the middle climber approaches and passes.

5. Once the previous lead climber is out of rope, the flip is complete and the team resumes with a new leader.

In conclusion, there will often be times when it is very tempting for the party to come together to rest, do transitions, or communicate. Although we wouldn't suggest this is "never" appropriate, we feel it should be done with great discretion. For this reason, much of what we discussed keeps the party separated for crevasse-fall protection. We believe if these transitions are practiced, they can be done with little time disadvantage. The decision to come together to simplify or speed things up should be based on terrain, not on an inability to perform a transition efficiently, or at all.

CHAPTER 11

Technical Ice

Ice and rock climbing share many basic techniques in terms of leading and technical systems. That shouldn't, however, let us approach climbing ice in the same way as rock. Several fundamental differences require climbers to adapt and change their techniques when it comes time to climb ice:

1. The environment. Cold, short days and a wet medium create brutal conditions in which to climb. It might seem obvious, too, but the cold requires us to wear far more clothing than in rock. More on that below.

2. With so many sharp objects attached to us, falling is very serious business and to be avoided almost as a rule. Stabbing yourself, or more likely catching a crampon and injuring an ankle, can occur even in very short falls (less than a meter!), leaving you non-ambulatory in a harsh environment.

3. Icefall, whether climber-generated or natural, is common. Climber-generated icefall happens on virtually every pitch.

4. Ice can be more tedious to climb than rock, because the falling hazard on ice starts at a lower angle. Most of the time this potentially awkward, low-angle ice is alpine ice—and luckily we usually climb alpine ice in the summer, which means the cold often becomes less of an issue on this terrain.

These considerations may sound like deterrents, but ice climbing also offers advantages. If we identify and capitalize on these potential advantages, we can mitigate some or all of the problems described above.

Ice is a pretty small word that denotes a big, complex part of what we call climbing. Depending on the circumstance, ice can be climbed in a summer alpine environment, a winter frozen waterfall, a mixed climb that is traditionally protected, or a mixed climb that has a sport-climbing quality, along with an ice screw or two. Each style of climbing demands a different approach.

Low-Angled Ice: Alpine Ice, Waterfall Ice, Mixed, Summer Glaciers

Since lower-angle ice is a problem in all types of ice climbing, let's attack that problem first. Slopes of relatively low angles—sometimes as little as 20 degrees—present significant falling hazard, unlike the rock environment in which friction offers much more protection and guards against a slip turning into a potentially lethal fall. Consequently, we often must protect for a fall on ice in places where you would just be hiking on rock. This low-angle falling hazard can make ice more tedious and slower than rock.

Even though this problem exists in all the various forms of ice, it tends to be most common and extensive in alpine ice, with waterfall ice second behind that and then mixed.

Alpine ice: Long, easy sections of alpine ice put climbers in a quandary—solo for speed or rope up for security? If we solo, our survival

If it were a rock slab you might elect to forego the rope, but on ice this feature—lower Willie's Slide in New Hampshire—has significant falling hazard. More than one guide has been surprised and ended up at the bottom in a heap. No names mentioned!

literally depends on our ability to avoid a fall. Reasonable for some, but unrealistic for others. Usually we have the rope at our disposal, but breaking it out seems less efficient, mostly because of a perceived loss in time. We'll discuss these considerations below.

Waterfall ice: In approaching a waterfall, we tend to see low-angle hazards during early season or in low-snow years. Places like Lincoln Falls in Colorado or Frankenstein Cliff in New Hampshire often have a tongue of ice extending down the hill

from the "real" climbing. When thinly blanketed in snow, these low-angle features can surprise climbers approaching the steeper climbing above.

We usually encounter these sections on approaches but occasionally on descents, too. While challenging, luckily these sections are usually short. Some areas, however, have fairly long approaches up a streambed or drainage and without snow can be very easy, but a slip can have severe consequences. Again, to solo or not to solo? Does the rope come out? How to keep moving efficiently?

Mixed terrain: We sometimes face low-angle, tedious ice on the approach to mixed climbs. Thankfully the hazards are usually short-lived, unless we're getting into the alpine—alpine gullies can present prolonged sections of awkward ice. Taking too much time in these shady gullies can be boring, but also brutally cold!

Summer glaciers: For folks in the Pacific Northwest, western Canada, and Europe, "dry" summer glaciers often throw very easy—but hazardous—terrain at us. What can be roped-up hiking terrain early in the season is all of a sudden pitched-out climbing later in the summer, once the seasonal snowpack has melted off.

Solutions

Without an efficient strategy, the terrain described above can end up taking an excessively long time (a hazard in its own right) or be extremely risky if climbers "wing it" and simply solo out of habit or to emulate more competent parties. So how do we solve the problem of this awkward, low-angle but high-consequence ice?

MOVEMENT SKILLS

As with most climbing, good movement skills enable us to move efficiently while simultaneously lessening our chances of falling. Having a fluid, practiced suite of techniques in one's toolbox speeds us up and protects us. Especially on low-angled ice, effortlessly combining French technique with one's front-pointing and *piolet traction* saves energy, improves security, and increases speed. We assume most practitioners know the fundamentals of French technique, but could use some practice. To some degree it's a dying art and one in which we see vastly different skill levels within the guiding community. Review and practice if you're lacking.

When following and top-roping ice, use that relatively secure time to see how little you need to swing and how relaxed you can keep your movement. This will translate into more fluid, faster,

and more secure climbing when you're leading or soloing.

THE TOOLS AS BELAY

After movement, the next thing we can look at is using the ice tool, or tools, as our main form of fall protection. Your tools' picks act as your first line of fall protection in the event of a slip due to sloppiness, unpredictable ice, or an equipment failure like a crampon popping. Unlike a fall in snow climbing, during which you self-arrest by embedding the pick after you fall, on ice you need to have the tool planted prior to moving so a slip doesn't turn into a fall.

SOLOING

Low-angle ice can be tiresome, and with a big pack, bending over to plant your tool becomes uncomfortable and strenuous. For climbers with good movement skills, climbing unroped may be an option if the section is short or you are so inclined.

If you choose to solo, some things to consider:

1. Check your crampons. If a crampon pops off, it can be difficult to fix and can quickly create a fall.

2. Wear a harness. You are going to need to put it on at some point, so getting it on before you put your crampons on is always a good plan, just in case you need to clip or tie in.

3. Have a sling/leash and an ice screw on your harness. That way should something go wrong, you can quickly get a screw in and clip yourself into it.

4. If you are carrying two tools, have the second tool handy if you are not using it; you might run into a section where two tools are preferable or you might drop or break a pick.

5. Check for tripping hazards on yourself and your kit. Dangling slings, rope, clothing, or baggy pants and gaiters have tripped up many an alpinist, resulting in falls.

6. If you are soloing with a partner, climbing side by side or timing sections with your partner so you are not hit with climber-generated icefall helps manage the hazard.

ROPING UP

If you decide to rope up, you can still keep things moving quickly by using simple anchors and sparse protection. This means the leader is still taking risks but the seconds (or second) are far more protected while they climb.

If the leader carries four ice screws and some quickdraws, a couple of locking carabiners, and the rope, this will lighten the team's packs. If the seconds take most of the other gear, this should reduce the leader's load to next to nothing. This allows the leader to easily hunch over to protect herself by swinging her tool(s). For the seconds, the protection of the rope allows them to be more upright using more French technique, making pack weight less of an issue.

If the leader places only one or two ice screws per pitch and uses only one-screw anchors, this system can reduce risk for the party with a reasonable compromise on time. The key is to not push the steepness with this type of system. A good indicator of the appropriate nature of this system is if you are climbing in a party of three, you should be able to comfortably use one rope with the seconds attached 10 to 15 feet apart at one end. The seconds should be able to climb most of the pitch upright with the ice tool in the cane position without swinging their tools. If the climbing is harder than that, you should manage the problem with a more conventional rope system.

With a little strategic thinking, using the rope skills covered earlier, you can keep the system simple without incurring undo risk. When the leader reaches the end of the pitch, she should place a good screw into solid ice and clip a locking carabiner into it and lock it. Into that "master carabiner" she should clip another locking carabiner

and clove-hitch herself into it. She should then clip another locking carabiner into the master biner and, using either a Munter hitch or a belay device, belay the seconds up.

Because the leader has a lighter pack, the best way to proceed is to block-lead so the packs do not have to be switched each pitch. So once the seconds arrive, the Munter can be flipped into a clove hitch or the rope can be cloved into the anchor. Once the climbers transfer the gear and the leader goes onto belay, she can begin the next pitch.

Somewhere within the first 30 to 50 feet, the leader should place some protection. After that the leader can continue climbing and should consider another piece of protection somewhere between 100 and 150 feet up the pitch. The leader should try to stretch the rope as far as communication allows, reducing the pitch count and therefore the anchoring transitions. In big, open, low-angle alpine ice faces, this will be easy and 200 feet will seem short. In streambeds when you are approaching waterfall ice routes or in mountain gullies with bulges or doglegs, communication can be more of a concern.

The leader needs to consider icefall in this mode of travel. She can take a slightly diagonal line on more-open ice or use terrain features to protect her seconds from icefall. Thinking about how the icefall she generates will impact her team below is important.

FAST LEADER, FASTER SECONDS

As mentioned earlier, good movement skill is important and will make a difference in your speed. This is crucial for both the leader and the seconds. For the leader, reducing the number of tool placements will be relevant. This, however, should not be at the expense of security. Whenever your feet are moving a pick should be imbedded, except for the easiest of sections or very near protection.

To reduce the number of placements, the leader should place the tool as high as comfortable then climb up until the tool is about waist high. His

The leader takes a smaller pack so he can cruise the pitch, while the followers will have heavier packs but a belay for security. Climbing pitches this way speeds the whole team up.

hand should simultaneously moved to the head of the tool. At that point, with feet placed securely, preferably with the lower foot in a flat foot position and the high one in a front point (*pied troisième*), the tool is replaced and the cycle repeats. A steady, methodical movement pattern that is not rushed, but is crisp and precise, is best. The pace should be such that the leader doesn't need to stop and rest until the belay.

For the seconds, because the rope is protecting them, they should not have to place their picks. Rather, they should be upright and use the tool as a cane—*piolet canne*. If the team deems this style of climbing is too difficult, we recommend a more conventional rope system. *Piolet canne*, with the feet in *troisième* or front-pointing, can be less strenuous and helps balance out the difference in pack weight. In the end, we are trying to mitigate the extra time that using the rope demands by reducing the time the seconds take to climb a pitch.

SIMUL-CLIMBING

What about simul-climbing? The technique in which everyone moves roped together 100 to 200 feet apart, with a screw or two between the climbers, may seem faster, but we believe that the difference in speed between a simplified, pitched-out system that is well executed and simul-climbing is not worth the potential (and small) time savings, nor the additional risk.

In simul-climbing you increase the chance of a leader fall twofold. At any time if one or more seconds fall, they will pull off the leader, creating a potentially high-force fall, not to mention a tumble that will probably result in one or all of the team getting injured. Some would say to mitigate that you should place more gear. To do this the team needs to carry enough screws to climb a significant distance, because once the leader is down to his last screw, he will have to belay to retrieve more gear from the followers.

Some quick math: If the team places three screws per 200 feet to combine three pitches, they will need nine ice screws, and that is only if they can be a rope-length apart. Since if any climber falls it creates a leader fall, that means all climbers will need to climb embedding their picks. Unless the team is incredibly fit, they will likely need to stop from time to time to rest if they are climbing more than 200 feet at a time.

That stop-and-start pacing, along with coordinating the timing of placing and removing screws, with potentially difficult communication, makes simul-climbing far more difficult to execute and ends up only being marginally faster—if at all—with a substantial increase in risk. We aren't saying it isn't possible for an athletic, well-practiced team to benefit from simul-climbing on an alpine ice face or an approach to a waterfall, but we feel it is overused and underestimated in difficulty and risk by most teams.

Steep Climbing

Let's transition from artfully moving in low-angled terrain to tackling steeper styles of climbing. Steep mixed, sport mixed, and waterfall climbing demand a different set of techniques and another array of considerations as we venture into them.

Traditional Mixed Climbing

This is arguably the scariest form of technical climbing, as it combines the hazards and challenges of ice climbing with the insecurity of rock climbing. On top of that, protection can be suspect due to iced up, mossy, vegetated cracks and poor rock from freeze thaw! The combination of skills required is impressive, and watching even the best of climbers on a serious traditional mixed pitch can be both scary and tedious. Don't be surprised to see a spark from a pick being swung into a

Despite guide-turned-photographer Jay Philbrick's relaxed smile, trad mixed can be spooky!

crack or a glancing blow when placing a piton. In short, it requires a battle that is both mentally and physically exhausting.

The rope techniques used to climb this kind of terrain are more like fifth-class rock than ice. The movement techniques and tools use in cracks and flakes go beyond what this book is focused on. Climbers often use a half-rope system and generally in the non-approved technique of separating the two lines rather than alternating clips in gear placements. In mixed, protection is often hard to come by and suboptimal in some way.

There is little else to say but to be as prepared mentally, physically, and technically as possible. You need to be exceptionally good, inventive, and ingenious at placing rock protection; understand how to place a Spectre in grassy cracks and hummocks; and carry more short screws than you want to rely on. You need to milk any time you can take advantage of the efficiencies and security of waterfall climbing. Get laps in crampons on rock. Think light and stay calm is the best advice we can give. This is awesome, serious fun.

Sport Mixed Climbing

Don't mistake similar names for similar hazards. Sport mixed is a way mellower beast than trad mixed! If traditional mixed climbing focuses on the mental and technical skills of climbing, sport mixed climbing focuses on the physical, gymnastic skills. This powerful, athletic form of climbing is some of the most entertaining to watch. Because the tools create consistent handholds, it is easy for a spectator to imagine the difficulty. In sport rock climbing how a hold feels—whether it slopes, is sharp, or is tilted—has an impact on the difficulty, but that is hard to sense as a spectator. In sport mixed climbing, seeing someone move across a roof, legs hooked over their arms in a figure four, is fun to watch. The power, training, and focus the sport mixed athlete brings to a problem are remarkable.

The thing that makes it so fun to watch also reduces the risk; that is, the steepness lowers the

Clipping bolts can take a little of the stress out of sport mixed, but it's still no cakewalk. PETER DOUCETTE/MOUNTAIN SENSE GUIDES

potential for injury due to the climber's crampons catching on ice or rock during a fall. Because most, if not all, of the protection is bolts, it makes the technical aspect of fall protection simple. Often, sport mixed climbers are cragging, doing a single pitch and lowering off. Climbers can have puff pants and warm boots to belay in, then strip down and wear very specialized ice boots and thin gloves for the send.

Multi-pitch bolted mixed climbs do exist, but are still pretty rare. In the few that do get climbed, hauling a pack is typical and often due to the "roofy" nature of the terrain, the party is never too far from the base.

Waterfall Ice

Mixed and sport mixed are sexy disciplines, but by far the most popular form of steep winter climbing is waterfall ice, whether in an ice park or on a frozen cascade in the backcountry. These formations present specific challenges, as well as unique advantages.

ENVIRONMENTAL CHALLENGES

Cold—this simple phenomenon impacts our climbing more than we might think. It can affect our judgment, sap our strength, and limit our dexterity. We know a small drop in body temperature can have an impact on higher brain function. That body temperature drop also has a direct effect on fine motor skills. For your body to keep itself warm, it has to burn more calories, potentially taking away from your energy reserves, particularly late in the day. Of course, the cold increases the severity of any accident or incident that slows the party down or makes it non-ambulatory.

Make the most of your tools and crampons! PETER DOUCETTE/MOUNTAIN SENSE GUIDES

Because of the cold, we wear warm clothes and gloves. The amount of energy it takes to bend and move with a significant amount of clothing on is surprisingly significant. To get a sense of this, take your bare hand and open and close it twenty times. Now pull on a warm glove and do the same thing. If you are like us, you'll notice a difference.

Working hard in the cold helps keep a climber warm, but remember you're gripping tools, too. This forces the blood out of your hands.
PETER DOUCETTE/MOUNTAIN SENSE GUIDES

At first you might not think this to be significant, but now imagine the number of times you open and close your hands over the course of a day and then extrapolate that to every joint in your body. You'll quickly realize why ice climbing can be so fatiguing. Gloves have the added impact of reducing your dexterity when working with gear, too. Clothing and in particular gloves significantly affect your ability to perform.

SHORTER DAYS

We climb waterfall ice in the winter, and that means shorter days. This puts time pressure on the party, particularly for longer routes. This pressure can, when combined with the cold, create a sense of urgency in the party that may lead to inappropriate shortcuts, especially later in the day.

Advantages on Ice

We've discussed a few of the challenges that differentiate ice climbing from rock. Ice offers us significant advantages, too, ones that can mitigate most of the hazards described above. Doing this depends upon us identifying these advantages and utilizing them; they're not necessarily automatic, nor obvious.

First, we can rely on our ice tools as protection on easier ground. When leading, you can have one good, solid tool in place such that if something went wrong, you could clip into it or put your rope over it and it would hold—you are protected. This is a mental shift from rock. You might feel moves in rock are more "secure" than others, but you can't use handholds as protection.

Compare Your Screws

Ever notice the threads are mostly the same length between sizes, gold and blue Black Diamond screws in particular? What you're really getting with different-length screws is the ability to find better ice, usually deeper. If the surface of the ice is aerated or too wet, a longer screw allows you to access more solid ice beneath. In firm, solid ice a longer screw isn't necessarily better.

In ice, our tools are embedded and are not subject to fatigue. Plant your tool and you've got a "jug." This idea is again an extension of self-arrest in snow. It shouldn't be over-relied on, but on easier sections this should allow you to minimize your protection, which in turns keeps you moving, which speeds you up, which keeps you warm with less clothing.

Second is the repeatability of the climbing movement. It is unusual to have to figure out an ice move. Ice climbing, when done well, is highly repetitious. This means you can move at a steady pace, again keeping yourself warm and speeding you up. Of course, there will be awkward or unusual moves now and again, but if you have a good eye for a line, you can be very methodical in your movement.

Third, we can place an ice screw virtually anywhere the ice is thick enough. This means you can stop in comfortable places and reduce the strenuousness of the climb. Also, during sections where you are relying on your tools as the primary fall protection, you know you can always place something if you have a malfunction of a crampon or a tool breaks. It also means that you can carry less gear. In rock, not only do you need enough pieces to protect a pitch, you need the right size and type. In ice, you might carry a few different lengths of screws, but for the most part a screw is a screw, so you don't need extra to make sure you have the right type. Also, given that we do longer runouts with reasonable security, this also reduces the number of screws you have to carry.

Fourth, on lower-angle terrain (up to about the angle you would put a ladder up against a wall), the leader plants his tools for fall protection, not necessarily for a handhold. A second who is already

Angle of Attack

Much has been written about the angle of attack when placing ice screws. The primary manufacturers of ice screws suggest 90 degrees. For many climbers, tilting the hanger end of the screw downward has become popular, due to more recent testing. So which one?

For us, 90 degrees is the go-to. We do this because testing suggests that in good ice, placing a screw tilted down is strongest, but 90 degrees is plenty strong enough. In a placement in poor ice, tilted down is not as strong as 90 degrees. Because it is impossible to see air pockets and imperfections that define poor ice, if you place at 90 degrees you will get a plenty strong screw in good ice and the best screw possible in poor ice. So unless you can be 100 percent sure that you're placing in good ice, 90 degrees is the best bet.

Even with significant falling hazard, the second can stand upright and make good time . . . provided she takes a belay.

protected by the rope should not have to swing a tool. On these easier sections, a second should climb like she slab-climbs a rock pitch—by just using her hands against the ice for balance. This should speed up the second and reduce her swinging, which preserves her strength for when she's in the lead.

Climbers need time, discipline, and practice to implement these skills and techniques. Like all aspects of climbing, they can be over-relied upon or incorrectly applied.

SUMMARY

So we see ice climbing presents different challenges than rock, but a few unique advantages, too. On ice, more than in rock climbing, movement skill is critical in risk management. To an experienced ice climber who rock climbs, this fact is often intuitive and unconsciously accepted. It is not unusual to see a climber who does not solo on rock, solo on ice.

Why? Simply put, this climber realizes the significant advantage the embedded pick gives him in fall protection. He also knows that at any time he can place an ice screw and clip into it for security. The key is to take advantage of this knowledge, and along with the rope, to make harder climbs possible and minimize the significant and unique challenges waterfall ice climbing presents.

Icefall

One of the most consistent hazards in waterfall ice is icefall. When it's warm, you need to be concerned about natural icefall. When it's cold, the ice gets brittle and climber-generated icefall becomes common. Seldom do you have days out ice climbing where you don't have to manage this hazard in some way. Icefall is such an overall concern it impacts where we put belay stances and the rope systems we use when we climb in parties of three.

Let's look at the two types of icefall and how they differ.

NATURAL ICEFALL

Many climbers rank heat as the main culprit in natural icefall, but extreme cold or a rapid change in either direction can be triggers, too. Avalanche-savvy readers will note some similarities in certain circumstances. For example, hanging icicles act like the unsupported slopes of icefall. Whatever the source of stress—heat, intense cold, rain—if the ice is stressed, you need to think icefall potential.

Fortunately, ice tends to be stronger than snow, so natural icefall isn't as common or as difficult to predict. It is easy, however, to overestimate the ice's strength. Waterfall ice also has the added complexity of liquid water flowing behind it, through it, or above it from the source that feeds (or fed) the climb itself. If you think of the often counterintuitive nature of things you've learned in the avalanche realm and how much those phenomena are studied, it shows how much we may err when predicting icefall.

Well-supported ice is very strong. In fact, we place ice screws in it and they hold significant falls. There is no need to be paranoid about natural icefall, but being vigilant is always a good idea. Watch for overhead hazards of hanging icicles and try to avoid spending large amount of time under them. We will try to describe some things we have seen or heard of over the years. Remember, however, icefall hasn't received the level of study that avalanche hazard has.

When ice forms, it forms in equilibrium, and if it melts at a constant, low rate, it will melt in equilibrium; that is, the changes are gradual rather than sudden or catastrophic. How quickly the ice forms or melts directly impacts its stability. If too fast, or if the water flow is overly strong, you tend to get problems like collapses, cracks, or unstable pillars.

Hanging ice is always suspect. As soon as a column touches down, the strength increases significantly. Icicles can be very strong, and we have all climbed under fairly big hangers. One thing to consider is the sun exposure: Does the hanger get sun while you are lower on the climb, nice and cold in the shade? Try not to be fooled by the temperature right where you're belaying, if the sun is baking the upper parts of the climb.

Next, look at how the hangers are attached. Does the ice flow over the top, then hit an overhang so it has a solid top, or does the icicle hang from below the overhang? Sometimes water flows out of cracks in a roof, so the icicle appears to be glued to the roof. This means the icicle is weaker and the rock can heat up as well.

Umbrellas are another variety of hanging ice. These form when water flowing over the ice gets blown up in an updraft. While sometimes pretty, these formations can be unstable and terrifying, too. They look like a classic, curved window awning with teeth. Again, watch the sun on these formations. Some climbs have them regularly, like *Wicked Wanda* in Canada and *Parasol Gully* in New Hampshire. Other climbs form them in some years but not others.

Rapid temperature changes, either up or down, can trigger a collapse of hanging ice. Although it

A dangler like this can make for dramatic, memorable climbing, but can also present significant risk.
DALE REMSBERG

Umbrella ice. DALE REMSBERG

seems it can be either cold-to-warm or warm-to-cold, the latter tends to surprise more people. Remember, ice is thick and it takes some time for temperature to penetrate. A relatively warm piece of ice, suddenly flash frozen, will have a surface that's cooling off rapidly, while at the core the ice is warm. This can cause cracking and send significant chucks of hanging ice down. If temperatures have been moderate and then you have a significant cold snap, be wary.

Ice dams can create significant icefall, too. These most often occur when a climber strikes a section of ice under tension. Hydraulic pressure causes the tension. After a warm spell, particularly one with a little rain that is followed by serious cold, the water flowing through or behind the ice can get dammed. The flow freezes and the dam builds up pressure. Sometimes the pressure creates a wave pattern on the surface of the ice, with a flat ledge above it. Striking these formations may just produce a spout

of water, but in some cases it can be so intense, it will knock you off the climb.

CLIMBER-GENERATED ICEFALL

Climber-generated icefall is far more predictable—if there's a climber above you, ice will likely be coming down. Not exactly true, but pretty close. The nice thing about climber-generated icefall is you know where it's coming from and roughly when. While relatively small, with the right velocity and a direct impact, it can definitely do damage.

When a climber generates icefall, how far to the side it can travel is related to how far it has fallen. Its trajectory resembles an upside-down V. This means that if you are 10 feet below a climber and 5 feet to the side, your chances of getting hit are pretty slim, but if you are 100 feet below someone and 5 feet to the side, you are practically centered in the drop zone. Also, the ice gets going only so fast in 10 feet, but it usually has far more

The Sweet Spot

At popular spots like Lincoln Falls in Colorado or Frankenstein Cliff in New Hampshire, we often see parties climbing below other parties. If you must—and we're not saying it's a great idea—it's often smarter to be leading just below someone and to the side rather than waiting until he's 75 feet up. The sweet spot is 12 to 15 feet below and off to the side. This means any ice dislodged from the climber won't have time to angle too far to the side. You'll be far enough that the upper climber can't swing and hit you, but close enough that falling ice will be mostly below him.

As a friend once said, "If you're leading with your head up the ass of the second in the party ahead of you, it's hard to get hit with ice."

velocity after 100 feet. The one nice thing about ice is as it drops and hits things, it typically breaks up, so the chances of getting hit are higher but the damage tends to be a bit less.

This knowledge of trajectory should affect where you belay, how you time getting on a route below another party, and where you need to move quickly when crossing under other climbers. Many will say that climbing under a party should never be done, and on certain routes that's true. We know that one team to a flow is not realistic, however. We've seen crowded climbs and busy weekends and how tight things get with time pressure, etc. On some flows picking a line and timing your lead so that the party ahead is more to the side than above can work. Climbing midweek works better, though!

You'll have much better luck managing how your own climber-generated ice affects your belayer. We mentioned considering where you belay: Will it be under the icefall from the next pitch? On some routes, no matter how hard you try, there's risk to the belayer. In a party of three climbing in caterpillar mode, the third person ends up waiting while two people climb a pitch above him, potentially doubling the chances of getting hit. In a parallel system, we can often mitigate this, even though at first glance it appears the second follower

could be exposed to greater icefall hazard. Read on and we explain just how to do this.

PROTECTING THE THIRD CLIMBER

A little finesse and expert management in a party of three climbing parallel style helps, and this is where rope systems differ between rock and ice. We will use a number of strategies to keep the second follower (third climber) from having to suffer the consequences of the first second's icefall. Here we go:

1. Timing. The first follower climbs a section while the second follower stays off to the side. Once the first follower climbs to a ledge, he stops, allowing the second follower to catch up. In this technique we keep the climbers closer together, knowing that the shorter distance ice falls, the less it can hit climbers to the side.

   This is the simplest system for the leader. The leader climbs up the pitch clipping both ropes into each piece, just like parallel system in rock. That means there is no added stress in leading the pitch or worrying about the terrain assessment, other than for their lead. The seconds do all the work, communicating and making the terrain-assessment decisions.

   The downside is, without the seconds climbing simultaneously, there is little speed difference from caterpillar. The second follower

The higher climber can relax for a moment after a steep section, both to shake out and to minimize falling ice for the second follower.

does, however, stay warmer because he gets to move sooner than if he waits for the first second to complete the pitch.

2. Diagonal pitch. If the pitch diagonals a bit, then as long as the seconds don't get too far apart, the fall line for the ice is off to the side of the second follower. All diagonal pitches gain altitude, so the more the pitch climbs vertically, the closer the seconds need to be.

Timing and diagonal technique don't differ entirely, and often they can be combined. If there is a logical diagonal line, the leader does need to "see" it and follow it such that the seconds are protected. This puts some responsibility on the leader. The seconds will still need to make timing decisions, particularly if the diagonal is more zigzag. In that case, the first follower may need to stop for a short time as the second follower traverses under him to make the turn.

The more the seconds and the leader can incorporate the diagonal technique over the timing technique, the more it will speed up the party. Diagonal is fairly simple for the leader, as he can clip both ropes into each piece, but it

Diagonal climbing naturally protects the second follower from icefall.

requires finessing the terrain by the team. This is in most cases the fastest technique.

3. Separation. This means two completely separate lines of ascent. In parallel, if the leader separates the ropes so that her line (the line of the rope on which she takes a belay) is distinct from the line of the rope she trails, the seconds can climb independently of one another—more side by side than above one another. The leader can do this by using directionals or better yet, by building a well-planned belay stance over her trail line.

Separating the ropes requires a significant amount of mental energy for the leader and a fair bit of work at the anchor. First, the leader must separate the ropes to make completely sure there are no twists or tangles, as this could present problems for her while climbing. Second, if the ropes are separate for the entire pitch and then come back together, they'll likely form a bit of an angle at the plaquette, meaning they might not self-brake. The leader may need to use two belay devices, one for each rope.

This technique requires the most practice, demands good to excellent terrain assessment, and the leader must have enough bandwidth to lead competently, make sure the ropes remain

Separation means no risk of bombing each other with ice and the followers get to climb side by side, which is usually more fun. Seeing these opportunities on the fly allows the guide to deliver a much better experience for the guests. DALE REMSBERG

untwisted at each clip, and manage a more complicated belay. Team members can help the leader restack ropes, and when executed well, a separated system can be relatively fast and efficient.

The downside, though, is an unskilled leader can put herself or her followers at risk with a botched attempt at separation. Incorporate this technique on simple terrain with your teammates before using it in the mountains.

Guides employ separation, as it delivers a better client experience. It adds work to the guide's day, but on longer routes it speeds the party up. Whether guiding or just climbing with friends, the details and decision making required in separating ropes require care and attention to detail. Review the following synopsis to get an idea of the execution.

The leader must leave the seconds clipped in correct order at the belay, such that neither is trapped under the other's rope. The outside follower must have the backside of his clove hitch *over* the middle follower's tie-in. Remember the "outside-inside-under" mnemonic from stance management. Both ropes must be stacked or lap-coiled neatly. The leader must remove all twists before leaving the stance. He may have to untie from one of the ropes to do this.

The leader's choice of which line to climb determines the rope on which he'll take a belay. For example, if there is a line out to the right and one directly above the stance, he'll have to choose which one to lead. Should he leave the belay moving right and choose to lead the right line, he should take a belay on the rope going to the follower on his right. (The leader should consider clipping the rope going to the follower on the left through a carabiner on the anchor, just to keep it out of the belayer's way.) If the leader elects to climb the line directly above the

The leader heads out right, clipping a screw in the belay as he leaves.

belay, he'd take a belay on the rope going to the climber farthest away from him (on the left).

4. Pseudo-separation. This can be used on terrain on which a party almost feels comfortable using the low-angle technique of end-roping. If a leader puts only three or four ice screws in for protection on a steep slab, the leader can clip both ropes into each piece but the seconds can climb side by side. Since the protection is so spaced, the followers can be separated even though the ropes are running through the same protection. At each piece of protection both stop until it's removed, then they recommence climbing, staying side by side. The seconds need to feel comfortable, because there is a chance that if one fell, he might swing into the other.

All of these techniques have their strengths and weaknesses. What will determine the technique you choose for any given pitch are the climbing abilities of the leader and seconds and the terrain configuration of the pitch. By looking into the strengths and weaknesses of each technique, it should help identify the terrain in which to apply them.

Rappelling on Ice

For a recreational climber, rappelling on ice resembles rappelling on rock. Instead of clipping a fixed anchor, however, you will build most of the anchors you use with a thread.

Threads—Rope or Sling?

When building threads, we have two main choices—use a sling through the ice or thread the rope itself? If we decide on a sling, we need to acknowledge we're creating garbage at the end of the season, when it melts out. We also need to decide if we leave a carabiner or ring on the sling, or simply thread the rope through it. Adding a biner or ring means more garbage, and it's possible the anchor will get covered by more ice, so it's a pretty short-lived use for so much waste.

Adding a sling presents more controversy, too. Can we thread the rope through it? Some say no, but climbers have rapped through slings for years. In wet, damp ice, the risk of a frozen rope is real, so adding a sling might be a good idea, but then do you add a locker? Two non-lockers? Now we're leaving a sling and at least one locker, but if the ice is that wet (and potentially the rope, too), will it really melt the sling? How much will the rope move or saw in a rappel, anyway?

Predicting whether the rope can melt or abrade a sling is tough business. Certainly cold temps and wet material help guard against damage, but how much is a guesstimate at best. Inspect any material or anchor before clipping it and use your best judgment.

Rapping on ropes of different diameters can result in the rope moving at the anchor during a rappel, which effectively saws a rap sling. We've seen ropes move as much as 10 feet when the thinner rope travels more quickly through the rappel device, allowing it to feed out faster and the knot to begin creeping. A careful climber can reduce or stop the movement with attentive rappelling, but that's something a client isn't likely to know how to do. If you decide to rig rappel ropes of different diameters through a sling, put the fatter one through the anchor so it negates this sawing effect.

Ideally we can thread the rope in our V- or I-thread. Using the rope, sans sling, in the ice might be the environmental choice, but it presents other problems. Especially in damp conditions, the rope can freeze in the thread, making it impossible to pull. Huge bummer but hopefully avoided with some vigilance: The last climber down should make sure the rope is running smoothly in the thread before rapping.

BACKED-UP THREAD

Once a thread is built, you probably have a screw anchor as well since that was your belay. We would

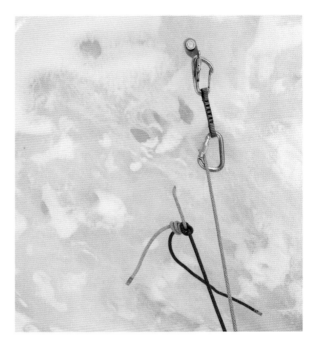

The backup screw is barely loose on the rope, so should the thread fail, the screw immediately takes the weight, but bears no weight as the first rappeller leaves the stance. DALE REMSBERG

suggest that before everyone is on his or her rappel device that you clip the anchor (or at least one screw) to the rope to back up a single thread. The backup should be slightly loose, but not taking any of the anchor's weight. If the thread were to fail or start to fail, the screw would take the weight. That way the thread gets a good test before the last rappeller removes the backup and descends.

Guided Rappels

For the guide, doing a multi-pitch rappel on ice has challenges that are rare on rock.

GUIDE DOWN FIRST?

It is common to back up a thread on an ice rappel, but if the guide goes down first to locate and build the next anchor, that leaves the last client to clean the backup. At first that seems reasonable, until we seriously consider the reasons for the backup. If an experienced climber saw cracking or heard creaking, she could make the decision of whether it was significant or not, to replace the thread, or to add a second. This may not be outside of a client's ability. We certainly don't want to make clients sound completely incompetent, but given the contract it seems that the guide should be the one making those critical decisions and relying on her judgment.

We know that threads are very strong and seldom does the backup seem important. It is almost a routine thing to do, as we often have a screw (or screws) in when we have a thread. If we are going to do it, however, we need to take it seriously. Having a client remove the backup isn't necessarily wrong, but we have to really think about how experienced the client is and balance that out with the alternatives.

There are two reasonable alternatives and one exceptional one:

1. Have the client remove the backup or don't bother even having one.

2. Send the client down first.

3. Leave an ice screw.

We've already discussed having the client remove it. Not having one might seem a bit extreme, but if we seriously bounce-test the thread with a backup and once satisfied remove it, we've in fact tested it as much or even more than rappelling will.

We could send the client down first, but he would have to build an anchor and/or remain protected from above.

Screws are easy enough to place, and because we have techniques to protect clients from above (from our alpine rock section), we know this is possible.

PROTECTING CLIENTS FROM ABOVE

First we'll cover how to do this with two clients and two ropes, in parallel mode. (If you are in caterpillar, it is virtually the same transition except the ends you thread and join come from the guide and the end of the rope on the middle climber coming from the third client. Because the ropes are separate, the rope handling and station management is easier in caterpillar.)

1. Guide arrives and anchors in normally and belays the clients.

2. When the clients arrive, the guide anchors them in with clove hitches.

3. The guide grabs the backside of the clove from the client who will go down second, ties a clove hitch into it, clips that to her belay loop, and unclips from her clove hitch.

4. The guide drills out the thread. While she does this, it would be a good time for her clients to stack or lap-coil their ropes.

5. The guide unties from her ends, removes any twists, feeds the end of the rope on which she'll lower the first client, then joins the ropes. The guide must make sure she threads the rope on which she'll lower the first client.

6. The guide ties a big bight knot into the rappel ropes just below the thread and attaches a backup sling from the anchor to the ropes.

7. The guide now builds an anchor that the first client will take down with him. This will be the anchor for the next stance. It's a leash girth-hitched to the client, connected with a locking carabiner to a prebuilt two-point cordelette. One way to carry this rig down is for the legs of the cord to be clipped together so they create a loop that fits around the client's head and shoulder.

8. Using the big bight knot as the masterpoint, the guide builds a lowering system (Munter or a plaquette) for the first client and lowers him down. When the client arrives at the anchor point for the next rappel, he places two screws and clips the pre-rigged anchor to them.

9. The guide takes the brake strand of the lower and ties a clove hitch and clips that to the screw anchor. This secures and protects the lower client.

10. The guide disassembles the lowering system and unties the big bight knot. She pulls all the rope she can through the thread until it comes tight to the clove hitch securing the client below. She ties a bight knot on that strand and clips it with a locking carabiner to the strand going down to the lower client. (This is the classic GriGri rappel setup.)

11. The guide unclips the clove hitch at the anchor securing the client below (the GriGri rappel system is now protecting him).

12. The guide puts a device on the single rope going down to the lower client and clips into it with a leash, then ties a big bight knot below her device using *both* strands of rope. Recall we do this so we're not belaying off the blocked knot, but rather on both strands of the rope through the thread.

13. The guide unclips from the clove hitch on her belay loop.

14. The guide puts the next client on belay using the big bight knot as the masterpoint. The screw anchor should still back up the thread.

15. The guide can lower or more likely do a belayed rappel for the second client. The rappel should be extended with a shoulder-length sling, girth-hitched to the client's harness. (If the guide lowers this client, the girth-hitched sling must be clipped with a locker to the rope going down to the first client. This will protect the second client once he arrives at the new anchor.) The second client should also have another sling he can use to leash into the anchor at the next stance (the anchor first client built in step 8).

16. Once the second client is down, he keeps his rappel device on the rope and clips into the anchor.

17. The guide disassembles the lower/belay, cleans the screw anchor, puts a friction-hitch backup on the rappel, unties the big bight knot, and rappels.

For a party of two with two ropes, the process is very similar but requires the guide leash in.

1. The guide arrives at the top of the pitch, builds a screw anchor, and clips in using a leash.

2. Once the client arrives, the guide ties a catastrophe knot on the brake strand.

3. The guide drills out a thread.

4. The guide unties from his ends of the ropes, threads an end (either one will do), and joins them with the knot of his choice.

5. The client unties from one end of a rope. The one from which he unties should be the one that was not threaded. The client stays tied into the rope that is through the thread—this is an important detail.

6. The guide ties a big bight knot just below the thread using the rappel ropes.

7. The guide has to separate the ropes.

8. The guide clips a sling with a locker from the screw anchor to the rope that's been threaded.

9. The guide puts the client on belay and pre-rigs an anchor system.

10. The guide lowers the client to the next stance.

11. The client puts two screws in and clips the pre-rigged anchor into the screws.

12. Once the client is anchored, the guide ties a clove hitch in the brake strand from the lower and clips it to the existing screw anchor. This secures the client.

13. The guide disassembles the lower and unties the big bight knot. He now pulls all the rope he can through the thread until it comes tight to the clove hitch securing the client below. He ties a bight knot on that strand and clips it with a locker to the strand going down to the client. This is the classic GriGri rappel setup.

14. The guide puts his rappel device and a backup on the strand going to the client, cleans the screw anchor, and descends.

We'll admit this technique is a lot of work and may be rarely used. Guides may feel more comfortable bounce-testing or even having an experienced client make the judgment call to remove a backup screw, or some combination of these options. Regardless of the frequency of using this technique and others, knowing them and having them as options in an unusual situation distinguishes the professional standard.

While pulling the rope through the thread at the end of a rappel, you shouldn't stop. The heat generated by pulling ropes may melt the ice a bit and then refreeze if you stop. It may take some force to get it back moving. We like to simultaneously thread the next anchor while we're pulling, as it prevents dropping the ropes. When you do that, however, you again melt the ice a bit due to friction. Remember to "unstick" the ropes before you leave the stance. The last climber should pop the ropes and verify they're running smoothly, then descend.

If you want to repeat the process of getting your clients down first, the procedure is similar. Once you thread a rope end, hand it to your client and have him tie into it. Now stack it as you pull it through the thread. When the junction knot arrives, tie the big bight knot, back up the thread with a sling from the anchor, and repeat the process.

On low-angled ice with long sight lines (like an alpine ice face), lowering your client down as far as possible and watching him place a screw or two, then clip into them, is often all you need to do. In this case adjusting the rope isn't necessary, because you're lowering him nearly the entire rope length. This will make this process much easier and quicker.

The above techniques are for rappels on steep terrain, with the occasional ledge. The ledges determine where the next anchor will be, and that's rarely a precise rope-length away. This means shortening the client's strand to manage the risk of his falling.

Ice: The Slippery Medium

Water ice is a slippery medium that presents a falling hazard at much lower angles than rock. Self-arrest doesn't work, and a reliance on tools opens you up to a falling hazard due to equipment failure. Make sure you properly perceive the falling hazard and do the basic things that are required when risk management depends almost entirely on your gear. Things like regular inspections of crampons, basic maintenance, and being ready for a malfunction by having a harness on, an ice screw racked, and sling prepared are the basics that are easily forgotten or ignored. Don't let complacency creep into your practice.

CHAPTER 12

Self-Rescue

So many books have been written on this subject that we considered not including it in this one. We expect that most of you already have a baseline level of self-rescue skills, and hopefully you own any of the books on the subject.

What convinced us to include some thoughts on self-rescue is the fact that many of the techniques can be used to solve problems not considered accidents. We hope to introduce some new tools, but more important, give you an expanded sense of the application of them—in short, how to apply your self-rescue techniques more often and how to incorporate them into your daily practice. Using our self-rescue techniques outside of the context of a rescue can help us, as climbers and mountain guides, deliver good client care, help increase client reward, and plain have a better time climbing.

Three Main Skills

When we think of true self-rescue, we think in terms of three main skills, all of which are simply techniques to move a hurt or incapacitated climber:

1. Hauling
2. Counterbalance rappelling
3. Tandem rappelling

Hauling. Hauling is pretty self-explanatory: We need to be able to build a mechanical advantage system to haul our partner up.

Counterbalance rappel. Counterbalance rappelling is for the most part unique to self-rescue and even unique to rescuing a following climber. To the uninitiated, it resembles a toprope up on

the cliff: the hurt climber tied to the rope, his rope running up and through an anchor, then down to a rescuer on a rappel device. For the rescuer and the hurt climber to move together, the rescuer connects himself to the hurt climber's rope. He does this affixing a Prusik to the patient's rope, then clipping it to his belay loop with a long sling and a carabiner. This connection has no real purpose when the climbers are together, except it makes both climbers move simultaneously when the rescuer feeds rope through his rappel device.

Tandem rappel. The tandem rappel has both the rescuer and hurt climber hanging on one rappel device so they can descend together. The rescuer ties a two-point cordelette, and what would normally be the masterpoint becomes the attachment to the rap device, with each climber clipped into the two legs.

Why not just use a counterbalance rappel, some might ask? With the counterbalance, for the rescuer and hurt climber to move down 1 foot you need 2 feet of rope to pass through the device. That makes the descent tedious and a bit jerky. Once the climbers can get to an anchor and build a proper rappel system, connecting both to the same device is much more efficient.

The goal of most self-rescue is to go from a typical leader or second belay to a tandem rappel and descend with the victim to the base of the cliff. Many times that requires a "pick-off" of the second from mid-pitch, so the counterbalance allows us to accomplish it. With leader rescue, the counterbalance rappel isn't as relevant. Similarly, when rescuing a follower who is close to the belay (and not

The Best by Silas Rossi

Silas Rossi. COURTESY SILAS ROSSI

I met Marc Chauvin when he was an examiner while I was taking my American Mountain Guides Association (AMGA) Alpine Exam in the Cascades. I was immediately impressed by the quality of his instruction and his feedback to me and other guide candidates. Marc's depth and breadth of understanding of climbing-related systems and techniques is unparalleled. In addition, Marc is a master educator, understanding exactly what his audience needs to know, when. He is able to break down his 40 years of experience and decision making into bite-size chunks that are easy to understand and apply—and convey them to students in a way that is relatable, logical, and fun.

For the last several years I've had the honor of co-teaching many professional guide-training courses with Marc. On one course in Rocky Mountain National Park the two of us and six AMGA Alpine Guide Course candidates were mock-guiding a moderate mixed route called *Dreamweaver* on Mount Meeker.

Halfway up the technical portion of the route, we caught a team that had just had an accident and were in need of help. We abandoned our objective for the day and offered our assistance as the rescue team. I did an initial patient assessment while Marc radioed for outside help. The patient had a significant, but non-life-threatening, lower leg injury. Without going into too much detail, we managed to improvise a 2,000-vertical-foot technical rescue with minimal gear in less than two hours. We left no gear behind and safely got our two teams of four people and the victim and his partner to the meadow below Chasm Lake before RMNP rangers arrived.

With the knowledge that a helicopter was on its way, we handed off the patient and his partner to the rangers and began our hike to the trailhead. I was feeling good about how things had gone on the rescue and was excited to get Marc's take on it. While Marc agreed that things had gone well, he wasn't interested in patting himself on the back for a job well done. He was already replaying the entire morning in his head and finding the weaknesses of the big-picture event.

"We did a good job," he said. "And we can do better. I want us to be the best. Not just the best in Colorado, not the best in the US . . . I want us to be the best in the world. And there's no reason we can't be that."

It's his desire to constantly improve that has elevated Marc to the level of expertise he has today. Marc's discipline and ability to reflect on the decisions he makes in a very objective way is what drives him to be so good at what he does. By the same token, Marc has not become the educator he is by accident. His progression has been purposeful and measured, and has allowed Marc to be at the cutting edge of his craft.

—*Silas Rossi is an IFMGA mountain guide based in New Paltz, New York. He lives with his wife, Cheryl, and their basset hound, Oliver.*

The rescuer transitions to a counterbalance rappel, and once he's close to the victim, he engages a friction hitch on the victim's strand and clips it to himself on his belay loop. PHILBRICK PHOTOGRAPHY

too seriously hurt), hauling him up to you may make more sense.

Ultimately, getting together with the hurt climber at a stance at which you can build, or already have, an anchor is the first step. After that, descending together in a tandem rappel is usually the best option for getting an injured climber down the cliff.

Looking at the big picture, we consider the entire process, from belaying until the point we can tandem rappel, a transition. How complex that transition is depends on whether the belay is above or below the hurt climber, what the distance is from the hurt climber, and the availability of terrain like

ledges, cracks, etc. The true expertise of self-rescue is the ability to use every advantage terrain gives you to minimize the technical difficulty of the transition from belaying to tandem rappel. In other words, cheat as much as you can.

Self-Rescue—Your Best Option?

Before we embark on the technical systems of self-rescue, we should discuss the appropriateness of a self-rescue. Self-sufficiency is a highly respected trait in climbing. That self-sufficiency needs to be tempered with reality. Once you get someone out of technical terrain, you will likely need help getting

To build a tandem rappel, start by doubling a 15-foot cordelette and tying a small bight knot at one end of the doubled loop. Notice the rescuer trapped the knot joining the cordelette ends inside the bight knot, or masterpoint. This protects the rescuer and victim from a junction knot failure, as the masterpoint is redundant. Try to make the two other loops slightly different lengths by offsetting them when you tie the bight knot/masterpoint—this allows you to place the victim below you during the rappel. You can also add a sling basketed through the victim's belay loop to extend her tie-in.

the injured person to a road. If you are going to get help for that, it may be prudent to get a rescue started sooner rather than later.

In some areas you might find a helicopter ready to extract you before you can finish first aid. In others you may wait for hours and find that only a small group is available to help. Executing a self-rescue is hazardous, difficult, and stressful. There are people who have trained extensively and are professionals working in some areas; to think you can do better or to ignore these professionals makes about as much sense as treating

someone for their injuries at home once you get down rather than going to the hospital. Of course, if you are in an area with inexperienced rescue personnel, you may very well be the most experienced person for some time. In that case, making your best effort seems the best choice. Remember, if self-rescue is your best option, make sure the scene is safe and do no harm.

Planning for Rescue

Any time you visit a new area, you should inquire as to the availability and quality of rescue. That can have an impact on what you bring and how you strategize your planned climb. It may seem strange having rescue in mind when planning. If, in fact, an efficient, professionalized team exists, you may decide to carry less emergency gear. If rescue resources are scarce, you might carry more or even plan a multiday trip to have more resources nearby.

In areas with ample rescue infrastructure (like many parts of Western Europe), you should use it if an accident occurs. It's hard to deny that traveling lighter has advantages: It increases your ability to move, lowers fatigue, and enhances your speed. Those things in and of themselves can derail an accident. Knowing you have competent rescuers nearby might allow you to leave a few items at home. To ignore available rescue infrastructure may very well create a rescue situation by virtue of having too much gear along. Climbers must balance how much "in case" equipment they bring against the potential of that very equipment contributing to an accident.

If you do find yourself in a region with professional rescue personnel and helicopter access, consider the weather. The ability to fly needs to be considered. Can the helicopter fly? Professional pilots can often fly in weather worse than we want to climb in, but give some thought to your particular situation.

With this said, let's get into the nuts and bolts of self-rescue.

Second Rescue Hauling

Hauling is less about rescue than it is about problem solving. Truly hauling an injured climber should be rare. If the injury is minor, or is an upper-body injury like a shoulder the climber can guard, then it might be considered reasonable. A lower-leg injury might be manageable for a short distance. The idea, however, that you can haul a seriously injured or unconscious climber any distance is a fantasy. Without some assistance from the injured climber, it will be next to impossible to overcome the friction of his body on the rock. A serious leg injury would be extremely painful, if not unbearable, if the victim must hop along as you haul her.

Normally we haul and assist climbers with minor injuries, when they're close to the belay, or just partners who can't get past a particular move. In these situations, when the climber can assist with our hauling, the process is far easier.

When using a plaquette in guide mode, it makes building a haul system quick and easy:

3:1 Haul from a Plaquette in Guide Mode

1. Tie a catastrophe knot into the brake strand.
2. Place a friction hitch on the rope going down to the stuck climber.
3. Clip the brake strand into the friction hitch and remove the catastrophe knot.
4. Pull.

Improving Efficiency

If you're using a Prusik or sling longer than about a foot (a shoulder-length sling is two feet, for example), consider tying a knot in excess material after you've wrapped it. Extra material only shortens the length of each pull, slowing you down.

The foundation of our hauling systems, the 3:1 is our most commonly used technique. The plaquette acts as the progress-capture pulley and a simple Prusik as the tractor. Note the rescuer has knotted the tractor Prusik so he doesn't lose distance in his throws. PHILBRICK PHOTOGRAPHY

Assisted Haul (or Drop Loop)

With a climber just below the anchor, within one-third of a rope length, instead of using a friction hitch, drop a loop of rope to the stuck climber and ask him to clip it to his belay loop. This is known as an assisted haul or drop-loop 3:1.

1. Tie a catastrophe knot into the brake strand.
2. Grab the brake strand where it comes off the stack or pile and pull some slack out of it, creating a loop that hangs from the back of the plaquette and from the stack. Clip a carabiner into this loop.
3. Lower the carabiner-on-a-loop down to the stuck climber.
4. Have the stuck climber clip the carabiner into his belay loop. Make sure the loop does not have any twists.
5. Untie the catastrophe knot and pull. The stuck climber can also pull on the strand coming from the plaquette to assist, should he need to.

Climbers call this technique the assisted haul because the stuck climber can pull on a strand and it assists the raise.

To help the stuck climber identify which strand to pull, the rescuer simply starts pulling. In front of the stuck climber will be three strands—two will be moving upward and one will be moving down. The stuck climber pulls on the one moving down. If the stuck climber assists, he's actually doing most of the hauling. Keep in mind, too, the rescuer mustn't pull too quickly, because this will pull and pinch the stuck climber's hand into the carabiner on the loop.

Both of these systems create a 3:1 theoretical mechanical advantage. With the friction created by the plaquette and the rope going through the carabiner on the friction hitch, you end up with somewhere around 2:1. This will be enough to assist someone as he climbs. For an overhang, you need a lightweight climber and little friction in the system, so no rope drag and properly extended protection pieces!

Mechanical Advantage in Hauling Systems

Understanding the fundamentals of mechanical advantage in our systems helps us execute a better rescue and avoid problems. We'll cover the basics, as there is far more detailed information available in books and online. We hope to give you enough information to understand the hazards and maintain efficiency when hauling, especially because these systems are improvised. You won't have the luxury of low-friction-bearing pulleys like professional rescuers or riggers do.

In the 3:1 system we have to pull 3 feet of rope to move the climber 1 foot. When we increase the mechanical advantage to a 5:1 or 6:1, we increase that ratio. So you can see, the goal is to increase the advantage just enough to work—and no more.

We need to avoid increasing the advantage to the point hauling becomes easy. Not only is it inefficient (remember you're pulling 6 feet of rope through a 6:1 for every foot it raises the climber), it adds force to the anchor, it can hurt the climber, and it can make the haul very inefficient through friction.

Forces on the Anchor

How do we add forces to the anchor? Let's take a 3:1 system as an example. Most people would say if they're hauling a 90-pound weight, they would have to pull 30 pounds to move that weight. But that doesn't take into consideration the friction of the system: The rope running through carabiners and over rock dramatically lower the advantage—from a 3:1 *theoretical* advantage to somewhere around a *real* advantage of 2:1, depending on the rock, the path of the rope, etc. So in a very real sense, the rescuer doesn't know how much weight he's pulling.

Now, the friction of the rope on rock and through carabiners is always there, so when the load is at rest (we're not hauling), the anchor takes the weight of the climber minus the friction in the system. To haul, we must overcome the climber's weight plus friction. So the anchor has to hold two-thirds of the weight plus friction when we are hauling.

Two-thirds—where is the other one-third? That is what you are pulling. In the system we described, you pull the rope up, so you are "one" of the "three" in that system. The anchor gets the other "two." It is that knowledge that's important. How

much force are you putting in the system? We don't really know because friction is incalculable for us, but we do know the anchor is getting double the forces we apply when pulling.

What if we increase the mechanical advantage? If we are pulling the rope up when we pull on a system, it is one of the 9x advantage. So if you are pulling a 9:1 system, the anchor gets eight times what you pull. If the weight you're pulling gets stuck and you pull as hard as you can, how much force can you generate? In a 9:1, multiply however hard you can pull by eight.

Imagine if you summon someone to help you haul—suddenly two people are pulling! Envision the forces generated by two strong climbers. All of a sudden, the weight gets stuck . . . but that weight is a climber. If the anchor holds, we are putting a lot of force on the stuck climber, and if he's pulled up against a roof, with his neck pinned, that could be disastrous.

If we create a system with which we can just barely move the victim, we are limiting how much force we put into the anchor and the climber. If the climber or rope became stuck, the increase of force in the system is minimal and we'll notice it right away. Suppose we were using a system of high mechanical advantage, like a 9:1. We might not notice the increase in forces and this could have dire consequences for both the anchor and more importantly the climber.

As far as efficiency is concerned, the higher the mechanical advantage, the more rope we need to pull. In a 3:1, as we mentioned, you must pull 3 feet of rope to move the climber 1 foot. In all systems, we will from time to time have to slide the friction hitch (the "tractor") to get another "throw." So if you increase the mechanical advantage to 9:1, you have to pull 9 feet of rope to move the climber 1 foot. This will require more throws, so we'll be sliding the Prusiks more often. This will make the haul very tedious, so *the easier the pull, the more tedious the system.*

With this basic understanding, let's work on increasing the mechanical advantage, because regardless of how much more tedious it may be, we need to be able to move the climber.

5:1 Haul

There are two common 5:1 hauls, and climbers debate which is better. The first one loses a little more to friction; the second one is harder to build. We'll describe both. We begin with the rescuer belaying with an auto-locking plaquette in guide mode.

BLOCK-AND-TACKLE 5:1

1. Tie a catastrophe knot into the brake strand.
2. Place a friction hitch on the rope going down to the stuck climber.
3. Clip the brake strand into the friction hitch.
4. Now pull the brake strand up and clip it to the anchor.
5. Clip another carabiner into the carabiner on the friction hitch.
6. Pull the brake strand down from the anchor and clip it into the new carabiner on the friction hitch.
7. Untie the catastrophe knot.
8. Pull.

The above 5:1 just loops the rope one more time from the friction hitch through the anchor then back to the friction hitch. Keeping the ropes untwisted helps with reducing friction. Any or all the carabiners can be non-locking since the self-braking plaquette backs up the system throughout.

Notice the block-and-tackle 5:1 requires just one rope, which makes it simpler than the backside 5:1. The downside is that it bends over one additional carabiner, increasing friction.
PHILBRICK PHOTOGRAPHY

BACKSIDE 5:1

1. Tie a catastrophe knot into the brake strand.

2. Place a friction hitch on the rope going down to the stuck climber.

3. Clip the backside of your clove hitch into the friction hitch.

4. Push the friction hitch almost as far as you can down the rope toward the injured climber.

The backside 5:1 runs through one less carabiner compared to the block-and-tackle version. You do, however, incorporate the backside of your clove hitch, making it slightly more complicated to build. The placement of the bight knot on the backside haul strand affects the system's efficiency.

PHILBRICK PHOTOGRAPHY

5. Tie a small bight with as small a loop as you can into the rope right where it comes out of the carabiner on the friction hitch. Using a small overhand on a bight helps keep the bight knot short.

6. Clip a carabiner into the bight knot and then clip the brake strand into that carabiner.

7. Untie the catastrophe knot.

8. Pull on the brake strand.

In step 4 you'll notice that you push the friction hitch down almost as far as you can. When you tie the bight knot, it is hard to get it as close as possible to the carabiner. Now when you push the friction hitch down, you will eat up the little bit of slack that inevitably occurs between the bight knot and the carabiner. This little bit makes a difference in the efficiency of your throws.

Comparing the two 5:1 systems, you'll notice the rope runs through one more carabiner in the first system, adding some friction. In the second system, getting the bight knot tied small and as close as possible to the carabiner on the friction hitch makes a big difference on the number of throws and the efficiency. It helps to be precise with tying and the placement of the knot.

9:1

The 9:1 is the next easiest to set up and it will be the first to require two friction hitches, so you will need to do double throws. It is essentially a 3:1 on top of another 3:1.

This is a last-resort haul—not very efficient but if you can't move someone with the 5:1, it might be necessary. The maximum force you can put on the anchor is eight times what you can pull. If for a short time you pull with 100 pounds of force, then it will put 800 on the anchor. Be very careful if at some point someone comes to help you. Two people potentially double that force, which means you

The 9:1 is similar to the block-and-tackle 5:1, but instead of clipping the last bend through another carabiner, you build a friction hitch on the strand and clip the rope to it. This creates a 3:1 on top of a 3:1, yielding enormous mechanical advantage.

PHILBRICK PHOTOGRAPHY

could further injure the victim and it puts far more forces into your anchor.

Remember, only enough mechanical advantage to move the load. If it is too easy, the potential for problems increases.

1. Tie a catastrophe knot into the brake strand.
2. Place a friction hitch on the rope going down to the stuck climber.

3. Clip the brake strand into the friction hitch.
4. Place another friction hitch on the brake strand and move it close to the carabiner on the first friction hitch.
5. Clip the brake strand to the anchor.
6. Now clip the brake strand to the second friction hitch.
7. Untie the catastrophe knot.
8. Pull.

Rescuing a Second, Counterbalance Transition (Unweighted)

Self-rescue becomes much more difficult with a weighted system. In reality, though, our transition from belaying to rescue is unweighted because we transfer the load to a temporary system. Once on the temporary system, our transitions become easier because we're dealing with an unweighted system.

The temporary system adds visual and material complexity. If we go through the transition first without weight and then add the temporary system, it is far easier to learn.

So could this transition actually take place unweighted? If you imagine how a second could get injured, one method might be hitting a ledge due to rope stretch or slack. If there is a ledge, the second may be able to sit on it or somehow otherwise take his weight off the system. Unweighted doesn't mean we can sacrifice security, though: At all times the second climber must remain protected!

1. The rescuer ties a bight knot into the brake strand and clips it into his belay loop with a locking biner.
2. He clips the rope going to the injured climber to the anchor with a locking carabiner. (Notice you're essentially building an LSD lower, which means the plaquette will not lock should the second slip. The bight knot on your belay loop is absolutely critical in this situation.)

3. The rescuer unclips the belay device from the anchor, slides it down the rope, and clips it to himself in rappel mode with a short extension. A basketed, shoulder-length sling through the belay loop is about the perfect length.

4. He places a third-hand backup on the ropes behind the rappel device.

5. He snugs everything up by taking up any slack through the rappel device and then tests it.

6. The rescuer unclips his clove hitch from the anchor.

7. He rappels down. When he reaches the bight knot he clipped to his belay loop, he engages his third-hand backup, tests it, and if it holds, unclips from the bight knot and unties it.

8. He finishes the rappel down to the injured climber.

1. Unweighted transition to counter-balance. To begin the transition, tie a bight knot in the brake strand and clip it to your belay loop. In the event you're short on locking carabiners, you can use two non-lockers (reversed and opposed) on the belay loop. This is a great spot to conserve lockers, and note the rescuer in this photo has done just that. PHILBRICK PHOTOGRAPHY

2. Feed or pull some slack through the plaquette to the climber's side and clip it through a locking carabiner on the masterpoint.
PHILBRICK PHOTOGRAPHY

3. *Unclip the plaquette from the anchor, slide it down the rope toward you, and clip it in rappel mode to a sling basketed through your belay loop. Clean the extra carabiner off the ear.* PHILBRICK PHOTOGRAPHY

4. *Add a friction-hitch backup to the brake strand below the device.* PHILBRICK PHOTOGRAPHY

5. *Unclip your clove hitch at the anchor, as well as the bight knot from your harness. Rack your carabiners, untie the bight knot, and rappel to the victim.* PHILBRICK PHOTOGRAPHY

During this transition the rescuer ties the bight knot and clips it to his belay loop, creating a very secure counterbalance anchor. Until the rescuer unclips his clove hitch from the anchor, both the rescuer and the injured climber are secure. This means any mistake made during the transition might create 3 to 5 feet of slack but will not be catastrophic. This simple move of tying a bight knot into the brake strand and clipping it to the rescuer will be common in our rescue/problem-solving transitions.

The Temporary Ledge

The above transition took place while the injured climber sat on a ledge. But what if there is no ledge? We'll build one—not a real one, but a temporary one.

In reality, our temporary ledge is just the technical solution to creating an unweighted scenario, like our natural one above. The temporary ledge simplifies our rescue. So, in the event your follower is injured and fully weighting the rope, consider building a temporary ledge with the following transition:

1. The rescuer ties a bight knot into the brake strand (he leaves 3 to 4 feet of slack this time) and clips it into his belay loop.

2. He ties a friction hitch on the rope going to the injured climber and clips a carabiner onto it. He uses a locking carabiner if he has a spare. *The rescuer should avoid using his best Prusik cord as he'll need it for the far more important application of his third-hand backup.*

3. He grabs the backside of his clove hitch and with this rope ties a Munter mule overhand on a locking carabiner clipped to the friction hitch built in step 2.

Now the rescuer releases the belay device and lowers the injured climber onto the Munter mule overhand. To do that, he first tries to lever the blocking carabiner back and forth on the plaquette.

1. Building the temporary ledge. Tie a bight knot on the brake strand and leave approximately 1 meter of slack in the system. Clip the knot to your harness with either a locking carabiner or two non-lockers reversed and opposed if you're short on lockers. Once you've backed up the victim, tie a friction hitch on his strand of the rope. Remember not to use your dedicated Prusik/third-hand, as you'll need it later during the rappel. We'd rather have our best material available for the rappel, as we'll be on it longer. With the backside of your clove, tie a Munter mule overhand to the friction hitch. Remember to orient the Munter in the "lower" position before tying it off, so it doesn't snarl once you weight it. PHILBRICK PHOTOGRAPHY

2. Ratchet the blocking carabiner back and forth to lower the victim onto the temporary ledge.

PHILBRICK PHOTOGRAPHY

This should slowly feed rope out until it produces enough slack, then he can pull the device from the back and release it. If that doesn't work, he can clip a carabiner (or a nut tool) to the lower hole on the plaquette and use it as a lever to orient the pla-quette to release. The Munter mule overhand setup should be as snug as possible, so little rope is needed to lower the injured client onto it.

Releasing the device takes a little thuggery. Don't worry about it releasing quickly, because the injured climber can't drop too far—the Munter mule backs it up, and in the unlikely chance it slips,

you have the bight knot on your belay loop secur-ing everything.

Once you've unloaded the plaquette, you can begin the transition. There is very little change in the process until step 6. Since the bight knot is already clipped onto the rescuer's belay loop, the process starts from there:

1. The rescuer clips the rope going to the injured climber to the anchor with a locking carabiner.

2. She unclips the plaquette from the anchor and clips it to herself in rappel mode with a short extension. A shoulder-length sling basketed through the belay loop is about the perfect length.

3. She places a third-hand backup on the rappel strand.

4. The rescuer snugs everything by taking up any slack through the rappel device, then tests it.

5. She unties the mule and with the Munter low-ers the weight onto her rappel. As she does this she needs to be well braced, so she does not get pulled into the anchor. The rescuer takes the Munter off the rope once the second's full weight is on her rappel rig and she's in control of the counterbalance rappel.

6. The rescuer unclips her clove hitch from the anchor.

7. She rappels down the slack behind her device. When the bight knot clipped to her belay loop comes tight, she tests her third-hand backup and unclips the bight knot and unties it. Once the bight knot is untied, the rescuer needs to make sure she will not be pulled into the anchor. If that were to happen, the rappel device would jam into the anchor, and then the friction hitch would pull upward and into the rappel device. The third hand will likely fail. *Dropping the vic-tim is a real hazard here.* The rescuer needs to be very careful until she is fully off the belay ledge. If she's still in danger of being pulled upward,

she can tie another catastrophe knot farther down the rope, rappel to it, then remove it and continue.

8. The rescuer rappels down to the injured climber.

In step 7 we talk about the potential for a catastrophic failure. With the victim's weight on the rescuer while she's close to the anchor, she must resist being pulled up and into it. We suggested adding 3 to 4 feet of slack before she ties the bight knot. This is to accommodate the length she'll need to lower the victim onto the Munter mule and still have rope to move away from the anchor before removing the bight knot. She must try not to waste the slack behind her device by failing to fight to move down (rather than lowering the victim). If she is close to the anchor and the bight knot is tight, she can tie another bight knot below the original and clip it to her belay loop before untying the original one. Being pulled into the anchor and dropping the victim at this point is the most likely mode of failure in this system and it is very serious. If there's any chance of this, the rescuer should have a bight knot behind her device and below her friction-hitch backup.

Beyond Rescue: Tools for Everyday Climbing

The temporary ledge and even small parts of the system like clipping a bight knot on the brake strand can be used to solve problems unrelated to rescue. By incorporating these techniques into our everyday systems, it allows us to stay practiced and feel less stressed should a rescue ever happen.

The Backup Bight Knot

The first tool that can be very useful is tying a bight knot into the brake strand of a plaquette and clipping it into you. Since you are usually clove-hitched into an anchor, this can be considered another anchor, but it doesn't cluster your system. Of course, in the worst-case scenario (a belay or haul-system failure), you would get a violent pull, but it will be more than survivable. Having a bight knot clipped to you gives you peace of mind whenever you're working with a plaquette for any reason.

Lowering the second a significant distance offers a good scenario in which the bight knot becomes useful. Imagine the second can unweight the system but still needs to be protected during the change to a lower.

You first tie a bight knot into the brake strand and clip it to your belay loop. Now you decide to use a Munter hitch for the lower. You tie a Munter hitch on the climber's rope and begin to disassemble your belay device. At that point you realize you incorrectly built the Munter and it is just a double loop through the locking carabiner. With the bight knot clipped to your belay loop, you still have your partner secured, and because the rope

Don't Break Down the Device!

Moving the belay device from the anchor into a rappel does not require that the rope be removed from the device. The device seldom if ever needs to be disassembled, just clipped in a different orientation. When changing the device from self-braking mode into rappel mode, the rescuer simply clips the blocking biner in the back to her harness, without removing the rope from it. The less the device is dismantled the better, because it reduces the chances for a mistake in feeding and clipping the rope into the device and/or dropping it.

A Bight Knot vs. a Clove Hitch

We clip a bight knot into our belay loop rather than building a clove hitch because of the seriousness and complexity of the things we are trying to accomplish when we need this tool. There are times a clove hitch's adjustability would be useful, and if that's a consideration, it's a reasonable thing to do. The nice thing about the bight knot, though, is that even when unclipped, it still acts as a catastrophe knot. This means it may work even if you prematurely unclip it or forget to clip it in the first place.

goes through a carabiner at the anchor, there isn't much slack.

Whenever you need to unlock your plaquette, if you first tie a bight knot into the brake strand and clip it into your belay loop, you have created (in seconds) security with no extra confusion at the anchor.

The temporary ledge solves the problem of unlocking and/or lowering a second who cannot unweight the belay. Once the ledge is built and weighted as described above, you can transition the plaquette to a lower. For us, if we need to do any weighted transition, we look to the temporary ledge, along with the bight knot clipped into the belay loop, as a possible solution.

A WEIGHTED KNOT PASS

Using the temporary ledge also facilitates a very easy, secure knot pass, using very little in the way of additional gear beyond a Prusik cord. Notice, too, the original Munter hitch used to lower is *not* broken down in this sequence. Because you've successfully used the Munter to lower the first rope-length, you know it's been built correctly, so why retie it? Using the temporary ledge, we simply pop the junction knot through the Munter, saving the steps of untying and retying it behind the junction knot, as well as eliminating the risk of retying it incorrectly. Simplify, simplify, simplify!

1. Knot pass. Use your temporary ledge rigging as a backup during the first lower. Note the temporary ledge pictured here is built using the backside of the rescuer's clove hitch. When the joining knot approaches the Munter, the rescuer engages the temporary ledge.
PHILBRICK PHOTOGRAPHY

2. The rescuer has engaged the friction hitch attached to his temporary ledge, verified that it's grabbing, and then tied an figure eight on a bight and clipped it to his belay loop to back up the knot pass. PHILBRICK PHOTOGRAPHY

4. The order in which you perform the following steps is important. First, release the Munter mule overhand on the temporary ledge and load the Munter used in the first lower. Second, engage your friction-hitch backup and verify it grabs. Third, while maintaining control of the brake strand, unclip the figure eight on a bight form your belay loop, untie it, and continue to lower. PHILBRICK PHOTOGRAPHY

3. The rescuer feeds the junction knot through the Munter hitch on the anchor, then puts a friction-hitch backup on the brake strand.
PHILBRICK PHOTOGRAPHY

Scenario: Assisting a Climber at the Crux

Let's see how these techniques can be put together in a new way to aid a guide or instructor wanting to coach a client at the crux on a multi-pitch climb. Using a few simple tools, a guide or instructor can set up a toprope on an upper part of a multi-pitch climb, using a system very similar to the counterbalance self-rescue transition.

In our scenario the guide is belaying 40 to 50 feet above a crux; there is a small ledge just below the crux, maybe 15 feet below the difficulties. The client can almost do the moves but not quite. There is no real time pressure. The client wants to focus on difficulty, not efficiency or moving quickly. To help the client, the guide wants to coach, and being closer allows better communication and helps keep the stoke high. Perfect situation to give the client a fun, challenging day!

Our transition begins with the client hanging on the rope, struggling a bit, and uninjured. He can unweight the rope, but cannot make the moves free.

1. The guide ties a bight knot into the brake strand and clips it to his belay loop.

2. The guide puts a third-hand backup on the brake strand, just above the bight knot.

3. The guide clips a locking carabiner into the masterpoint of the anchor where the belay device is clipped.

4. The guide now asks the client to temporarily get on the rock and unweight the rope. As soon as it's unweighted, the guide clips the climber's strand into the locking carabiner; this sets up the load strand direct (LSD) lower. *Note:* Although the LSD lower does not normally require a locking carabiner, in this scenario it does, as that carabiner will also be used for the counterbalance rappel.

5. The client re-weights the rope. The guide engages the third hand, checks everything, unclips and unties the bight knot on the brake strand, and lowers the client to the ledge below the crux.

6. Once the client is comfortable on the ledge, the guide ties another bight knot on the brake strand below the third-hand backup and clips it to his belay loop with a locking carabiner. *This is absolutely critical.*

7. The guide preps a sling on his harness for an extended rappel. A sling basketed through the belay loop is a very good length for this application.

8. The guide now unclips the belay device from the anchor and clips it in rappel mode onto his extension. *Note:* The guide only needs to unclip the biner hanging the device from its ear, slide the device down the rope, open the blocking carabiner, and clip that to his sling/tether—no need to disassemble it only to reassemble it on the sling/tether.

9. The guide checks and weights the rappel system, unclips his clove hitch at the anchor, then unclips and unties the bight knot and rappels to the client. This puts an upward tug on the client, so a little warning is a good idea.

10. Once down on the ledge, the guide again ties a bight knot into the brake strand and clips it to his belay loop, securing the team.

11. The guide now takes a locking carabiner and clips it to the top of the belay device and clips that back to his belay loop. This puts the device into guide mode on his belay loop.

12. The guide can now belay and coach as the client works the hard section.

13. Once the client is through the crux and gets to a rest, the guide ties another bight knot into the brake strand and clips that to his belay loop and takes the older one out. The guide now ascends to the anchor, using the belay device in locking mode and a friction hitch with a foot loop. The foot loop should be built above

his plaquette; a double-length sling is a good length. Ascending will put a tug on the client, so another warning is in order.

14. Once at the anchor, the guide ties another bight knot into the brake strand and clips it into his belay loop. He removes the one he tied at the ledge afterward.

15. The guide secures himself with a clove hitch to the anchor on the climbing rope. *Note*: The guide never untied, only dropped his clove when he rappelled.

16. The guide unclips the belay device from his belay loop, clips it into the anchor in self-braking mode (reversing the maneuver from step 8), and finally cleans the foot loop off the rope.

17. The guide checks everything, unclips and unties the bight knot on his belay loop, and belays the client up to the stance.

This process isn't theoretical—it is a technique we have used in our work and allows us to maximize our clients' enjoyment and progress. For a careful, competent guide, techniques like these not only deliver a more customized day to a paying client, but employing them also acts as training and practice for a rescue situation.

This scenario does not include the temporary ledge because the client can unweight the rope. For a routine instructional system this is typical, but if you were to add that component to a practice you have a pretty complete scenario you can use to gain the skills necessary to deal with a problem.

The Tandem Rappel

Guides use the tandem rappel in a variety of situations—an injured or nervous client, or a child being the most obvious. Working with a family, the tandem allows the adults to be pre-rigged above the guide with a smaller child as a tandem.

We can also use the tandem in the recreational setting. A recreational team can employ the tandem to replace the simul-rappel. Because both climbers are on the same device, the problems and hazards of the simul-rappel don't exist. If you're not careful with the lengths of the arms of the cordelette, the tandem can be awkward and uncomfortable. With a little forethought, however, and staggered-length arms on the cordelette, it can be much more comfortable.

On multiple rappels, two climbers can attach to each new anchor with one clip of the masterpoint using a tandem. This makes the transition from one anchor to the next very efficient.

Leader Rescue

While leader rescue is typically much easier than rescuing a follower, it presents more risk. In most leader rescues, the belayer and leader are already set up in a counterbalance. Problem is, that counterbalance is anchored by what is most likely a single piece of protection, which the rescuer can't inspect, clipped with a non-locking carabiner. The whole team is counterbalanced on that piece, though with additional pieces below it.

Fortunately, in most cases the belayer can simply lower an injured leader down to the anchor. Most wouldn't even consider this scenario a "rescue." As we said, this is the situation in a vast majority of cases. Consider: A 200-foot rope is pretty standard, and although we do sometimes stretch the rope out on a climb, we find it far more common for pitches to be somewhere between 120 and 150 feet. Many times—especially in places like Eldorado Canyon—pitches are less than 100 feet.

So, unless the leader is near the end of a long pitch, chances are you'll be able to lower her back to you. Unless . . . the leader's highest piece is more than 100 feet from your belay. (We'll chat about traverses in a moment.) This presents a special, albeit less common, problem.

Rescues without the Option of Lowering

In the event you cannot lower the leader back to your stance, the goal becomes getting both you and the leader to a secure anchor, hopefully at a decent stance or ledge. From there you'll transition into a descent of some sort, most likely tandem rappelling.

Reuniting with the leader may require some combination of the rescuer ascending and/or lowering the injured leader. Remember, the rescuer is already rigged in a counterbalance rappel. That means the rescuer has three obvious options available:

1. The rescuer can stay put and lower the injured leader.

2. The injured leader can stay put and the rescuer can ascend.

3. The rescuer can climb with his device locked off, so that as he climbs, the leader lowers.

Initially the rescuer has all three methods at his disposal and can transition from one to the other as he sees fit. Eventually either the injured leader or the rescuer will get to the ledge first. At that point, options narrow. Before we go too much further, let's go over the transition from belaying the leader to a position where we can have these options.

1. The rescuer ties off his belay device.

2. He ties a bight knot into the brake strand and clips it into his belay loop with a locking carabiner.

3. He unclips his clove hitch from the anchor and disassembles the anchor.

4. Using the anchor material (cordelette), the rescuer ties a friction hitch on the rope going up to the injured leader and makes a foot loop.

5. He stands in the foot loop, which will take the weight off his belay device. He then clips the ear of the belay device to his belay loop and unclips the locking carabiner with the rope in it from his belay loop; this becomes the blocking carabiner. This flips the belay device into guide mode on his belay loop.

6. The rescuer unties the belay device (from step 1) and is ready to effect the rescue.

Once this transition is complete, you have all three options available to you: moving the rescuer, moving the injured leader, or both. If at this point the rescuer started to climb, the leader would lower down the cliff. Or, the rescuer could start to ascend the rope, which would keep the leader in place while the rescuer moved up. Finally, the rescuer could flip the device and lower the leader.

Had the rescuer deemed a lower an appropriate first step, he would have lowered the leader prior to doing the above transition. For this reason, we can likely assume the rescuer will be going up. Once he gets a better handle on the situation, he may want to do a lower; for example, if the rescuer gets to a ledge within 100 feet of the highest piece of protection and he then decides to lower the leader to it. From this point on, how the rescue takes place has everything to do with the terrain, nature of injury, and how much risk the rescuer decides is appropriate.

Risks While Rescuing

The risks are real, but not excessive. Ascending may seem extreme because we have removed the anchor. The reality, however, is that for the worst to happen, all the leader's protection would have to fail. Of course, if the top piece were to fail and the rescuer was ascending the rope or hanging on it, it would result in a fall. The distance the rescuer and the leader would fall is the distance to the next piece. The key for the rescuer is to get in a position where they can improve security "on the fly."

That security can come in two ways:

1. The rescuer gets to a ledge that is within 100 feet of the top piece of protection and clovehitches into a piece he places or a piece of protection already on the pitch.

2. The leader is lowered or can get himself to a piece of protection and secures the rescuer's strand of rope to it.

The rescuer will have some gear with him, because as he's already cleaned the anchor and as he ascends, he removes more gear. This may seem to add risk, but leaving the anchor and the gear does not reduce the falling hazard.

By having that gear, he not only expedites the rescue, but also makes it less complicated and in the end less risky. The key is to not go so far as to limit how much protection remains above. At the least there should be three or four pieces of protection left, so the rescuer should not ascend above that point unless he can be secured in some other way.

If the injured leader gets to the ledge first, he can do a very simple procedure to secure the rescuer. If the rescuer and the leader can unweight the rope, the leader can tie a clove hitch into the rope going down to the rescuer and clip it to a piece at the stance. If the rope cannot be unweighted, the injured leader can use his Prusik cord and tie a friction hitch on the rope going to the rescuer and clip that into a piece at the stance.

When the leader does this, in effect he creates a two-piece anchor for the rescuer. There's the top piece on which the leader probably took his initial fall and now a friction hitch connecting another piece in the system to the strand the rescuer is ascending. The two pieces are not perfectly equalized, but at least now the rescuer is ascending a rope that's secured by two individual pieces. If the top piece blows, the friction hitch will go tight, and instead of falling the distance between the top piece and the next, the friction hitch will arrest the rescuer's fall. This increases the security substantially for the rescuer.

The rescuer ascends the rope with a foot loop installed above his plaquette, which he has flipped into ascension/guide mode. The rescuer is counterbalanced with the leader through the top piece of protection in their system. The leader has increased security for the rescuer by affixing a friction hitch on the rescuer's strand of rope to a piece of protection, effectively creating a two-point anchor on which to ascend.

A close-up of the friction-hitch attachment to the rescuer's strand. The leader added his friction hitch directly into the quickdraw on the nearest piece of good protection.

PHILBRICK PHOTOGRAPHY

Provided the leader and rescuer can communicate, the leader can connect the rescuer's rope to a piece with a clove hitch, offering more security than a friction hitch. To do this, the rescuer must leave a bit of slack in the rope, allowing the victim to tie a clove hitch.

PHILBRICK PHOTOGRAPHY

The Impossible Scenario

We often get questions about seriously injured leaders and seconds. Much has been discussed about the viability of rescuing an unconscious victim. In a self-rescue you need to be realistic as to what is solvable. A truly unconscious leader who stays unconscious and who is a significant distance from advanced medical care is likely not going to make

it. People die and they die climbing; you cannot save everyone.

That said, if you have a critically injured leader, you need to alert authorities and you need a team—preferably with a helicopter—that has the means to extricate your partner. That is his only real hope. For you to take extreme risks to save someone you can't save may make you feel better . . . but it might just kill you, too. Take a deep breath and work with deliberate and thoughtful patience doing your best, but with an accurate perception as to the risks and benefits. Rescue is serious business—take it seriously.

Special Problems and Terrain as the Solution

We can anticipate and design solutions for many of our problems, but in most cases the individual terrain demands a unique solution. Imagine the scenario of a leader who has traversed far to the side of your belay. You can go through many techniques and systems to devise "the solution," but if you notice the long ledge 75 feet below the injured leader and lower him to it, then counterbalance rappel to it and traverse, you'll look far smarter.

In our work it is easy to see terrain as the enemy. It is terrain that creates the falling hazard, the route-finding problems, and the pendulums for our clients on traverses. But if we also notice a ledge or a particular weakness or a horn on which to belay, these become opportunities. When you start to look at terrain for solutions, you start to see terrain as the solution.

When, due to stress or inexperience, we see terrain solely as the problem, the only solution we have is the rope. We see this time and time again, the hope for a technical solution via the rope, instead of the simpler, perhaps less sexy, solution within terrain. So, it's nearly axiomatic in guiding—terrain before the rope, and the rope before despair. Burn this into your consciousness!

Complex Second Rescue

As we mentioned, rescuing the leader counts as a special circumstance due to the fact that it is rare

you won't be able to lower the leader down to you. The same situation applies to the second.

We described a rescue of your second, assuming he is within half a rope length of your stance. But what if he is farther down? In that situation you'll need to descend to another stance to anchor and then transition to the new lower anchor. This complicates the rescue because as we'll see, the top belayer may already be short on gear.

The rescuer has already led a pitch, decreasing the size of his rack, and now he needs to descend, leaving an anchor above. As he descends he'll remove gear as he rappels past, hopefully replenishing his options. He may not have another cordelette, either, because he left it at the stance above and the second probably has the other below. Perhaps the rescuer could replace the top cord with slings or an improvised system.

So, we will describe the process assuming two things: 1) the rescuer knows the second is more than half a rope length below, and 2) the rescuer did *not* recoup the cordelette from the stance above.

1. The rescuer needs to find a place to anchor within 100 feet of the second, but with about 5 to 6 feet of slack left in the counterbalance rappel.

2. The rescuer builds an anchor at this stance and leashes in.

3. The rescuer places a friction hitch onto the rope going down to the injured second and attaches it to the anchor using a mariner's hitch. He allows rope through his device to load the friction hitch/mariner's hitch.

4. Once the friction hitch/mariner's hitch bites, he feeds out a few inches more, introducing slack into the rope above the friction hitch/mariner's hitch.

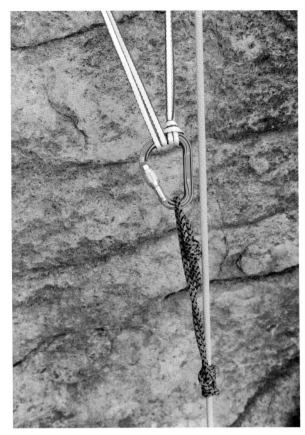

1. Build a mariner's hitch by clipping a double-length sling to your anchor, and attach it with a Munter hitch to a locking carabiner on a friction hitch on the load strand of the rope.

PHILBRICK PHOTOGRAPHY

2. Now wrap the sling around itself until you're left with several inches of material, and thread the end between the two strands of the sling. Notice the rescuer positioning the bartacks such that it's the portion of the sling threaded through itself at the end. PHILBRICK PHOTOGRAPHY

5. The rescuer takes the slack and clips the rope going to the injured second through the new anchor with a locking carabiner, then ties a bight knot and clips it to his belay loop.

6. The rescuer disassembles his rappel device, unties from the end of the rope, and pulls the rope down from the anchor above. He should then pull the rope back up and either tie back into the end or tie a stopper knot in the end of the rope. This closes the system so he can't rappel off the end of the rope.

7. He now rebuilds his rappel, adds a third-hand backup below it, and releases the mariner's knot to weight his next counterbalance rappel.

8. The rescuer unclips his leash.

9. He must again be wary of getting pulled into the anchor, as doing so can unlock his device.

He *must* resist the upward pull when starting his counterbalance rappel. Once he gets established on rappel, he can untie the bight knot on his belay loop and continue.

Most would assume that if the rescuer has a cordelette, he will use it for anchoring. Depending on the configuration of the pieces, this may very well be the best use. If he can save it, though, it may come in handy later in the rescue. In that case using the cordelette to tie a friction hitch/Munter mule, instead of the mariner's knot, may be a better use.

There will likely be a shortage of locking carabiners, so using opposite-and-opposed non-lockers becomes important. We mention in step 9 that the hazard of getting pulled into the anchor, which then allows the third-hand backup to travel upward and hit the rappel device and fail, is a realistic concern. Notice, though, at that point the rescuer still has the bight knot clipped to his belay loop. The rescuer must try to avoid this, but the bight knot prevents dropping the second—though it would be unnerving for the second to be dropped several feet!

In step 9 the rescuer should rappel 6 to 10 feet below the anchor before unclipping and untying the bight knot—this distance protects him from risking a failure of the rap system. Due to a large weight discrepancy or just a low-friction system, if the rescuer still feels in danger of being pulled upward, he can replace the bight knot with one farther down the rope and put even more distance between himself and the anchor.

Multiple Seconds

You've already thought to yourself, *what about multiple seconds?* For the recreational party, a team of three may make things easier, while for the guide it will likely complicate things. How exactly you solve the problem will depend on so many variables that you cannot have a specific system. What we will do is discuss some ideas and the strengths and weaknesses of each.

CATERPILLAR

In a caterpillar system, if the injured second is the first follower, the rescue system can stay the same (counterbalance to him) because the other second is well anchored below. Once the rescuer gets to the point of a tandem rappel, the second follower (who remained at his belay) can rappel with the team, either prior to the rescuer so she can set up the next stance or as a pre-rigged rappeller in a client/guide situation.

If the team is in caterpillar and the second follower is injured, there are far more options. In a recreational party the first follower can be lowered and do a pick-off. Once down to the injured partner, the rescuer would attach the injured climber to the rescuer's rope with a friction hitch and back it up with a sling from one belay loop to the other. The leader can then lower the injured climber onto this system. The key to this system is coordination, and therefore communication will be critical.

In a guided situation the uninjured follower's rope can be set up as a 100-foot rappel. Remember, he's already at the stance and can be pre-rigged on his rope; then the guide can do the rescue to a new stance and give a fireman's belay to the client. In this system the guide will have to delay getting to the injured climber so that she can set up the pre-rigged rappel for the uninjured second.

PARALLEL

In parallel systems the problems are more complex since both seconds' ropes are probably in the belay device. In a recreational setting a well-coordinated lower of both seconds connected by an extended friction hitch connecting the victim to the rescuer can work, but now the communication is made more difficult because the leader and the healthy second are rarely close enough to develop a plan.

For a guided party the guide may decide to have the healthy second finish the pitch, then free up the rope and set up a pre-rigged rappel—as she did in the caterpillar system. Again, this prolongs the time it takes the guide to get to the injured climber.

In almost all systems a guide could secure the healthy second and leave him in place, get the injured second stabilized, then re-ascend to belay the healthy second to the stance. Regardless of the situation, a thoughtful plan needs to be hatched and then executed. There will be no easy answer or cookie-cutter process because of the sheer number of variables.

Complex Systems and Simple Solutions

No self-rescue is a cookie-cutter process with two followers, in caterpillar or parallel. Each rescue requires considering all the skills at your disposal to solve the problem. We have described some basic tools and systems, but there is no way to develop and learn a step-by-step process to solve every possible permutation. Self-rescue is far more advanced than that and requires a comfort with rope systems and a good vision for terrain.

Climbers must have a complete toolbox of techniques, as well as a high level of comfort in vertical terrain, to execute a complex self-rescue. What we think you'll find, however, is that many minor injuries or simple accidents can be surprisingly easy to manage. As you practice more-complex systems, don't allow their complexity to blind you to the simple solutions before your eyes.

Afterword

We've come full circle, all in a cycle of risk management for climbing. From first identifying risks and hazards to prioritizing them to then devising solutions to mitigate and manage them, we hope to have shared with you two mountain guides' approaches to climbing rock, snow, and ice.

We started with the fundamentals of the craft—gear selection, how to use it, and the basic techniques. After introducing these, we moved beyond the individual tools and presented them as part of an advanced, holistic system that goes beyond rules-based solutions into the realm of judgment-based decisions and expert application of the tools themselves.

In parting ways, we hope you've learned some new techniques for your own practice, but even more so, developed a new mindset for climbing and leading others into the mountains.

Index

glacier travel, 199–200; ascending in, 225–27; belaying across bridges in, 228–35; crevasse hazards in, 212–14, 239; crevasse rescue in. *See* crevasse rescue; descending in, 246; downclimbing in, 246; drop loops in, 216–17, 222–23; falling hazards in, 212–14, 239; guiding in, 241–43, 245–46; hauls in, 218–23; lap-coiling in, 240; on low-angled glaciers, 213–14; maintaining space in, 235; rappelling in, 223, 246; rescuing other parties in, 223–24; rope types for, 243–44; roping up for. *See* roping up; route-finding, 212–14; short-roping in, 244–46; staying protected through transitions in, 235–36; transitions from glacier mode to pitching, 235–39; transitions from pitching to glacier mode, 239–43. *See also* summer glaciers

gloves, for ice climbing, 255

Grand Teton National Park, Wyoming, 136–37

GriGri system, 197–98

ground: anchors on, 63–64; belaying on, 62–64

guide transition techniques: belayed rappel, 122–23, 127–31, 183–86; doubling up on devices for, 124; for glacier travel, 241–43; long lowers, 186–87; lowering, 123–24, 131–33, 183–86; lowering two clients into insecure stance, 193–98; pre-rigged rappel, 122, 124–27, 182–83; short-roping in glacier travel, 245–46

guiding alpine rock: belayed rappels, 180–81, 183–86; caterpillar transitions with one rope, 167–68; caterpillar transitions with two ropes, 168–70; descents, 179–98; end-roping, 171–72; equivocation hitch, 180, 189–93; knot pass, 187–89; lowering, 180–81, 183–87; lowering two clients into insecure stance, 193–98; parallel transitions with one rope, 170; parallel transitions with two ropes, 170–71; pre-rigged rappel, 182–83; rope lengths for, 167; rope systems for two clients, 163–66; short-pitching, 166; short-roping, 161–63, 181–82, 198

guiding glacier travel, 241–43, 245–46

gullies, 142

half-rope systems, 6–7, 85–86

hammer. *See* ice hammer

hanging ice, 258–59

harness, seconds belaying off of, 75–76, 82–84

hauling: assisted haul, 275; crevasse rescue, 218–23; 5:1, 276, 277–78; mechanical advantage in, 275–77; 9:1, 276, 278–79; self-rescue, 270, 272, 274–79; 3:1, 274–77

Hawse, Angela, 188–89

heuristics, in risk management, 3

hexes, in rack, 17–18, 24

hip belay, 82–84

horizontal cracks, mitigating secondary pulls with, 30

horns, on ridges, 141–42

hydration: judgment ability and, 5; strategies for achieving, 5

ice axe, 199

ice climbing, 199–200. *See also* technical ice

ice dams, 260

icefall: climber-generated, 260–61; natural, 258–60; protecting against, 261–65

ice hammer, 199

ice screws: angle of attack for, 256; fall protection with, 256–58; for glacier travel, 217; length of, 256; mitigating secondary pulls with, 31

judgment, in risk management, 4–5, 207–8

knot pass: rescue application of, 188–89; weighted, 285–86; when lowering, 187–89

knots: backup bight, 284–85; catastrophe, 71; for creating friction in glacier travel, 215, 217; dynamics of, 42; limiter, 60

Kong GiGi, 76, 80–81, 124

lap-coiling, in glacier travel, 240

lead belaying: on cliff, 65–70; direct, 68–70; factor 2 fall protection in, 70–75; on ground, 62–64; pull-off prevention strategies for, 64–65; in special situations, 67–70

physical stress, judgment ability and, 4–5

pickets: angles of, 205; mid-clip, 202–4

pieces: back cleaning of, 18–19; mitigating secondary pulls through placement of, 28, 30–33; omnidirectional, 31; oppositional, 28, 33; practicing placement of, 19; in rack, 17–18, 24; removal of, 25, 33–34; secondary pull forces on, 26–29; security of, 25–26; strength of, 25–26

pitching: in glacier travel, 235–43; maintaining same leader going into, 238–39; in snow climbing, 201; switching leaders going into, 236–38

plaquettes: belaying seconds with, 76–82; failure of, 77–81; flipping, 11–12; hauling with, 274–75; lowering with, 14, 79

pre-mortem, 4

pre-rigged rappel, 122; in alpine rock, 182–83; one leader, one student, one rope, 124; one leader, one student, two ropes, 124–25; three people, two ropes, caterpillar technique, 125–26; three people, two ropes, parallel technique, 126–27

protection system. *See* fall-protection system

Prusik, for glacier ascensions, 227

psychological skills: biases and experiences affecting, 2; strengths and weaknesses in, 1–2

pulley effect, 74–75

pulling off, of leaders, 64–65

Purcell Prusik, 150

quad: in combination anchors, 56–58; three-point, 54–56, 58; two-point, 48–49, 52–54

quickdraws: mitigating secondary pulls with, 28–30; in rack, 20–21, 24

racks, 16; back cleaning and, 18–19; management of, 17; planning and prediction for, 18–19; sample traditional, 24; sizes and shapes of pieces in, 17–18, 24; slings, carabiners, and accessories in, 20, 24

rappelling: in alpine rock, 143, 173–80; backside rap-feed for, 114–16; belayed. *See* belayed rappels; caterpillar transition techniques for, 117–20; climbing tools for, 13–14; counterbalance, 270, 272, 279–84; in crevasse rescue, 223; double-rope system transition techniques for, 113–16; doubling up on devices for, 124; extended with friction-hitch backup, 108–9; fireman's belay, 109; first encounters with, 13–14; in glacier travel, 223, 246; moving on, 178; parallel transition techniques for, 120–21; pre-rigged. *See* pre-rigged rappel; safeguarding in, 177; single-rope system transition techniques for, 108–13; in snow, 206, 209–11; tandem, 270, 272–73, 288; on technical ice, 265–69

redirected belaying, 76, 84, 103–4

Red Rock Canyon National Conservation Area, Nevada, 84

redundancy, at belay anchors, 42–48

reepschnur, 197–98

rescue: assisting other parties in, 223–24, 271; knot pass application in, 188–89; from rope-built anchors, 23; tools used in everyday climbing, 284–88. *See also* crevasse rescue; self-rescue

reversed-and-opposed non-lockers, at belay anchors, 48

ridges: assessment of, 139–42; in parties of three, 153–56

risk management: bias and experience effects in, 2–3; communication and teamwork in, 3–4; experience, education, and educated guesses in, 2–3; heuristics in, 3; judgment in, 4–5, 207–8; proper planning and, 22–23; skill strengths and weaknesses in, 1–2; stress mitigation in, 5; three kinds of skills for, 1

rope: anchors built from, 21–24; carrying of, 148; categories of, 7, 86; coiling of, 144–48, 158, 240; creating friction for glacier travel, 215, 217; dynamics of knots in, 42; for glacier travel, 243–44; lengths for alpine rock, 143–44, 148, 167; marking middle of, 111; properties of, 6, 42, 74–75; in rappel transitions, 108–11; spare, 153; stashing of, 144–48; threads built from, 265–66; as transition tool, 107–8; tying off, 144–48, 158

rope drag, secondary pull and, 27, 29

rope-grabs, 225–27

fireman's belay, 109; from glacier mode to pitching, 235–39; for guides and citizen leaders. *See* guide transition techniques; for leader rescue, 289; leashes for, 106, 108; long lowers, 186–87; lowering, 123–24, 131–33, 183–86; lowering two clients into insecure stance, 193–98; new tools for, 107–8; for one guide with two clients in alpine rock, 167–72; parallel to caterpillar, 100; from pitching to glacier mode, 239–43; practicing for, 133–34; pre-rigged, 122, 124–27, 182–83; rappel setup for caterpillar, 117–20; rappel setup for parallel, 120–21; rappel setup for parties of two, 113–16; rappel setup for single-rope system, 108–13; rappel to another rappel, 175–78; rappel to third- and fourth-class alpine rock, 178–79; short-roping in glacier travel, 245–46; short-roping to technical descents, 181–82; stance management during, 99–100; technical descents to short-roping, 198; third- and fourth-class into fifth-class alpine rock, 144–49, 153–59, 167–71; third- and fourth-class to end-roping, 154–55; traditional tools for, 106; types of, 106

traverses, protection of, 38–40

Tricams: mitigating secondary pulls with, 31–33; in rack, 17–18, 24; removal of, 34

T-slots, 202

twin-rope systems, 6–7, 85–86

two-point belay anchors: in combination anchors, 56–58; comparisons of, 52–54; crossed sling. *See* crossed sling; direct tie-in, 50–54; quad, 48–49, 52–54; situations for, 52–54; traditional cordelette, 49–50, 52–54

tying off: belay devices, 9; coils, 144–48, 158

UIAA. *See* Union Internationale des Associations d'Alpinisme

umbrella ice, 258, 260

Union Internationale des Associations d'Alpinisme (UIAA), 7

upward-pull piece, 67–68

visual contact, with clients, 100–103

waterfall ice: low-angled, 248; steep, 254–55

water intake. *See* hydration

weighted knot pass, 285–86

Willie's Slide, New Hampshire, 248

workspace, for rope management, 92

zippering, secondary pulls causing, 28

About the Authors

Marc Chauvin and **Rob Coppolillo** are both certified by the International Federation of Mountain Guide Associations (IFMGA). Chauvin was the third American to be certified; Rob was the ninety-seventh. Chauvin also helped create the American Mountain Guides Association Certification Program and has assisted in developing its curricula over the past twenty-five years. He's a past AMGA President, Alpine Discipline Coordinator, and Instructor Team Member. Coppolillo is also an accomplished author. He has written articles for *Climbing* and *Skiing* and is a contributing editor for *Elevation Outdoors* magazine. In 2013 he published a how-to cycling book called *Holy Spokes: A Biking Bible for Everyone.*

Rob Coppolillo

Marc Chauvin